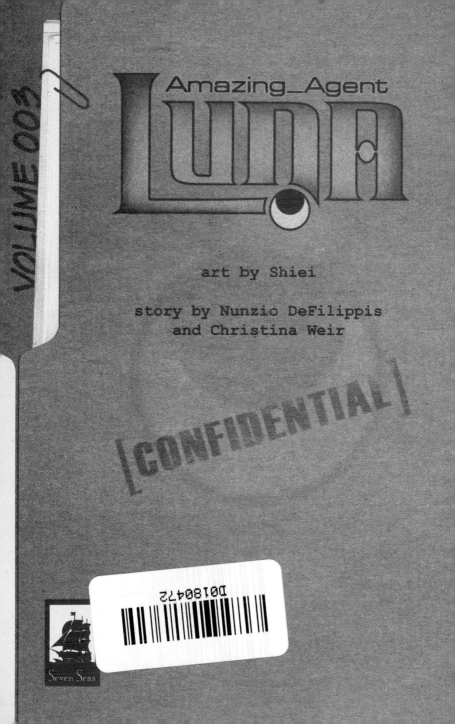

VOLUME 003

Amazing_Agent
LUNA

art by Shiei

story by Nunzio DeFilippis
and Christina Weir

[CONFIDENTIAL]

D0180472

Seven Seas

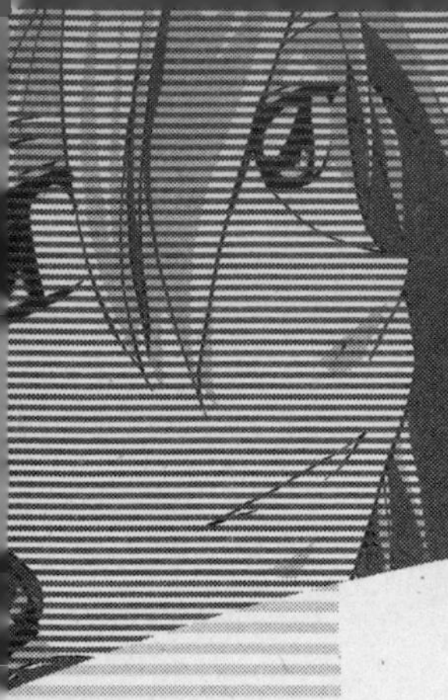

Amazing Agent Luna

VOLUME 3

story by Nunzio DeFilippis
Christina Weir

art by Carmela "Shiei" Doneza

STAFF CREDITS

toning	**Roland Amago**
lettering	**Nicky Lim**
	Cheese
graphic design	**Nicky Lim**
assistant editor	**Adam Arnold**
editor	**Jason DeAngelis**
publisher	**Seven Seas Entertainment**

Visit us online at www.gomanga.com.

ISBN 1-933164-10-7

Printed in Canada

First printing: April, 2006

10 9 8 7 6 5 4 3 2 1

AMAZING AGENT LUNA - VOLUME 3

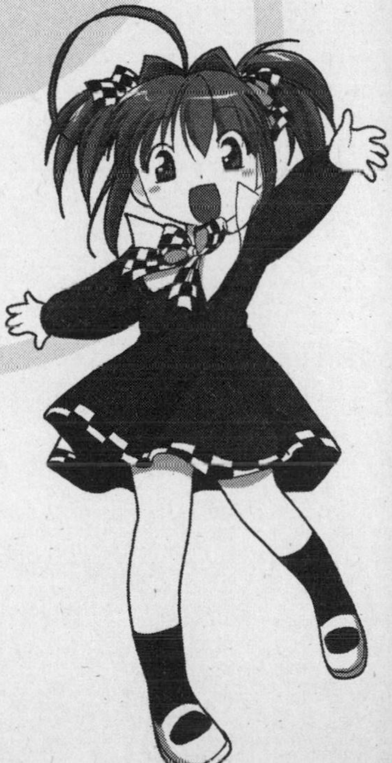

PERATIONAL STATUS REPORT

FILE NO. 013-a

PRODUCED AT: - 05i2

DATE PRODUCED:

FILE PROCESSED BY:

NATURE OF REPORT: [CLASSIFIED]

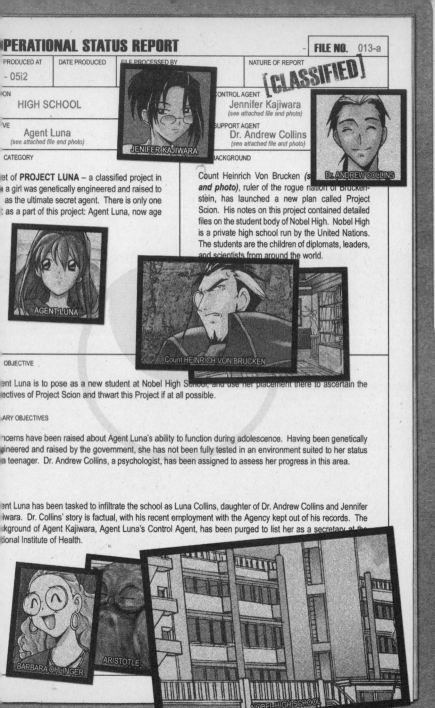

JENIFER KAJIWARA

Dr. ANDREW COLLINS

ON: HIGH SCHOOL

CONTROL AGENT: Jennifer Kajiwara *(see attached file and photo)*

VE: Agent Luna *(see attached file and photo)*

SUPPORT AGENT: Dr. Andrew Collins *(see attached file and photo)*

CATEGORY

et of **PROJECT LUNA** – a classified project in a girl was genetically engineered and raised to as the ultimate secret agent. There is only one as a part of this project: Agent Luna, now age

AGENT LUNA

BACKGROUND

Count Heinrich Von Brucken ***(s*** ***and photo)***, ruler of the rogue nation of Brucken-stein, has launched a new plan called Project Scion. His notes on this project contained detailed files on the student body of Nobel High. Nobel High is a private high school run by the United Nations. The students are the children of diplomats, leaders, and scientists from around the world.

Count HEINRICH VON BRUCKEN

OBJECTIVE

ent Luna is to pose as a new student at Nobel High School, and use her placement there to ascertain the ectives of Project Scion and thwart this Project if at all possible.

ARY OBJECTIVES

ncerns have been raised about Agent Luna's ability to function during adolescence. Having been genetically gineered and raised by the government, she has not been fully tested in an environment suited to her status a teenager. Dr. Andrew Collins, a psychologist, has been assigned to assess her progress in this area.

ent Luna has been tasked to infiltrate the school as Luna Collins, daughter of Dr. Andrew Collins and Jennifer iwara. Dr. Collins' story is factual, with his recent employment with the Agency kept out of his records. The kground of Agent Kajiwara, Agent Luna's Control Agent, has been purged to list her as a secretary at the tional Institute of Health.

NOBEL HIGH SCHOOL

ARISTOTLE

BARBARA OHLINGER

OPERATIONAL STATUS REPORT

FILE NO.

REPORT PRODUCED AT	DATE PRODUCED	FILE PROCESSED BY	NATURE OF REPORT
OB - 05i2		Jennifer Kajiwara	[CLASSIFIE

OPERATIONAL STATUS

Agent Luna has successfully infiltrated the school and is considered a normal teenage girl by the faculty ar students there. She has fooled Principal Barbara Ohlinger *(see attached file and photo)*, but seems to hav raised the suspicions of gym teacher Mark Dreyfus *(see attached file and photo)*. Dreyfus has taken over a acting principal upon the recent disappearance of Ohlinger. While background checks on Dreyfus show him ' be clean, his suspicions of Agent Luna make this a problematic development.

With regards to Von Brucken's Project Scion, we know very little. The Count has sent agents to infiltrate th school as science teachers on two occasions, including hiring current science teacher Professor Yves Tromper *(see attached file and photo)*, who has thus far managed to avoid any actions that would allow us to arrest hin The Project involved the creation of cloned owls, cloned copies of the school mascot Aristotle *(see attached fi and photo)*. These clones were super strong, and larger than the original. Our investigations indicate that th size was an error. All cloned owls were destroyed, save one. This owl was stolen from the animal shelter. W believe Tromperie to be responsible, but we cannot be certain of this.

Principal Ohlinger's disappearance may be linked to Von Brucken's plans. We have attempted to locate th principal, but with no luck yet. If Tromperie has captured her, we have been unable to ascertain where he ha taken her or why. If not, we have no leads on what might have happened to her.

With regards to our secondary mission protocol (Agent Luna's emotional status), Dr. Collins assures me that sh continues to fit in well at school, although the strain of deceiving her fellow students has begun to show c occasions.

Luna has made several friends – Francesca Aldana and Oliver Riggs *(see attached files and photos)*. Sh has struck up an acquaintance with Count Von Brucken's son, Jonah *(see attached files and photos)*, himse a student at Nobel High. This development is both promising and problematic. As a source of intelligence c his father, Jonah is invaluable. But Dr. Collins suspects Luna may be developing a crush on the boy, which cou complicate the mission. Additionally, the boy's loyalties remain unclear. It is probably best to assume he share his father's agenda, but we have no proof of this.

Our covers remain secure after the unexpected visit of this agent's parents to our base of operations. My paren' believe that Dr. Collins and I are married and that my departure from their home to join Project Luna was in fa a departure to start a relationship with Collins and have a child with him.

Dr. Collins goes so far as to suggest the visit was of great help to Agent Luna, who saw in my parents an extende family. He thinks that she will gain stability from seeing our cover story as a legitimate family. I am unsure of th wisdom in that.

There are many aspects of this assignment that remain incomplete, but thus far our progress has bee substantial. I will continue to report regularly on Agent Luna's status.

MARK DREYFUS · JONAH VON BRUCKEN · YVES TROMPERIE · OLIVER RIGGS · FRANCESCA ALDANA

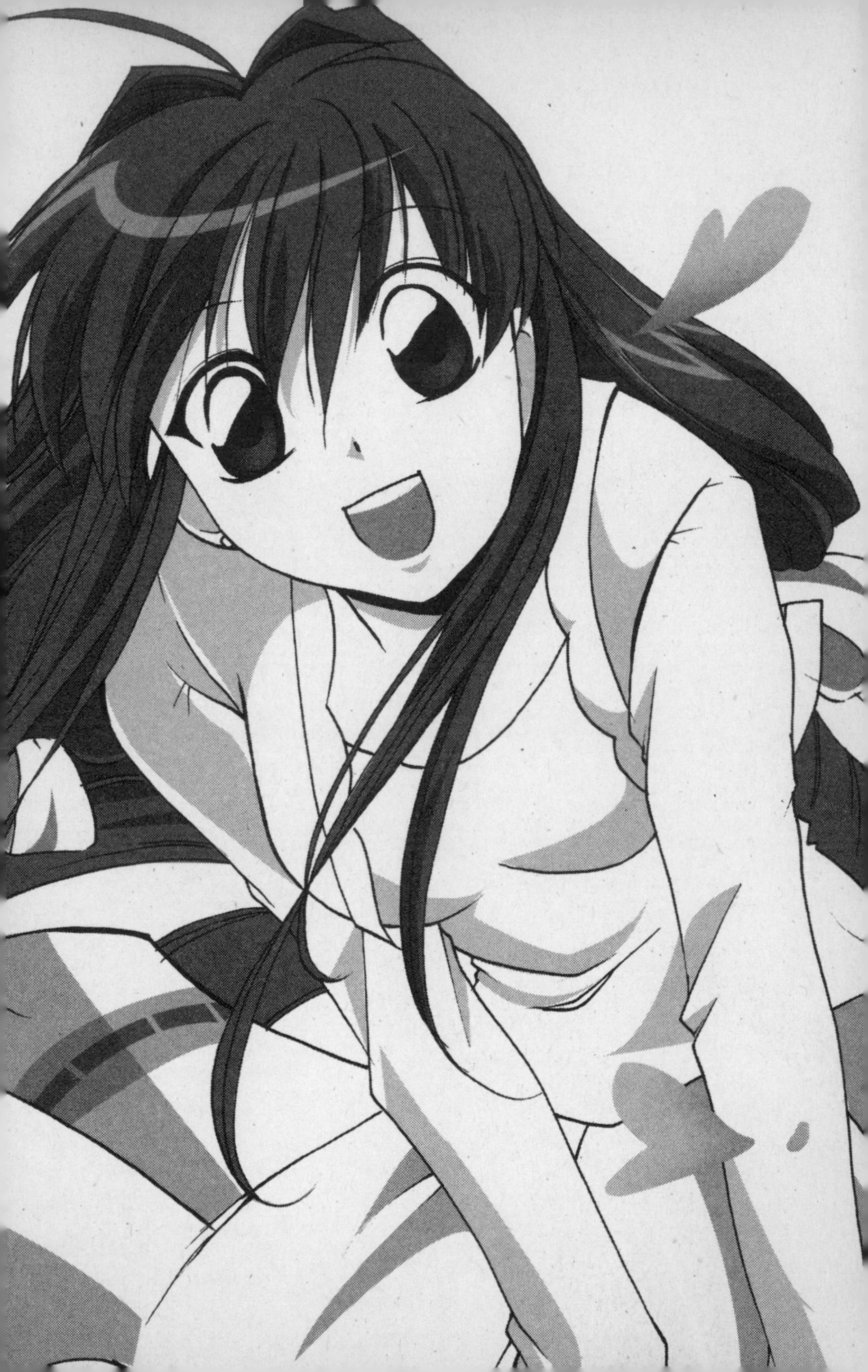

File 11
TEN YEARS AGO...

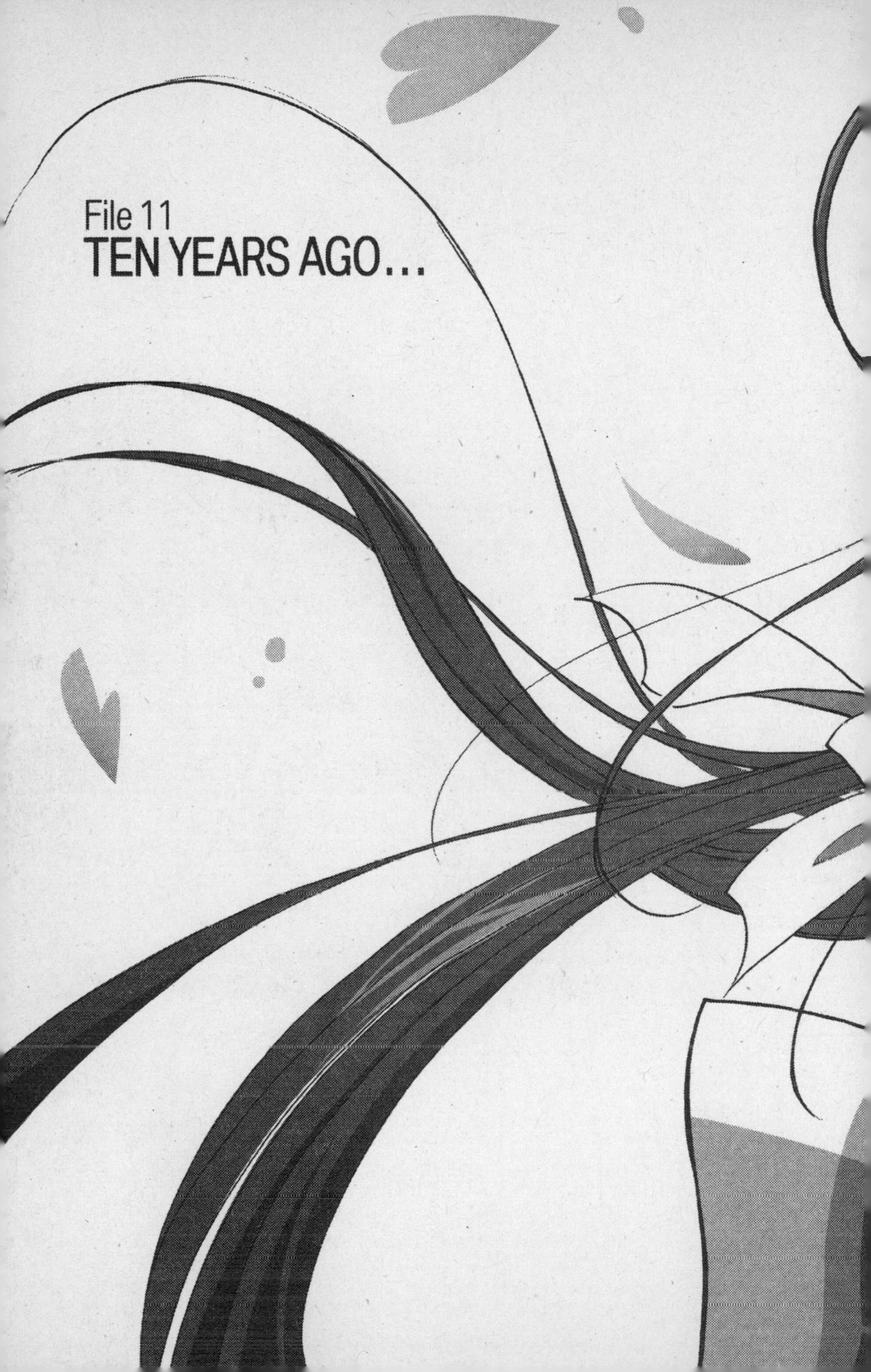

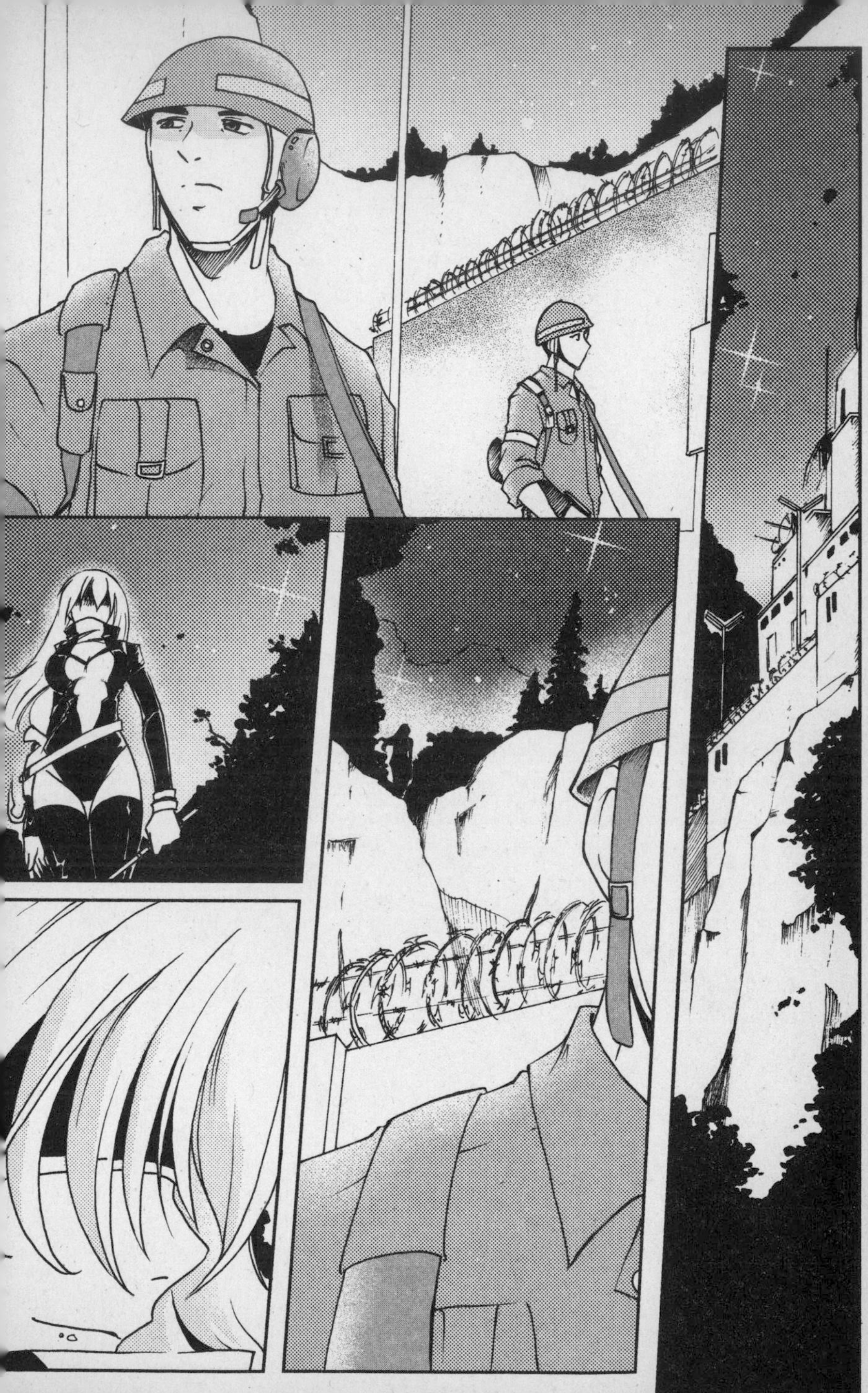

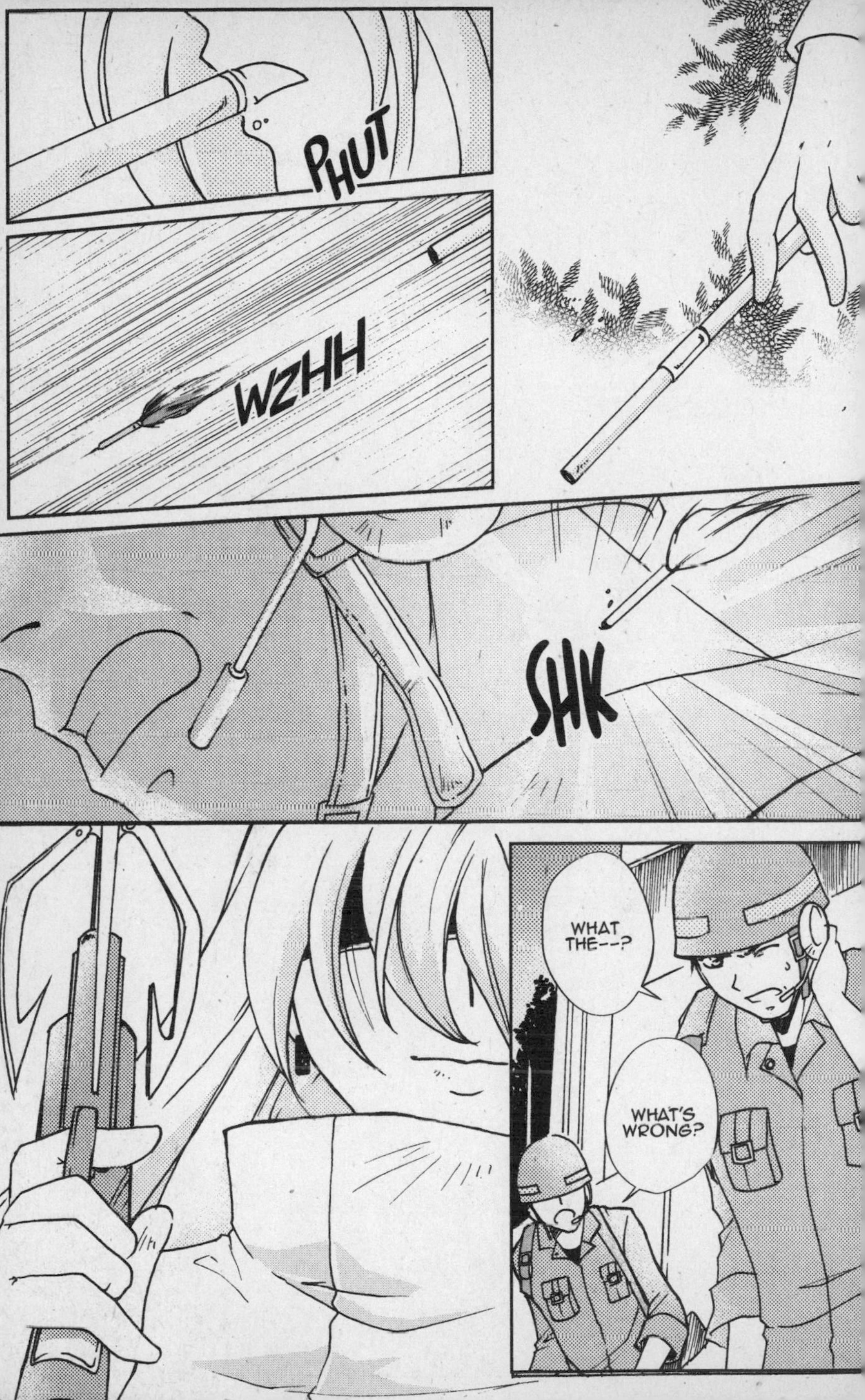
PHUT
WZHH
SHK
WHAT THE--?
WHAT'S WRONG?

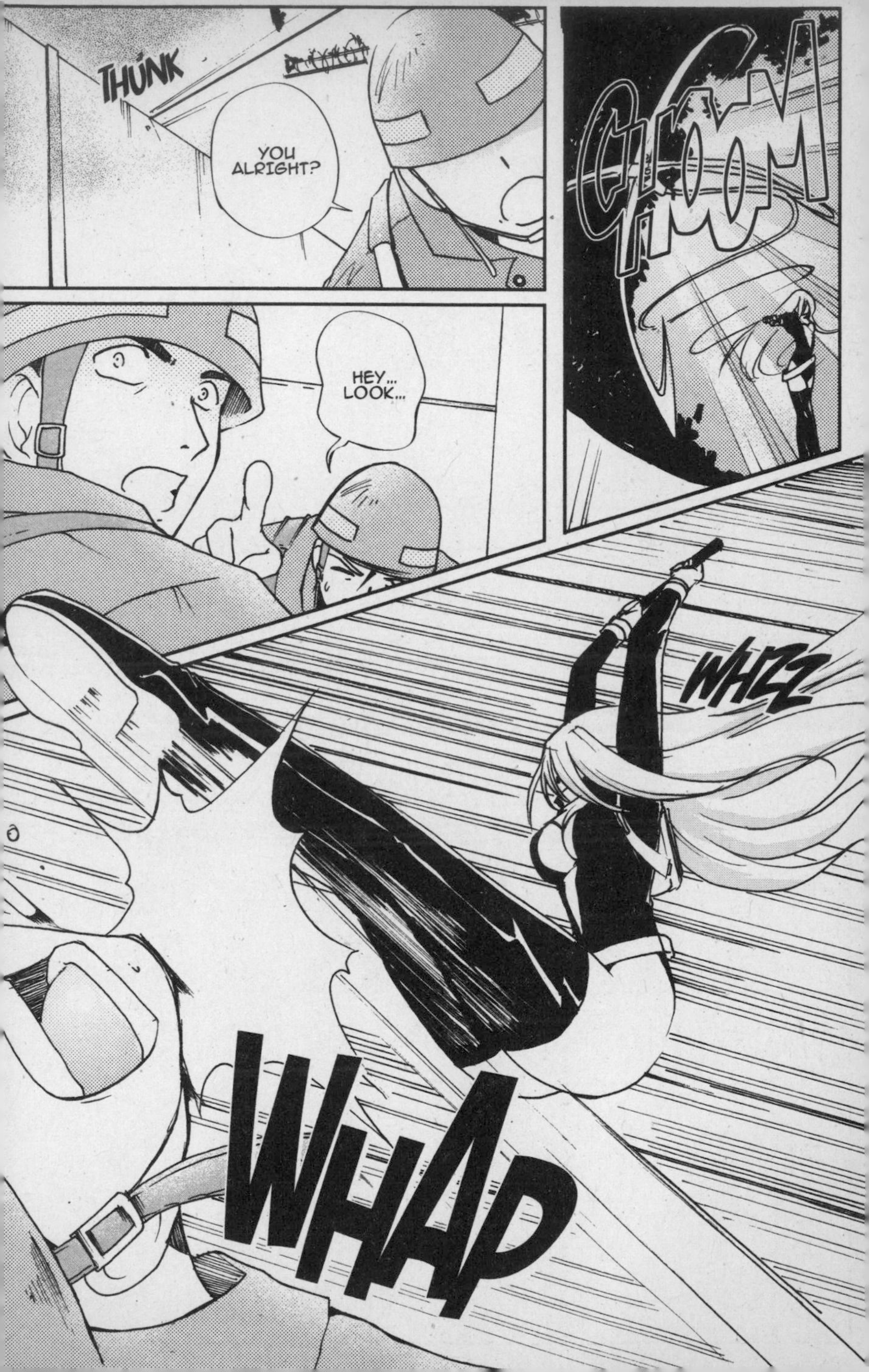
GROOM
THUNK
YOU ALRIGHT?
HEY... LOOK...
WHIZZ
WHAP

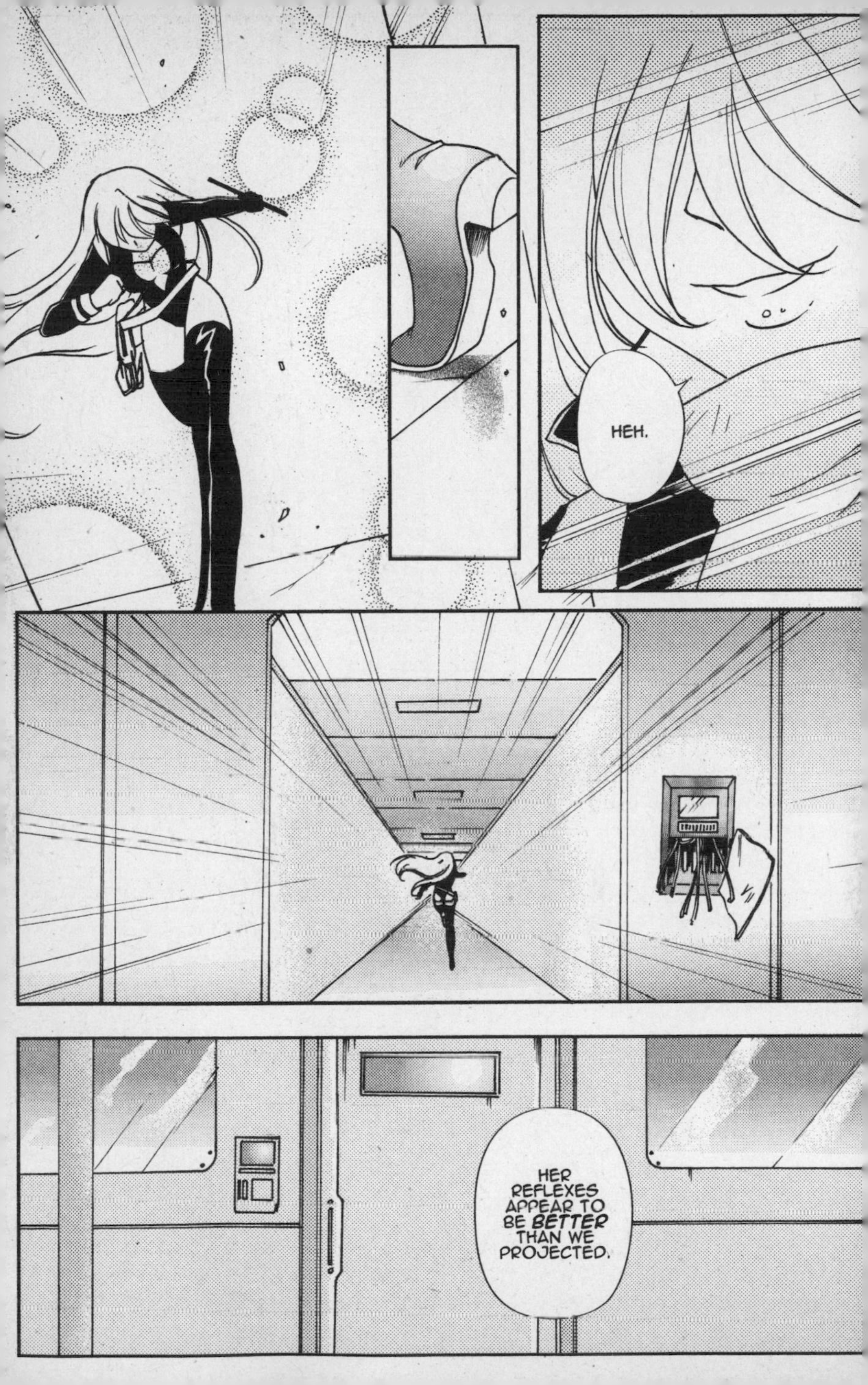
HEH.
HER REFLEXES APPEAR TO BE *BETTER* THAN WE PROJECTED.

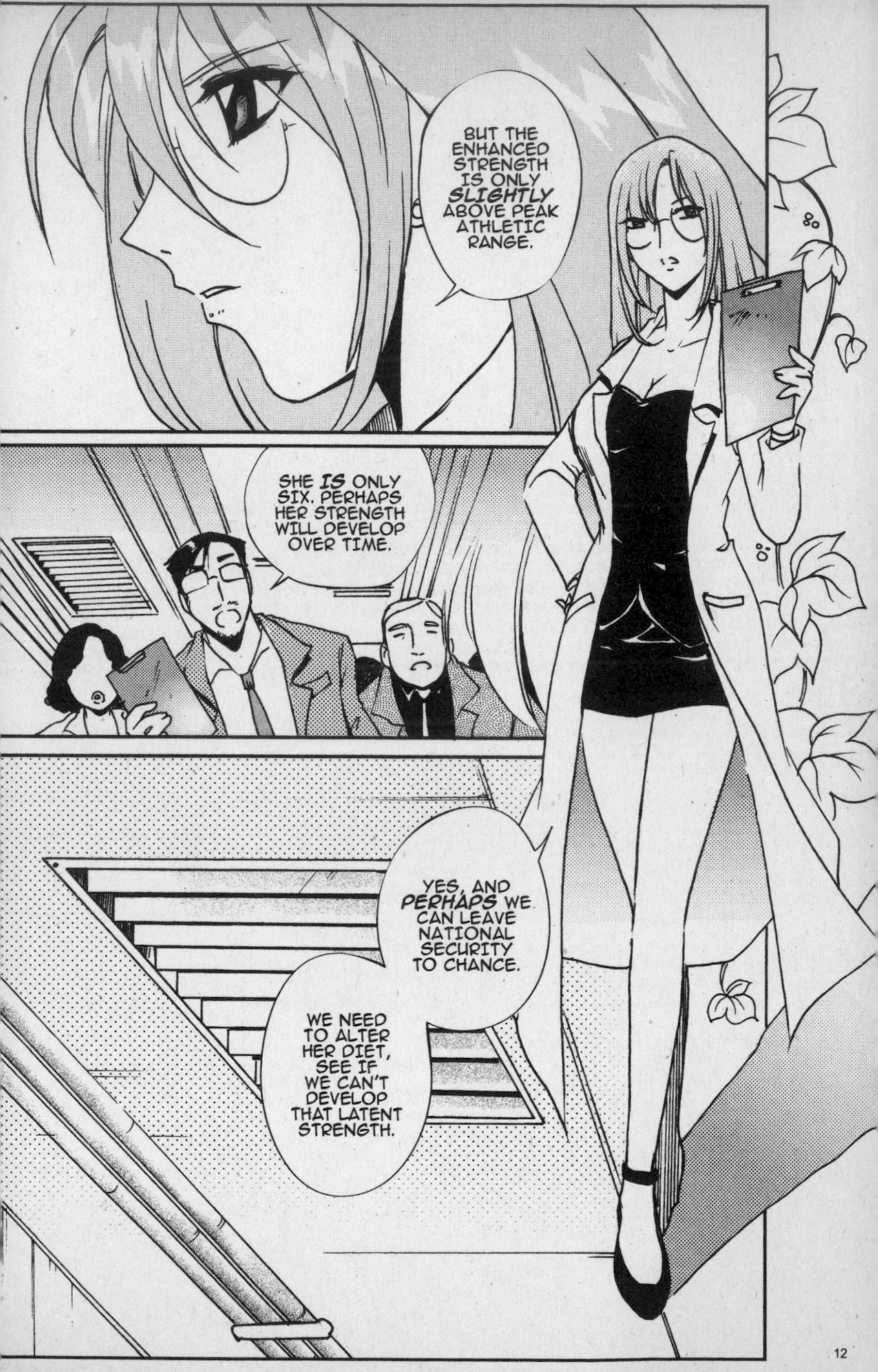
BUT THE ENHANCED STRENGTH IS ONLY SLIGHTLY ABOVE PEAK ATHLETIC RANGE.
SHE IS ONLY SIX. PERHAPS HER STRENGTH WILL DEVELOP OVER TIME.
YES, AND PERHAPS WE CAN LEAVE NATIONAL SECURITY TO CHANCE.
WE NEED TO ALTER HER DIET, SEE IF WE CAN'T DEVELOP THAT LATENT STRENGTH.

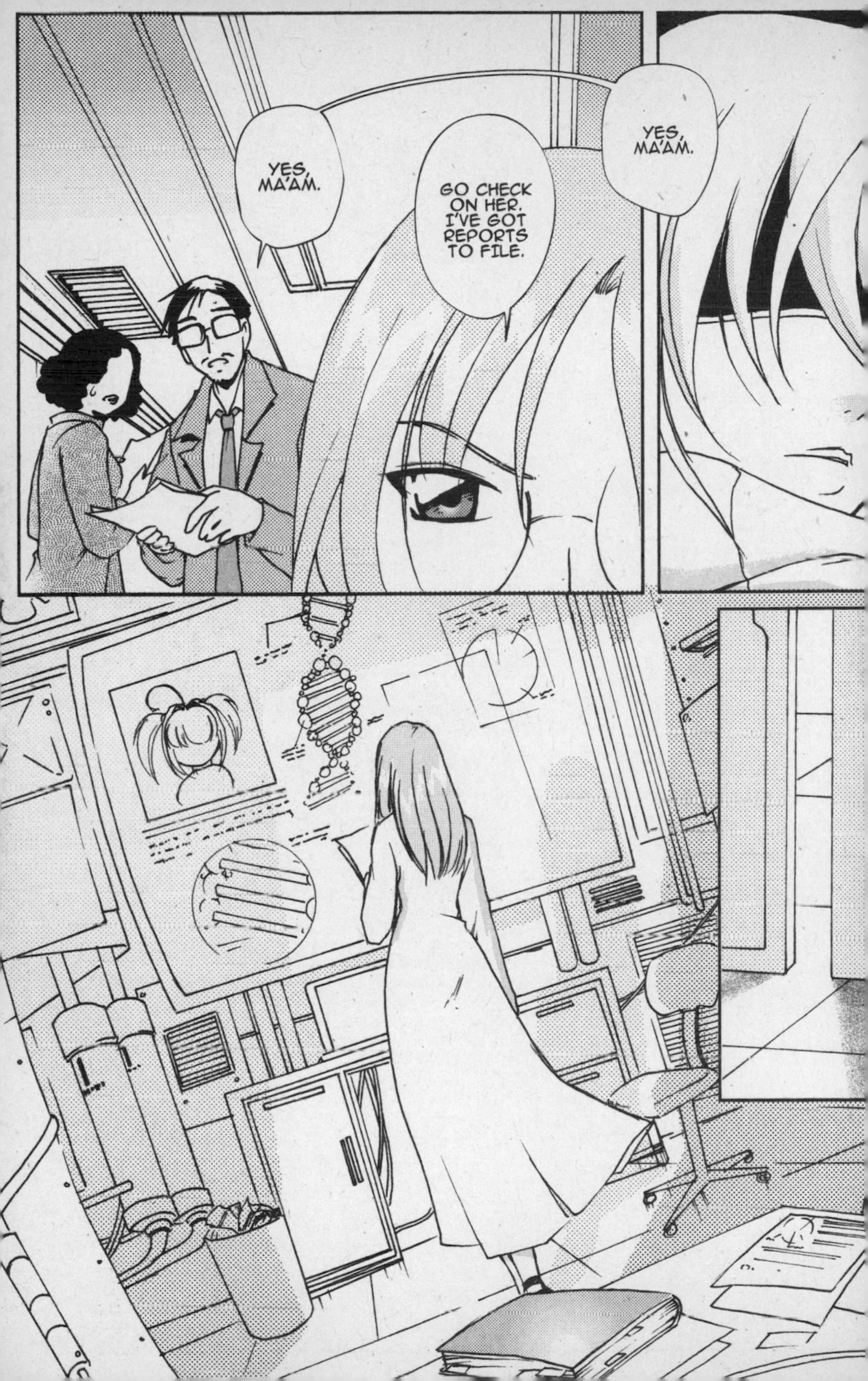
YES, MA'AM.
GO CHECK ON HER. I'VE GOT REPORTS TO FILE.
YES, MA'AM.

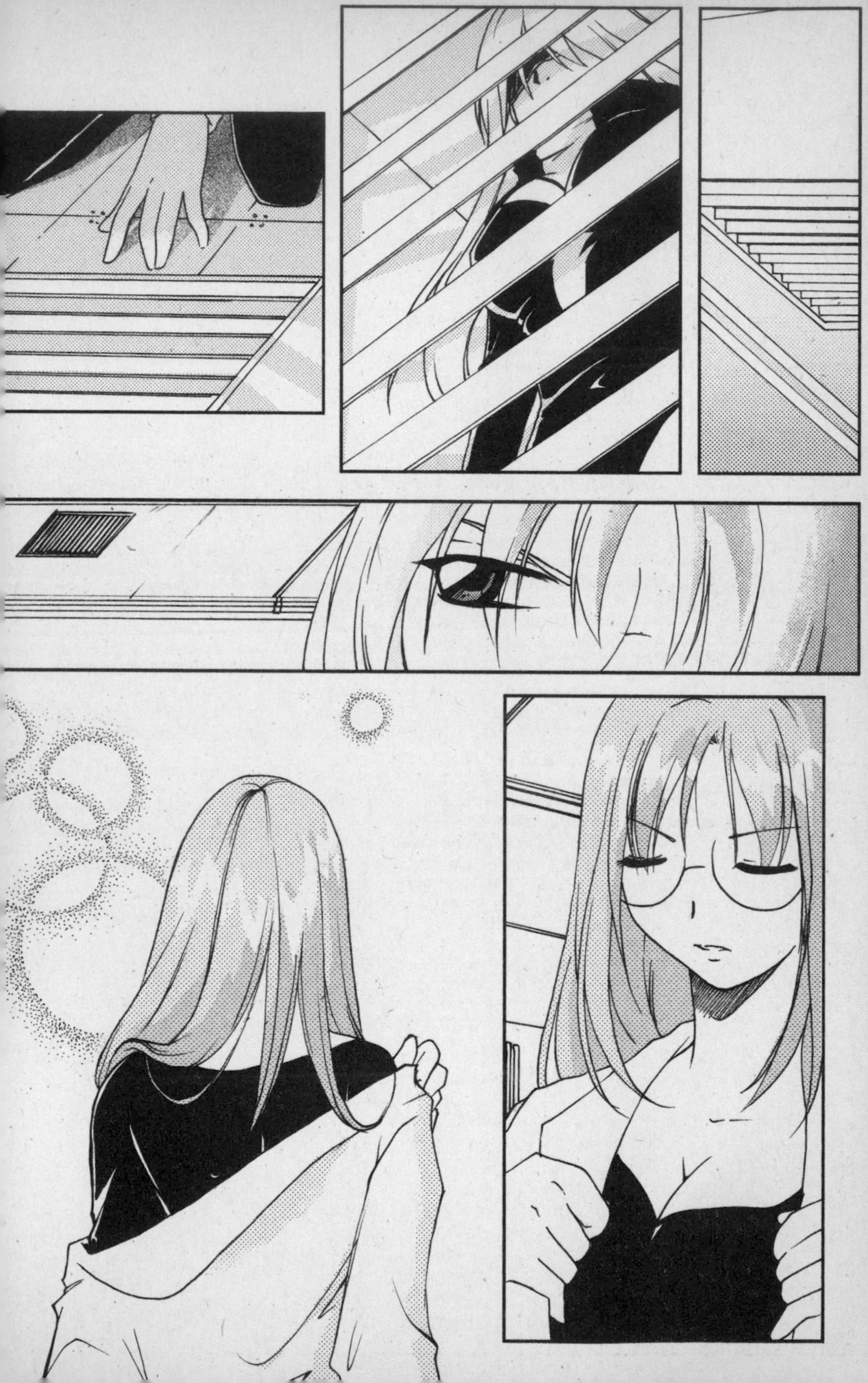

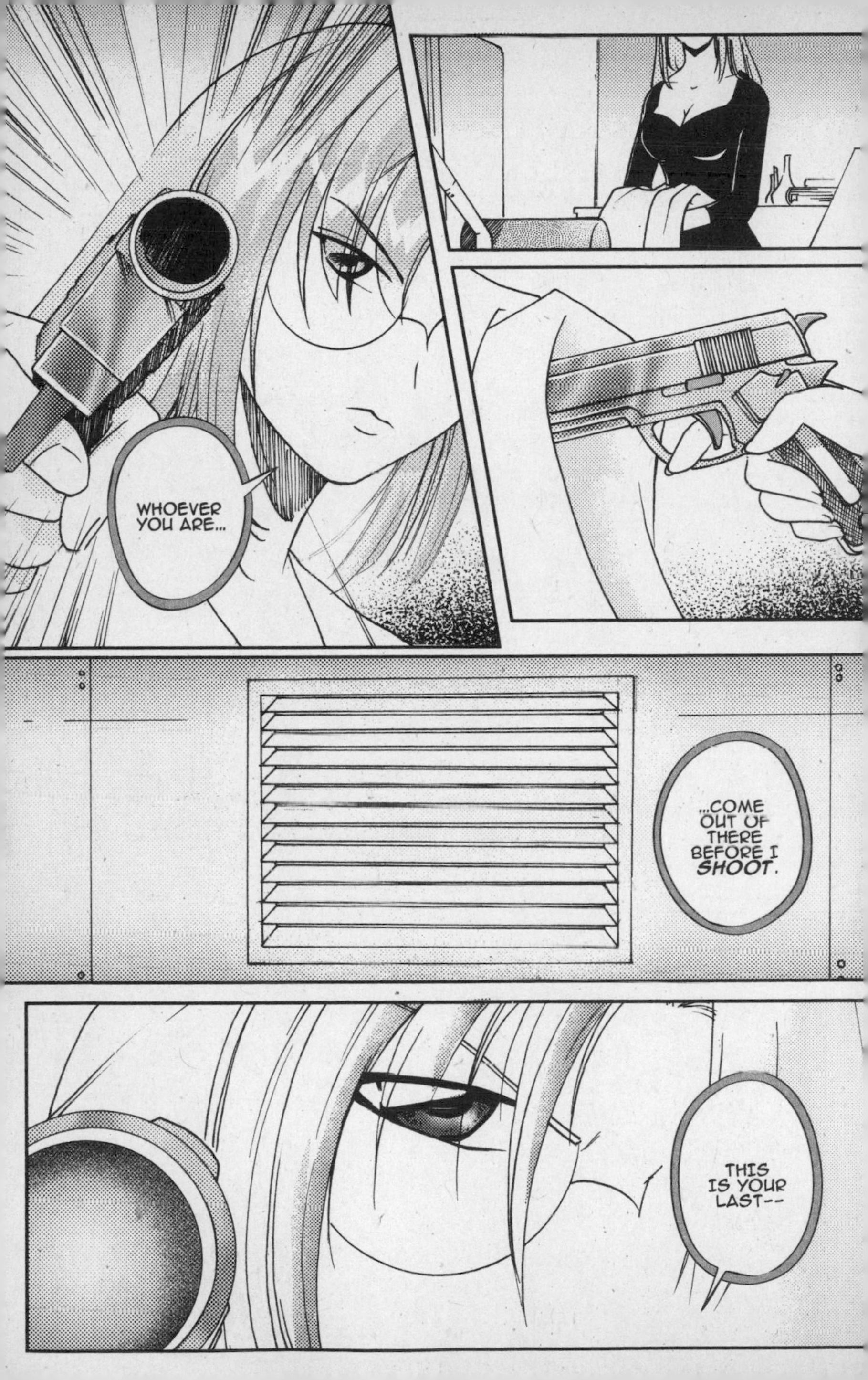
WHOEVER YOU ARE...
...COME OUT OF THERE BEFORE I SHOOT.
THIS IS YOUR LAST--

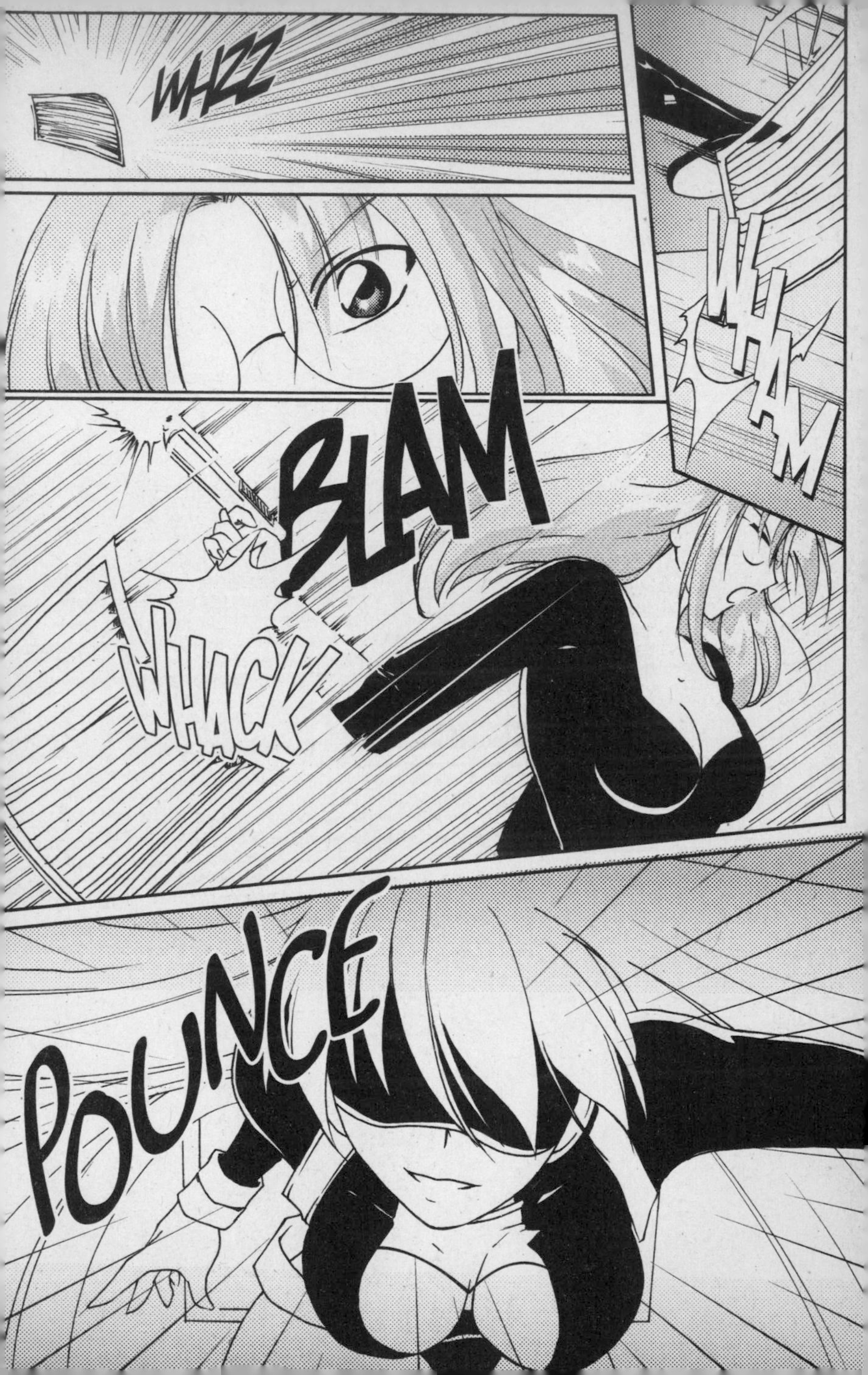
WHAM
WHIZZ
BLAM
WHACK
POUNCE

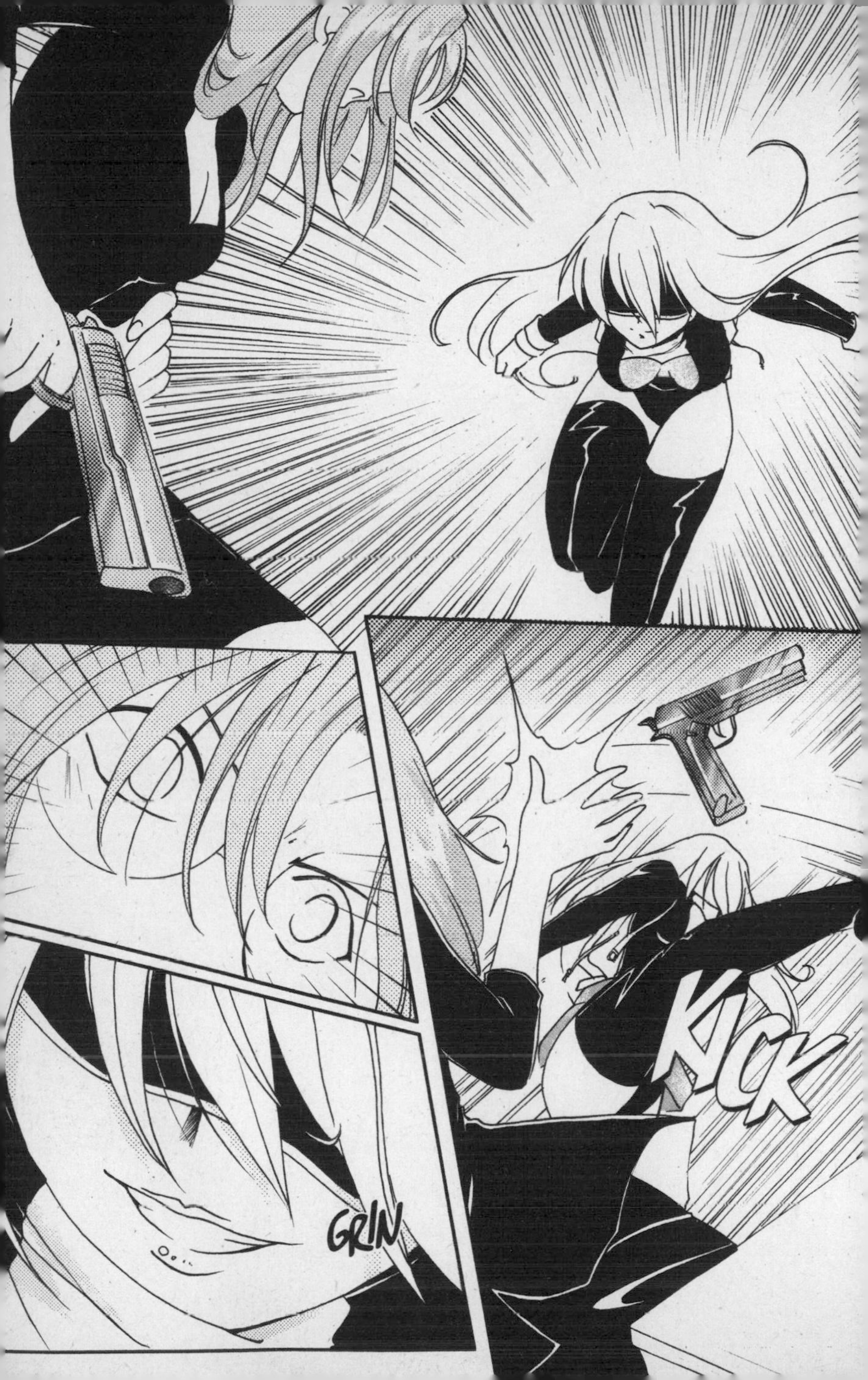
KICK
GRIN

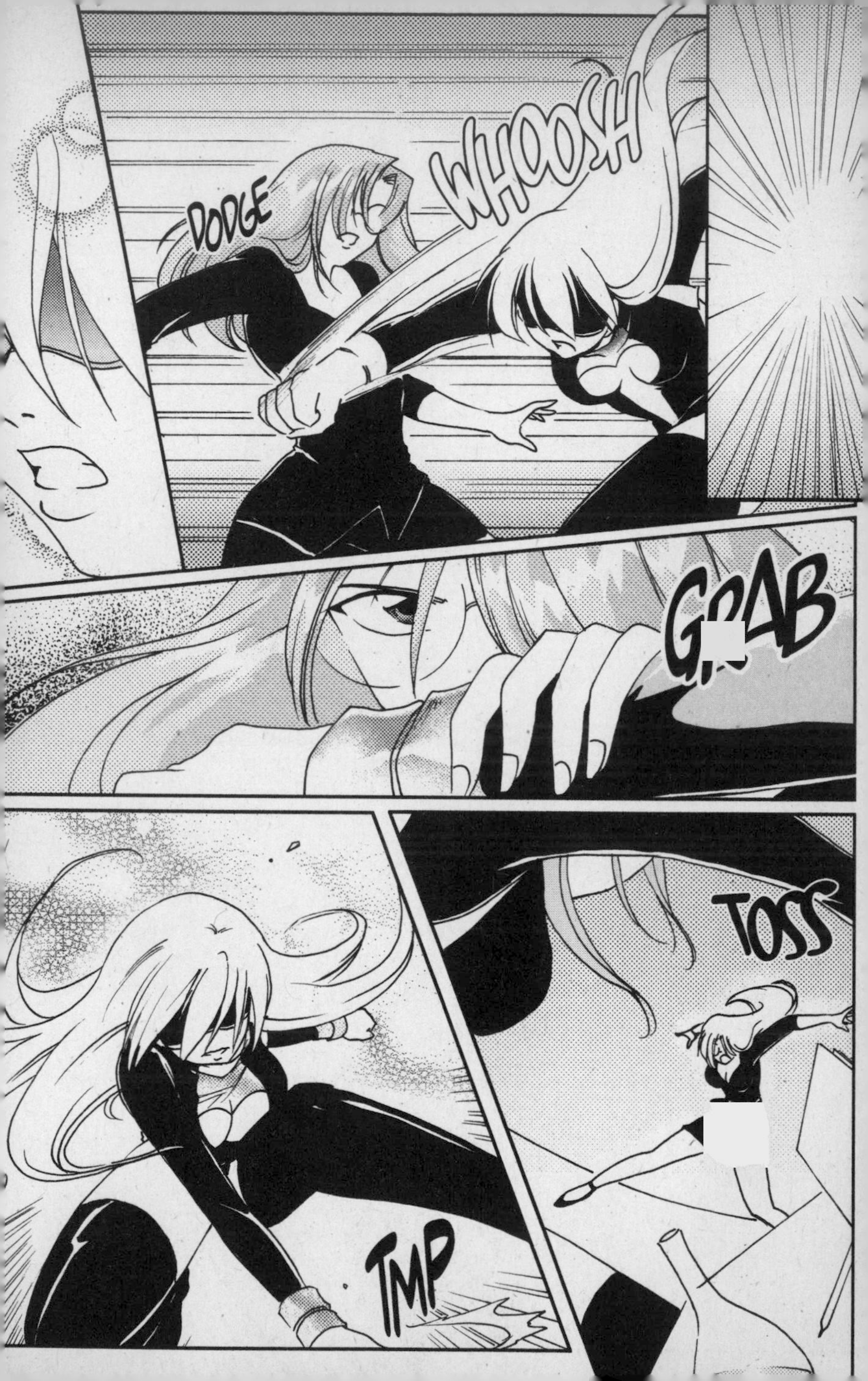
WHOOSH
DODGE
GRAB
TOSS
TMP

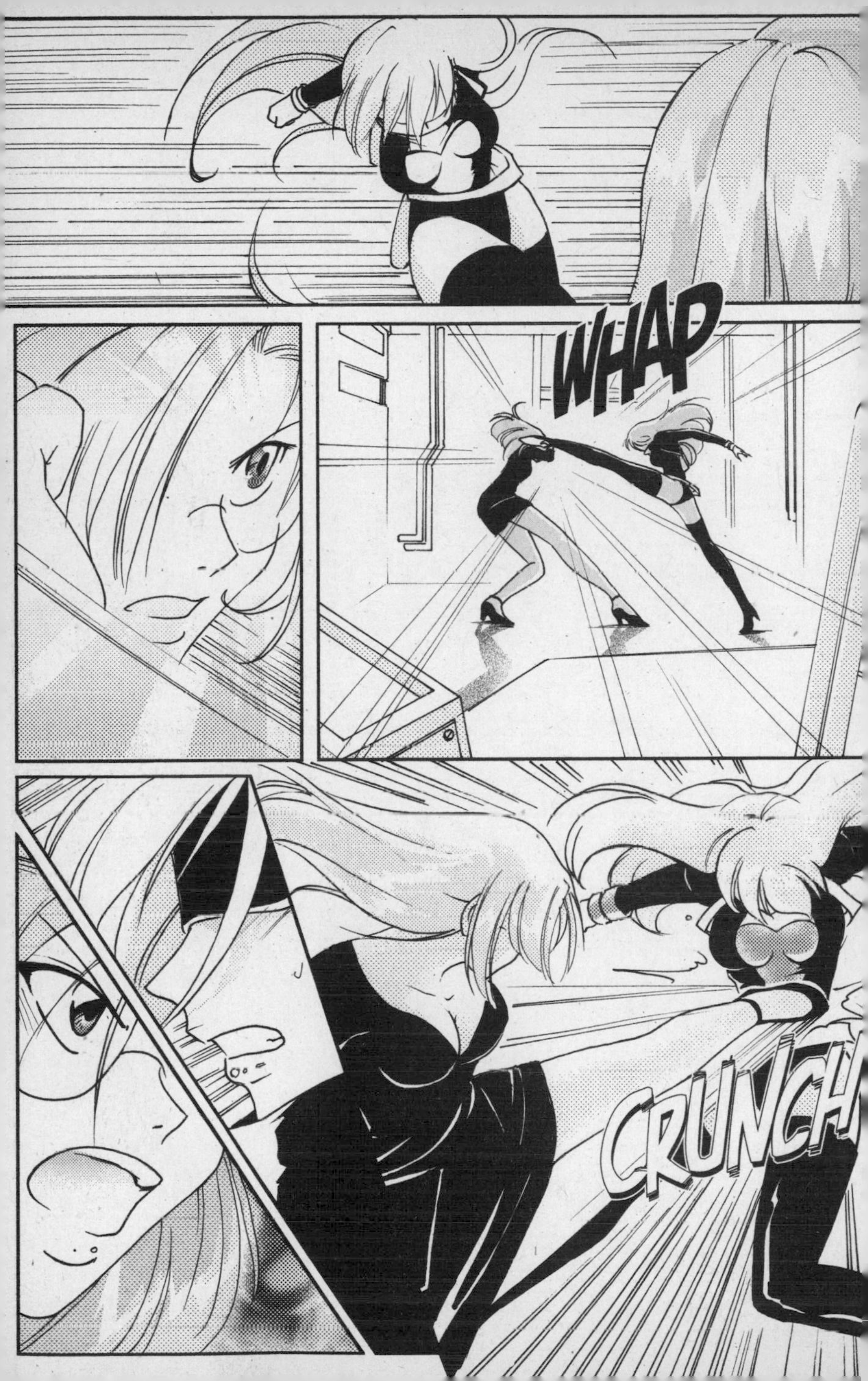
WHAP
CRUNCH

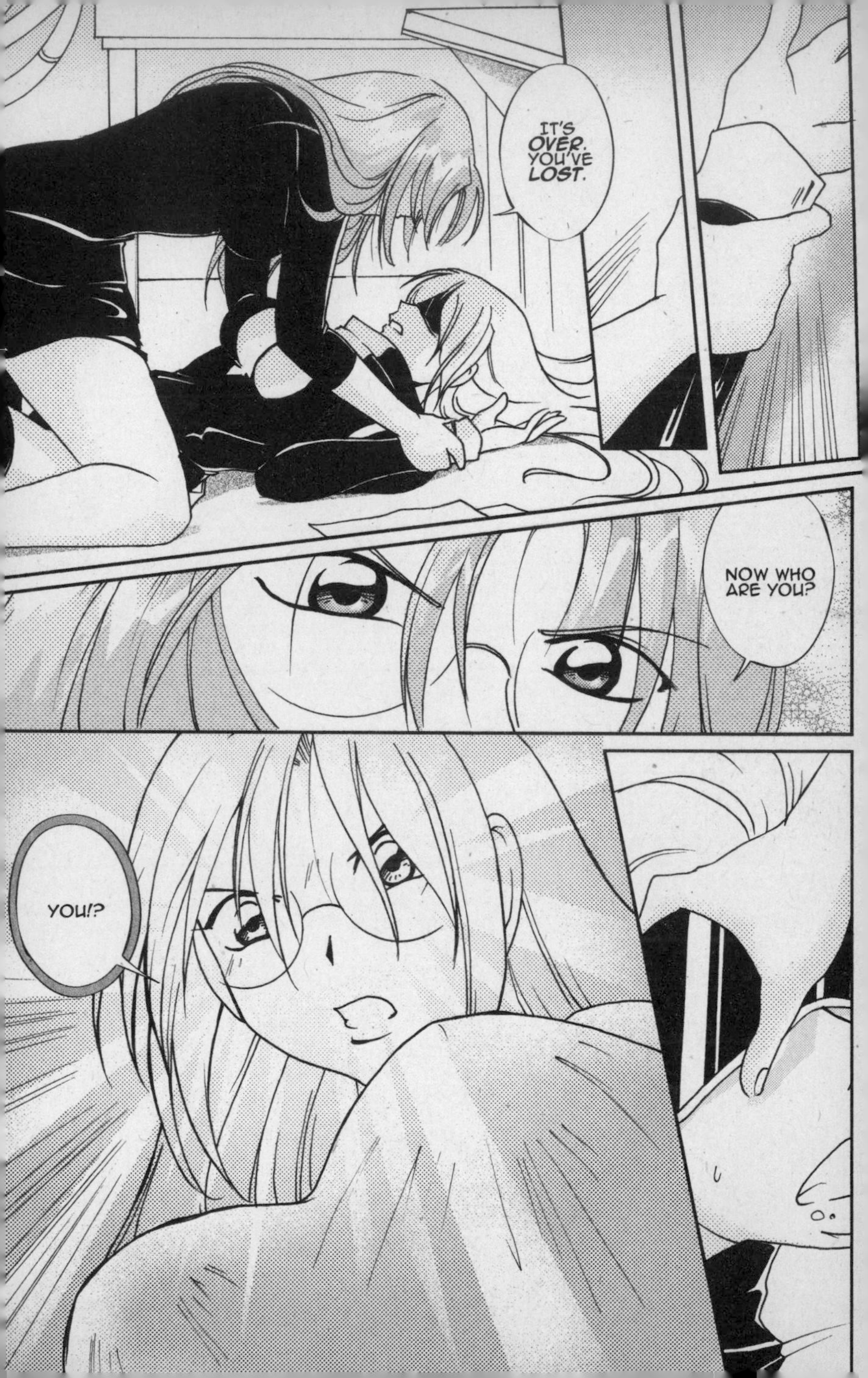
IT'S OVER. YOU'VE LOST.
NOW WHO ARE YOU?
YOU!?

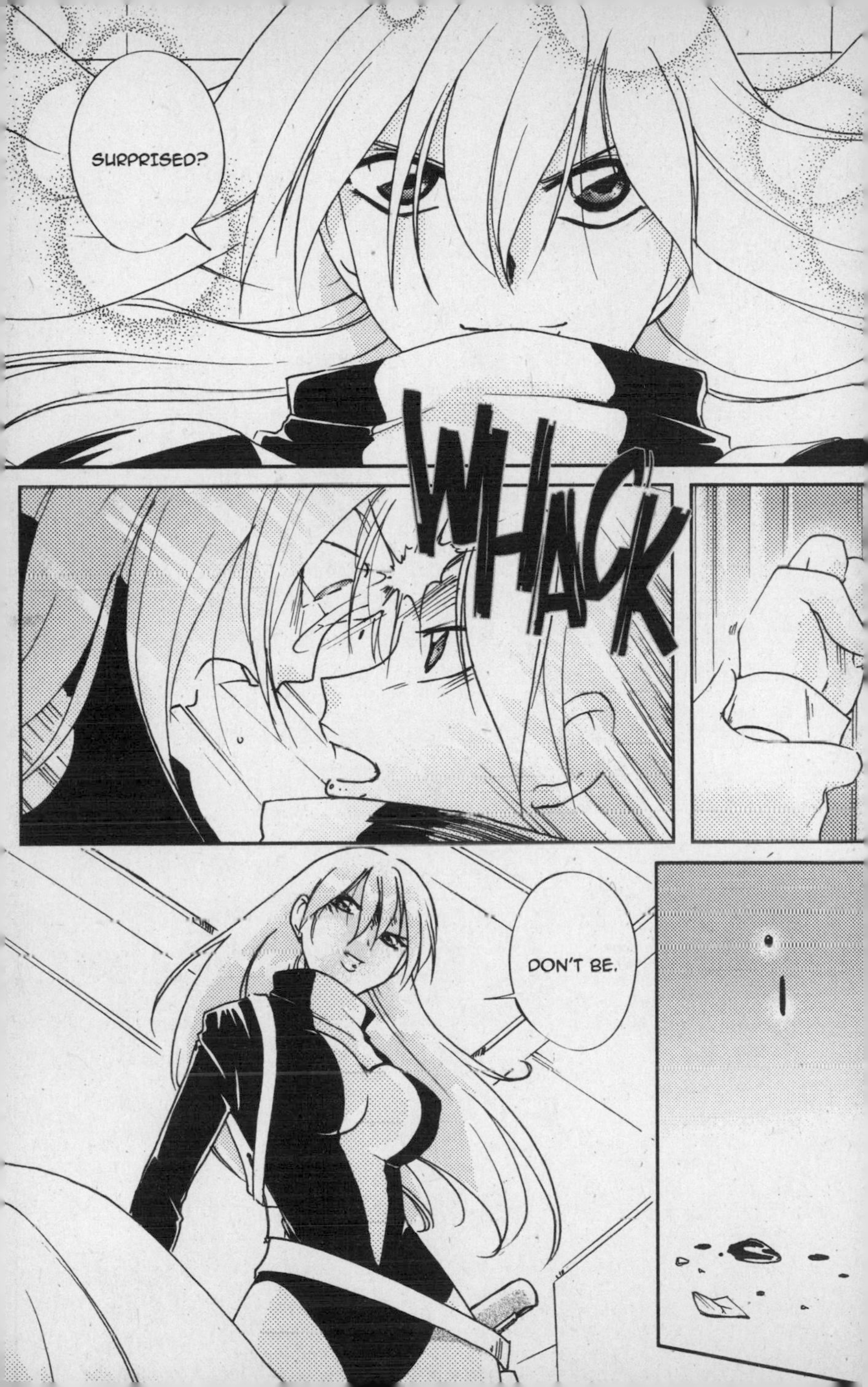
SURPRISED?
WHACK
DON'T BE.

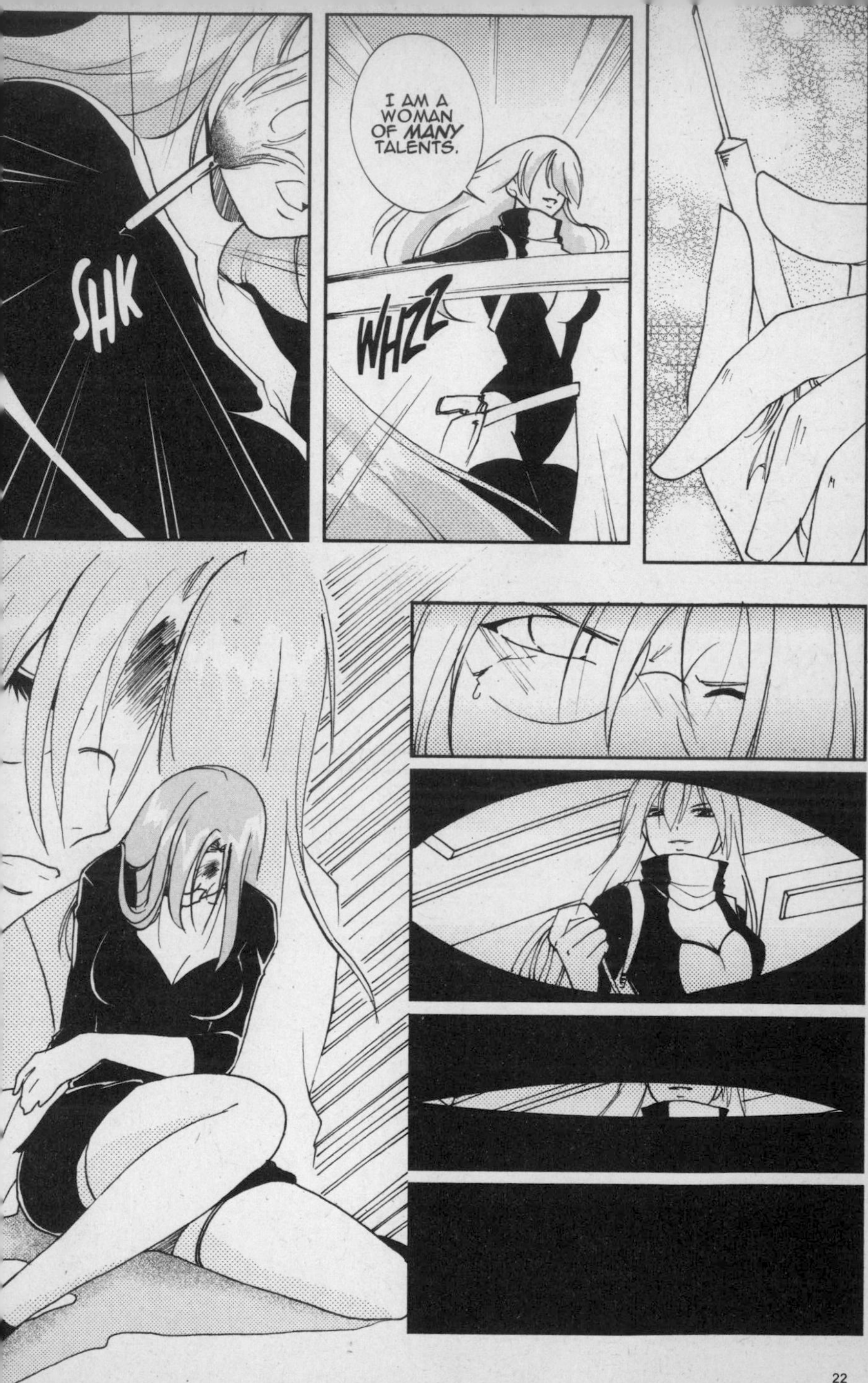
I AM A WOMAN OF MANY TALENTS.
WHZZ
SHK

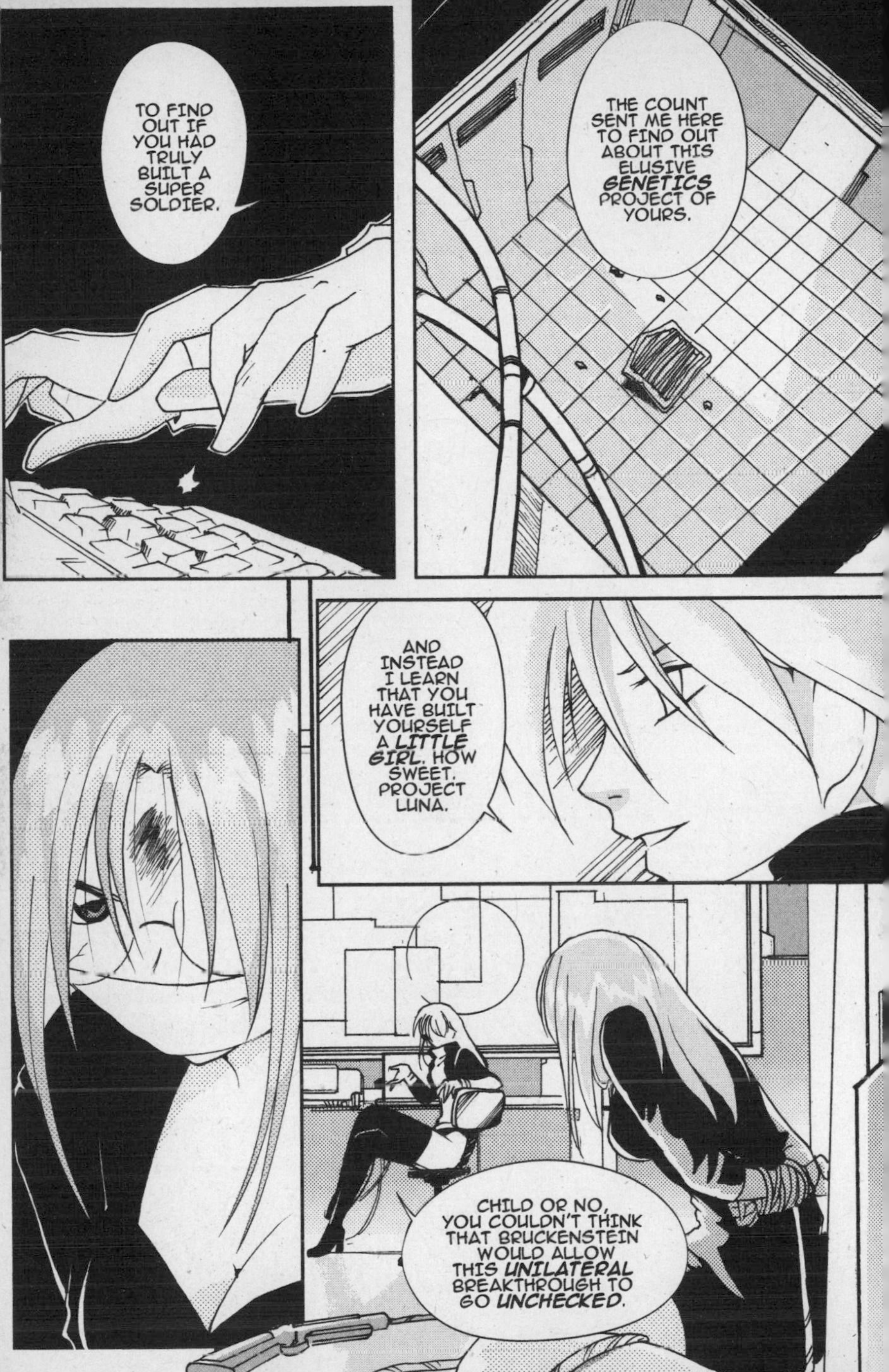
THE COUNT SENT ME HERE TO FIND OUT ABOUT THIS ELUSIVE GENETICS PROJECT OF YOURS.
TO FIND OUT IF YOU HAD TRULY BUILT A SUPER SOLDIER.
AND INSTEAD I LEARN THAT YOU HAVE BUILT YOURSELF A LITTLE GIRL. HOW SWEET. PROJECT LUNA.
CHILD OR NO, YOU COULDN'T THINK THAT BRUCKENSTEIN WOULD ALLOW THIS UNILATERAL BREAKTHROUGH TO GO UNCHECKED.

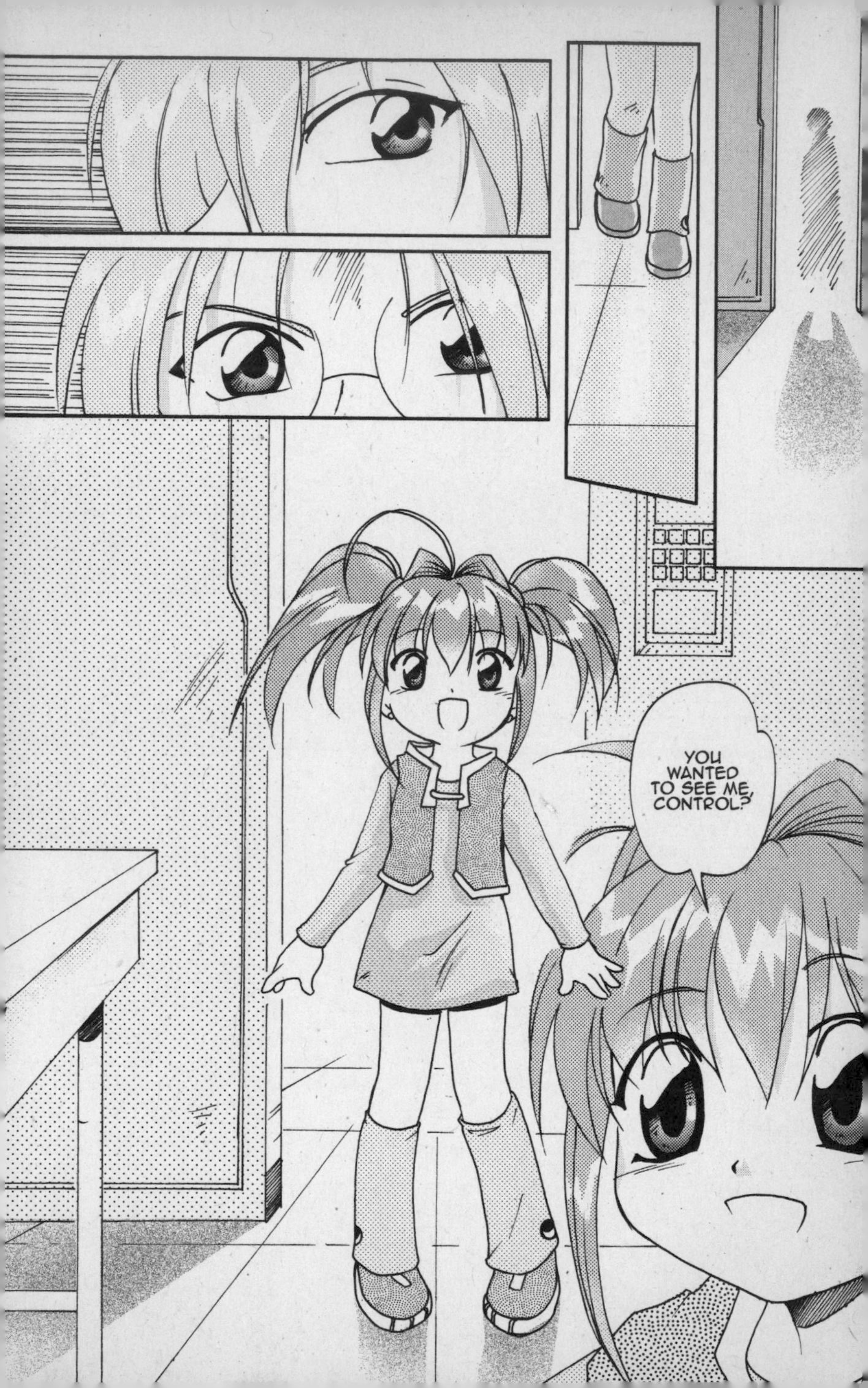
YOU WANTED TO SEE ME, CONTROL?

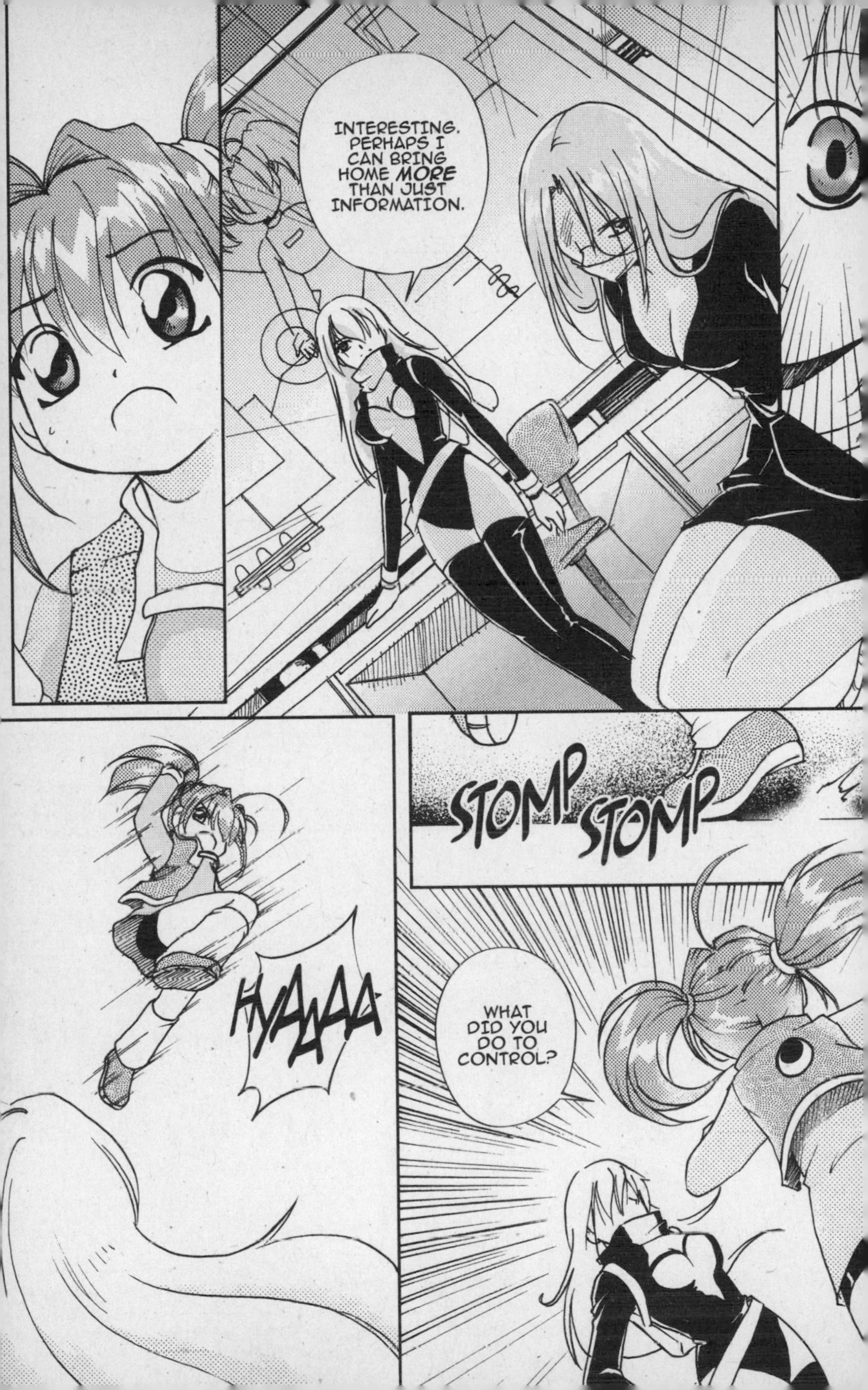
INTERESTING. PERHAPS I CAN BRING HOME *MORE* THAN JUST INFORMATION.
STOMP STOMP
WHAT DID YOU DO TO CONTROL?
KYAAAA

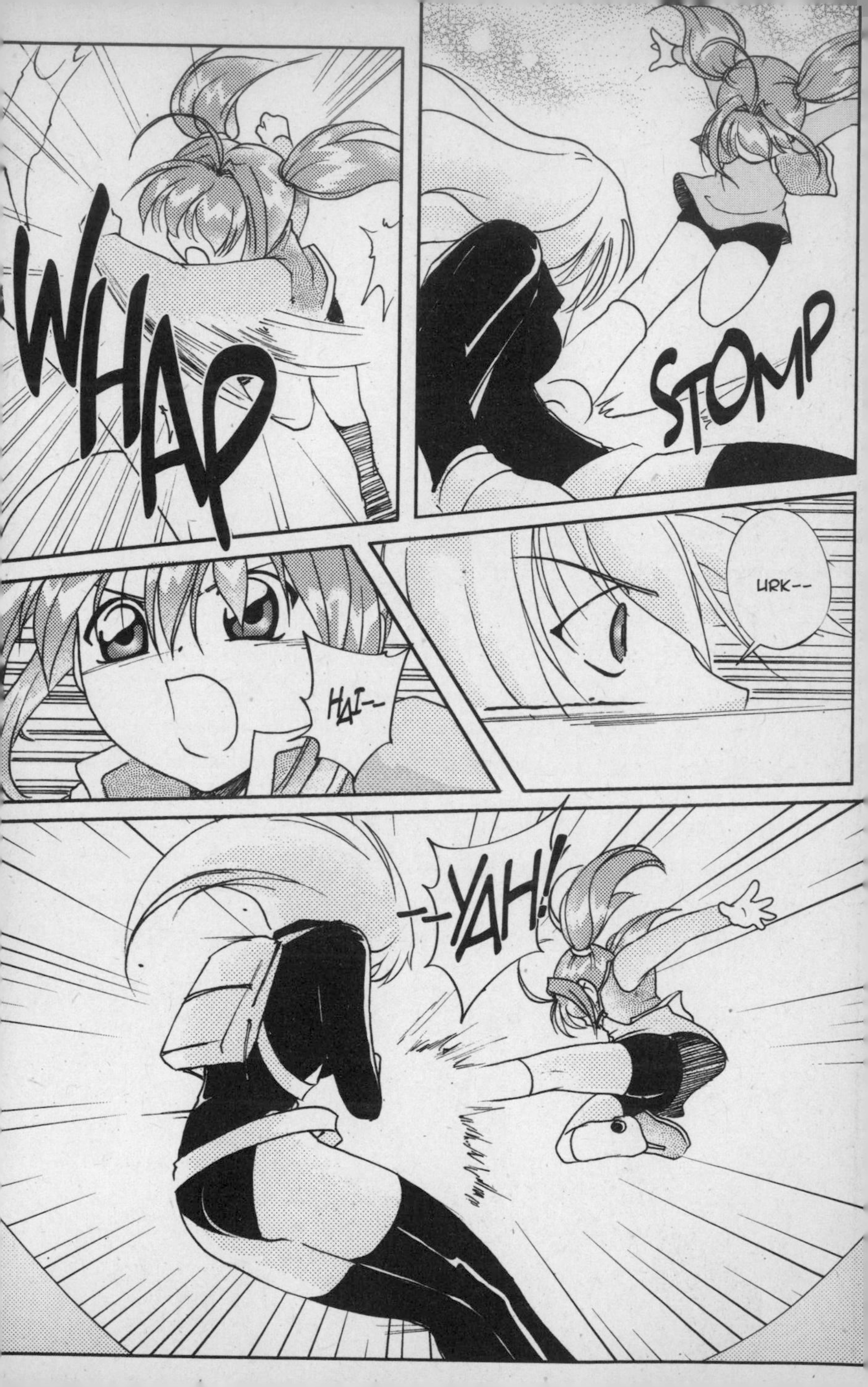
STOMP
WHAP
URK--
HAI--
--YAH!

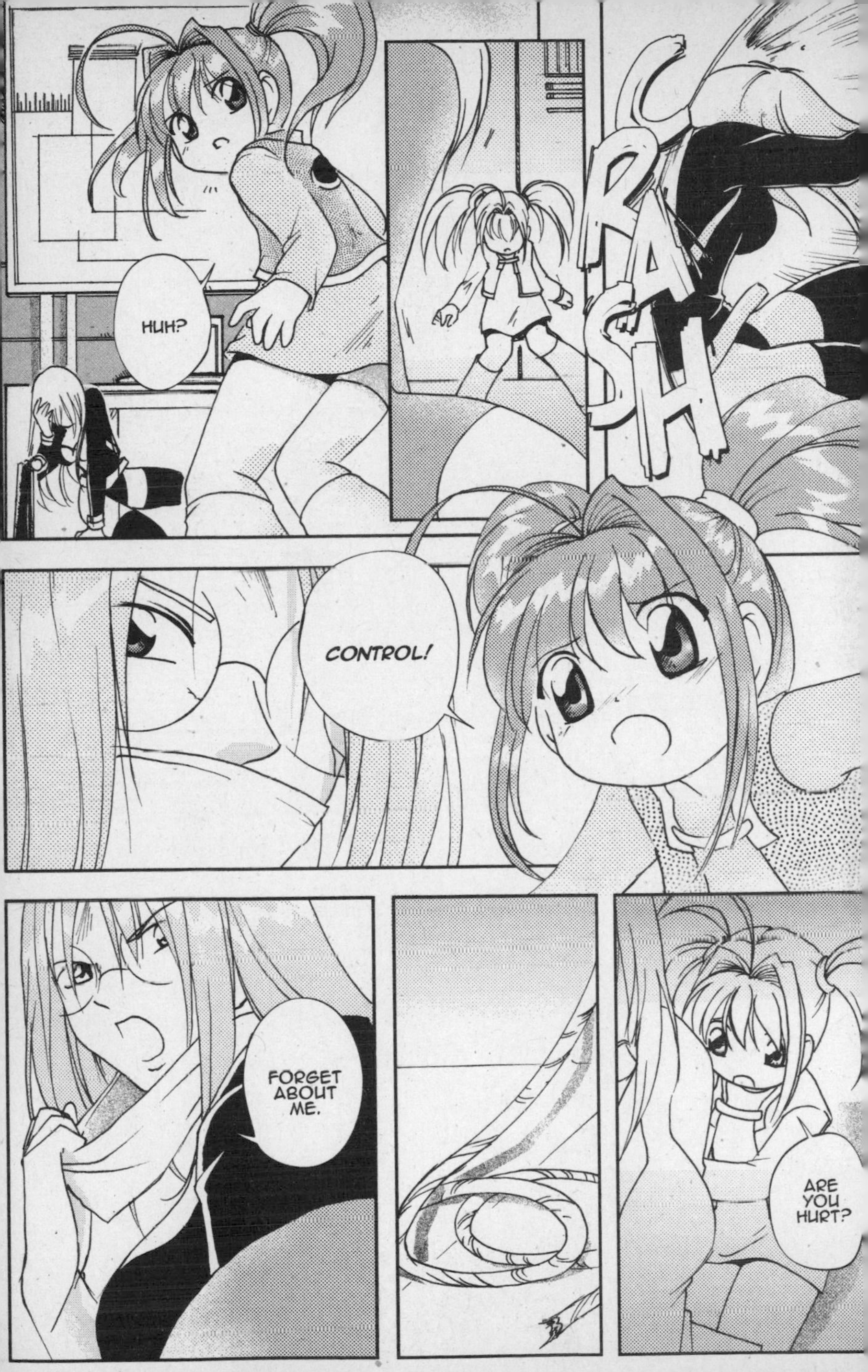
CRASH
HUH?
CONTROL!
ARE YOU HURT?
FORGET ABOUT ME.

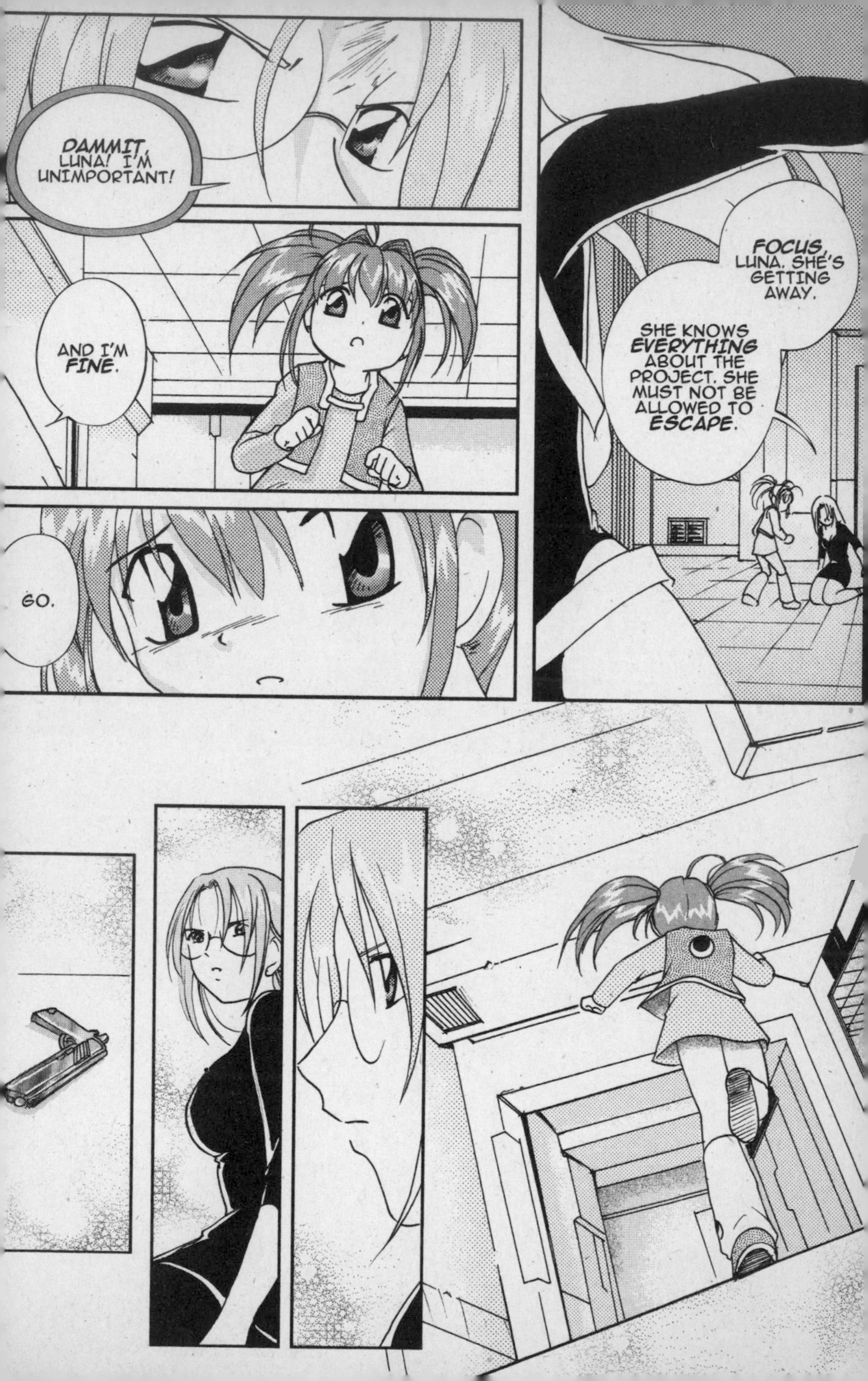
FOCUS, LUNA. SHE'S GETTING AWAY.
SHE KNOWS EVERYTHING ABOUT THE PROJECT. SHE MUST NOT BE ALLOWED TO ESCAPE.
DAMMIT, LUNA! I'M UNIMPORTANT!
AND I'M FINE.
GO.

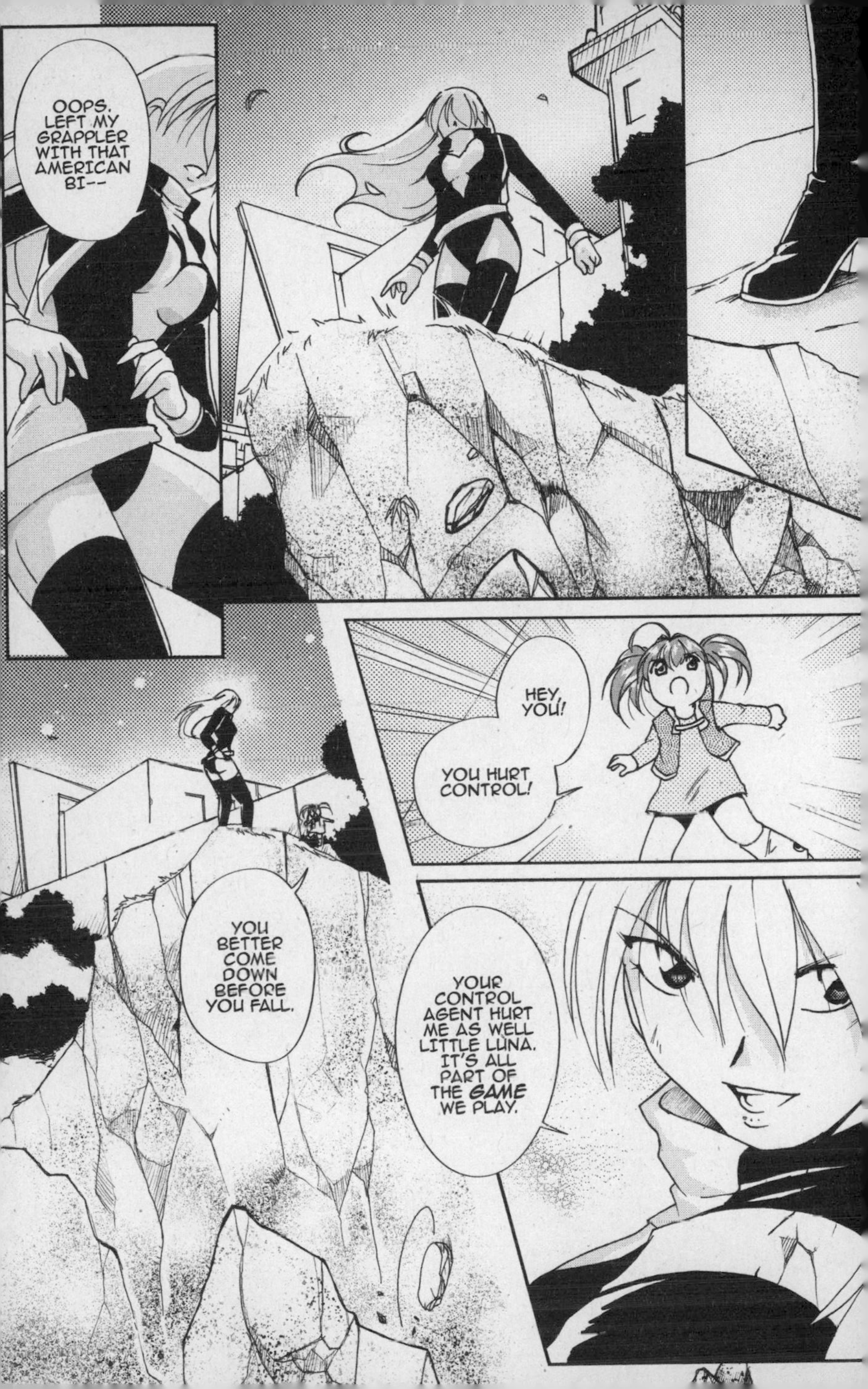
OOPS. LEFT MY GRAPPLER WITH THAT AMERICAN BI--
HEY, YOU!
YOU HURT CONTROL!
YOUR CONTROL AGENT HURT ME AS WELL LITTLE LUNA. IT'S ALL PART OF THE ***GAME*** WE PLAY.
YOU BETTER COME DOWN BEFORE YOU FALL.

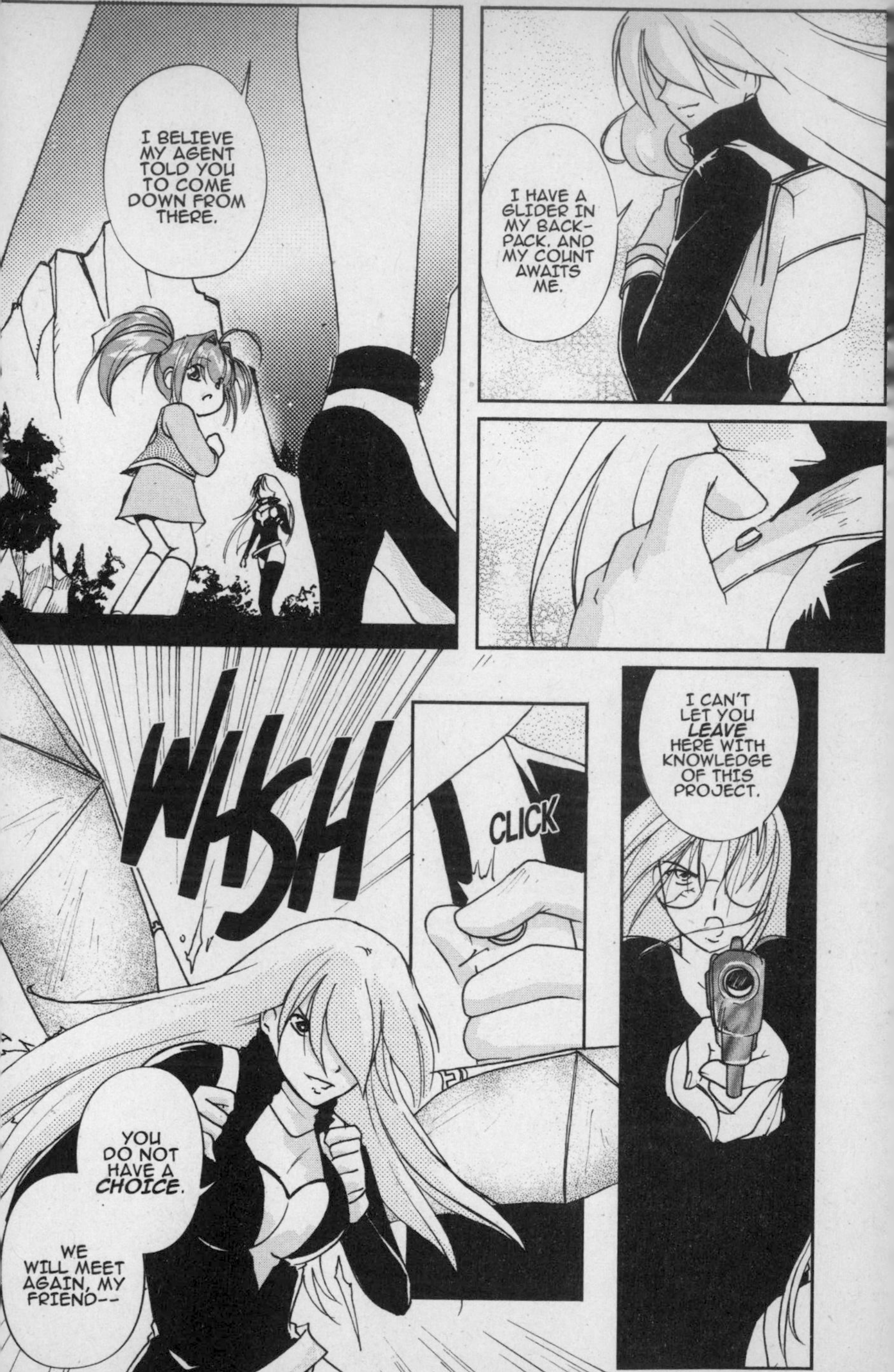
I HAVE A GLIDER IN MY BACK-PACK, AND MY COUNT AWAITS ME.
I BELIEVE MY AGENT TOLD YOU TO COME DOWN FROM THERE.
I CAN'T LET YOU *LEAVE* HERE WITH KNOWLEDGE OF THIS PROJECT.
CLICK
WHSH
YOU DO NOT HAVE A *CHOICE*.
WE WILL MEET AGAIN, MY FRIEND--

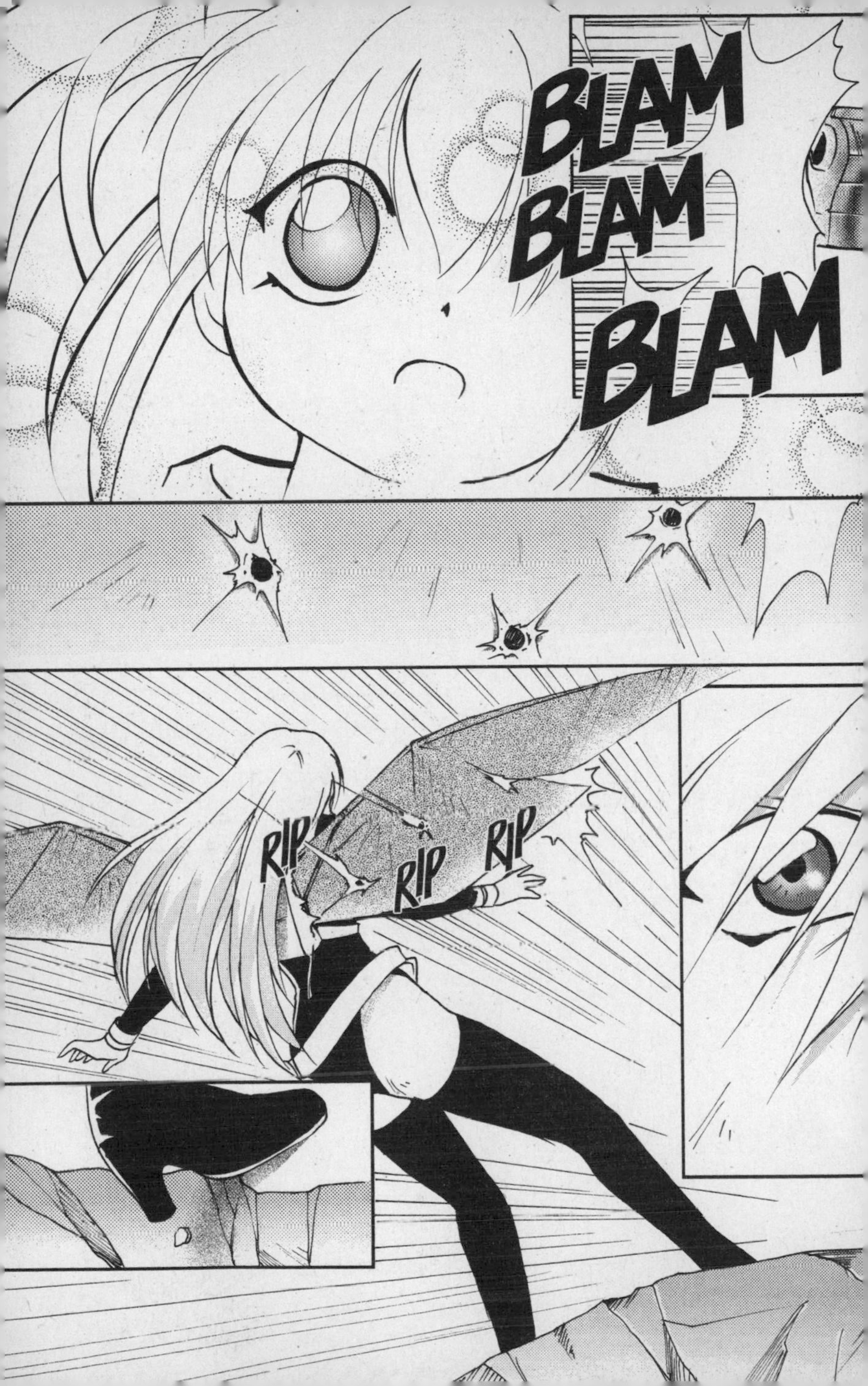
BLAM
BLAM
BLAM
RIP
RIP
RIP

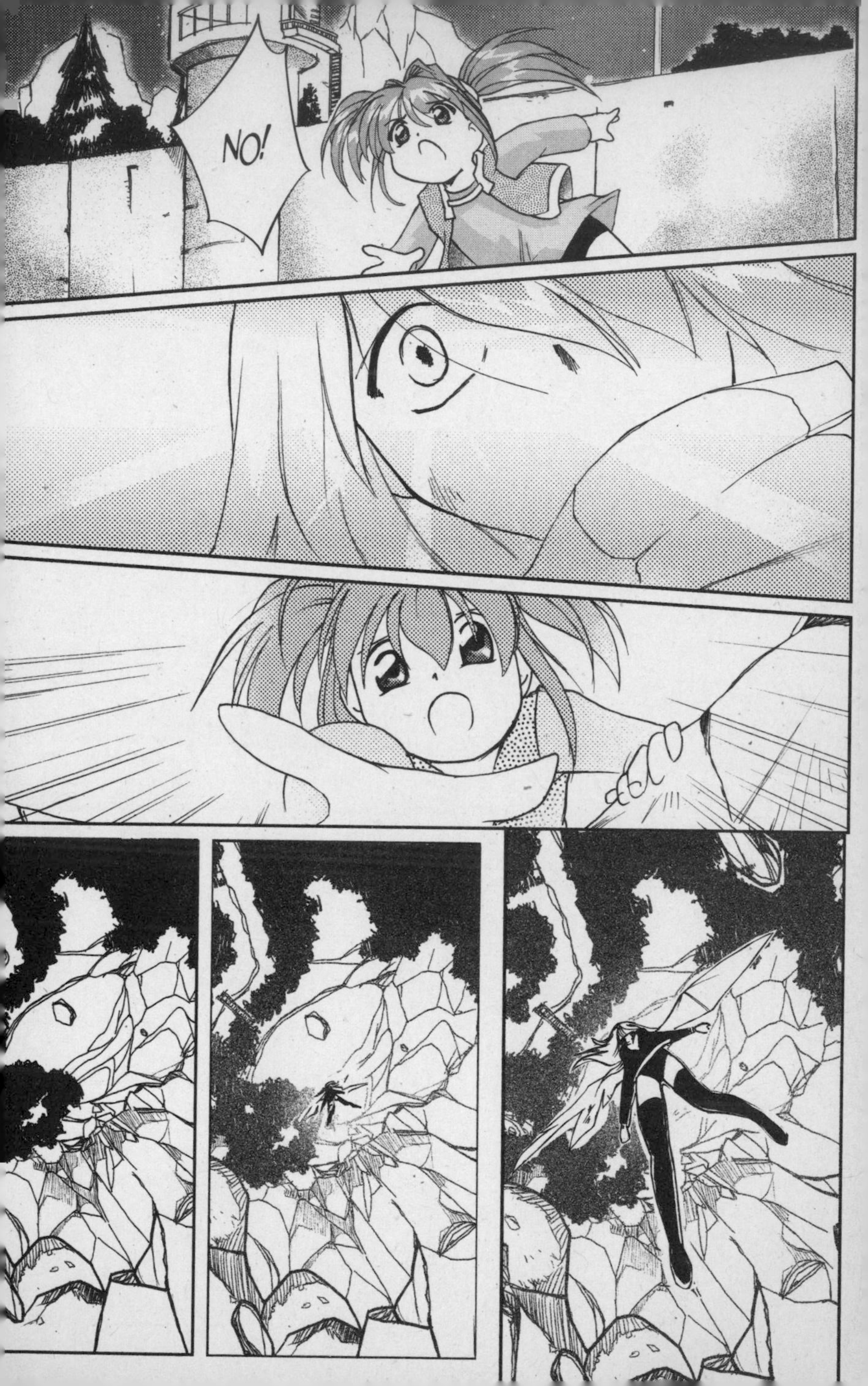
NO!

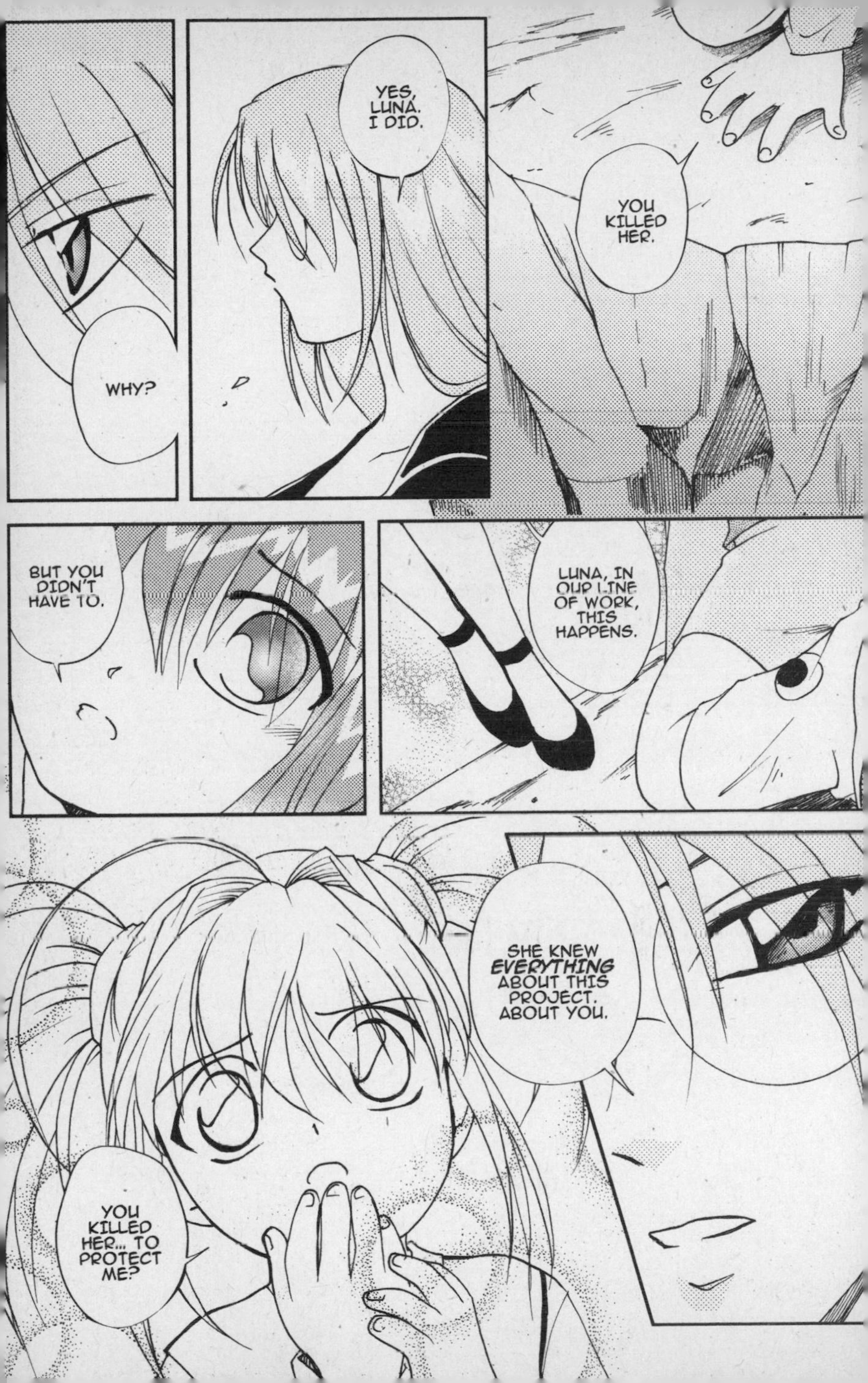
YOU KILLED HER.
YES, LUNA. I DID.
WHY?
LUNA, IN OUR LINE OF WORK, THIS HAPPENS.
BUT YOU DIDN'T HAVE TO.
SHE KNEW *EVERYTHING* ABOUT THIS PROJECT. ABOUT YOU.
YOU KILLED HER... TO PROTECT ME?

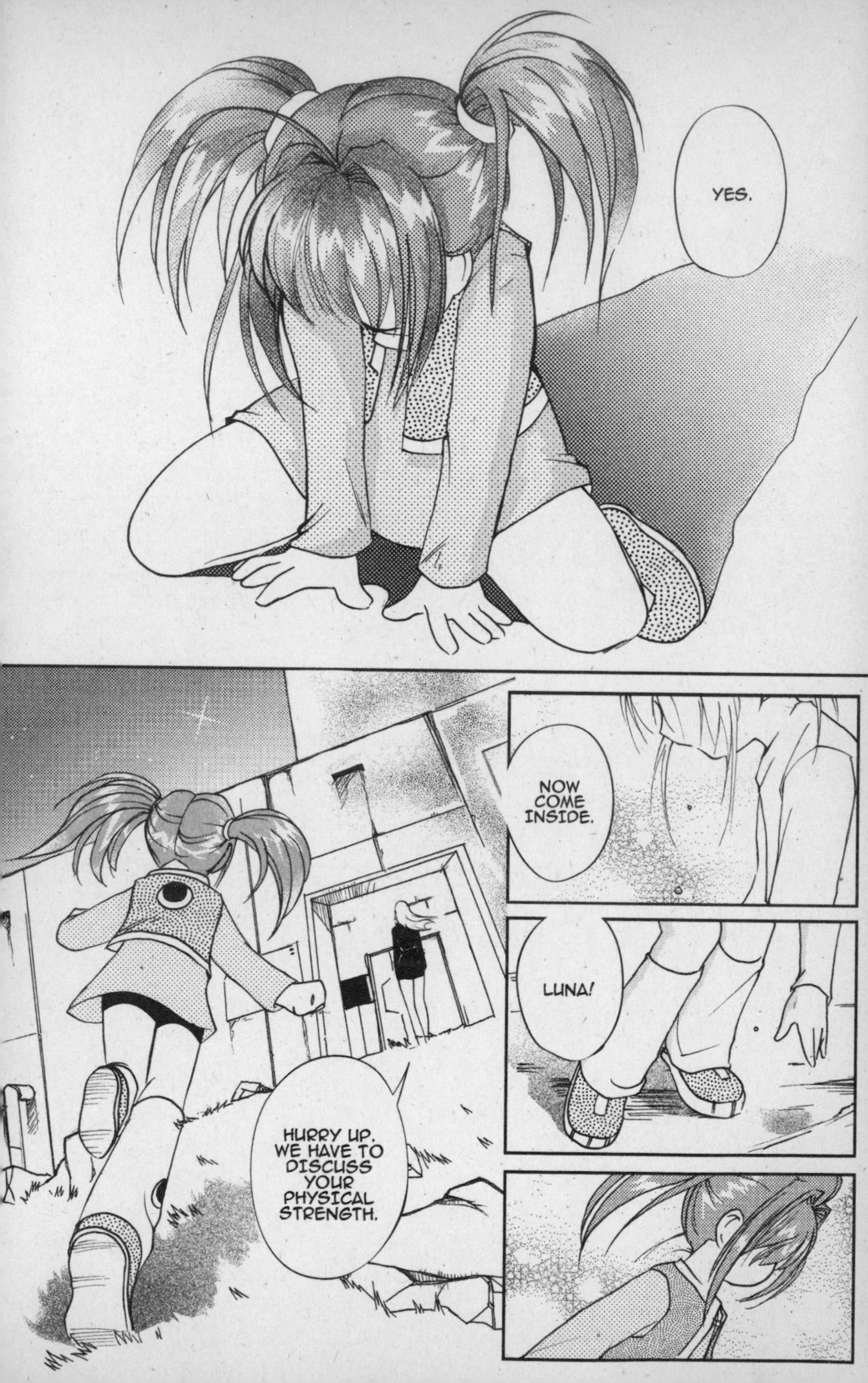
YES.
NOW COME INSIDE.
LUNA!
HURRY UP. WE HAVE TO DISCUSS YOUR PHYSICAL STRENGTH.

File 12
EVOLUTIONS

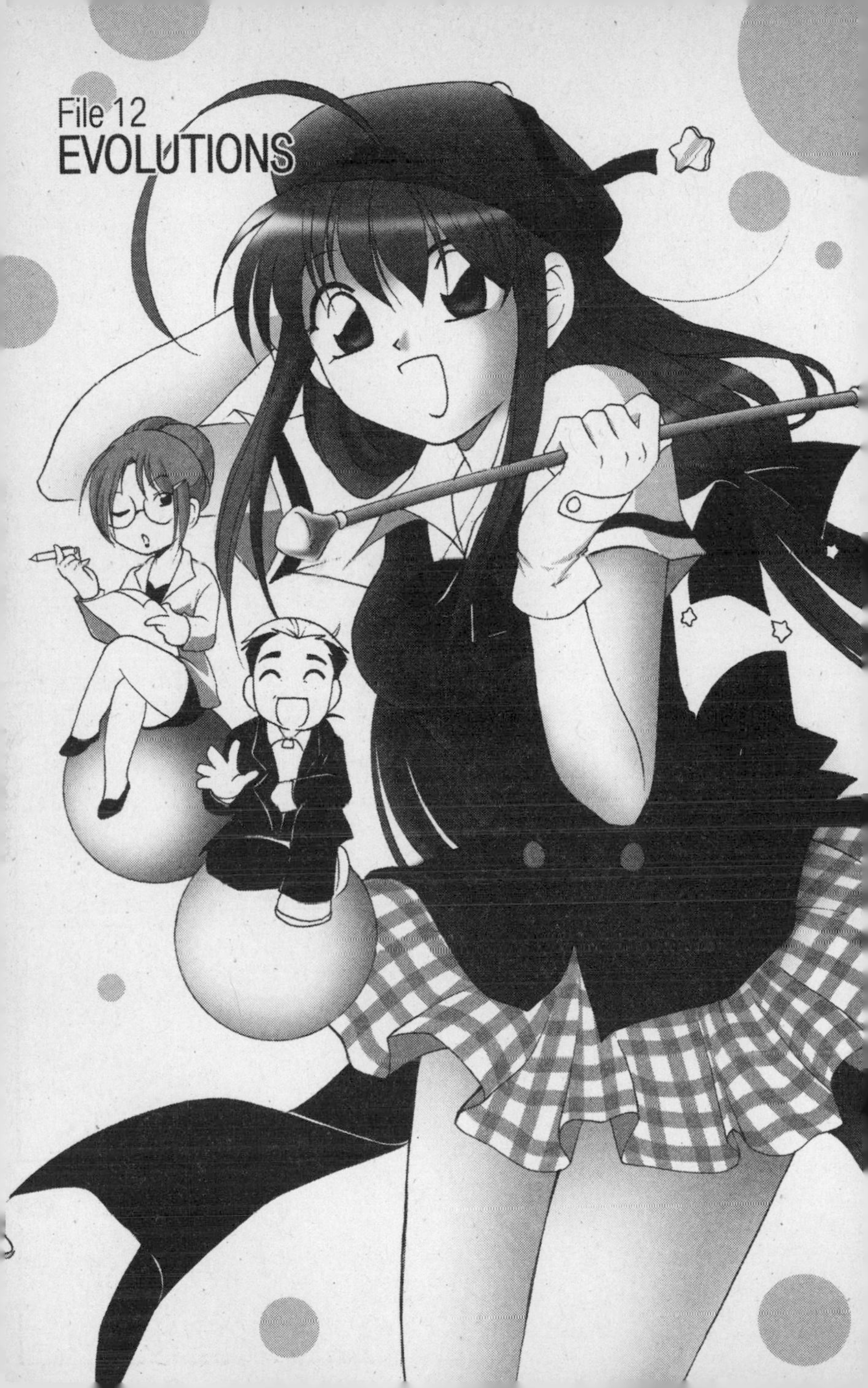

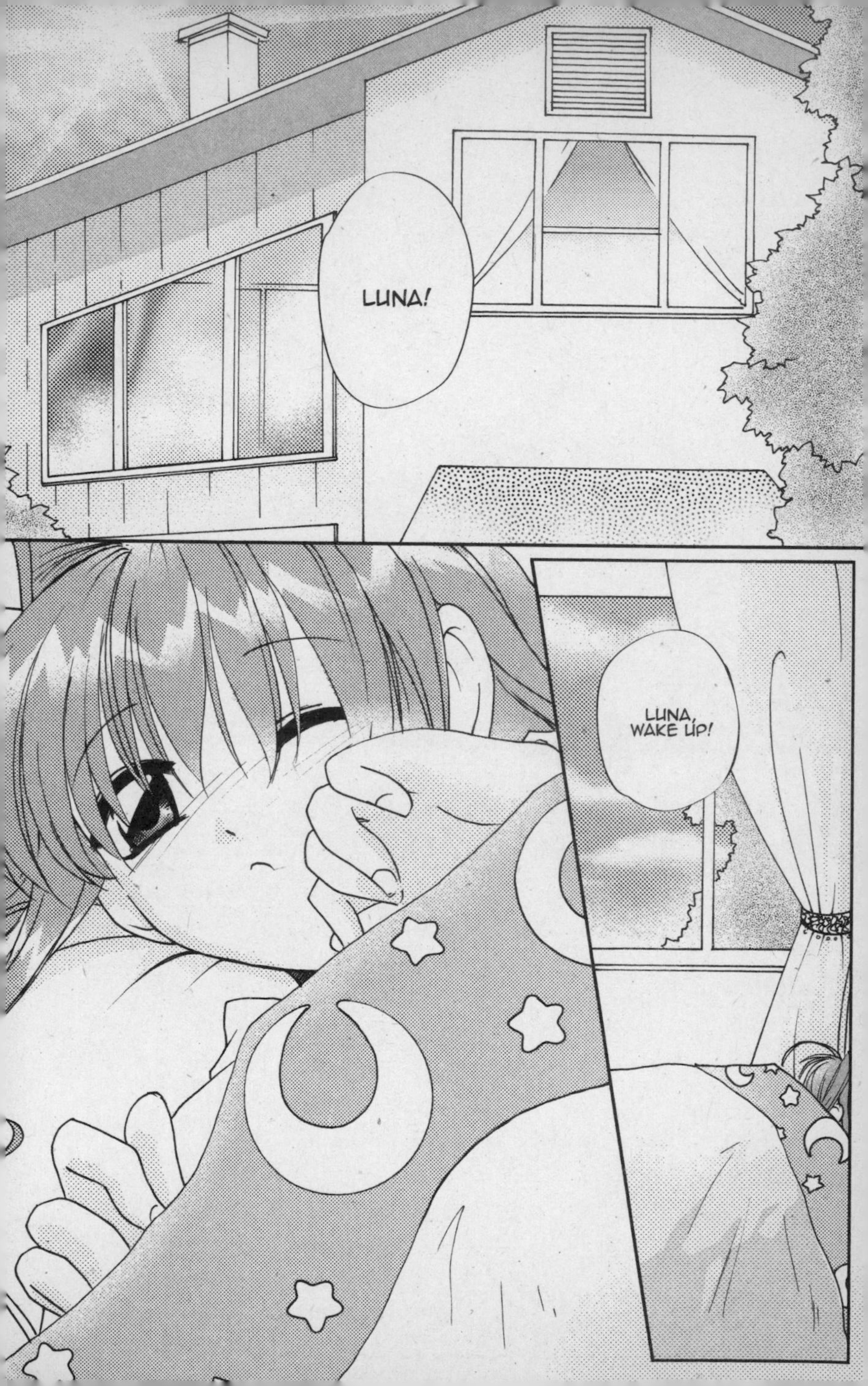
LUNA!
LUNA, WAKE UP!

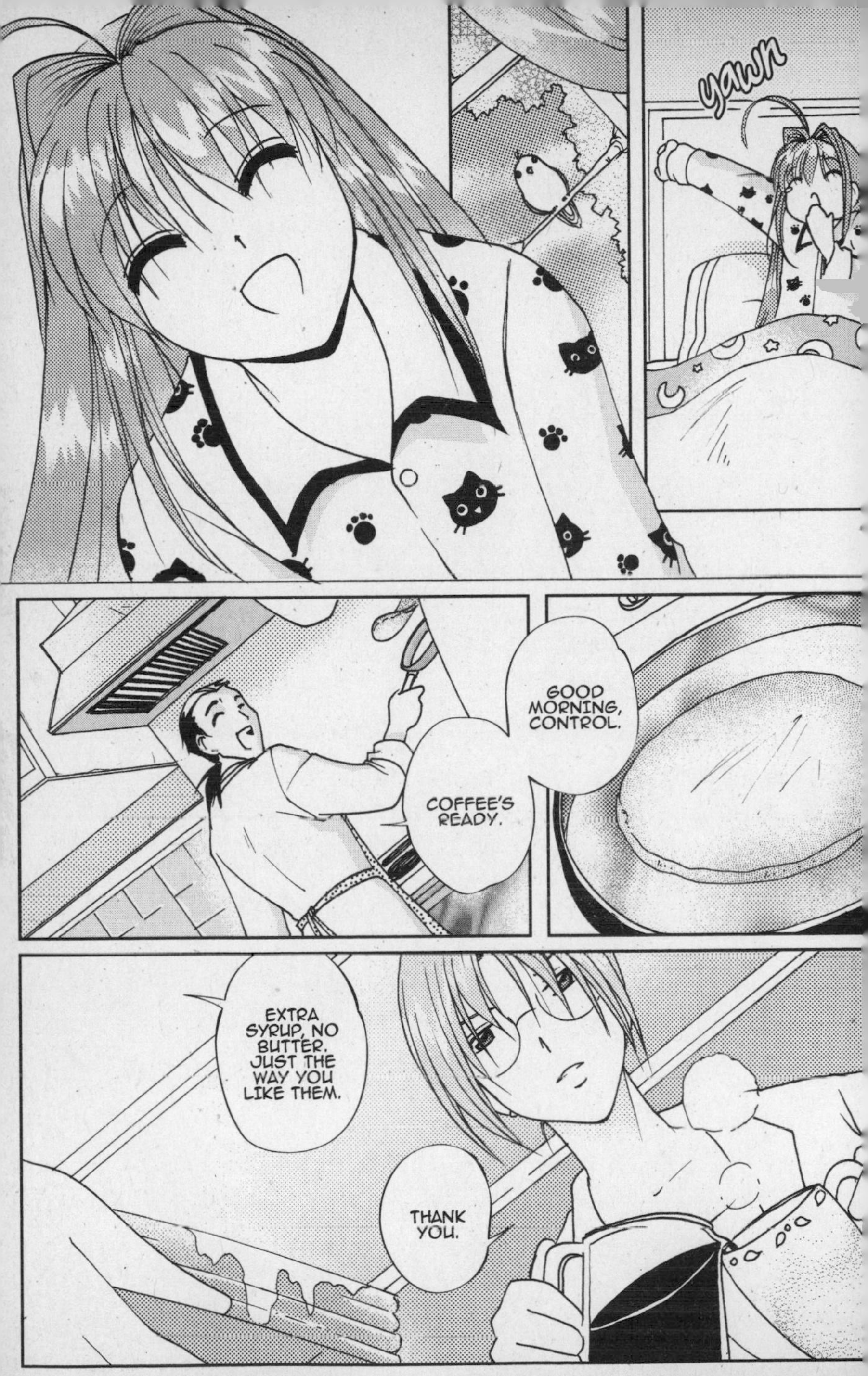
YAWN
GOOD MORNING, CONTROL.
COFFEE'S READY.
EXTRA SYRUP, NO BUTTER. JUST THE WAY YOU LIKE THEM.
THANK YOU.

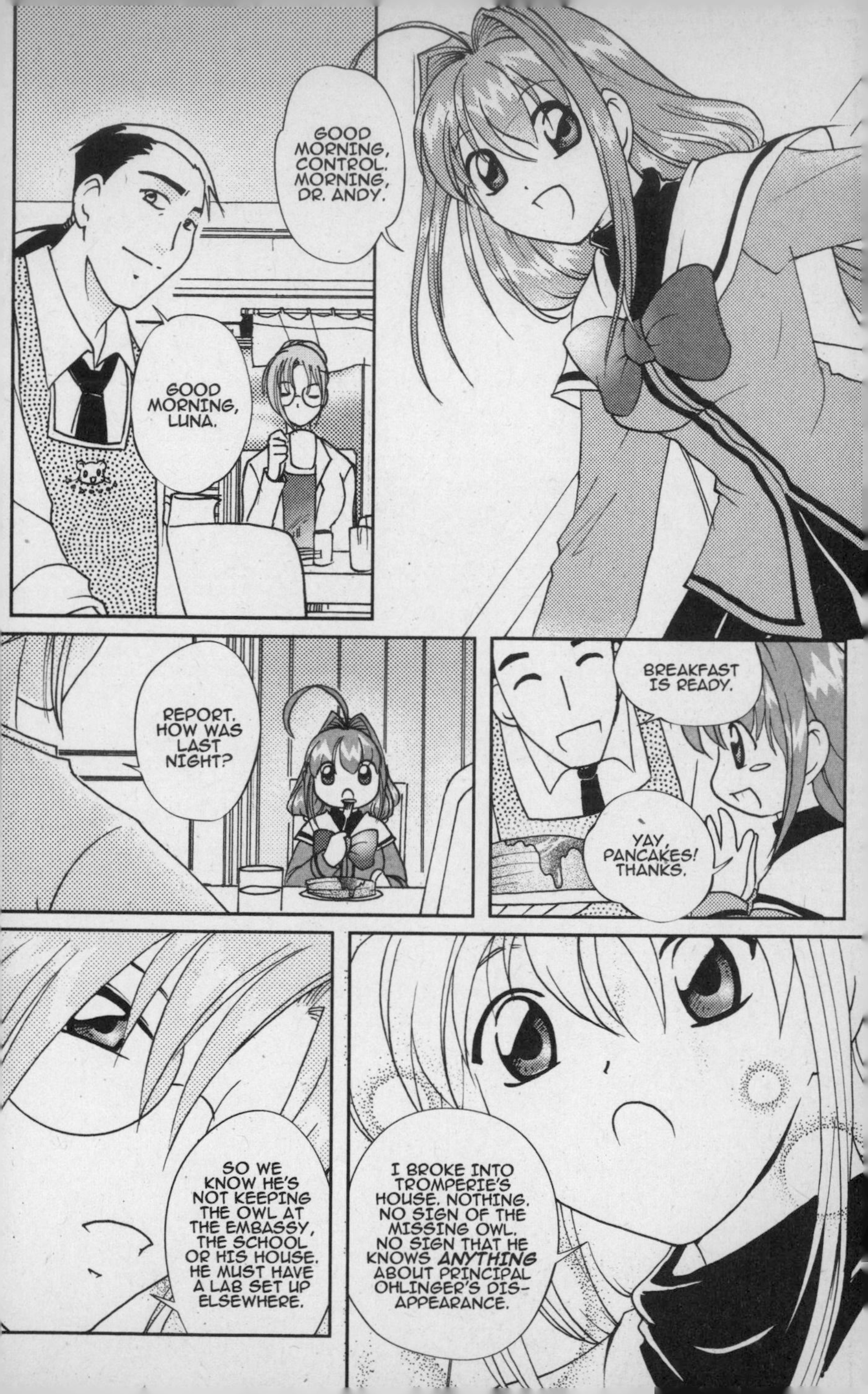
GOOD MORNING, CONTROL. MORNING, DR. ANDY.
GOOD MORNING, LUNA.
BREAKFAST IS READY.
YAY, PANCAKES! THANKS.
REPORT. HOW WAS LAST NIGHT?
I BROKE INTO TROMPERIE'S HOUSE. NOTHING. NO SIGN OF THE MISSING OWL. NO SIGN THAT HE KNOWS *ANYTHING* ABOUT PRINCIPAL OHLINGER'S DIS-APPEARANCE.
SO WE KNOW HE'S NOT KEEPING THE OWL AT THE EMBASSY, THE SCHOOL OR HIS HOUSE. HE MUST HAVE A LAB SET UP ELSEWHERE.

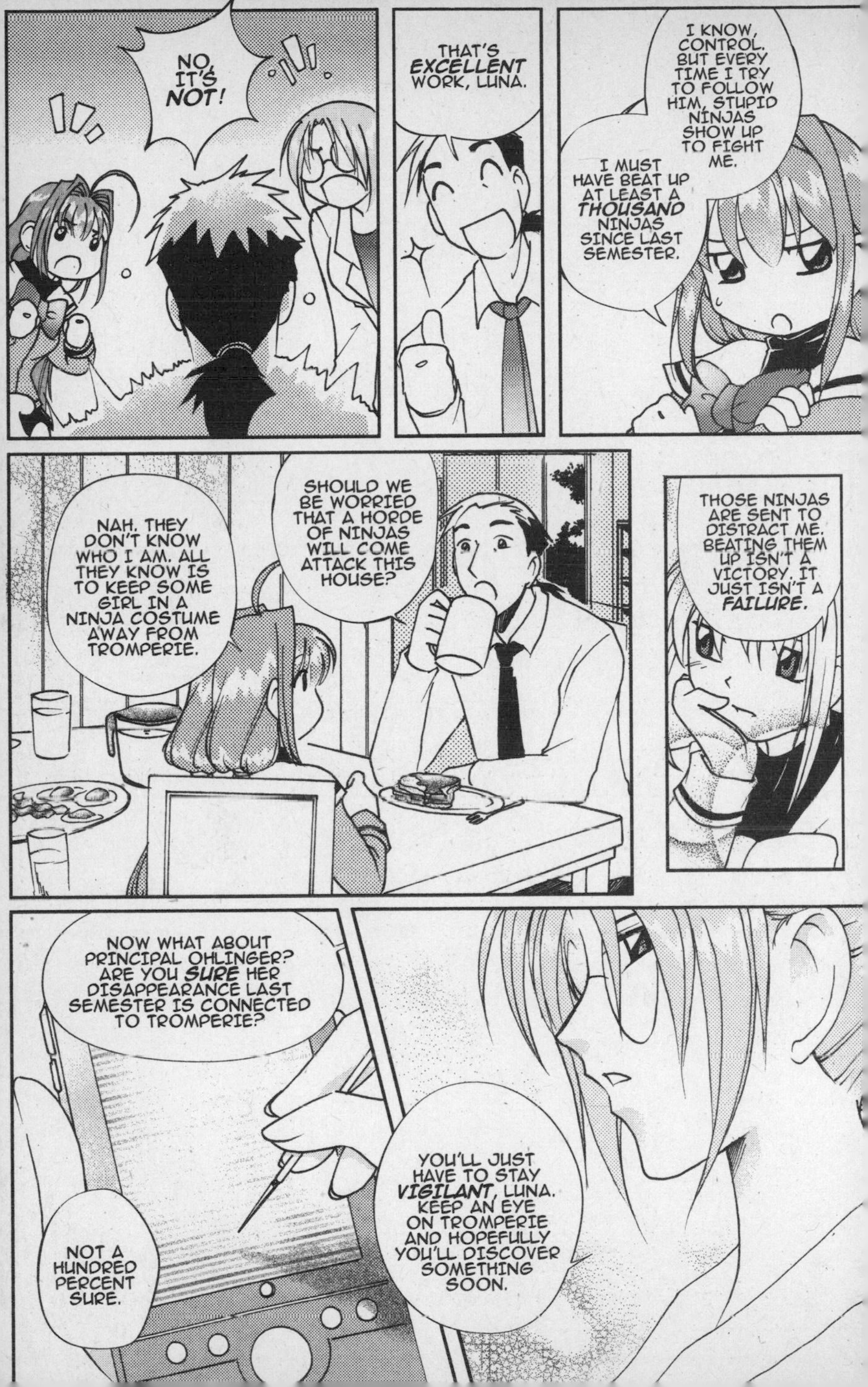
I KNOW, CONTROL. BUT EVERY TIME I TRY TO FOLLOW HIM, STUPID NINJAS SHOW UP TO FIGHT ME.
I MUST HAVE BEAT UP AT LEAST A *THOUSAND* NINJAS SINCE LAST SEMESTER.
THAT'S *EXCELLENT* WORK, LUNA.
NO, IT'S *NOT*!
THOSE NINJAS ARE SENT TO DISTRACT ME. BEATING THEM UP ISN'T A VICTORY. IT JUST ISN'T A *FAILURE.*
SHOULD WE BE WORRIED THAT A HORDE OF NINJAS WILL COME ATTACK THIS HOUSE?
NAH. THEY DON'T KNOW WHO I AM. ALL THEY KNOW IS TO KEEP SOME GIRL IN A NINJA COSTUME AWAY FROM TROMPERIE.
YOU'LL JUST HAVE TO STAY *VIGILANT*, LUNA. KEEP AN EYE ON TROMPERIE AND HOPEFULLY YOU'LL DISCOVER SOMETHING SOON.
NOW WHAT ABOUT PRINCIPAL OHLINGER? ARE YOU *SURE* HER DISAPPEARANCE LAST SEMESTER IS CONNECTED TO TROMPERIE?
NOT A HUNDRED PERCENT SURE.

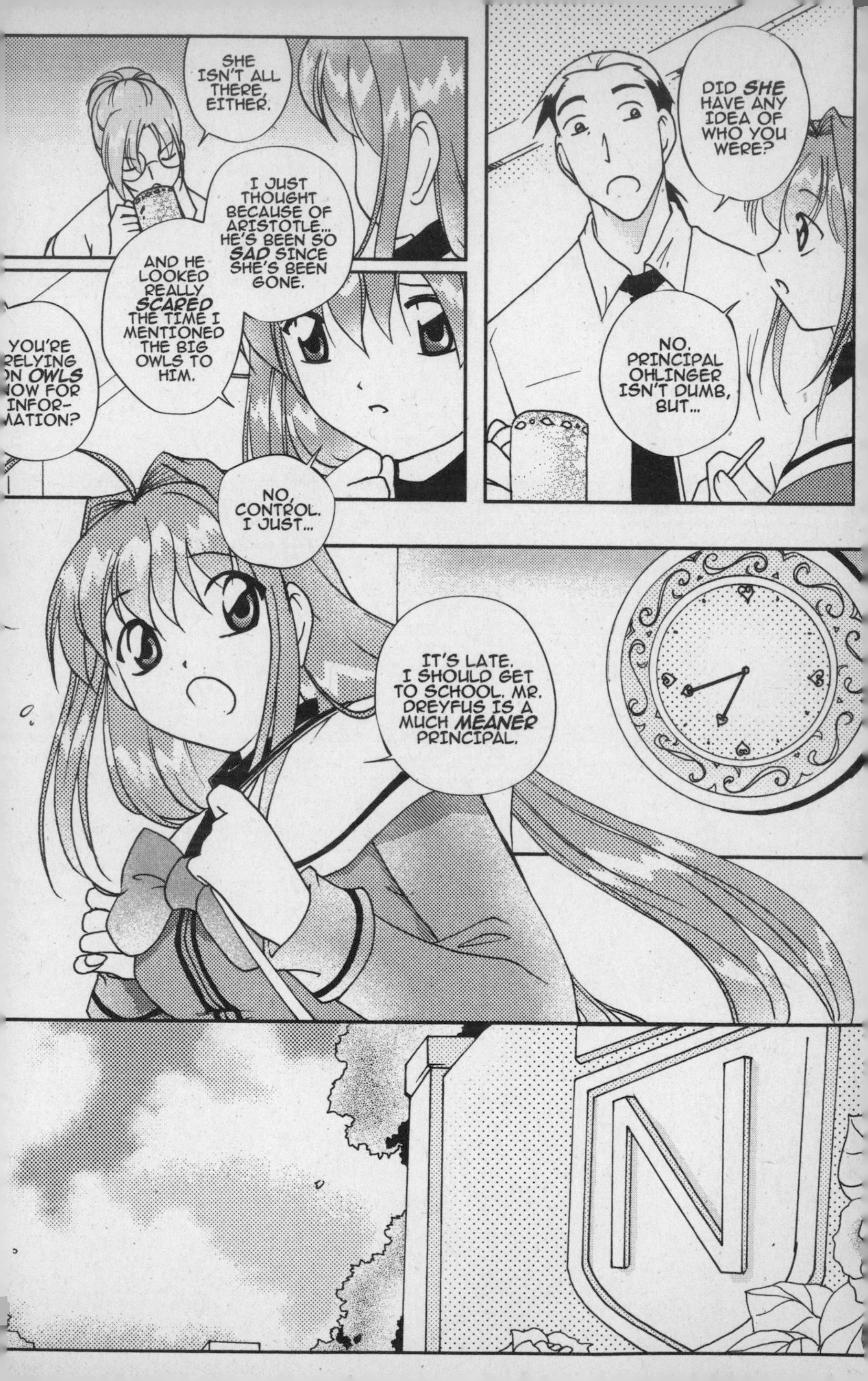
DID SHE HAVE ANY IDEA OF WHO YOU WERE?
NO. PRINCIPAL OHLINGER ISN'T DUMB, BUT...
SHE ISN'T ALL THERE, EITHER.
I JUST THOUGHT BECAUSE OF ARISTOTLE... HE'S BEEN SO SAD SINCE SHE'S BEEN GONE.
AND HE LOOKED REALLY SCARED THE TIME I MENTIONED THE BIG OWLS TO HIM.
YOU'RE RELYING ON OWLS NOW FOR INFORMATION?
NO, CONTROL. I JUST...
IT'S LATE. I SHOULD GET TO SCHOOL. MR. DREYFUS IS A MUCH MEANER PRINCIPAL.

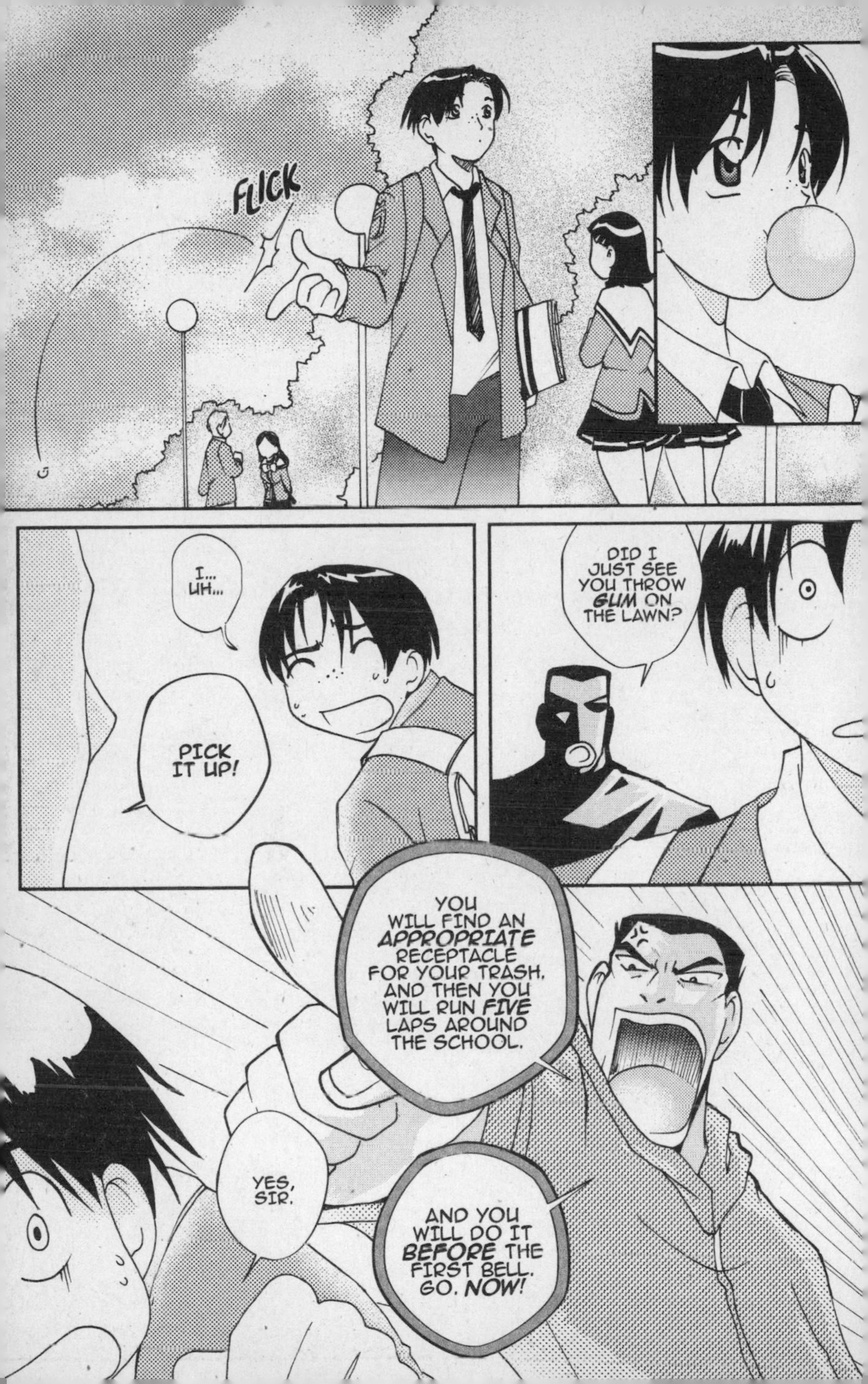

FLICK
DID I JUST SEE YOU THROW GUM ON THE LAWN?
I... UH...
PICK IT UP!
YOU WILL FIND AN APPROPRIATE RECEPTACLE FOR YOUR TRASH. AND THEN YOU WILL RUN FIVE LAPS AROUND THE SCHOOL.
AND YOU WILL DO IT BEFORE THE FIRST BELL. GO. NOW!
YES, SIR.

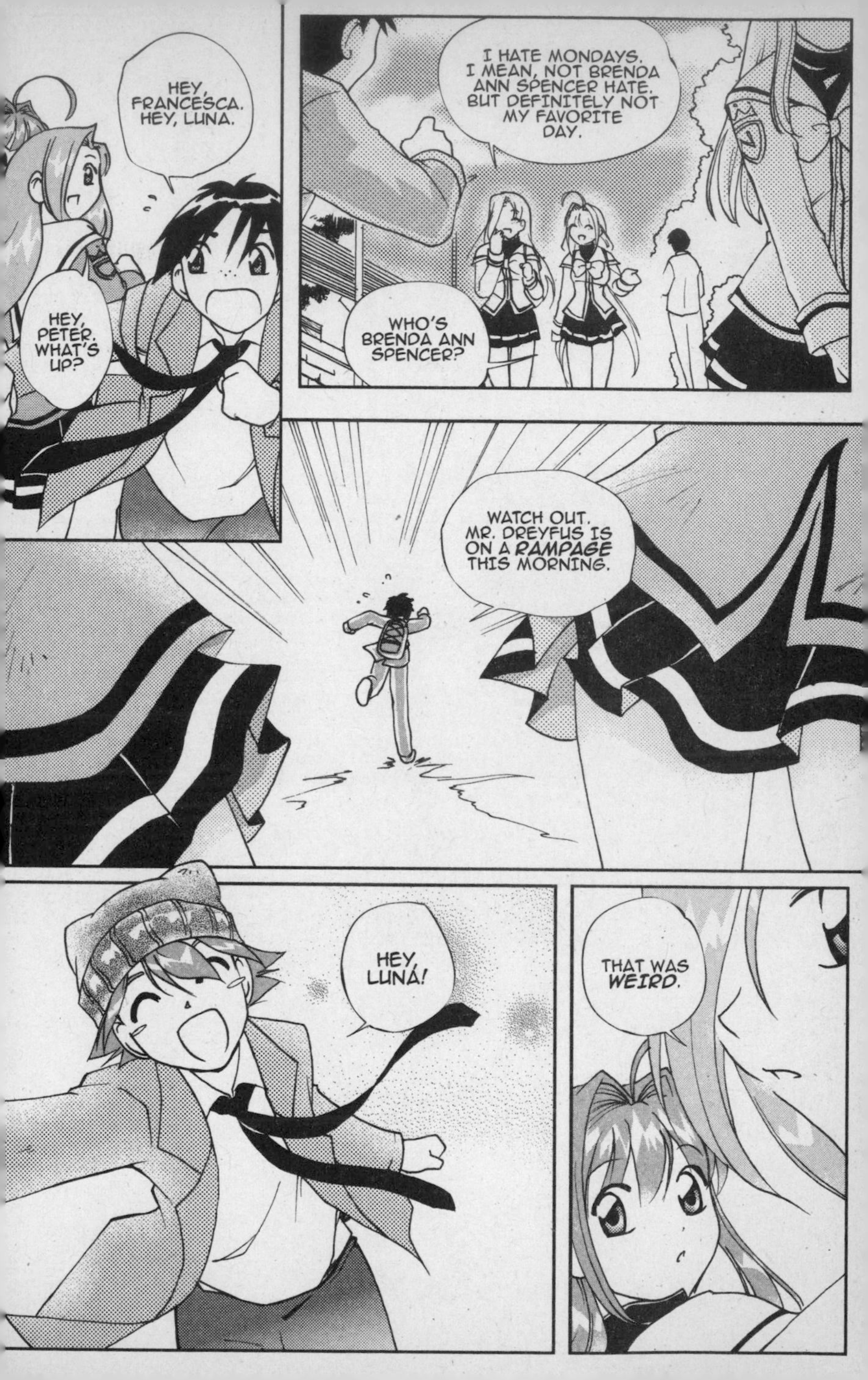
I HATE MONDAYS. I MEAN, NOT BRENDA ANN SPENCER HATE. BUT DEFINITELY NOT MY FAVORITE DAY.
WHO'S BRENDA ANN SPENCER?
HEY, FRANCESCA. HEY, LUNA.
HEY, PETER. WHAT'S UP?
WATCH OUT. MR. DREYFUS IS ON A *RAMPAGE* THIS MORNING.
THAT WAS *WEIRD*.
HEY, LUNA!

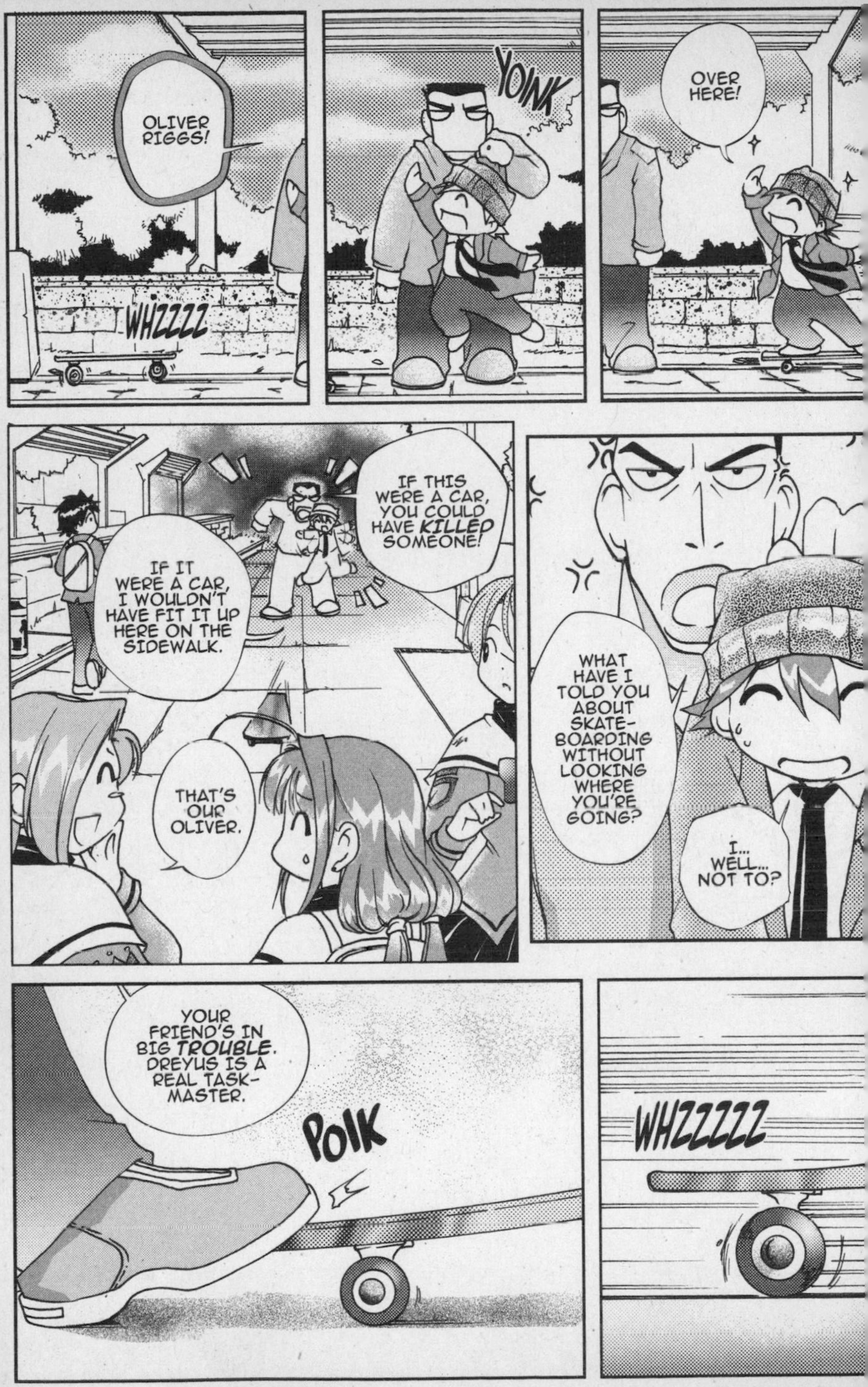
OLIVER RIGGS!
WHZZZZ
YOINK
OVER HERE!
IF THIS WERE A CAR, YOU COULD HAVE *KILLED* SOMEONE!
IF IT WERE A CAR, I WOULDN'T HAVE FIT IT UP HERE ON THE SIDEWALK.
THAT'S OUR OLIVER.
WHAT HAVE I TOLD YOU ABOUT SKATE-BOARDING WITHOUT LOOKING WHERE YOU'RE GOING?
I... WELL... NOT TO?
YOUR FRIEND'S IN BIG *TROUBLE*. DREYUS IS A REAL TASK-MASTER.
POLK
WHZZZZZ

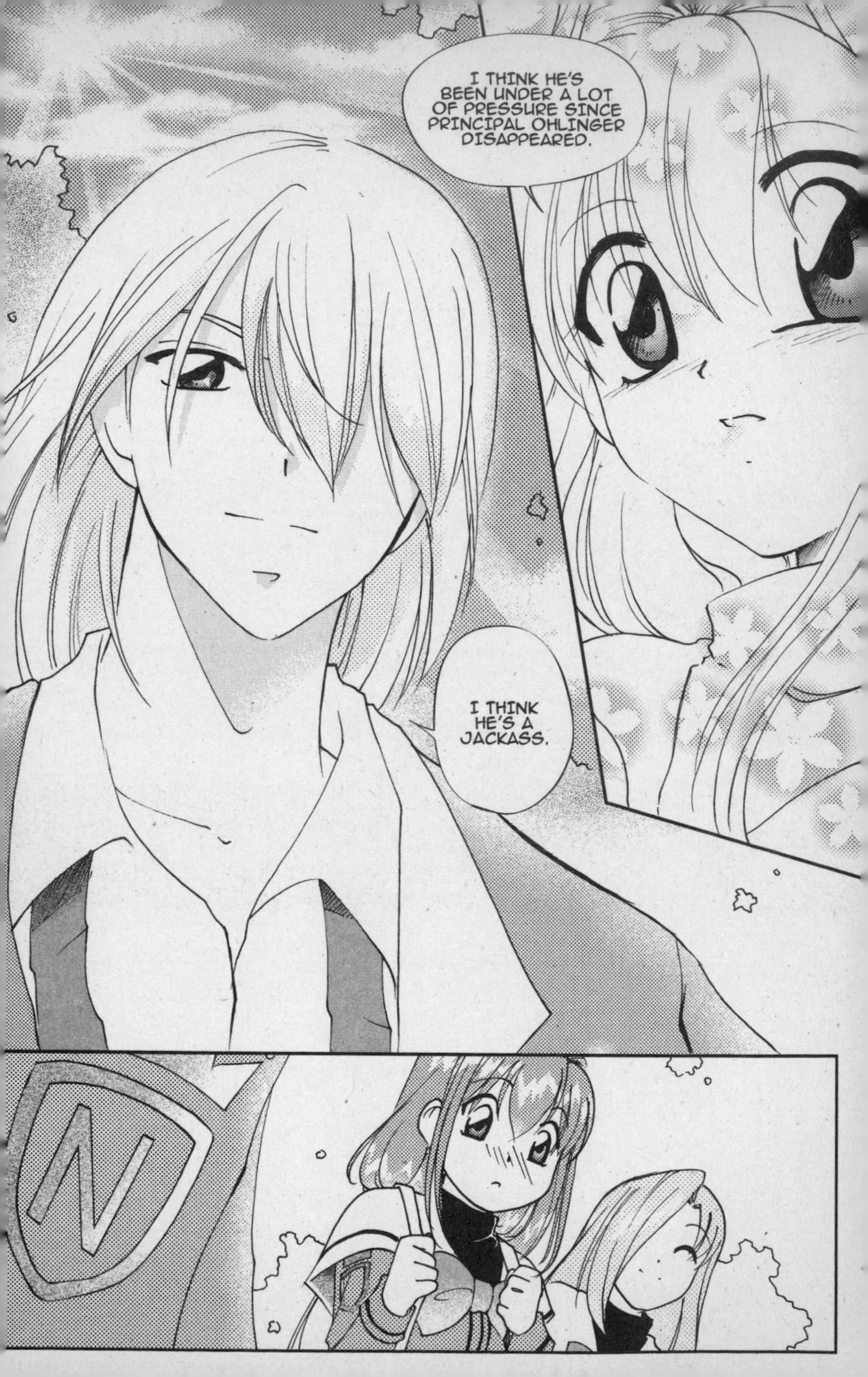
I THINK HE'S BEEN UNDER A LOT OF PRESSURE SINCE PRINCIPAL OHLINGER DISAPPEARED.
I THINK HE'S A JACKASS.

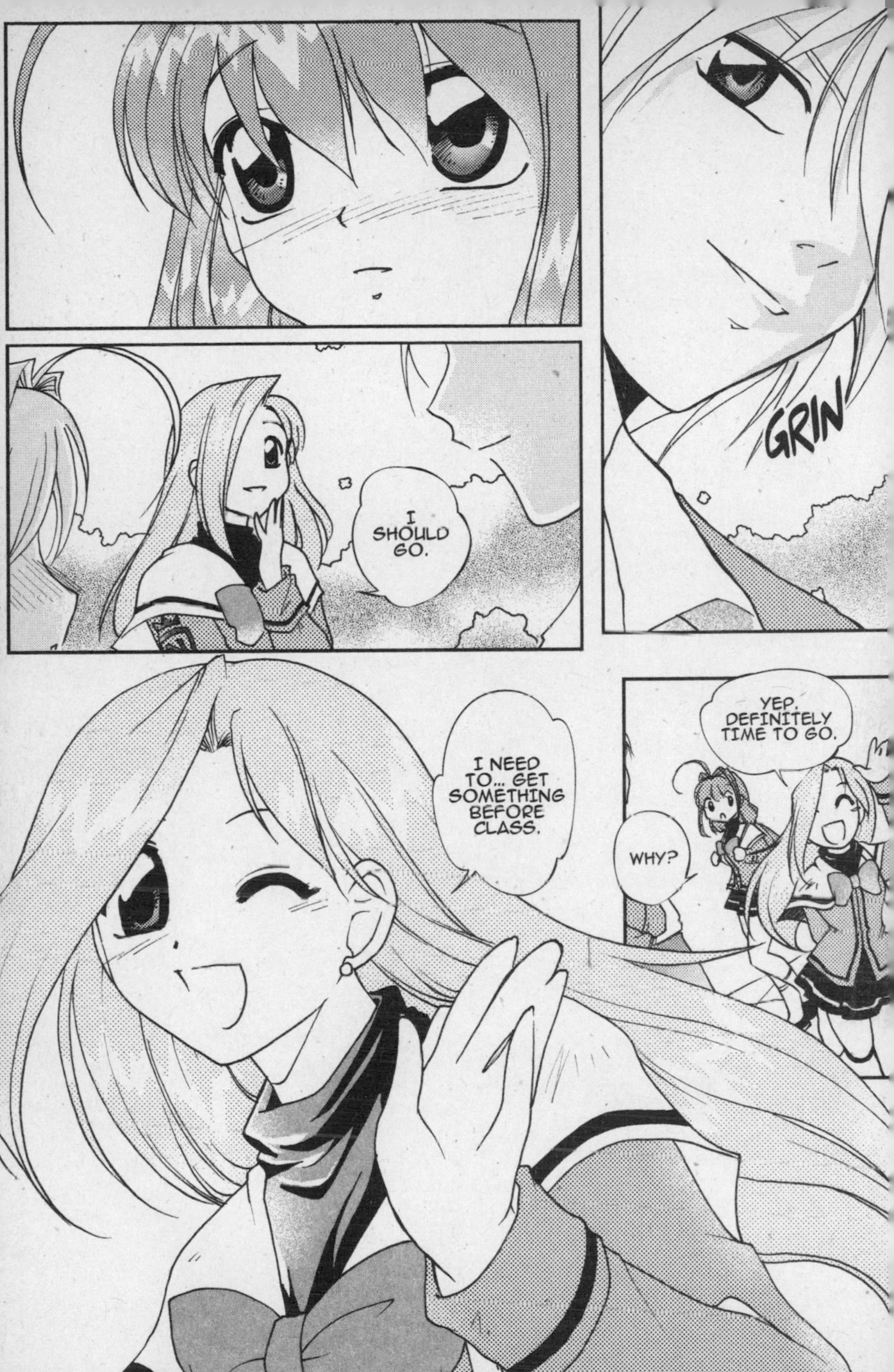
GRIN
I SHOULD GO.
YEP. DEFINITELY TIME TO GO.
WHY?
I NEED TO... GET SOMETHING BEFORE CLASS.

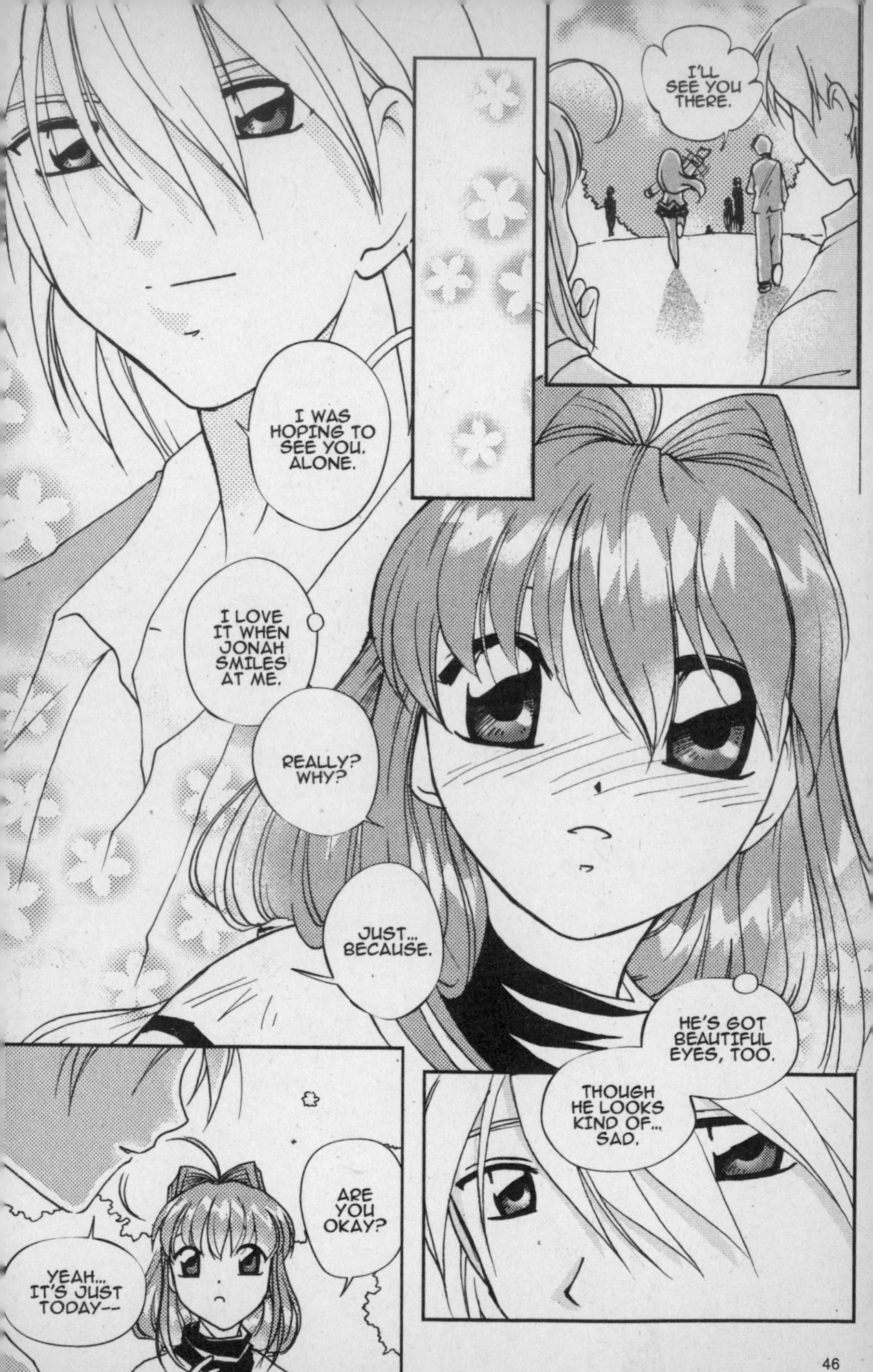
I'LL SEE YOU THERE.
I WAS HOPING TO SEE YOU. ALONE.
I LOVE IT WHEN JONAH SMILES AT ME.
REALLY? WHY?
JUST... BECAUSE.
HE'S GOT BEAUTIFUL EYES, TOO.
THOUGH HE LOOKS KIND OF... SAD.
ARE YOU OKAY?
YEAH... IT'S JUST TODAY--

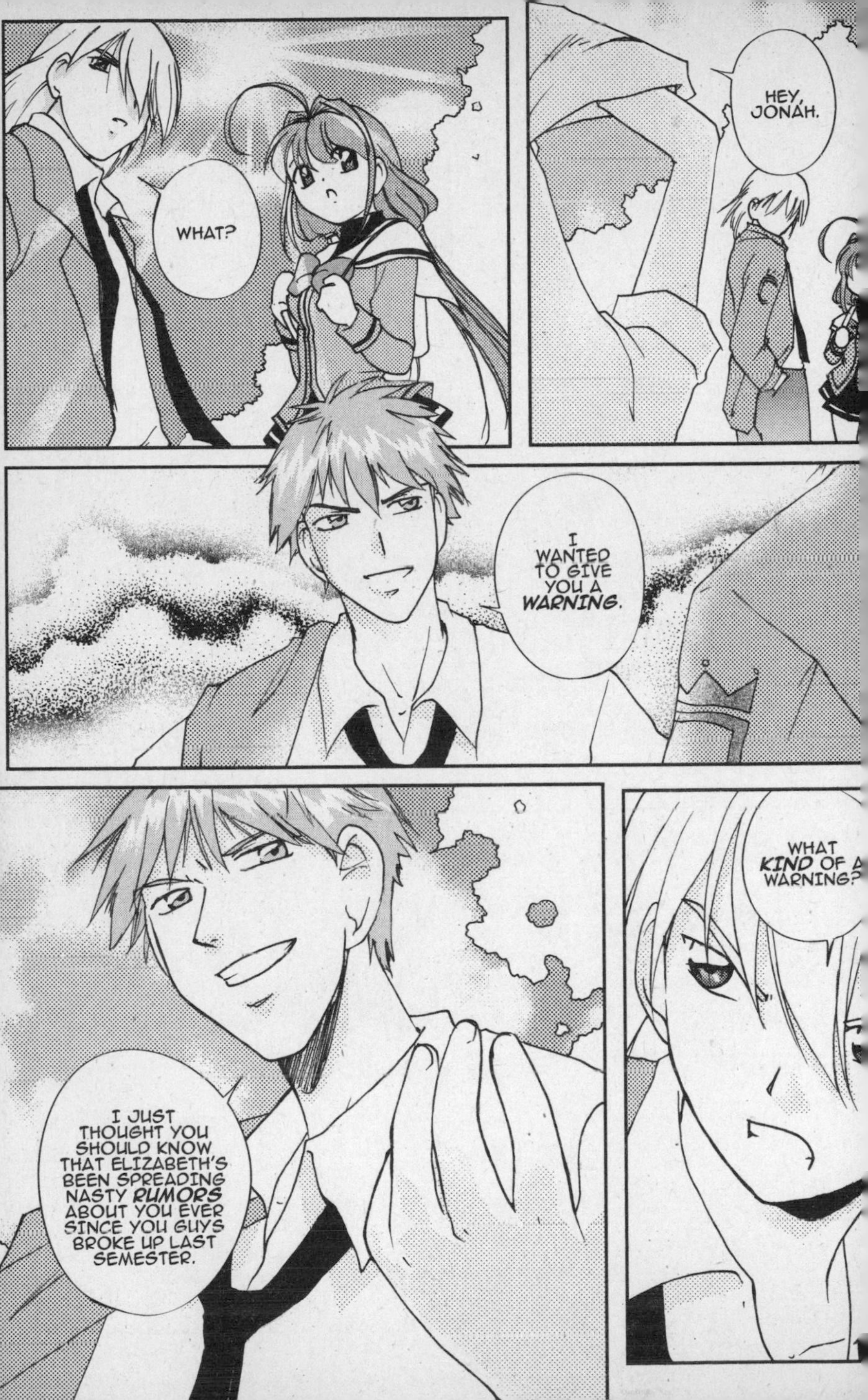
HEY, JONAH.
WHAT?
I WANTED TO GIVE YOU A ***WARNING***.
WHAT ***KIND*** OF A WARNING?
I JUST THOUGHT YOU SHOULD KNOW THAT ELIZABETH'S BEEN SPREADING NASTY ***RUMORS*** ABOUT YOU EVER SINCE YOU GUYS BROKE UP LAST SEMESTER.

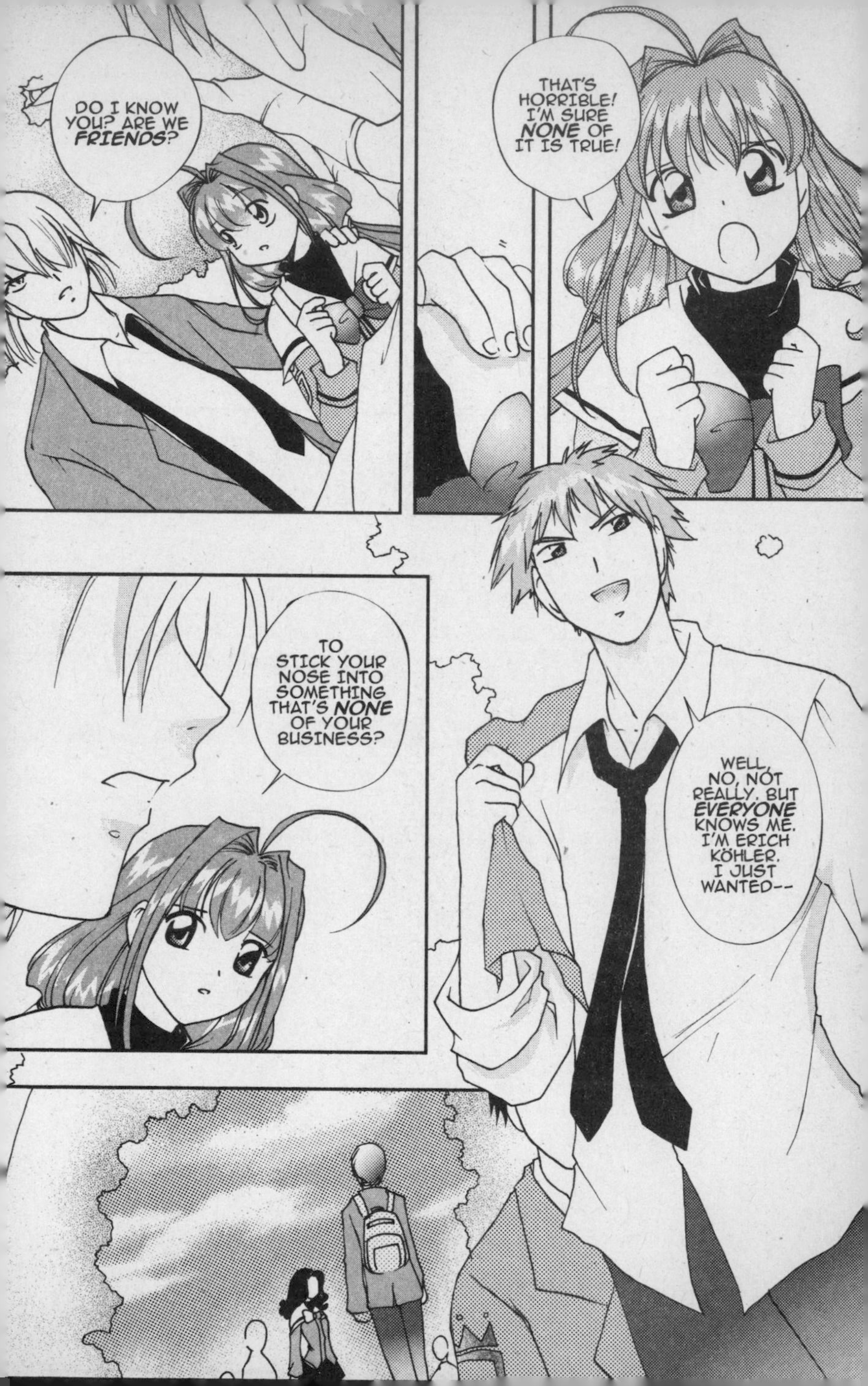
THAT'S HORRIBLE! I'M SURE *NONE* OF IT IS TRUE!
DO I KNOW YOU? ARE WE *FRIENDS*?
TO STICK YOUR NOSE INTO SOMETHING THAT'S *NONE* OF YOUR BUSINESS?
WELL, NO, NOT REALLY. BUT *EVERYONE* KNOWS ME. I'M ERICH KÖHLER. I JUST WANTED--

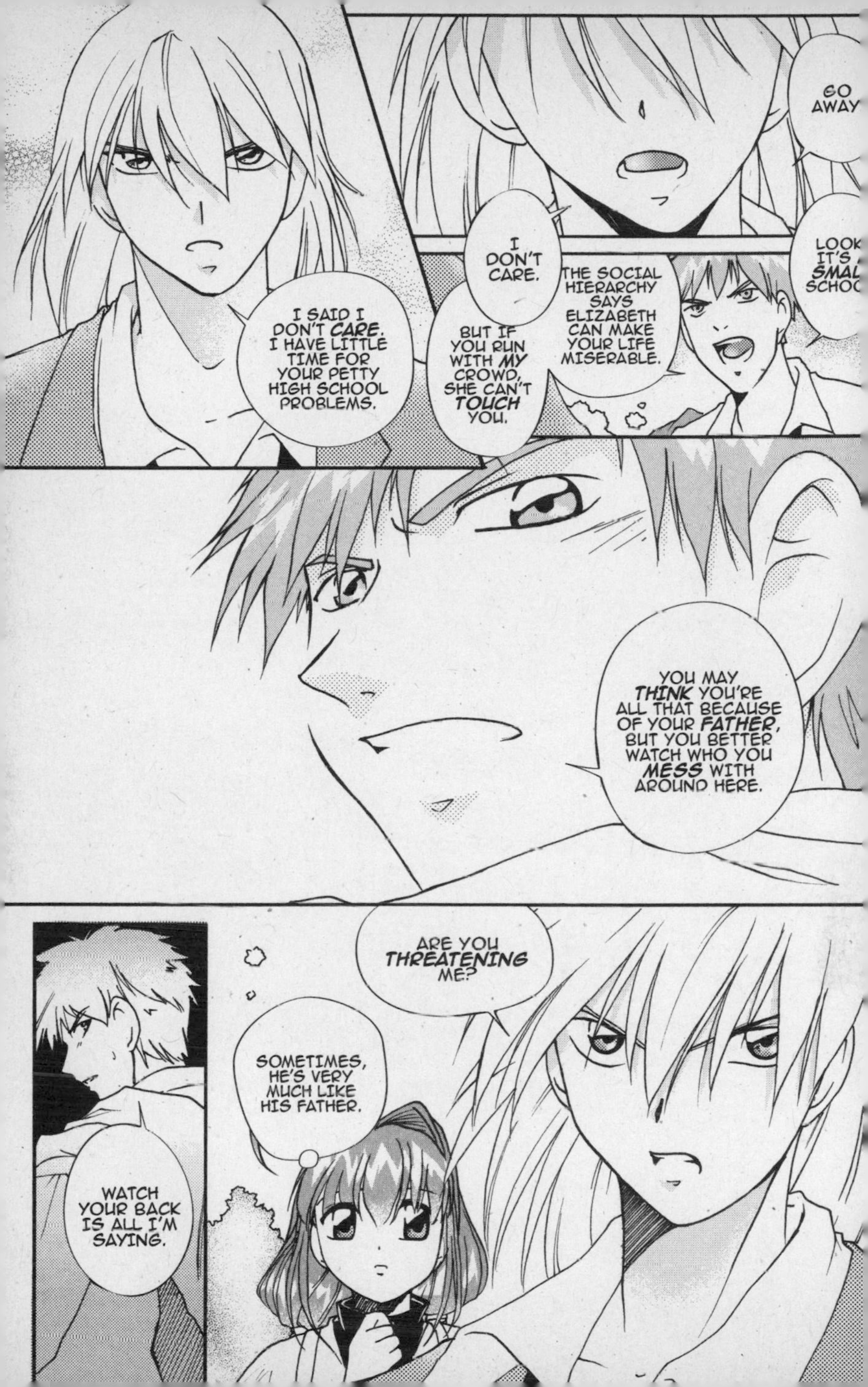

GO AWAY
I DON'T CARE.
LOOK IT'S SMAL SCHO
THE SOCIAL HIERARCHY SAYS ELIZABETH CAN MAKE YOUR LIFE MISERABLE.
BUT IF YOU RUN WITH MY CROWD, SHE CAN'T TOUCH YOU.
I SAID I DON'T CARE. I HAVE LITTLE TIME FOR YOUR PETTY HIGH SCHOOL PROBLEMS.
YOU MAY THINK YOU'RE ALL THAT BECAUSE OF YOUR FATHER, BUT YOU BETTER WATCH WHO YOU MESS WITH AROUND HERE.
ARE YOU THREATENING ME?
SOMETIMES, HE'S VERY MUCH LIKE HIS FATHER.
WATCH YOUR BACK IS ALL I'M SAYING.

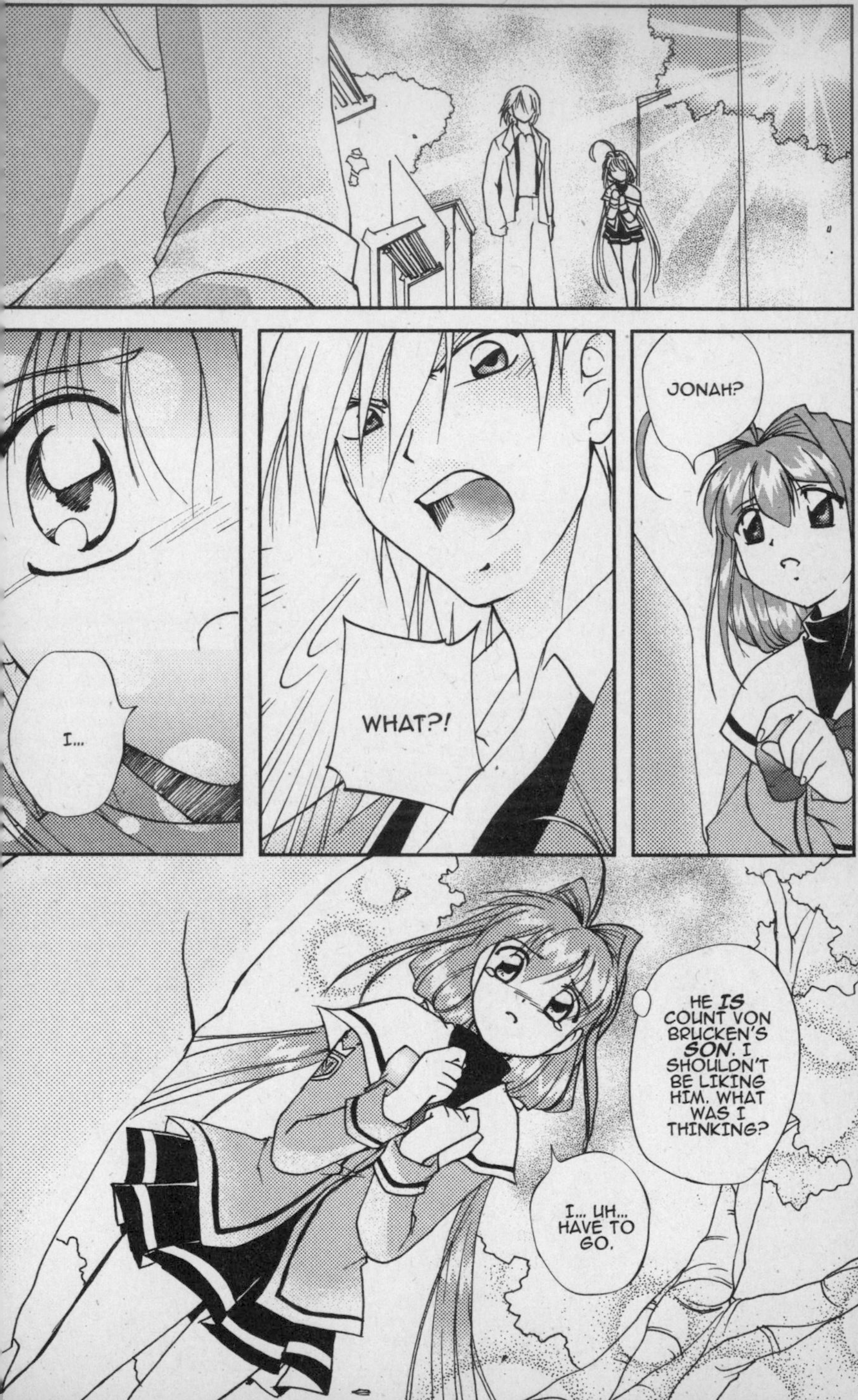
JONAH?
WHAT?!
I...
HE *IS* COUNT VON BRUCKEN'S *SON*. I SHOULDN'T BE LIKING HIM. WHAT WAS I THINKING?
I... UH... HAVE TO GO.

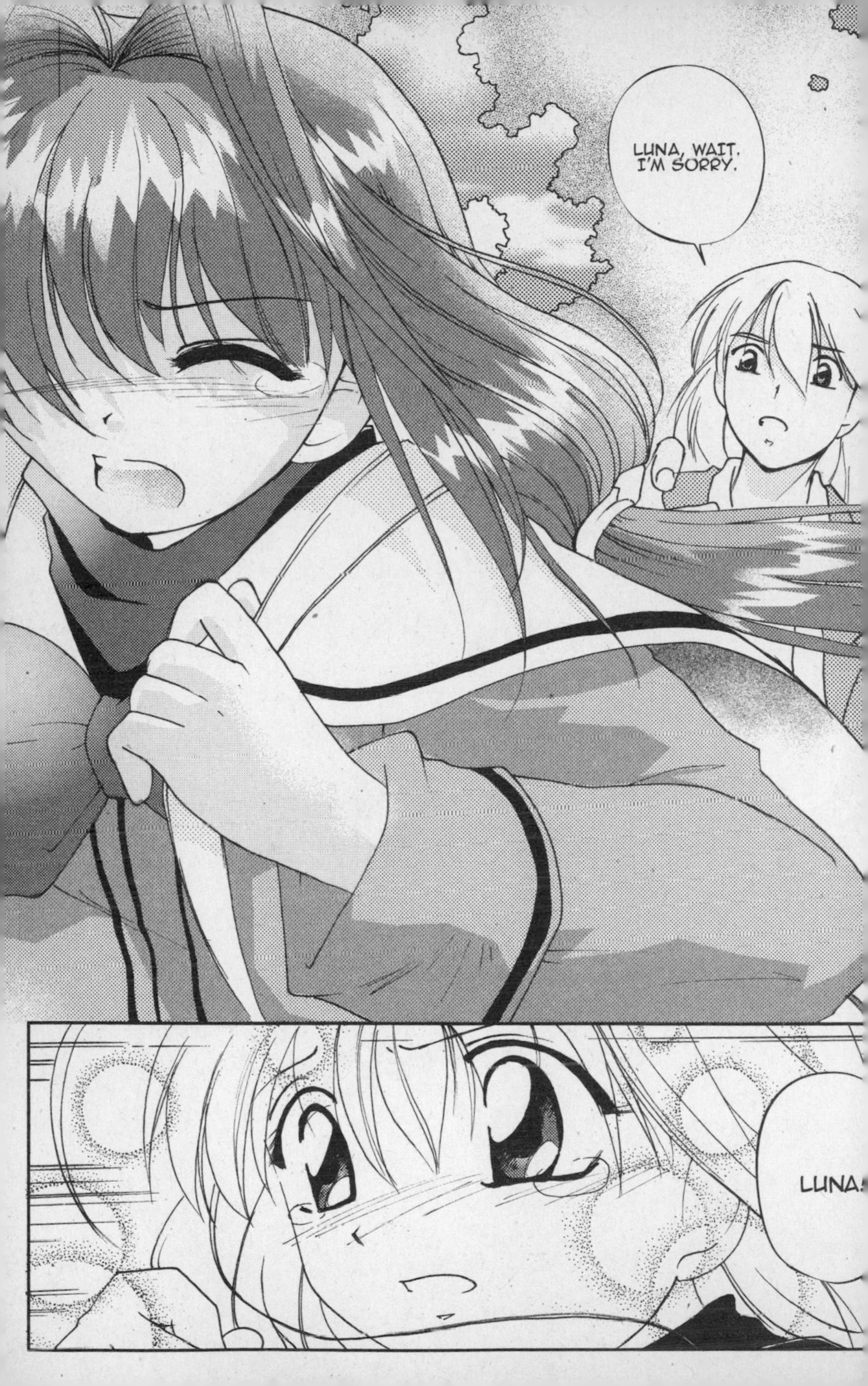
LUNA, WAIT. I'M SORRY.
LUNA!

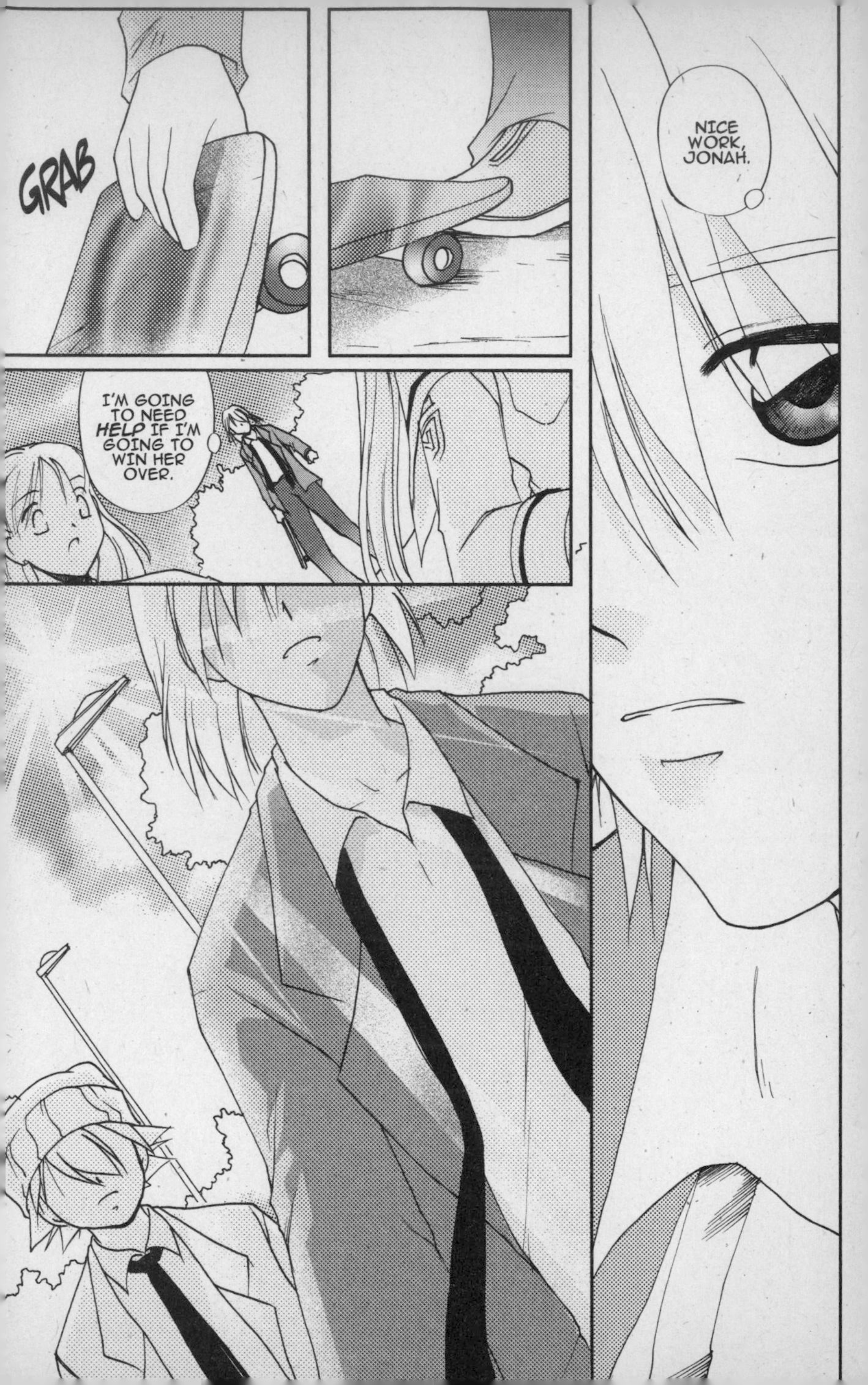
NICE WORK, JONAH.
GRAB
I'M GOING TO NEED **HELP** IF I'M GOING TO WIN HER OVER.

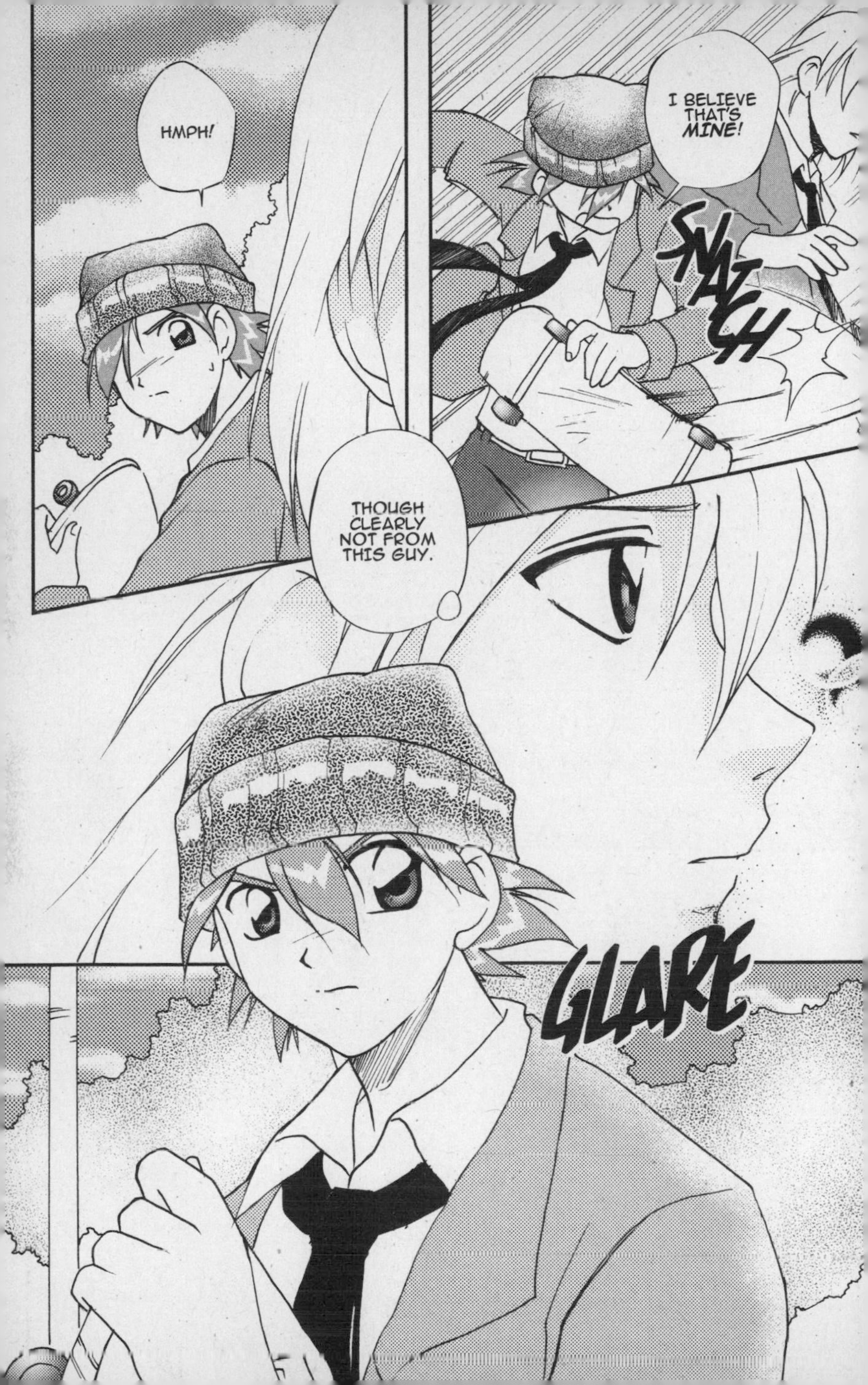
I BELIEVE THAT'S MINE!
SNATCH
HMPH!
THOUGH CLEARLY NOT FROM THIS GUY.
GLARE

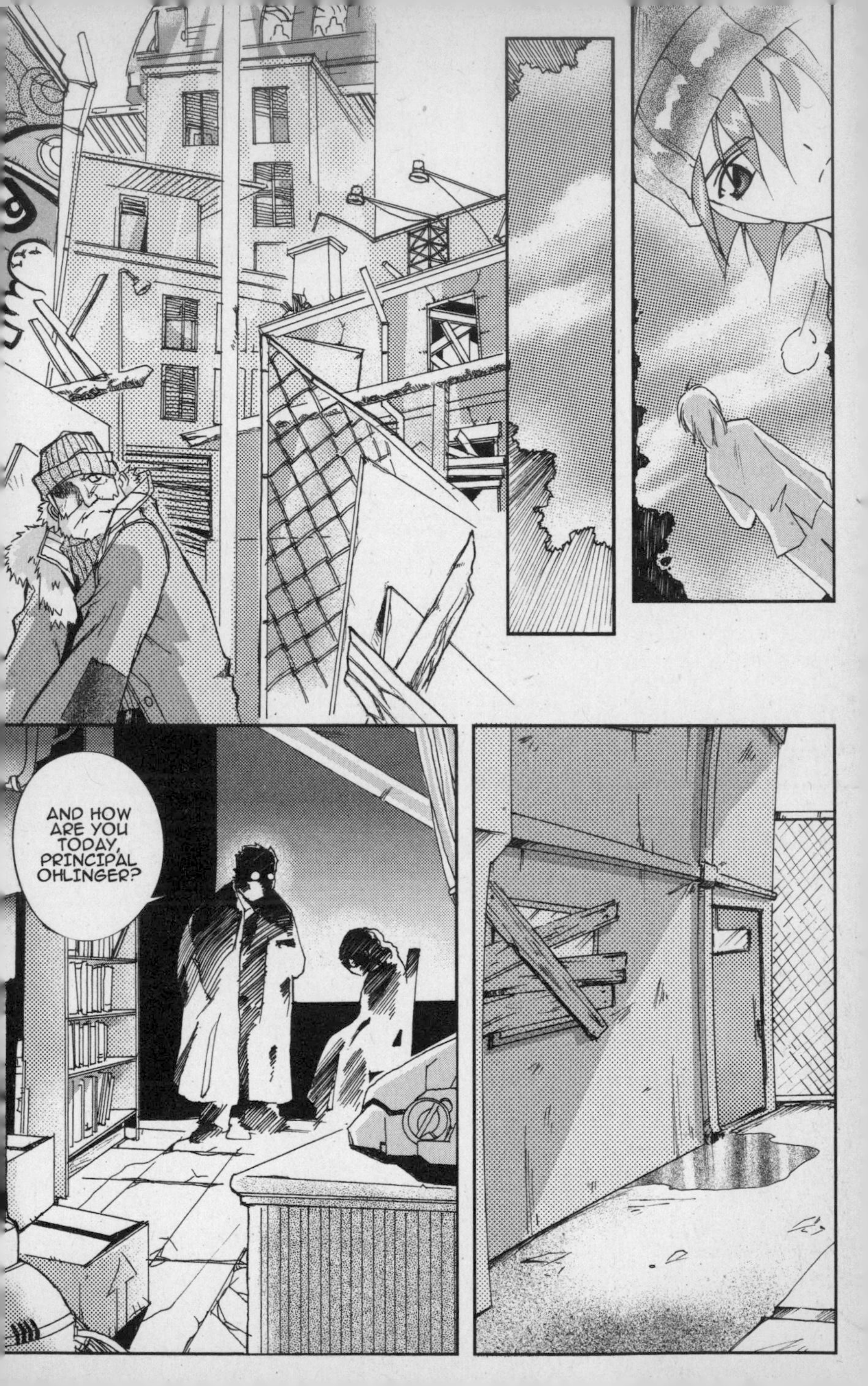
AND HOW ARE YOU TODAY, PRINCIPAL OHLINGER?

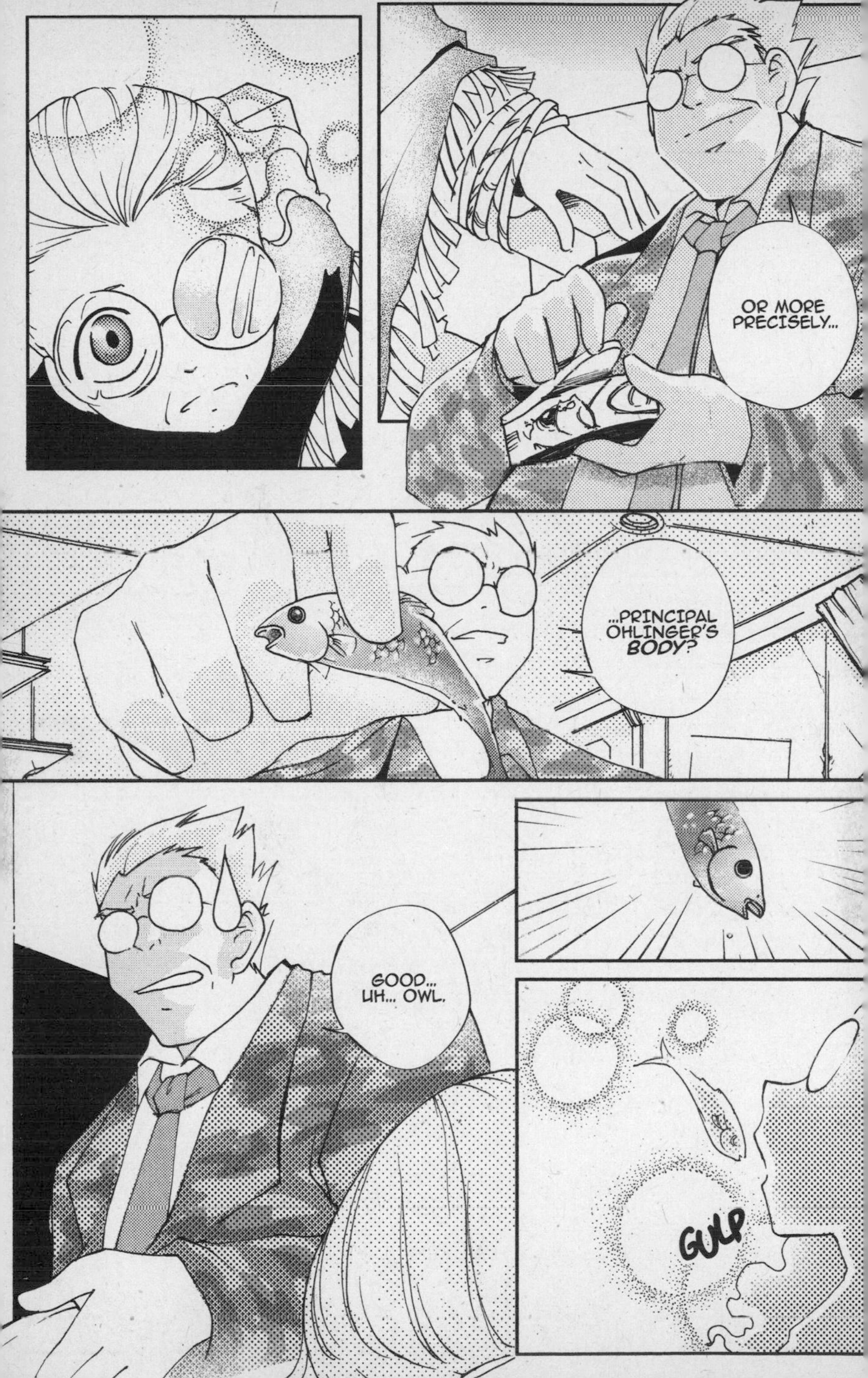
OR MORE PRECISELY...
...PRINCIPAL OHLINGER'S *BODY*?
GULP
GOOD... UH... OWL.

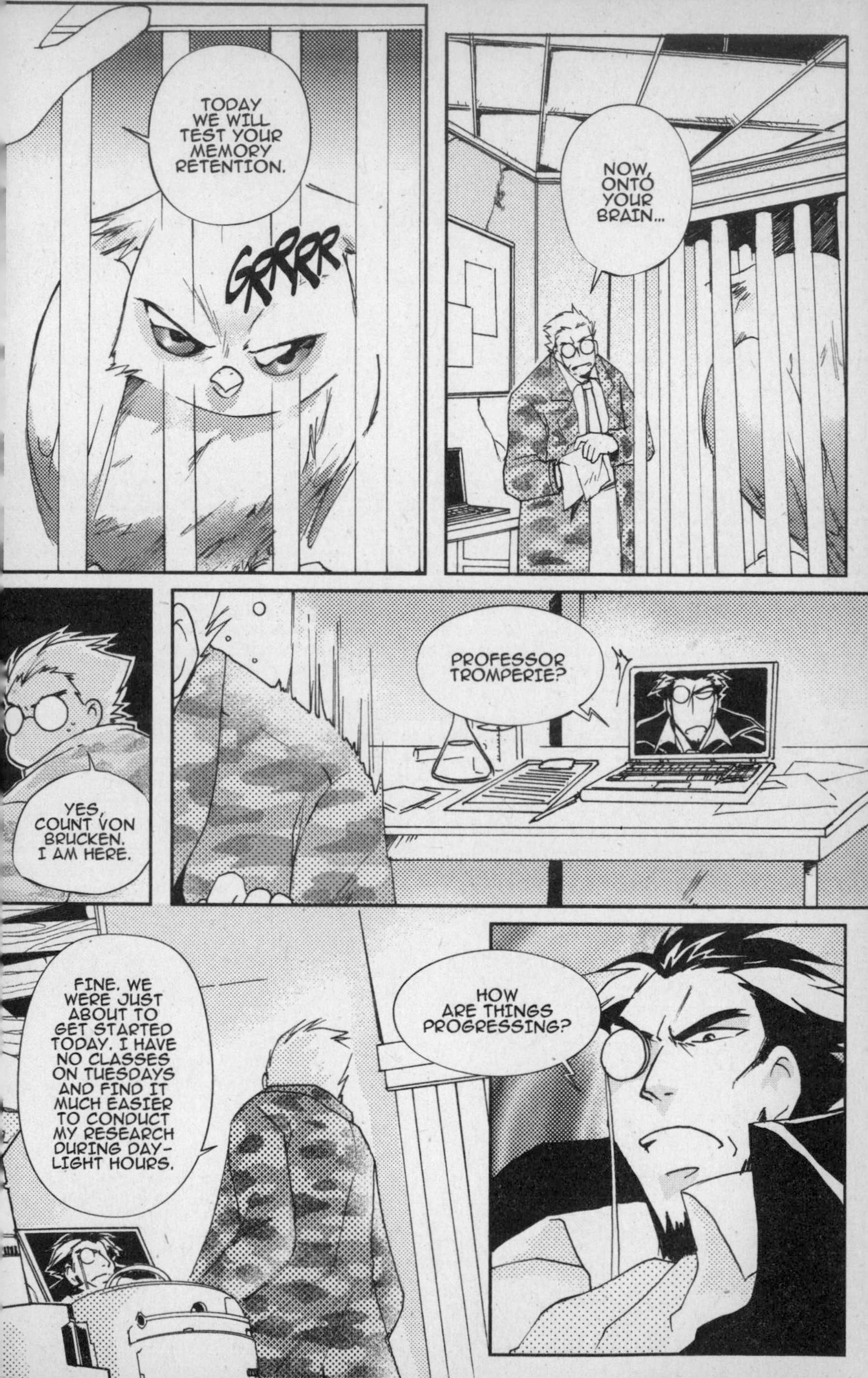
NOW, ONTO YOUR BRAIN...
TODAY WE WILL TEST YOUR MEMORY RETENTION.
GRRRR
PROFESSOR TROMPERIE?
YES, COUNT VON BRUCKEN. I AM HERE.
HOW ARE THINGS PROGRESSING?
FINE. WE WERE JUST ABOUT TO GET STARTED TODAY. I HAVE NO CLASSES ON TUESDAYS AND FIND IT MUCH EASIER TO CONDUCT MY RESEARCH DURING DAY-LIGHT HOURS.

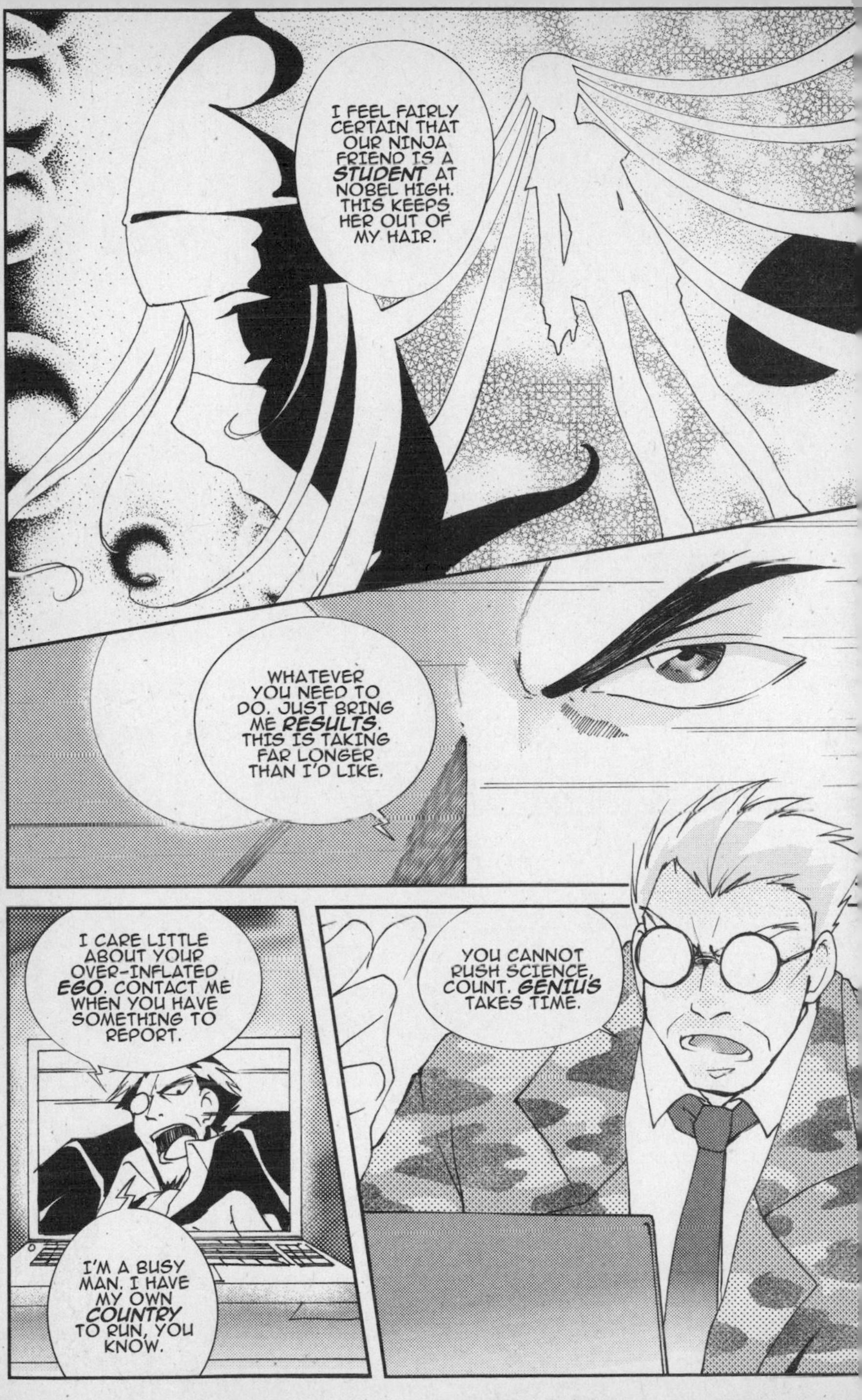
I FEEL FAIRLY CERTAIN THAT OUR NINJA FRIEND IS A STUDENT AT NOBEL HIGH. THIS KEEPS HER OUT OF MY HAIR.
WHATEVER YOU NEED TO DO. JUST BRING ME RESULTS. THIS IS TAKING FAR LONGER THAN I'D LIKE.
YOU CANNOT RUSH SCIENCE, COUNT. GENIUS TAKES TIME.
I CARE LITTLE ABOUT YOUR OVER-INFLATED EGO. CONTACT ME WHEN YOU HAVE SOMETHING TO REPORT.
I'M A BUSY MAN. I HAVE MY OWN COUNTRY TO RUN, YOU KNOW.

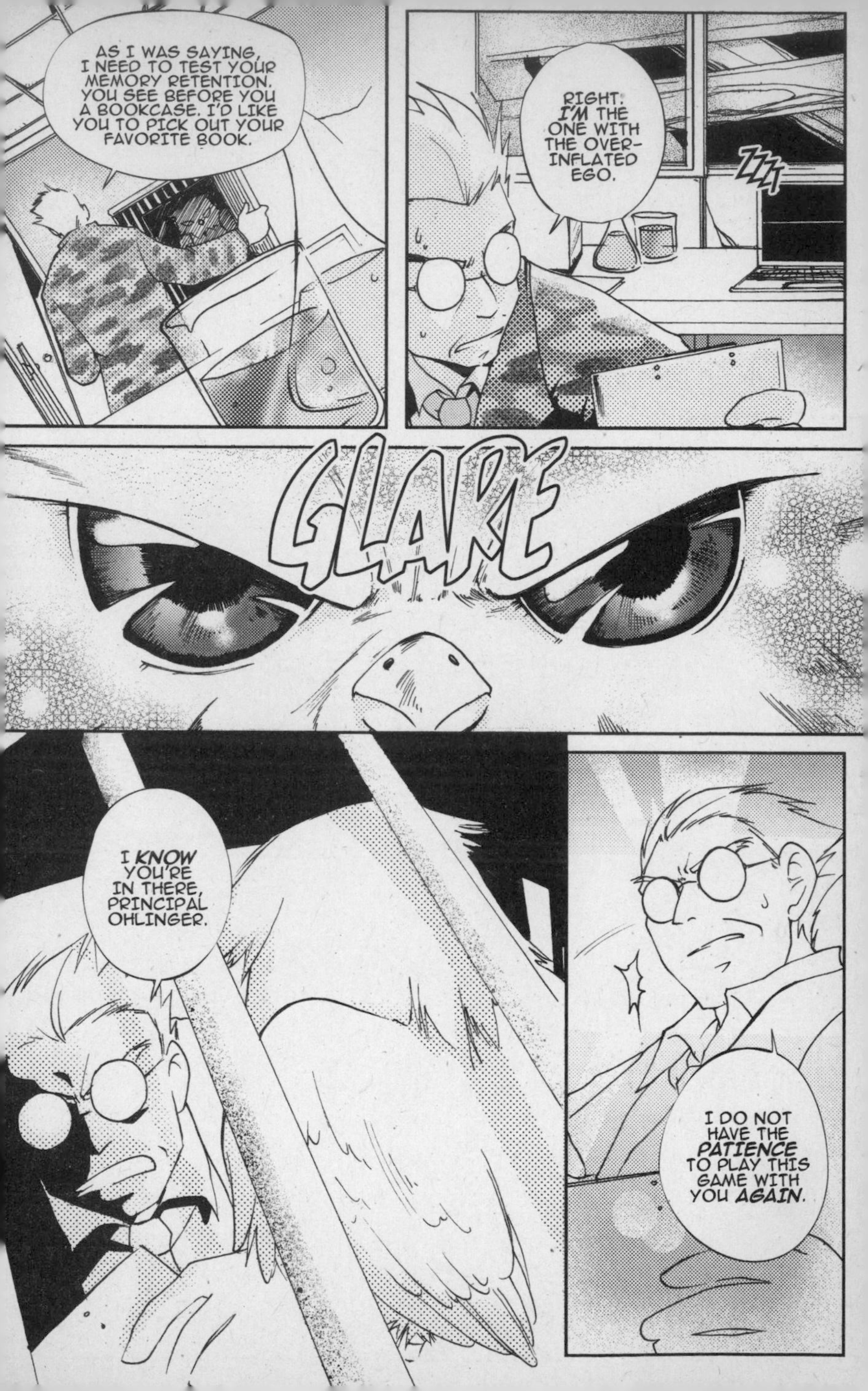
RIGHT. *I'M* THE ONE WITH THE OVER-INFLATED EGO.
ZZZT
AS I WAS SAYING, I NEED TO TEST YOUR MEMORY RETENTION. YOU SEE BEFORE YOU A BOOKCASE. I'D LIKE YOU TO PICK OUT YOUR FAVORITE BOOK.
GLARE
I DO NOT HAVE THE ***PATIENCE*** TO PLAY THIS GAME WITH YOU ***AGAIN***.
I ***KNOW*** YOU'RE IN THERE, PRINCIPAL OHLINGER.

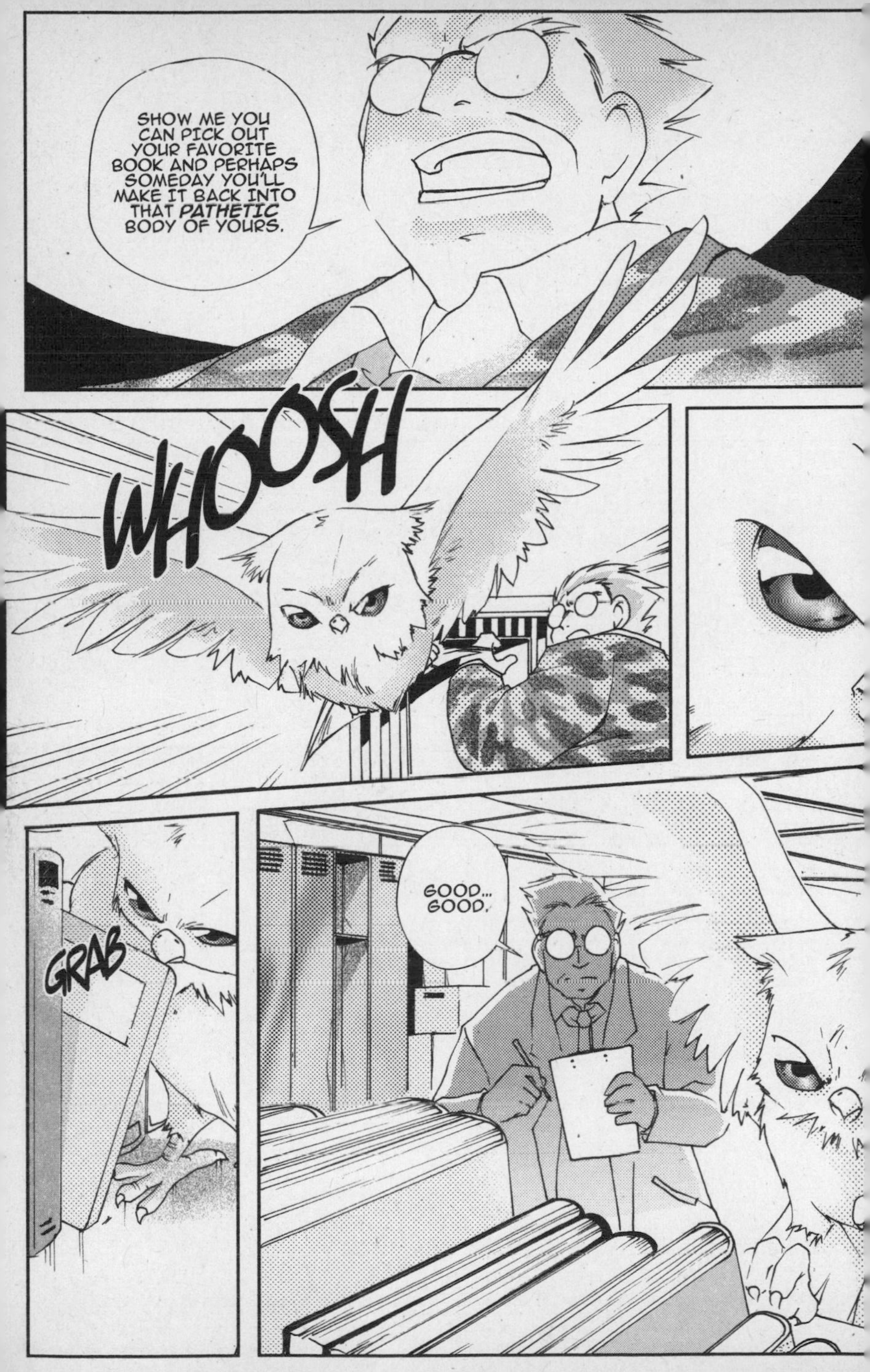
SHOW ME YOU CAN PICK OUT YOUR FAVORITE BOOK AND PERHAPS SOMEDAY YOU'LL MAKE IT BACK INTO THAT *PATHETIC* BODY OF YOURS.
WHOOSH
GOOD... GOOD.
GRAB

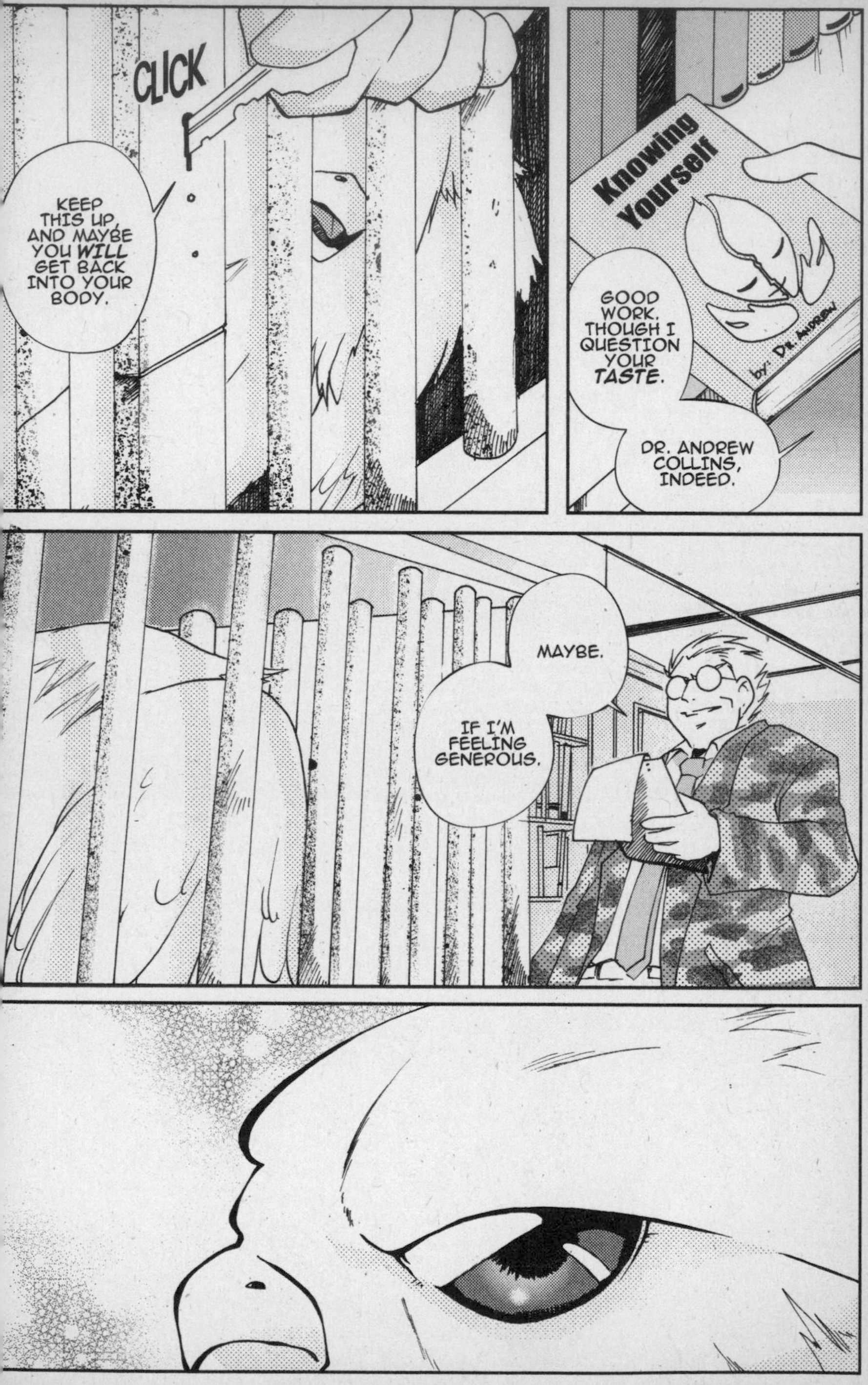
Knowing Yourself
by: Dr. Andrew
GOOD WORK. THOUGH I QUESTION YOUR *TASTE*.
DR. ANDREW COLLINS, INDEED.
CLICK
KEEP THIS UP, AND MAYBE YOU *WILL* GET BACK INTO YOUR BODY.
MAYBE.
IF I'M FEELING GENEROUS.

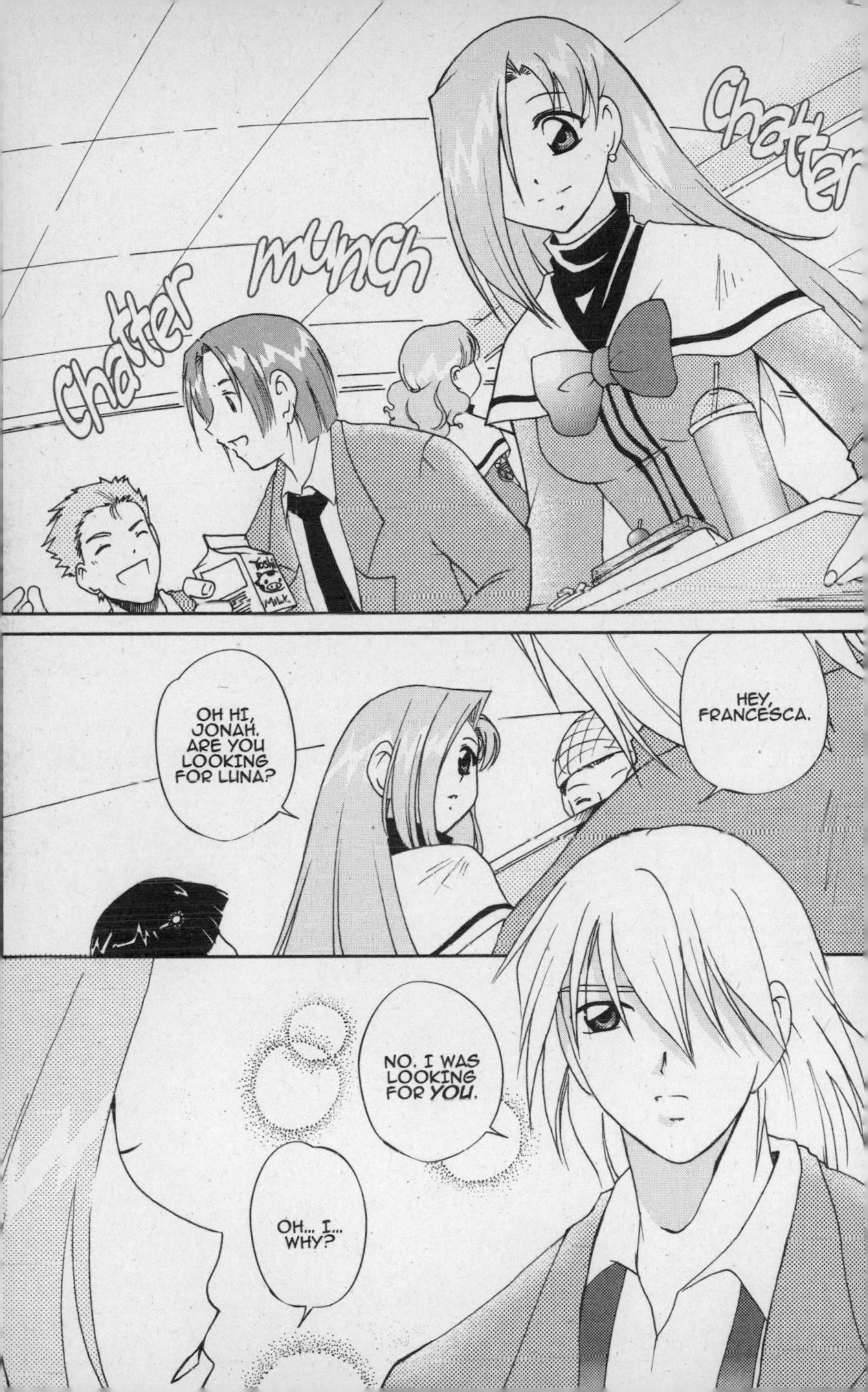
Chatter
munch
Chatter
HEY, FRANCESCA.
OH HI, JONAH. ARE YOU LOOKING FOR LUNA?
NO. I WAS LOOKING FOR ***YOU***.
OH... I... WHY?

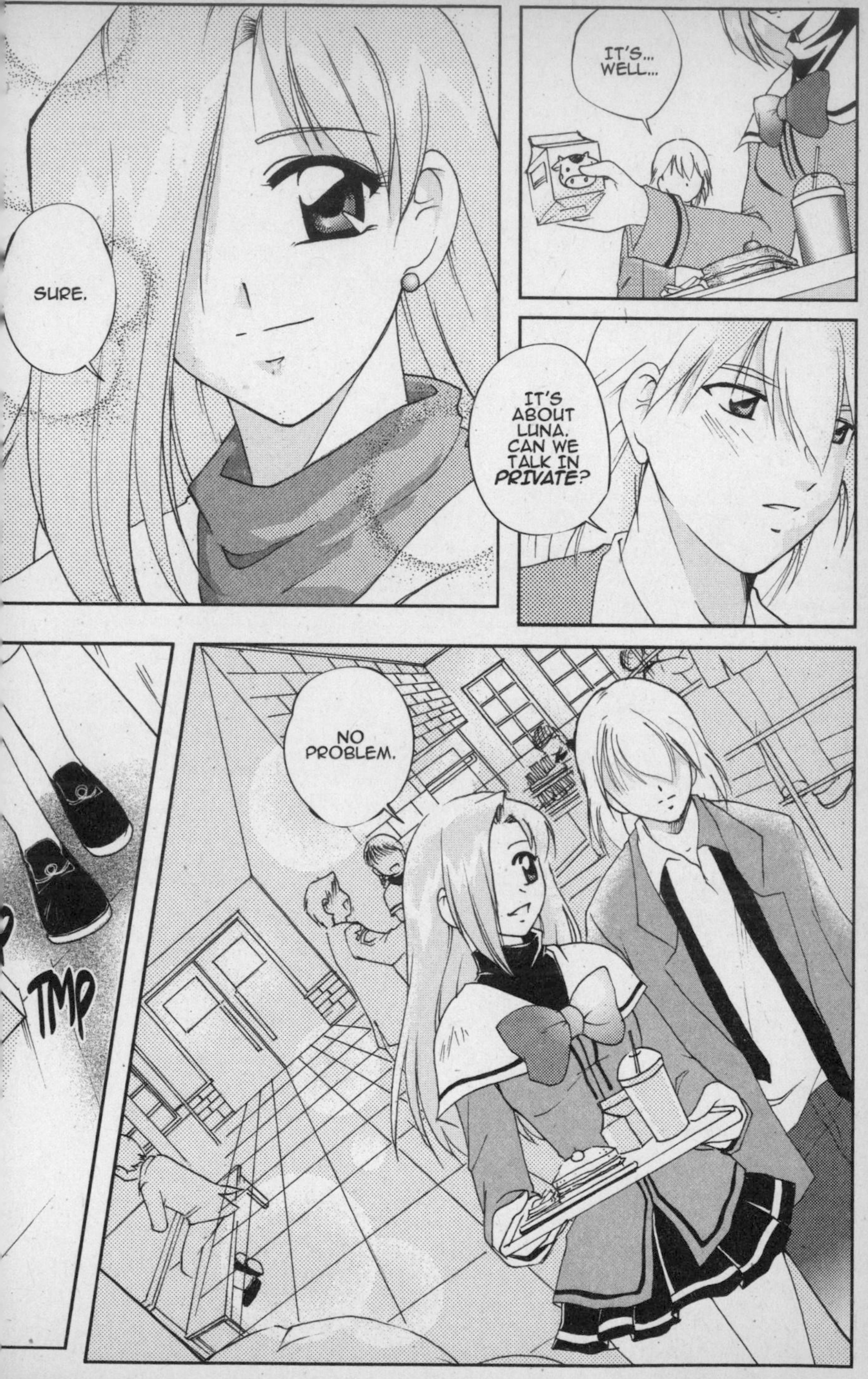
IT'S... WELL...
IT'S ABOUT LUNA. CAN WE TALK IN *PRIVATE*?
SURE.
NO PROBLEM.
TMP

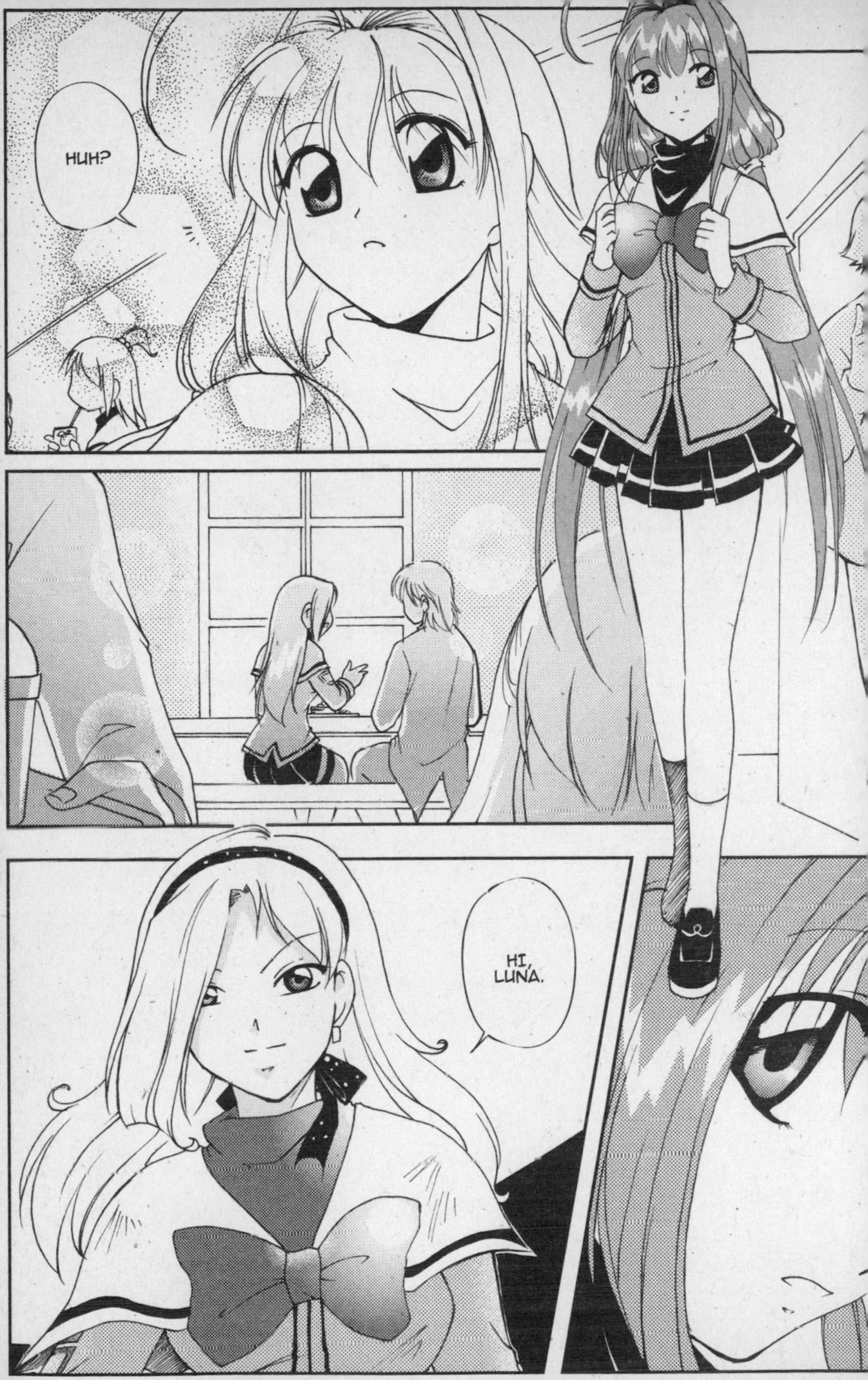
HUH?
HI, LUNA.

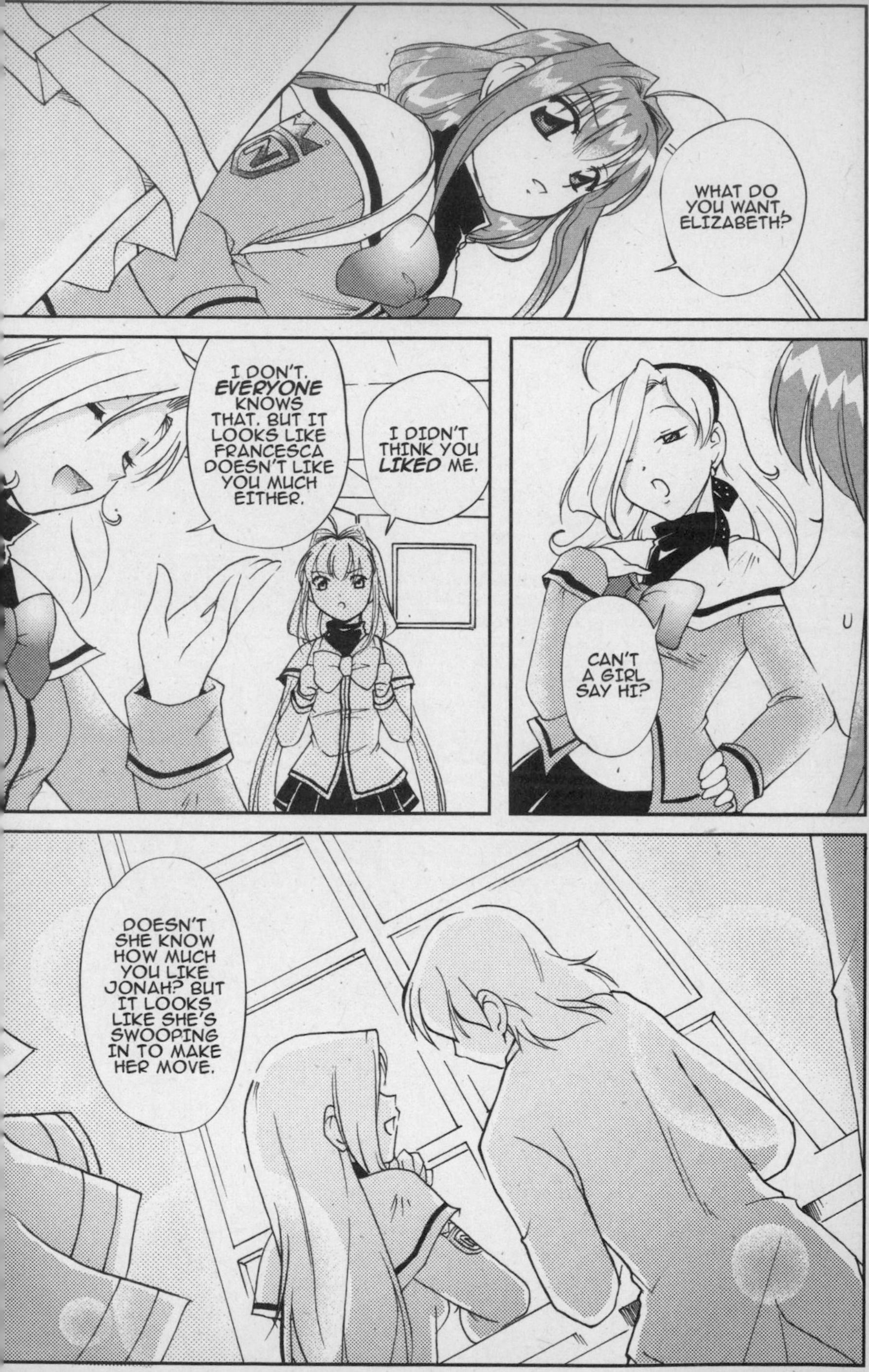
WHAT DO YOU WANT, ELIZABETH?
CAN'T A GIRL SAY HI?
I DIDN'T THINK YOU LIKED ME.
I DON'T. EVERYONE KNOWS THAT. BUT IT LOOKS LIKE FRANCESCA DOESN'T LIKE YOU MUCH EITHER.
DOESN'T SHE KNOW HOW MUCH YOU LIKE JONAH? BUT IT LOOKS LIKE SHE'S SWOOPING IN TO MAKE HER MOVE.

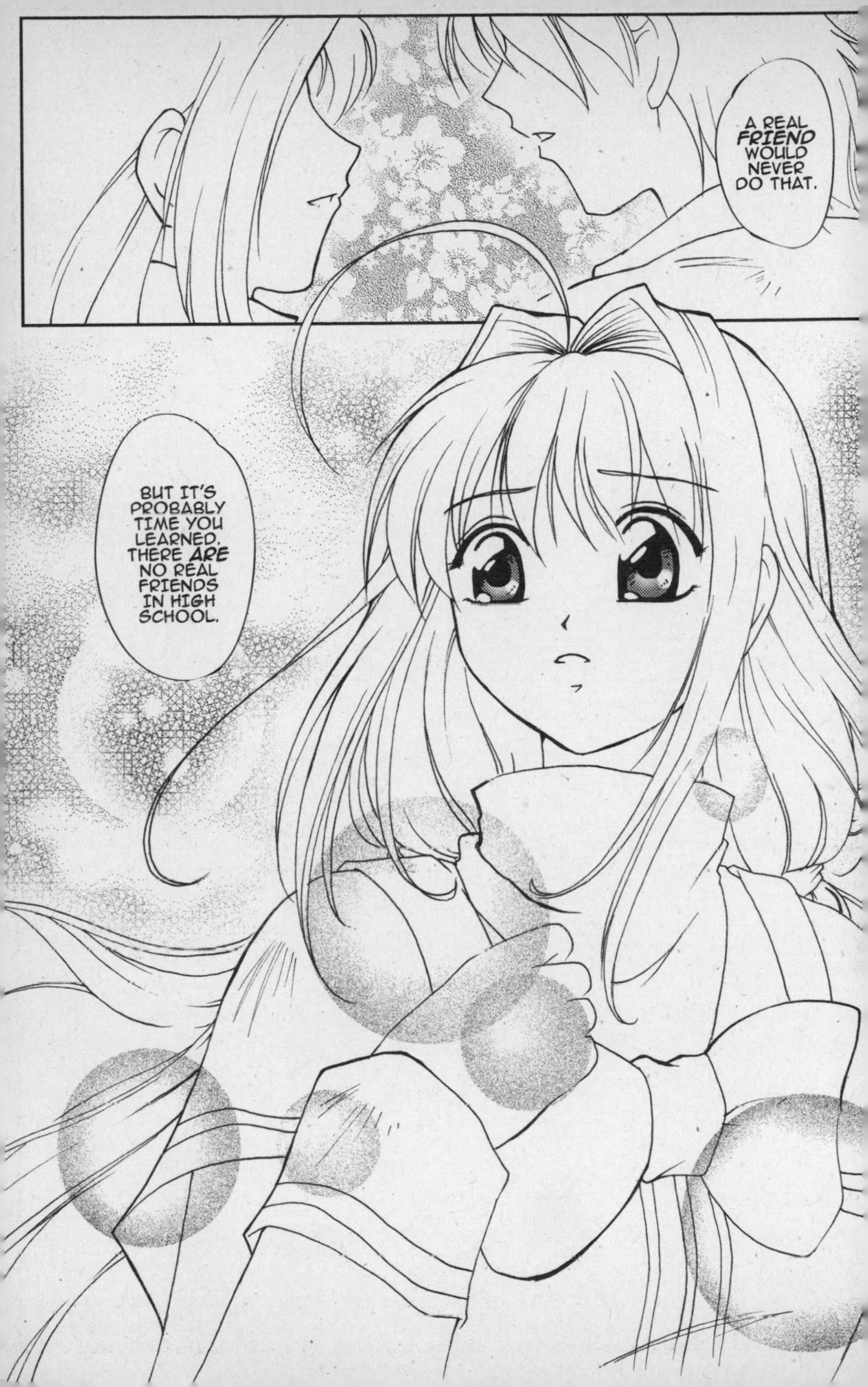
A REAL FRIEND WOULD NEVER DO THAT.
BUT IT'S PROBABLY TIME YOU LEARNED. THERE ARE NO REAL FRIENDS IN HIGH SCHOOL.

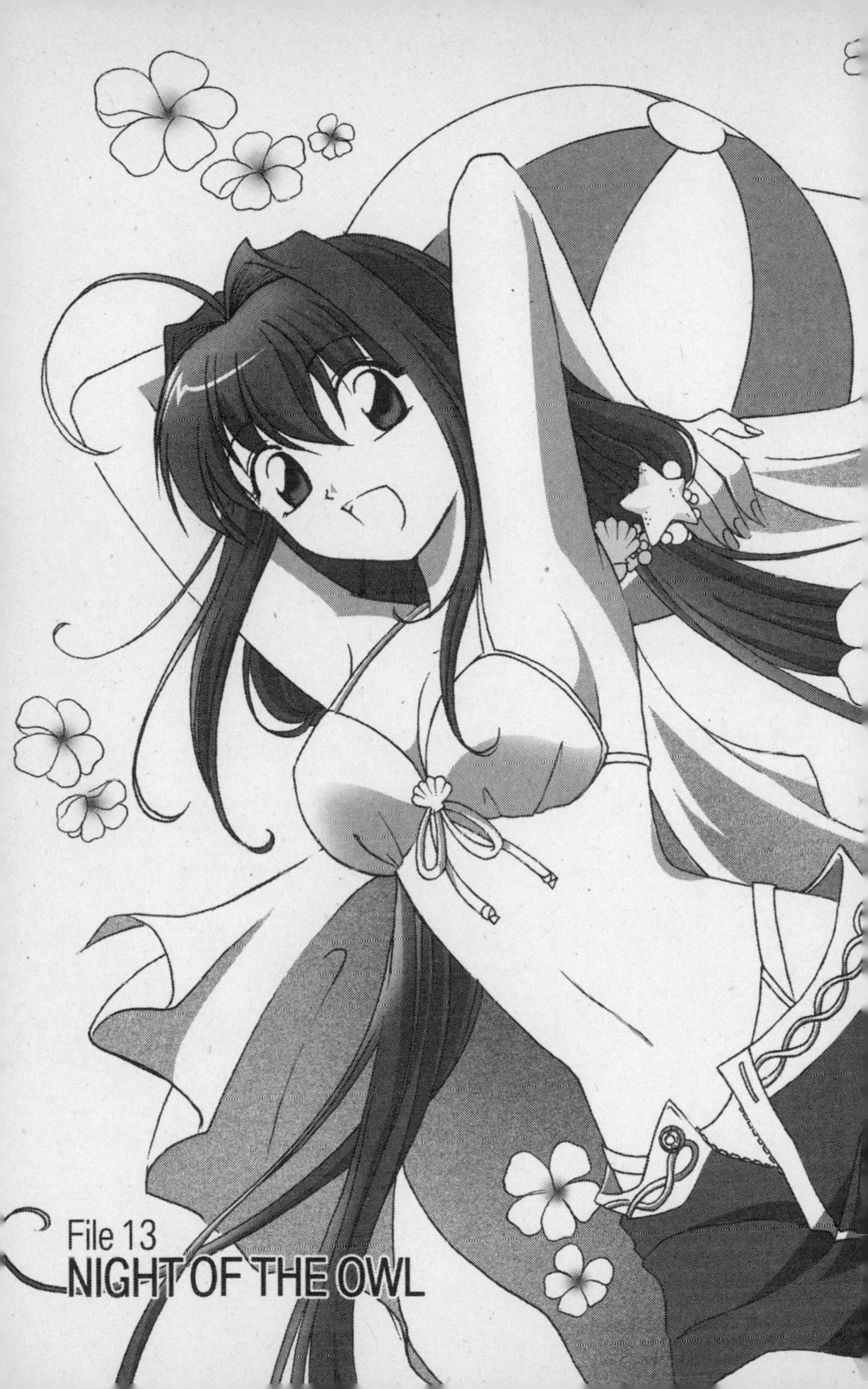

File 13
NIGHT OF THE OWL

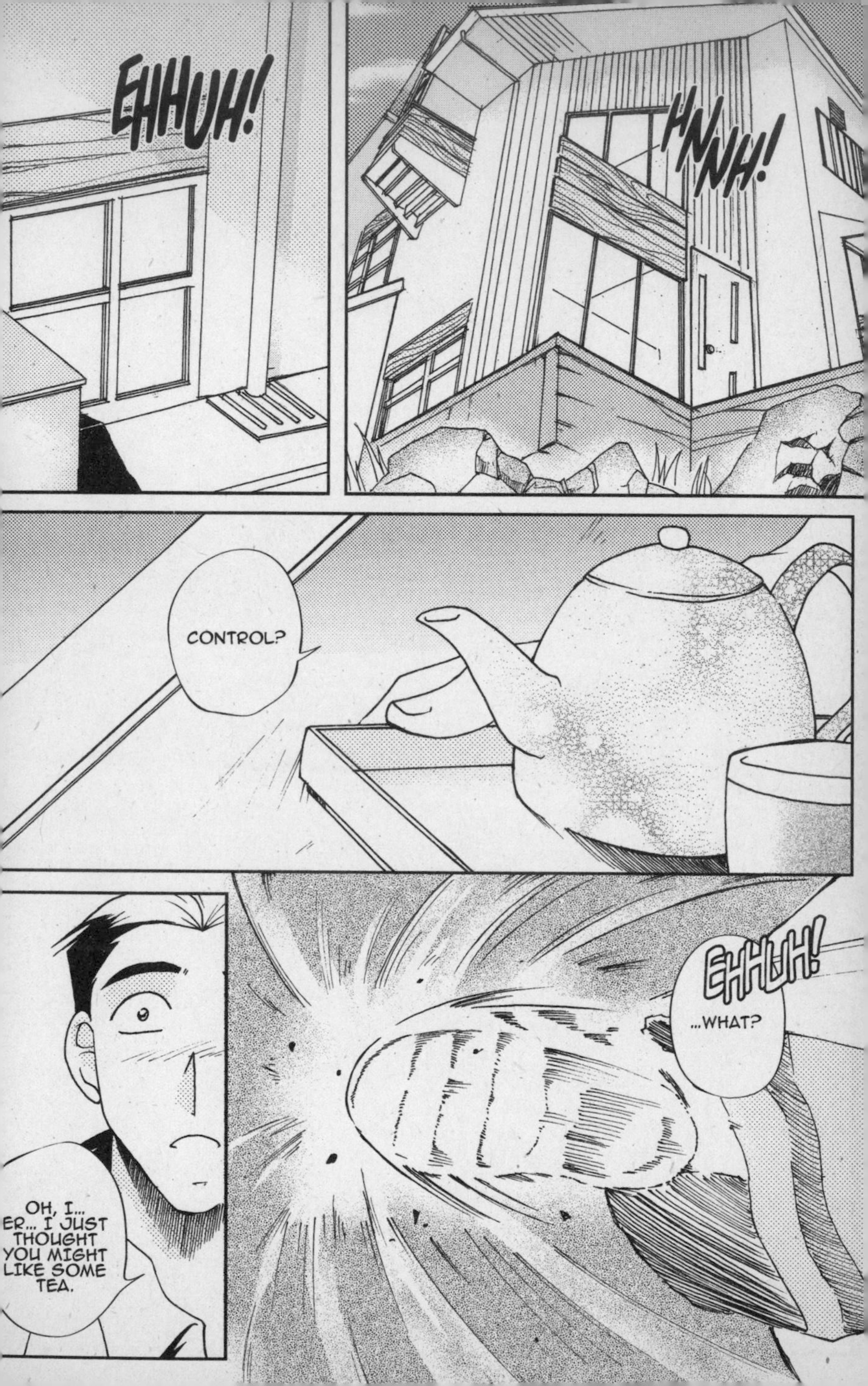
HNNH!
EHHUH!
CONTROL?
EHHUH!
...WHAT?
OH, I... ER... I JUST THOUGHT YOU MIGHT LIKE SOME TEA.

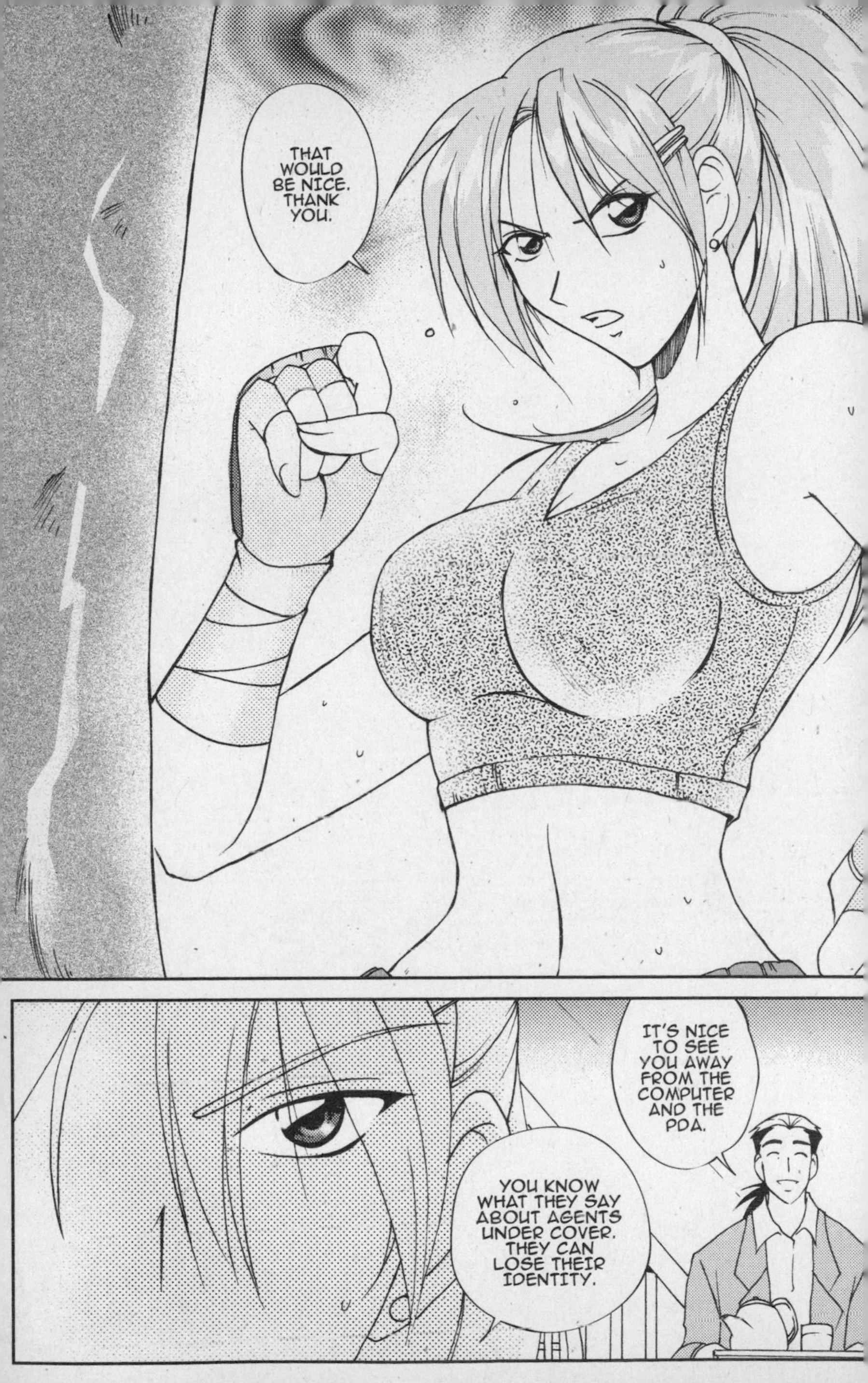
THAT WOULD BE NICE. THANK YOU.
IT'S NICE TO SEE YOU AWAY FROM THE COMPUTER AND THE PDA.
YOU KNOW WHAT THEY SAY ABOUT AGENTS UNDER COVER. THEY CAN LOSE THEIR IDENTITY.

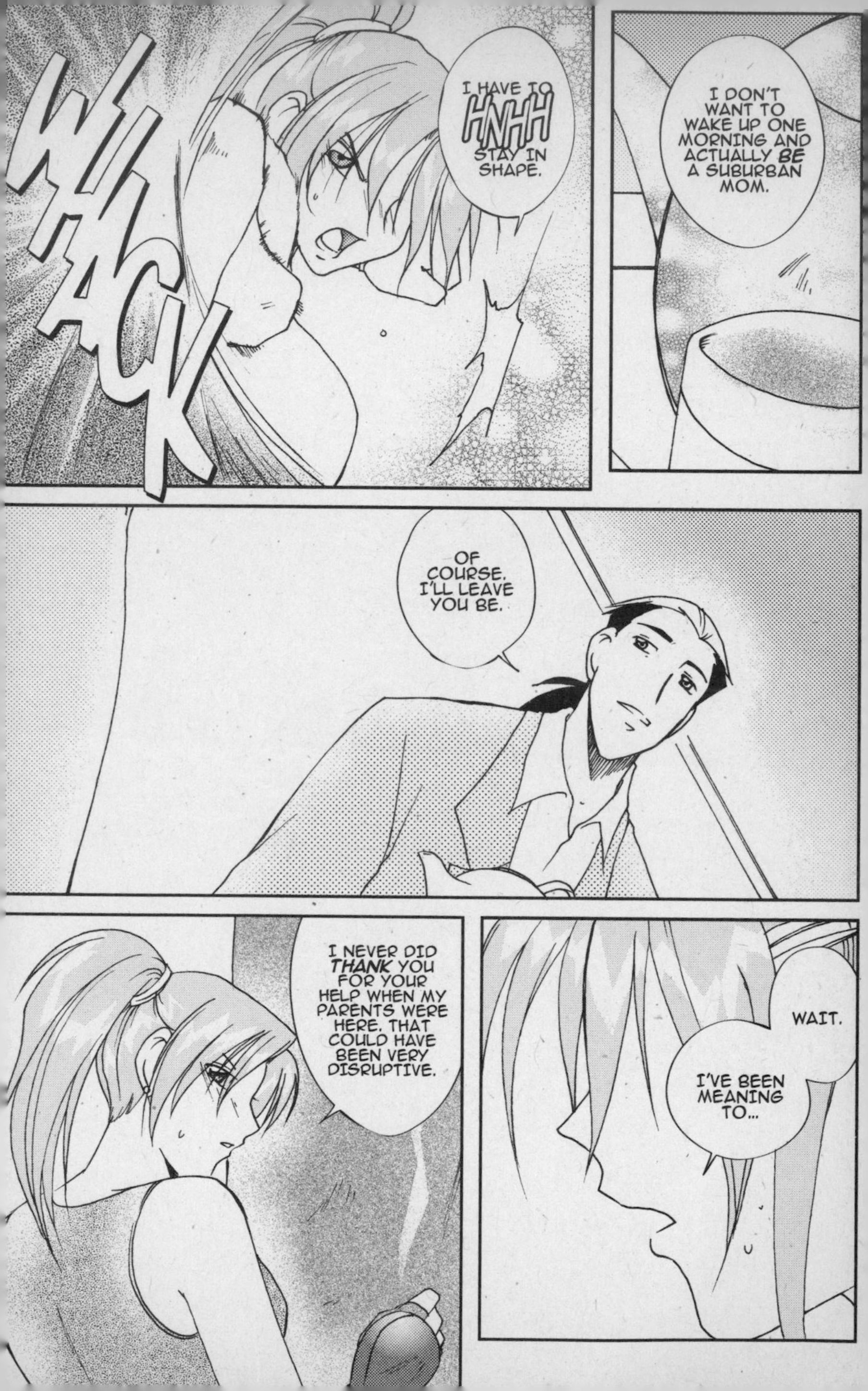
I DON'T WANT TO WAKE UP ONE MORNING AND ACTUALLY *BE* A SUBURBAN MOM.
WHACK
I HAVE TO HNHH STAY IN SHAPE.
OF COURSE. I'LL LEAVE YOU BE.
WAIT.
I'VE BEEN MEANING TO...
I NEVER DID *THANK* YOU FOR YOUR HELP WHEN MY PARENTS WERE HERE. THAT COULD HAVE BEEN VERY DISRUPTIVE.

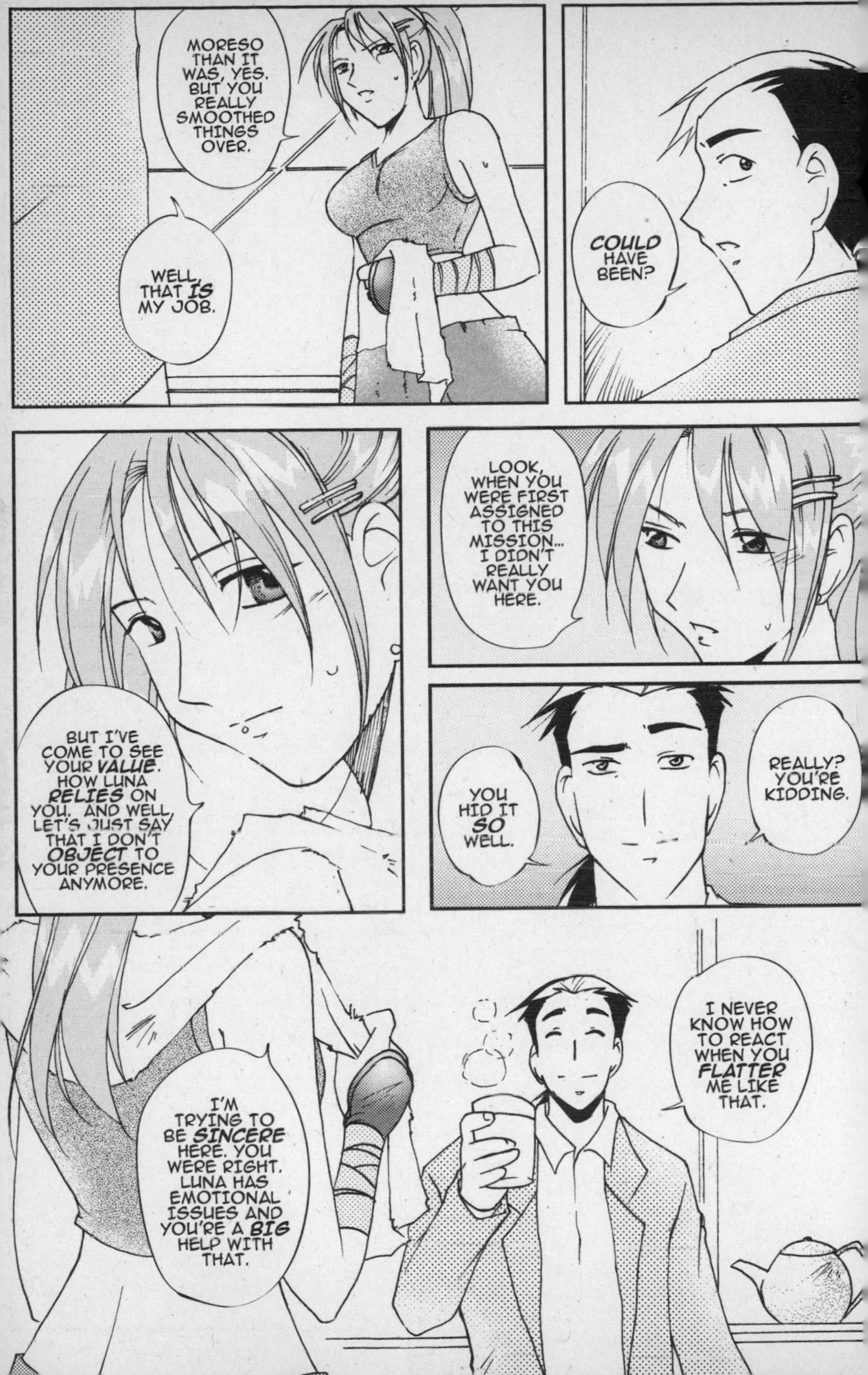
COULD HAVE BEEN?
MORESO THAN IT WAS, YES. BUT YOU REALLY SMOOTHED THINGS OVER.
WELL, THAT IS MY JOB.
LOOK, WHEN YOU WERE FIRST ASSIGNED TO THIS MISSION... I DIDN'T REALLY WANT YOU HERE.
REALLY? YOU'RE KIDDING.
YOU HID IT SO WELL.
BUT I'VE COME TO SEE YOUR VALUE. HOW LUNA RELIES ON YOU. AND WELL, LET'S JUST SAY THAT I DON'T OBJECT TO YOUR PRESENCE ANYMORE.
I NEVER KNOW HOW TO REACT WHEN YOU FLATTER ME LIKE THAT.
I'M TRYING TO BE SINCERE HERE. YOU WERE RIGHT. LUNA HAS EMOTIONAL ISSUES AND YOU'RE A BIG HELP WITH THAT.

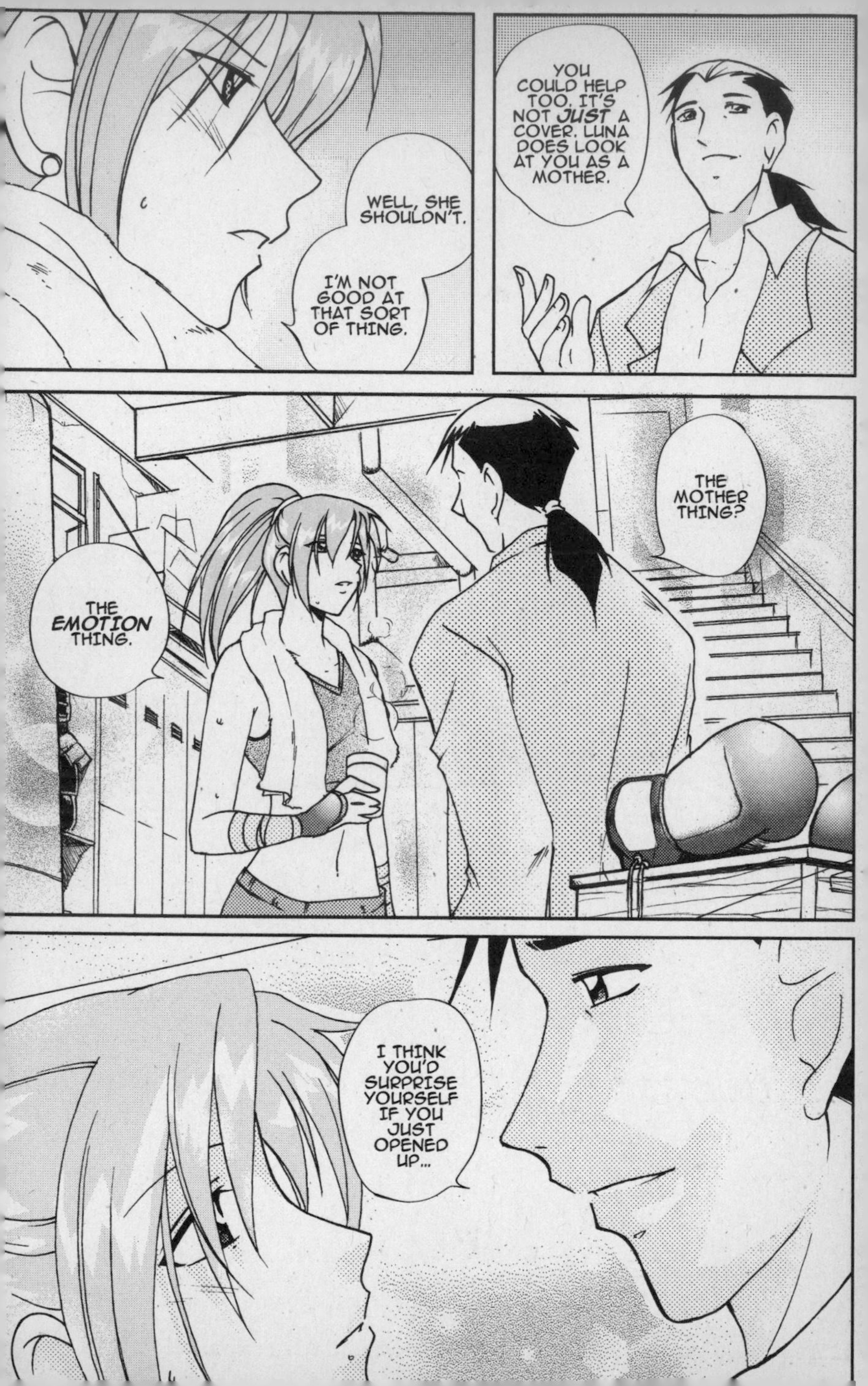
YOU COULD HELP TOO. IT'S NOT *JUST* A COVER. LUNA DOES LOOK AT YOU AS A MOTHER.
WELL, SHE SHOULDN'T.
I'M NOT GOOD AT THAT SORT OF THING.
THE MOTHER THING?
THE *EMOTION* THING.
I THINK YOU'D SURPRISE YOURSELF IF YOU JUST OPENED UP...

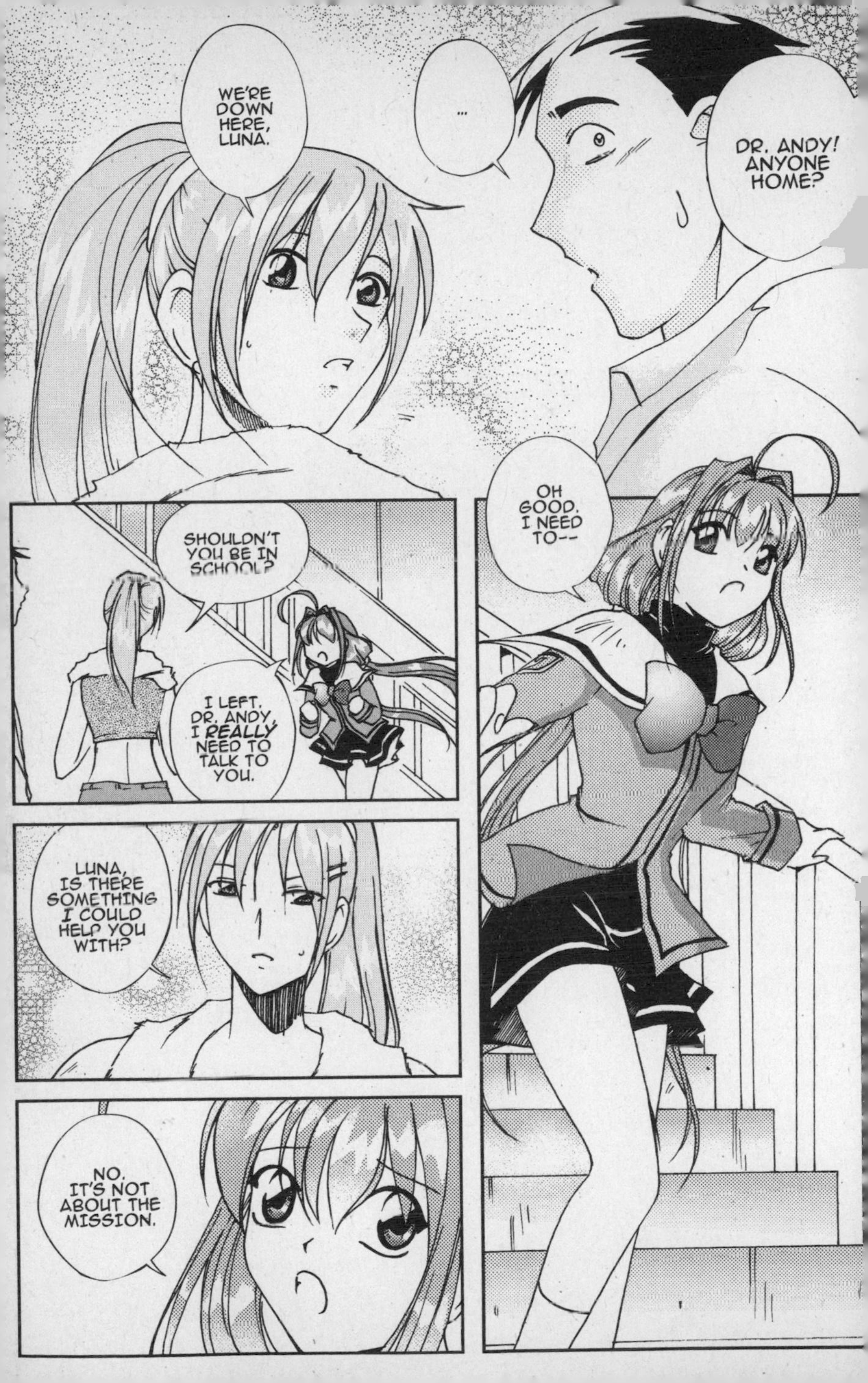
DR. ANDY! ANYONE HOME?
...
WE'RE DOWN HERE, LUNA.
OH GOOD. I NEED TO--
SHOULDN'T YOU BE IN SCHOOL?
I LEFT. DR. ANDY, I *REALLY* NEED TO TALK TO YOU.
LUNA, IS THERE SOMETHING I COULD HELP YOU WITH?
NO. IT'S NOT ABOUT THE MISSION.

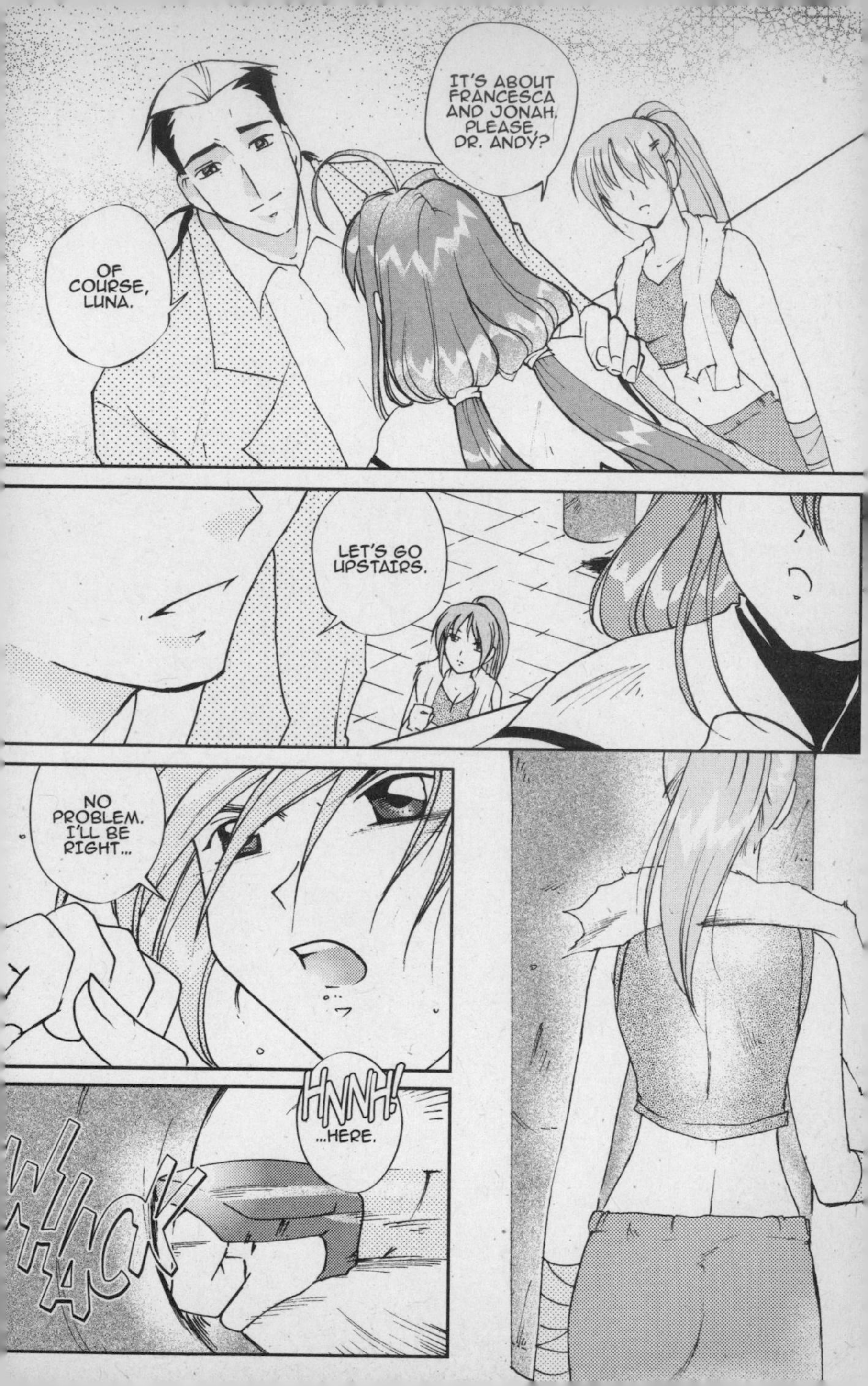
IT'S ABOUT FRANCESCA AND JONAH. PLEASE, DR. ANDY?
OF COURSE, LUNA.
LET'S GO UPSTAIRS.
NO PROBLEM. I'LL BE RIGHT...
HNNH!
...HERE.
WHACK

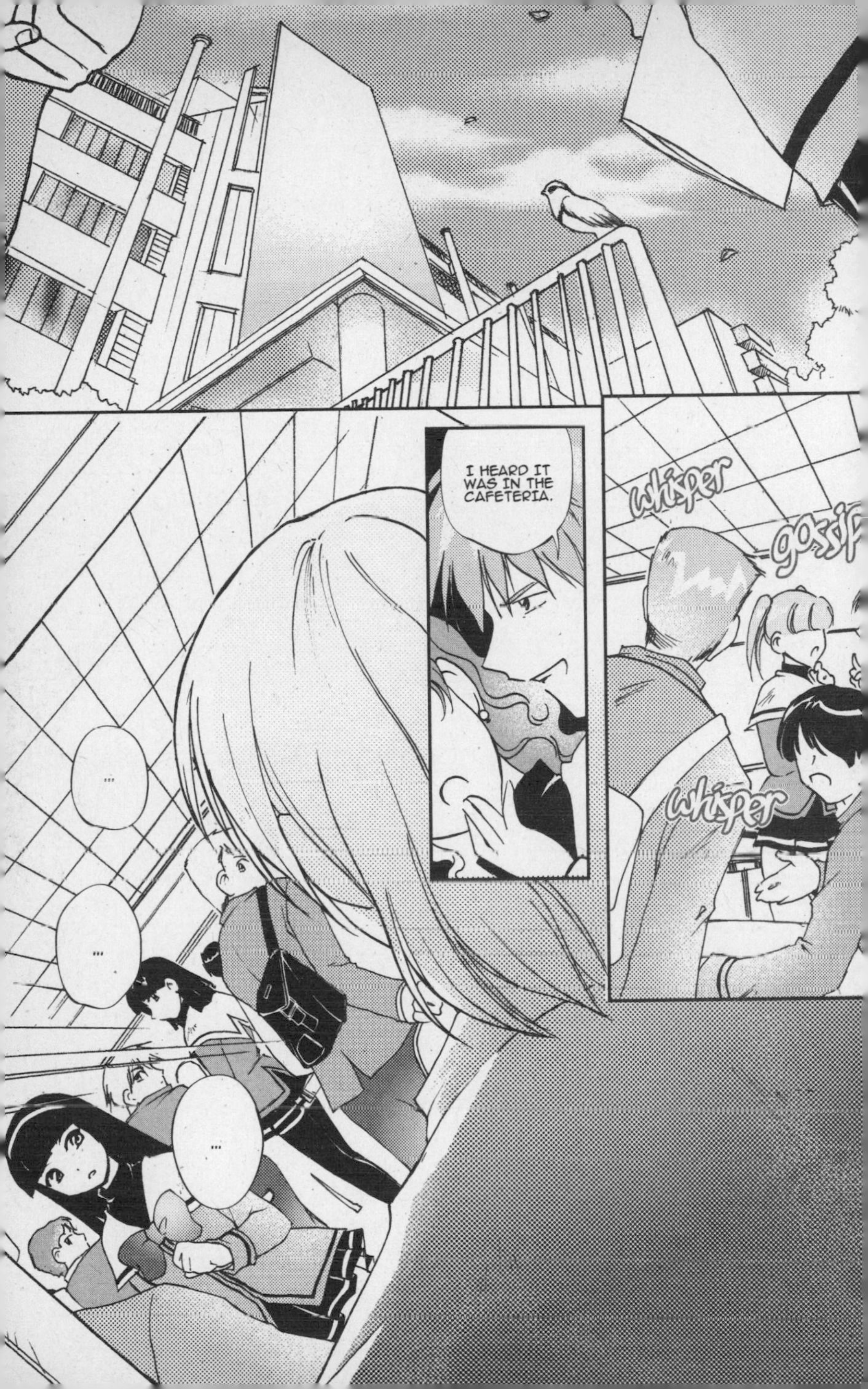

whisper
gossip
whisper
I HEARD IT WAS IN THE CAFETERIA.
...
...
...

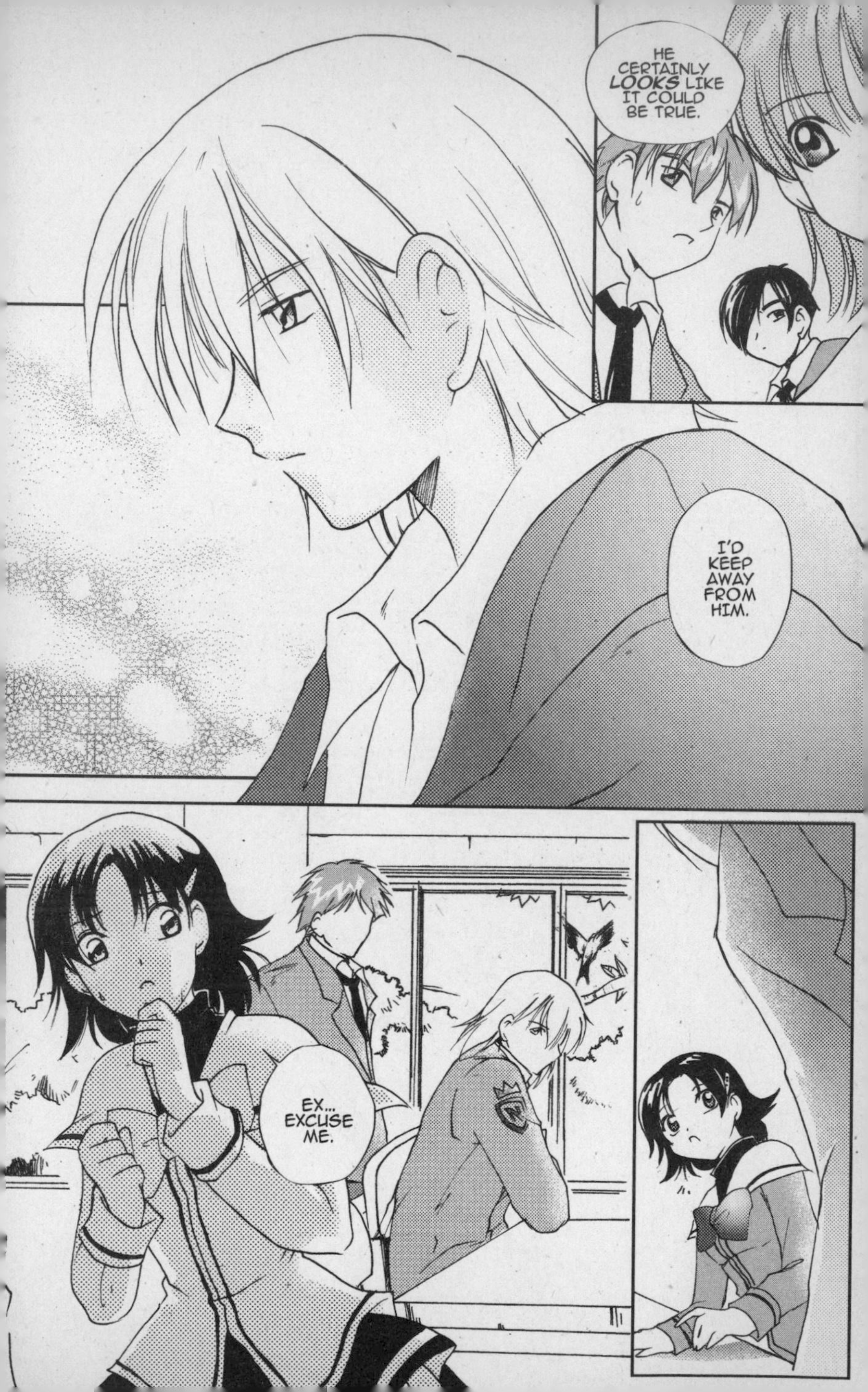
HE CERTAINLY **LOOKS** LIKE IT COULD BE TRUE.
I'D KEEP AWAY FROM HIM.
EX... EXCUSE ME.

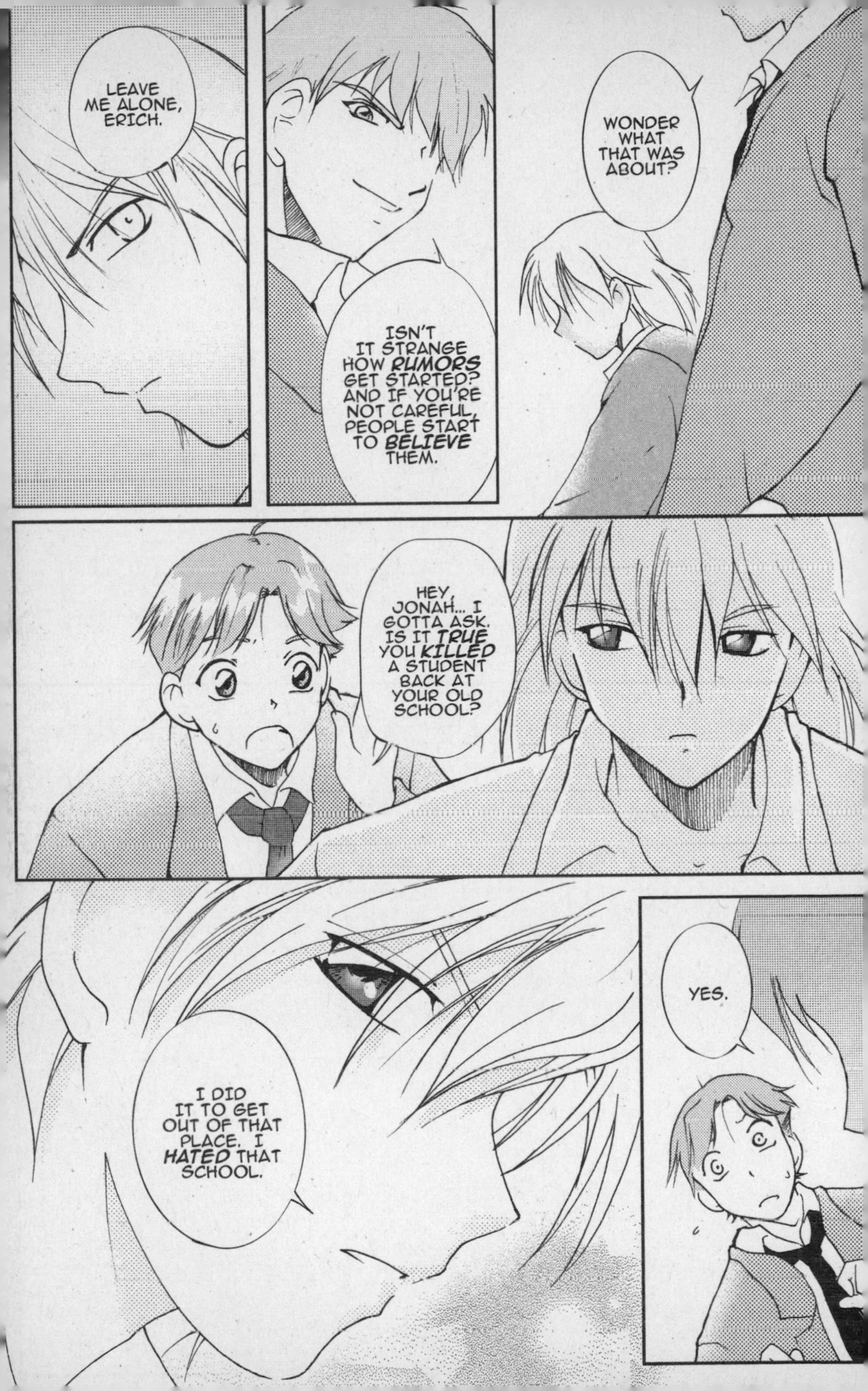
WONDER WHAT THAT WAS ABOUT?
ISN'T IT STRANGE HOW *RUMORS* GET STARTED? AND IF YOU'RE NOT CAREFUL, PEOPLE START TO *BELIEVE* THEM.
LEAVE ME ALONE, ERICH.
HEY, JONAH... I GOTTA ASK. IS IT *TRUE* YOU *KILLED* A STUDENT BACK AT YOUR OLD SCHOOL?
YES.
I DID IT TO GET OUT OF THAT PLACE. I *HATED* THAT SCHOOL.

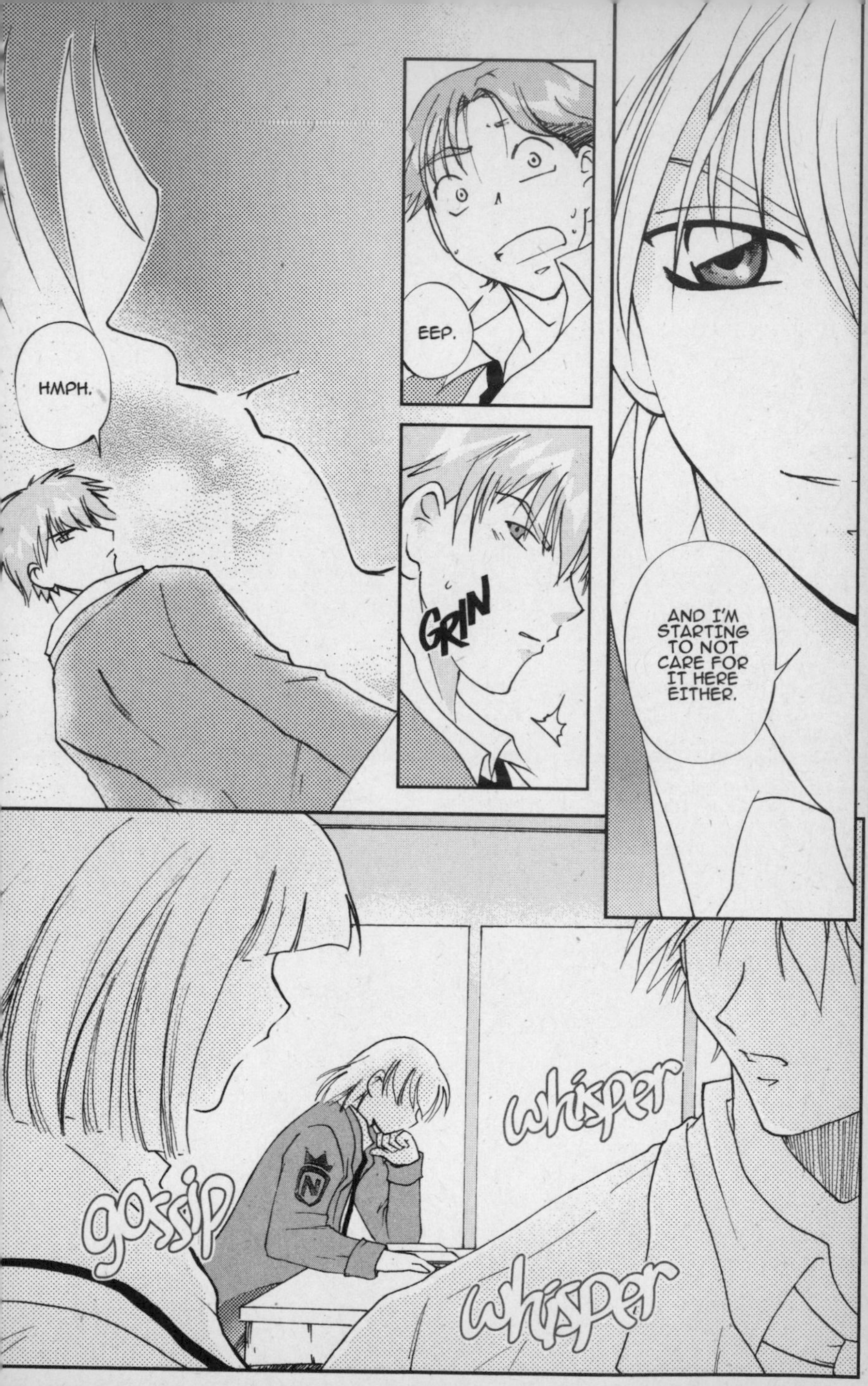
AND I'M STARTING TO NOT CARE FOR IT HERE EITHER.
EEP.
GRIN
HMPH.
whisper
gossip
whisper

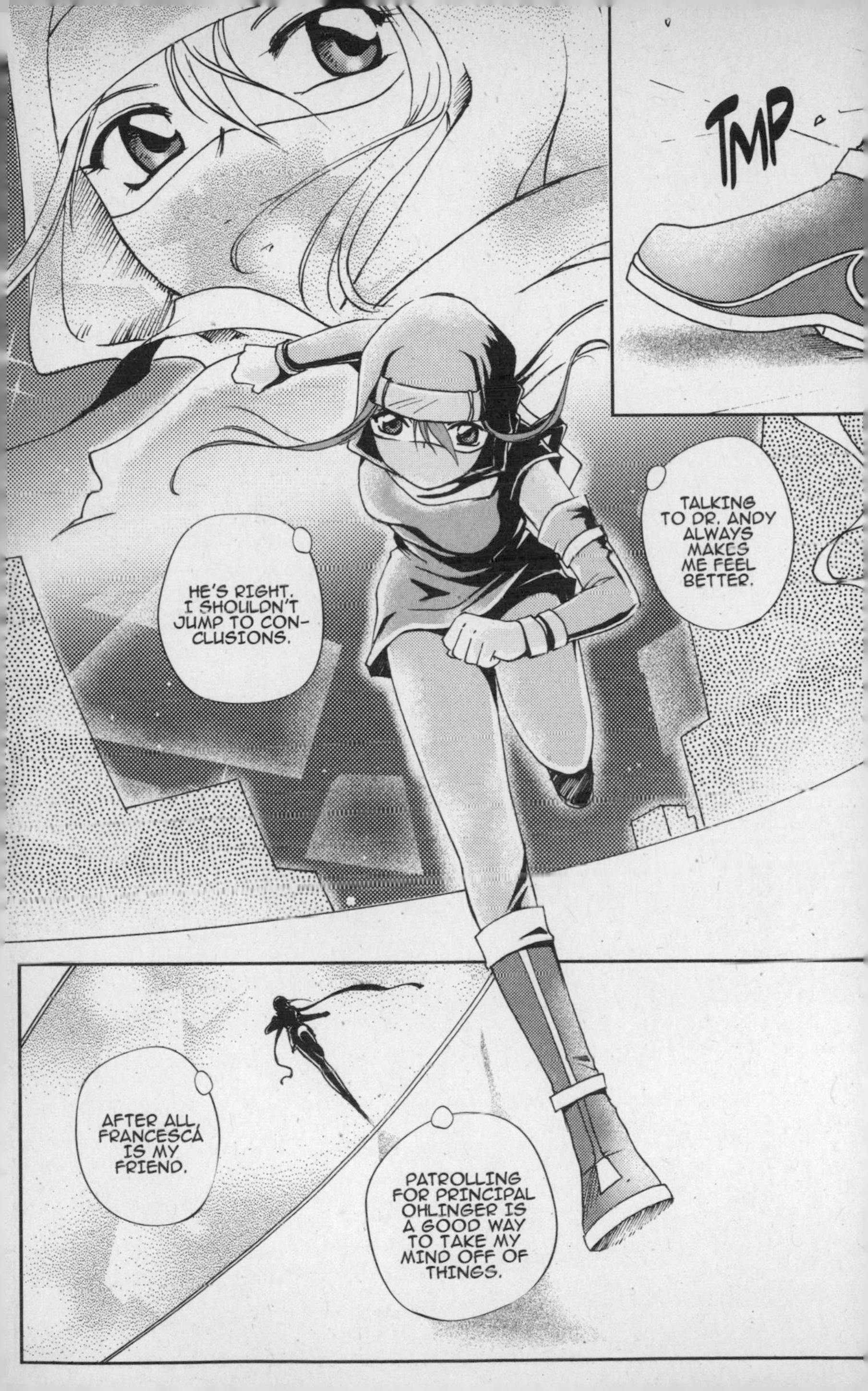
TMP
TALKING TO DR. ANDY ALWAYS MAKES ME FEEL BETTER.
HE'S RIGHT. I SHOULDN'T JUMP TO CON-CLUSIONS.
AFTER ALL, FRANCESCA IS MY FRIEND.
PATROLLING FOR PRINCIPAL OHLINGER IS A GOOD WAY TO TAKE MY MIND OFF OF THINGS.

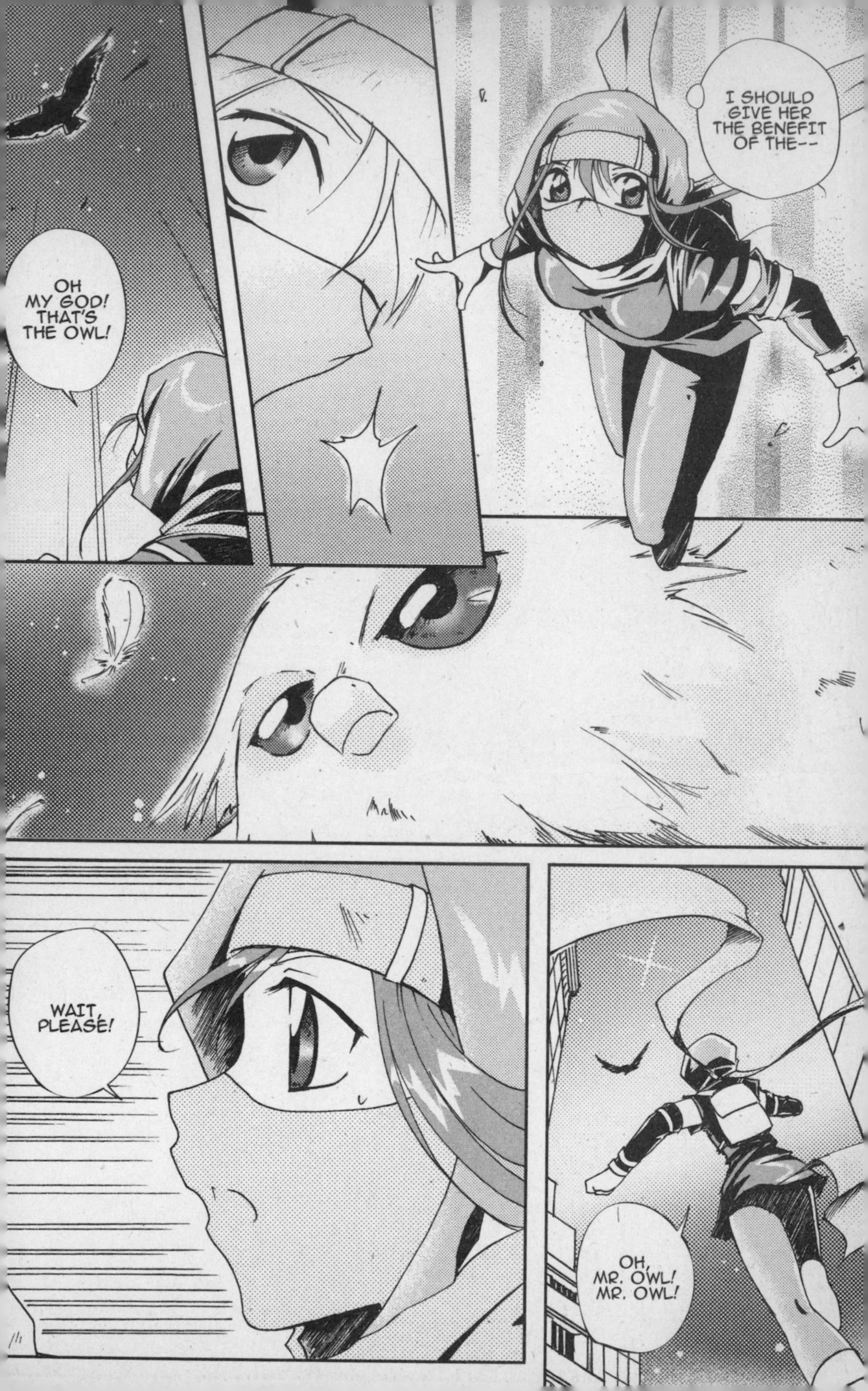
I SHOULD GIVE HER THE BENEFIT OF THE--
OH MY GOD! THAT'S THE OWL!
OH, MR. OWL! MR. OWL!
WAIT, PLEASE!

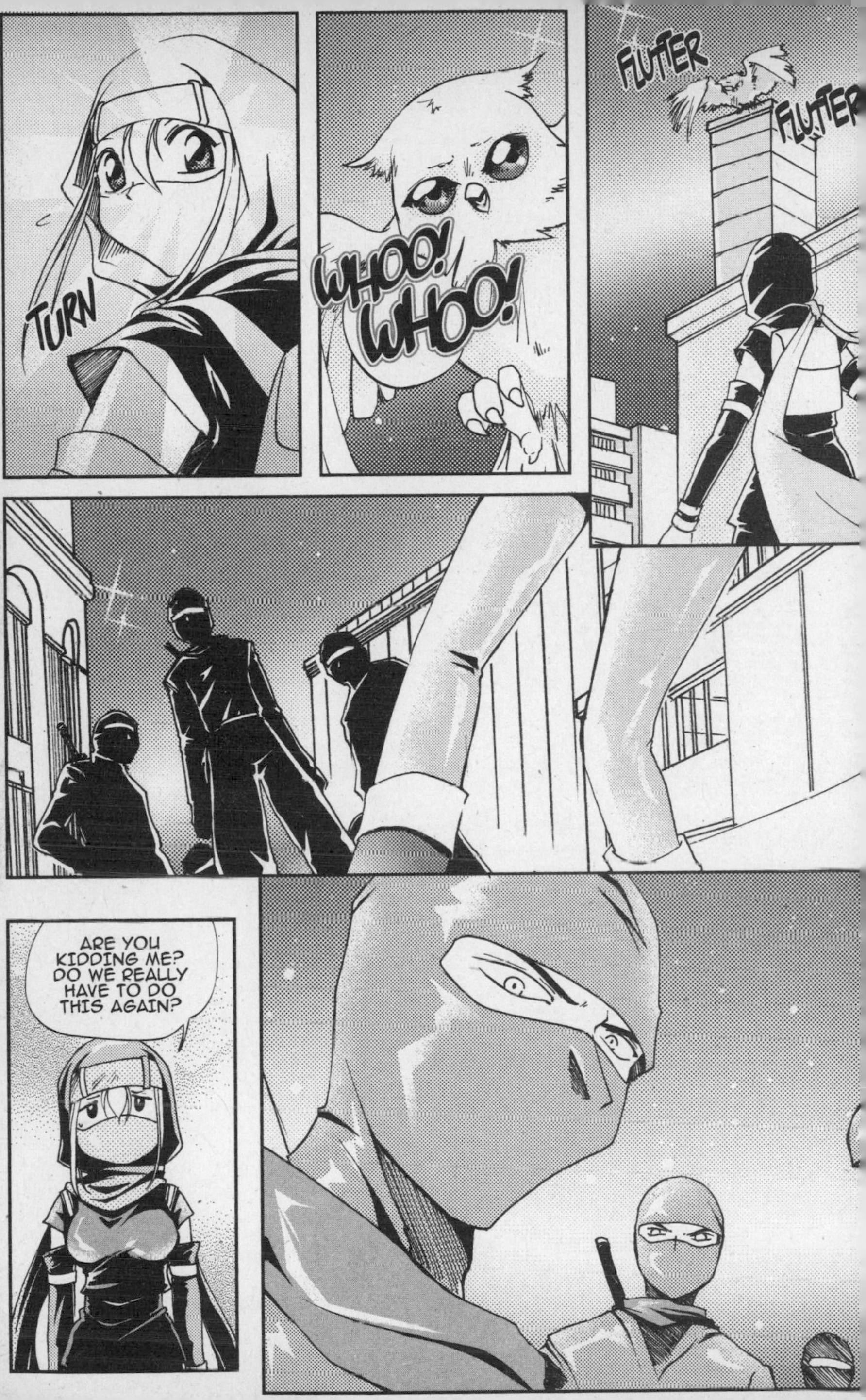
FLUTTER
FLUTTER
WHOO! WHOO!
TURN
ARE YOU KIDDING ME? DO WE REALLY HAVE TO DO THIS AGAIN?

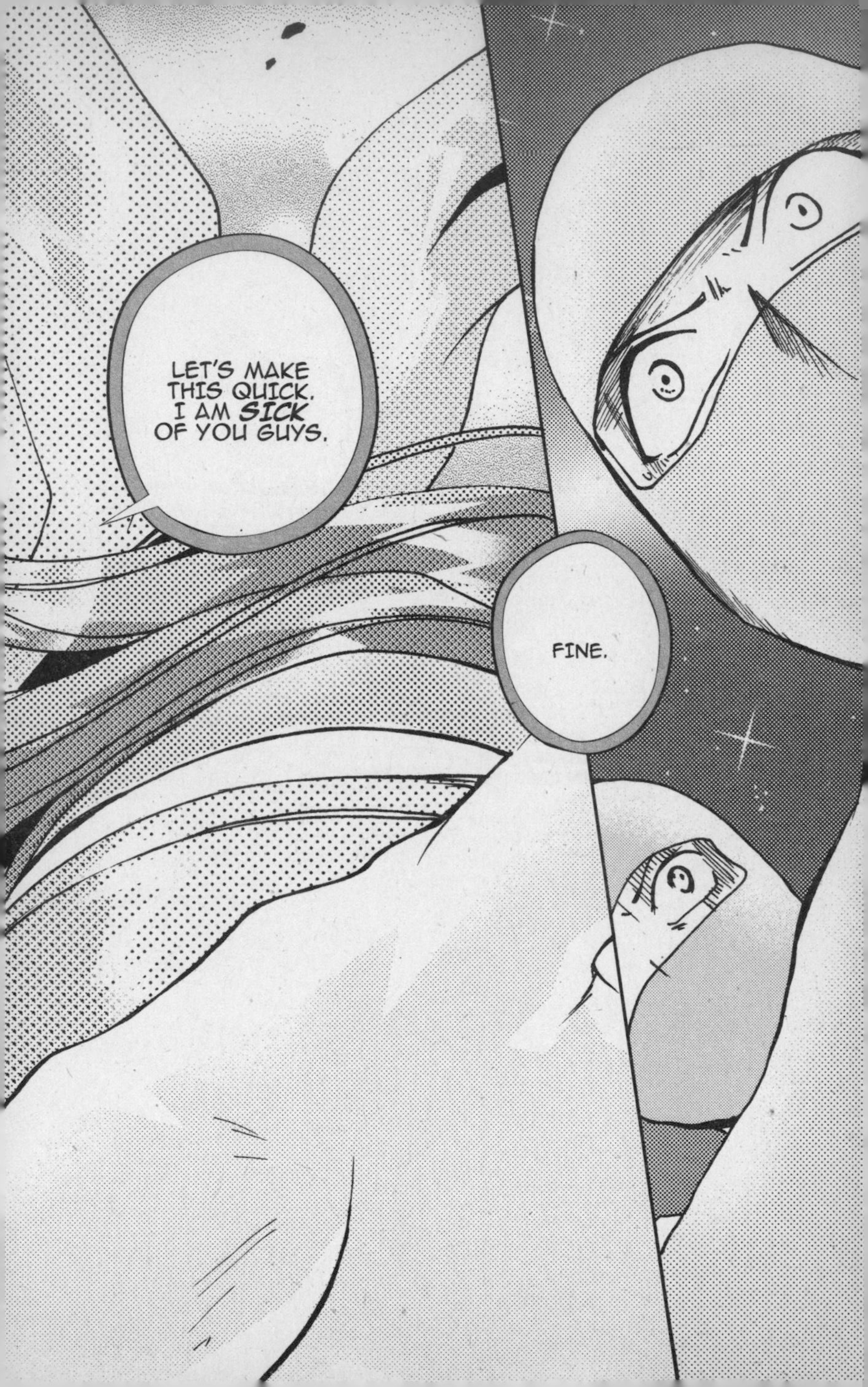
LET'S MAKE THIS QUICK. I AM *SICK* OF YOU GUYS.
FINE.

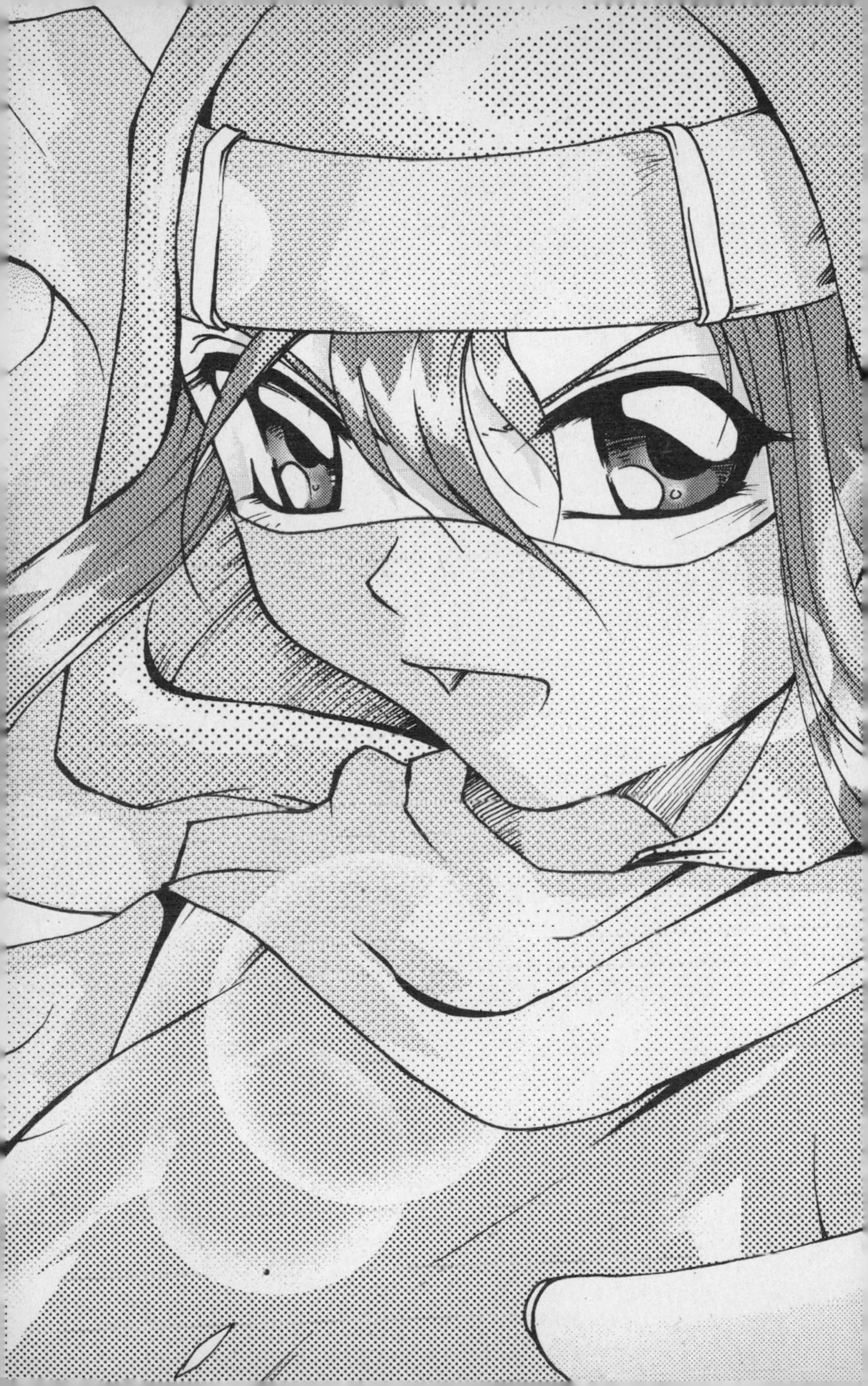

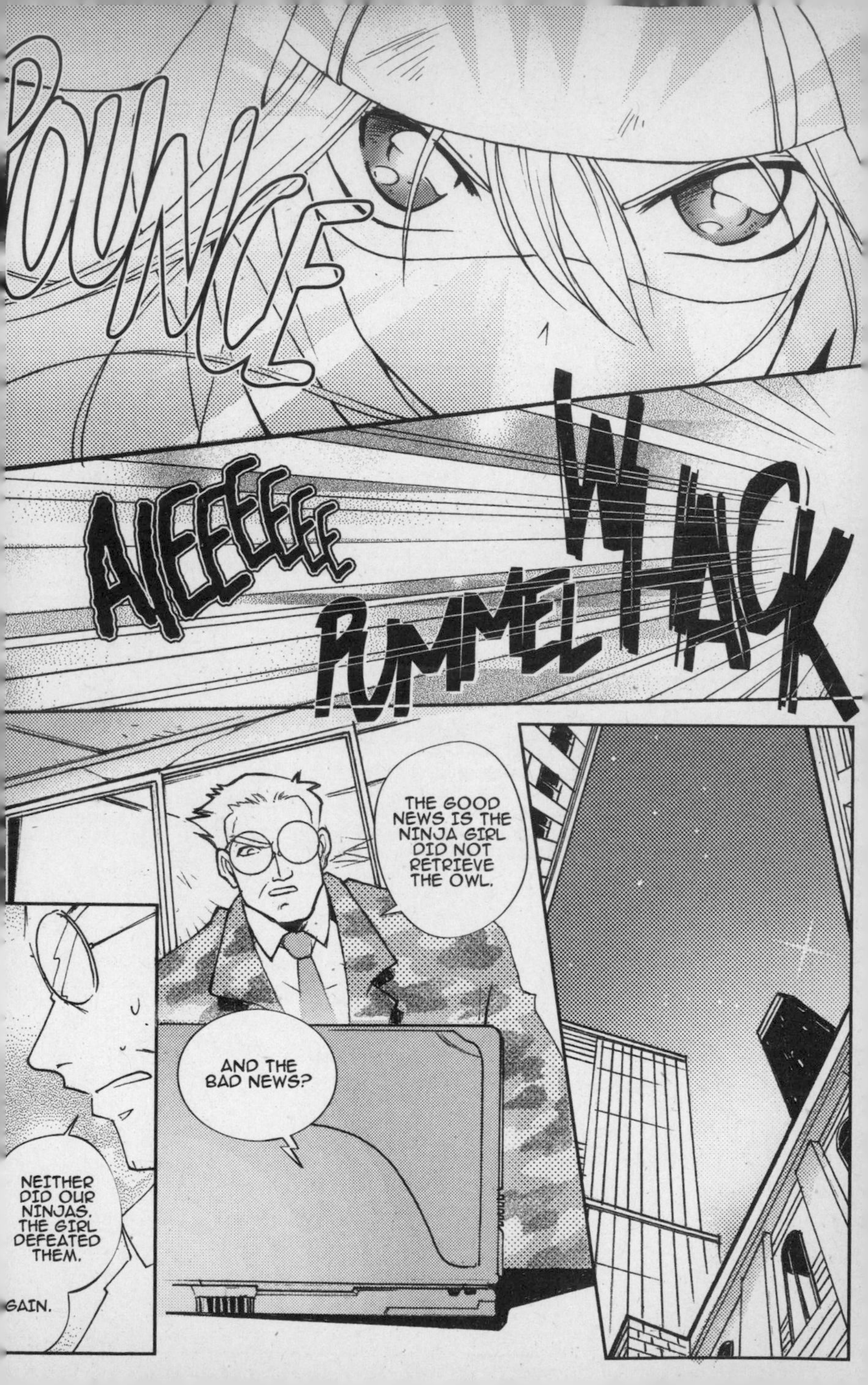
POUNCE
WHACK
HACK
PUMMEL
AIEEEEEE
THE GOOD NEWS IS THE NINJA GIRL DID NOT RETRIEVE THE OWL.
AND THE BAD NEWS?
NEITHER DID OUR NINJAS. THE GIRL DEFEATED THEM.
GAIN.

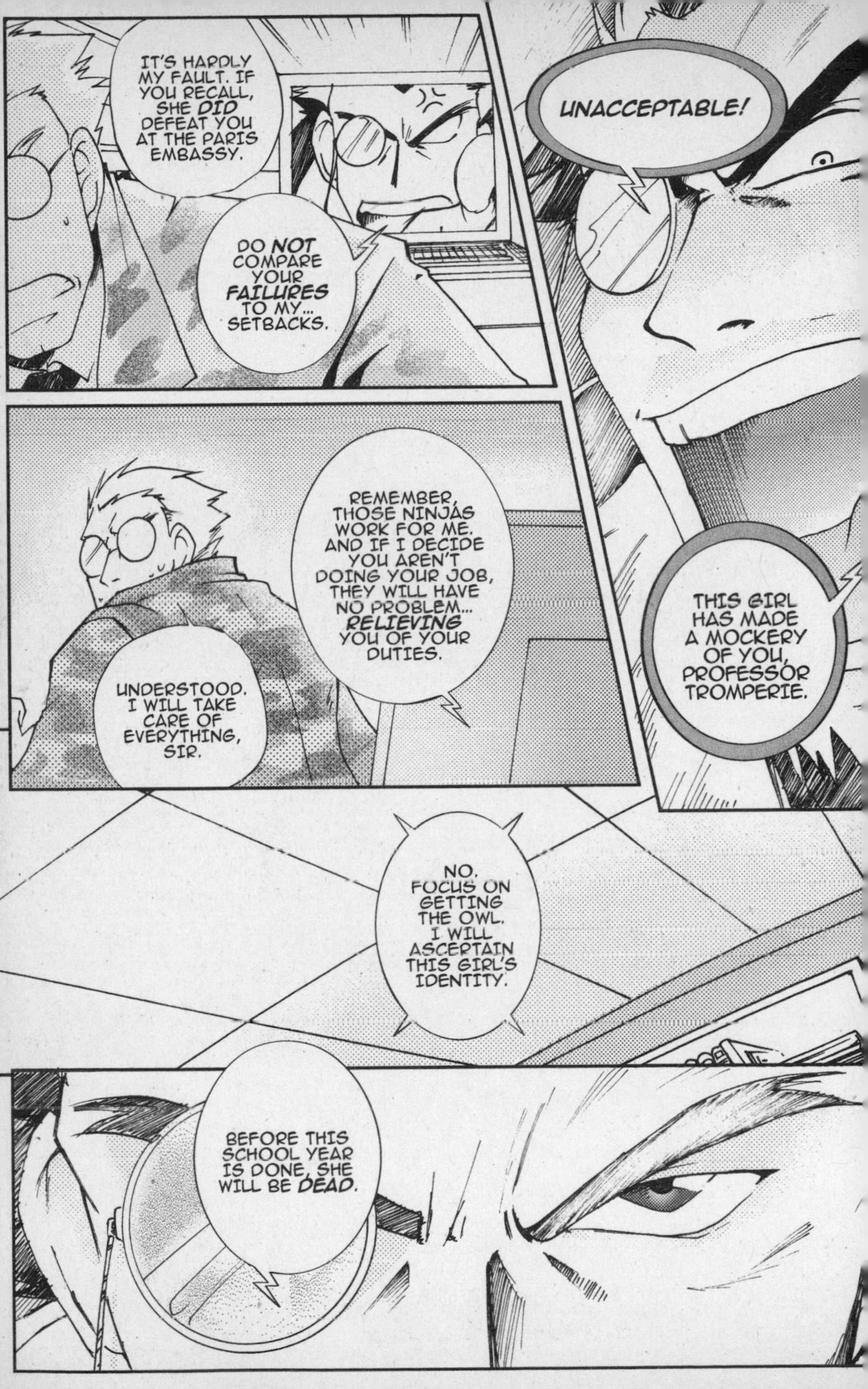
UNACCEPTABLE!
THIS GIRL HAS MADE A MOCKERY OF YOU, PROFESSOR TROMPERIE.
IT'S HARDLY MY FAULT. IF YOU RECALL, SHE *DID* DEFEAT YOU AT THE PARIS EMBASSY.
DO **NOT** COMPARE YOUR ***FAILURES*** TO MY... SETBACKS.
REMEMBER, THOSE NINJAS WORK FOR ME. AND IF I DECIDE YOU AREN'T DOING YOUR JOB, THEY WILL HAVE NO PROBLEM... ***RELIEVING*** YOU OF YOUR DUTIES.
UNDERSTOOD. I WILL TAKE CARE OF EVERYTHING, SIR.
NO. FOCUS ON GETTING THE OWL. I WILL ASCERTAIN THIS GIRL'S IDENTITY.
BEFORE THIS SCHOOL YEAR IS DONE, SHE WILL BE *DEAD*.

File 14
BEST FRIEND

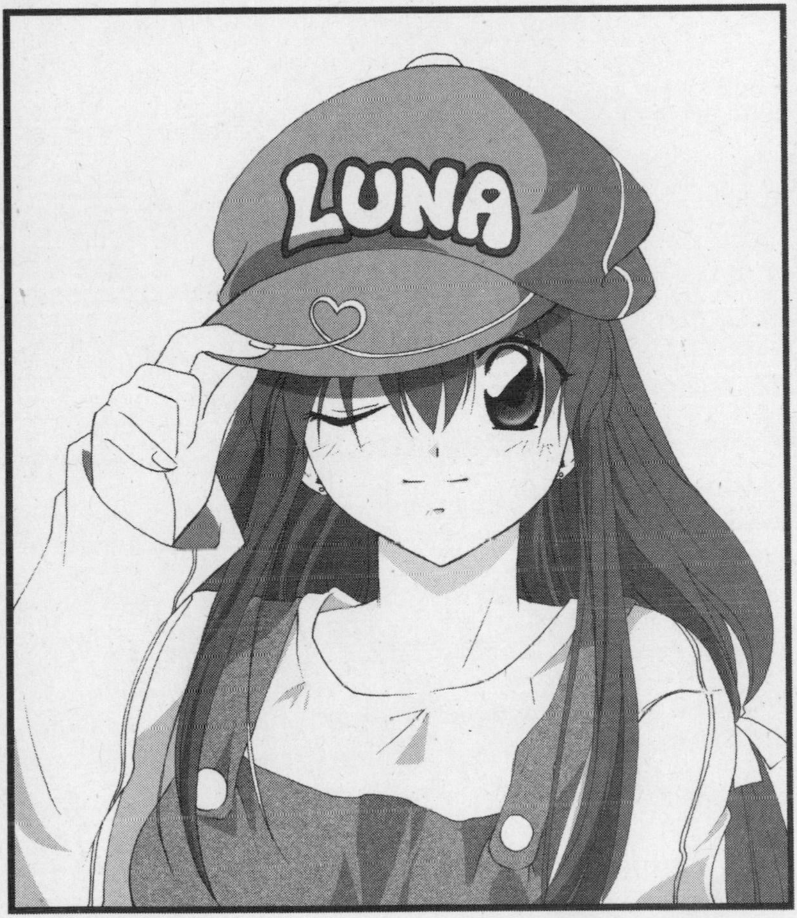
LUNA

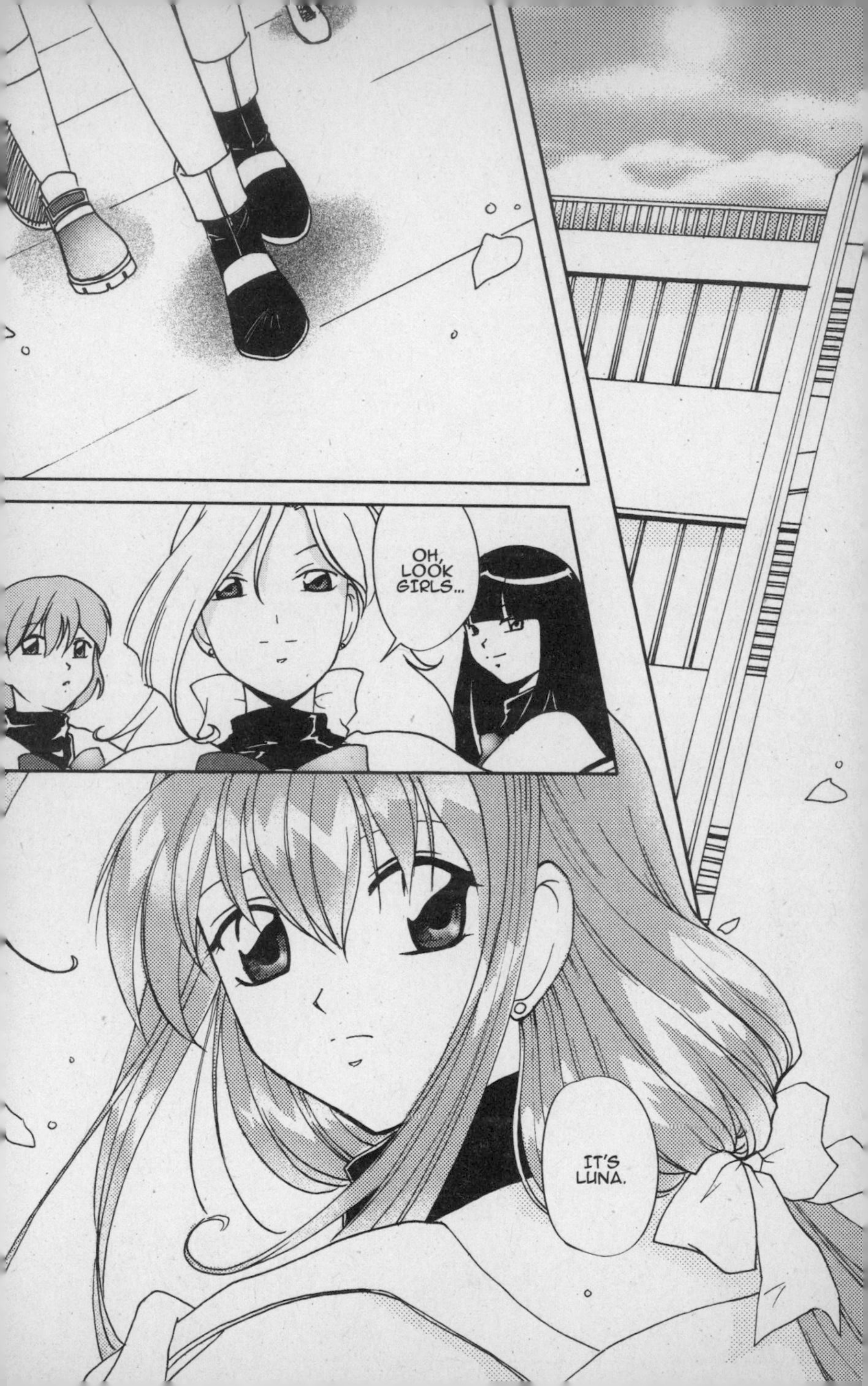
OH, LOOK GIRLS...
IT'S LUNA.

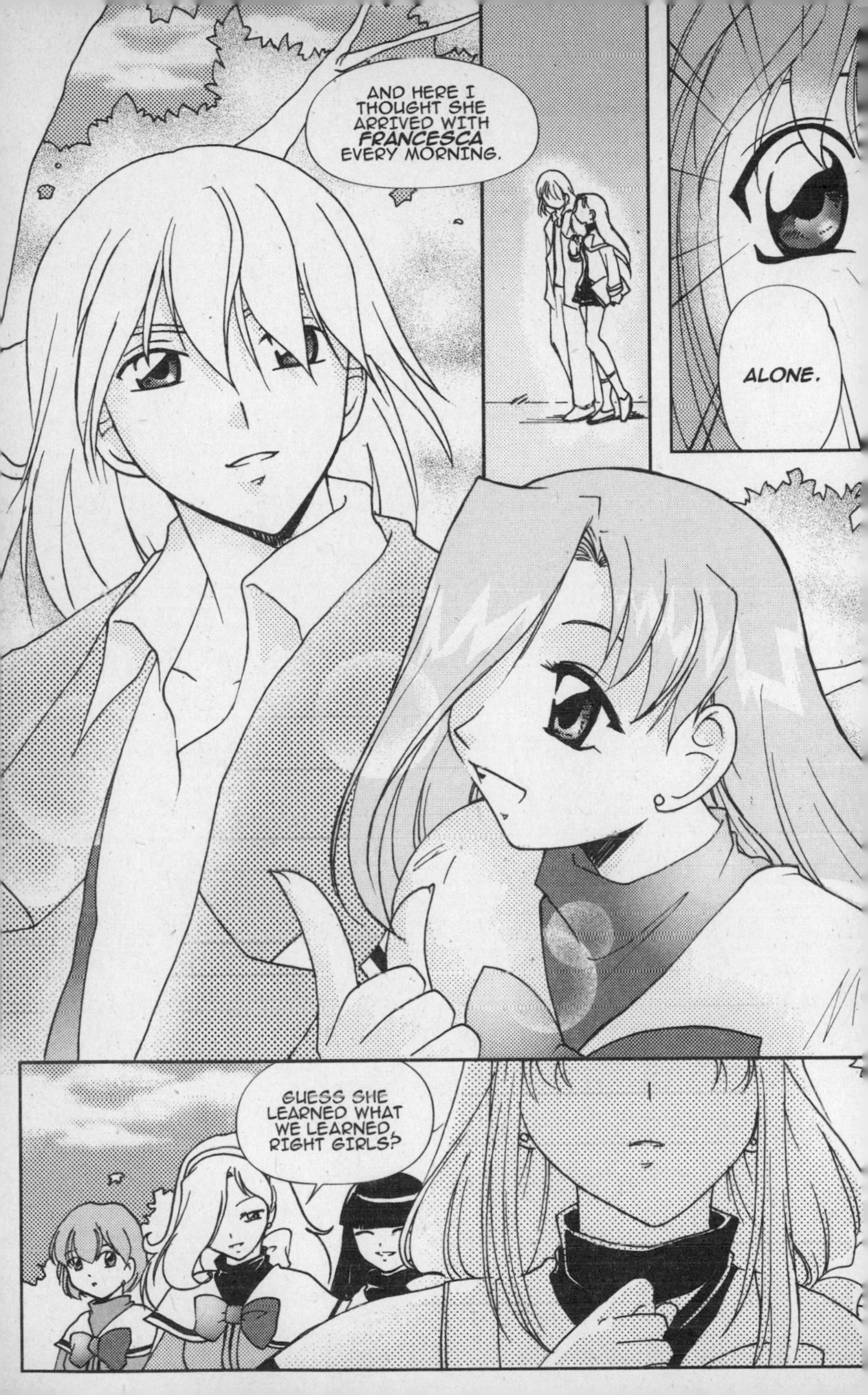
ALONE.
AND HERE I THOUGHT SHE ARRIVED WITH *FRANCESCA* EVERY MORNING.
GUESS SHE LEARNED WHAT WE LEARNED, RIGHT GIRLS?

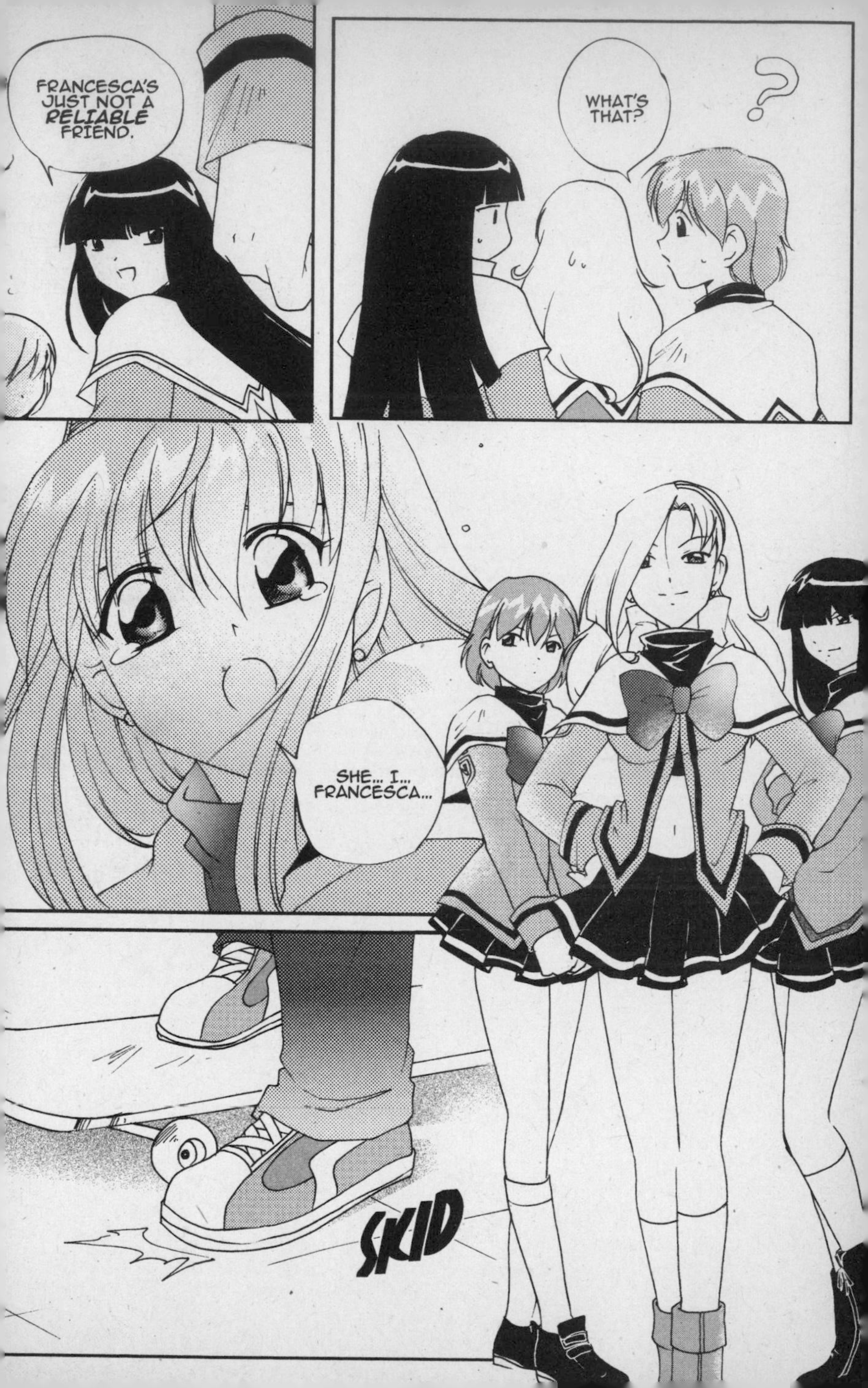
WHAT'S THAT?
FRANCESCA'S JUST NOT A RELIABLE FRIEND.
SHE... I... FRANCESCA...
SKID

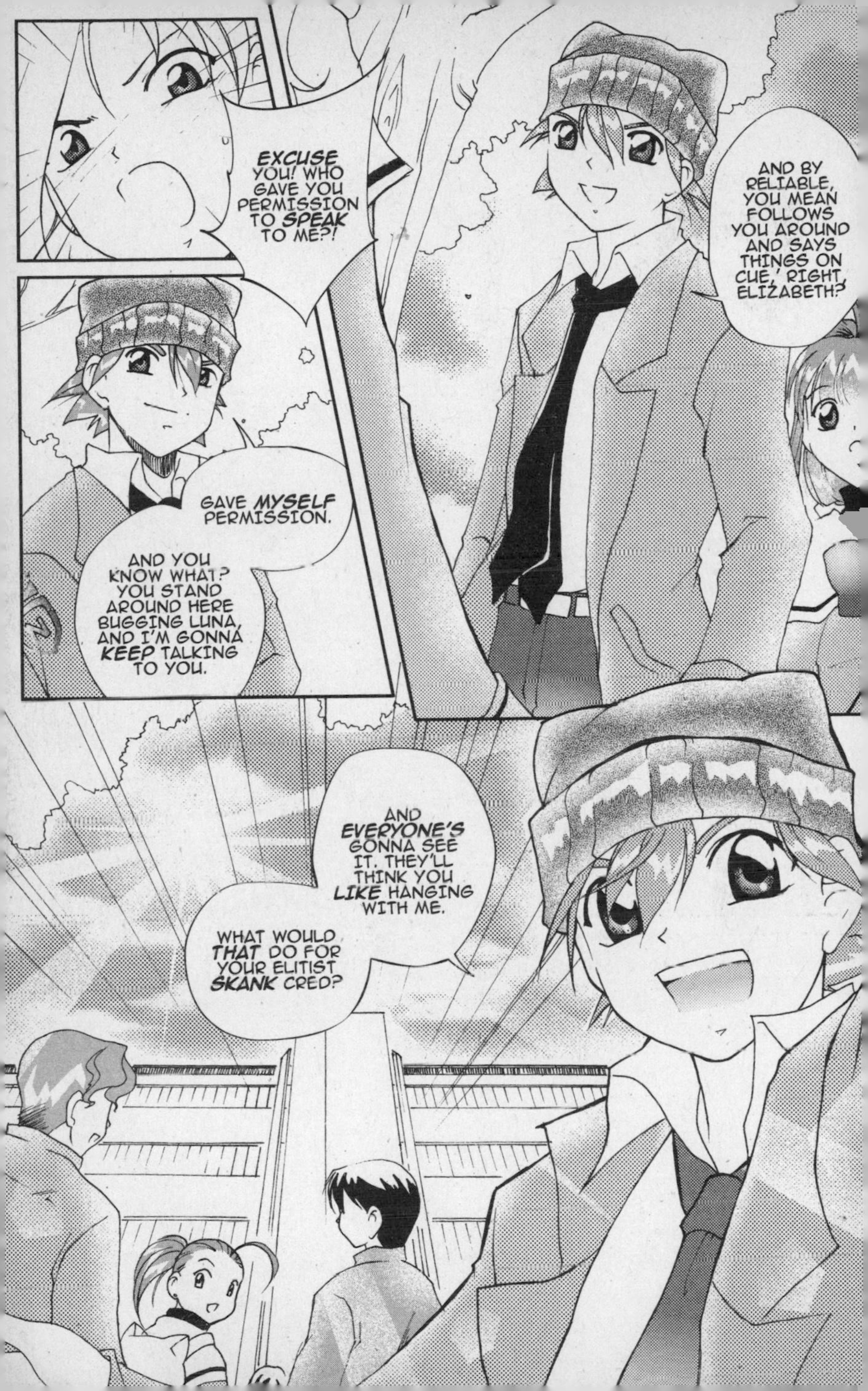
AND BY RELIABLE, YOU MEAN FOLLOWS YOU AROUND AND SAYS THINGS ON CUE,' RIGHT, ELIZABETH?
EXCUSE YOU! WHO GAVE YOU PERMISSION TO SPEAK TO ME?!
GAVE MYSELF PERMISSION.
AND YOU KNOW WHAT? YOU STAND AROUND HERE BUGGING LUNA, AND I'M GONNA KEEP TALKING TO YOU.
AND EVERYONE'S GONNA SEE IT. THEY'LL THINK YOU LIKE HANGING WITH ME.
WHAT WOULD THAT DO FOR YOUR ELITIST SKANK CRED?

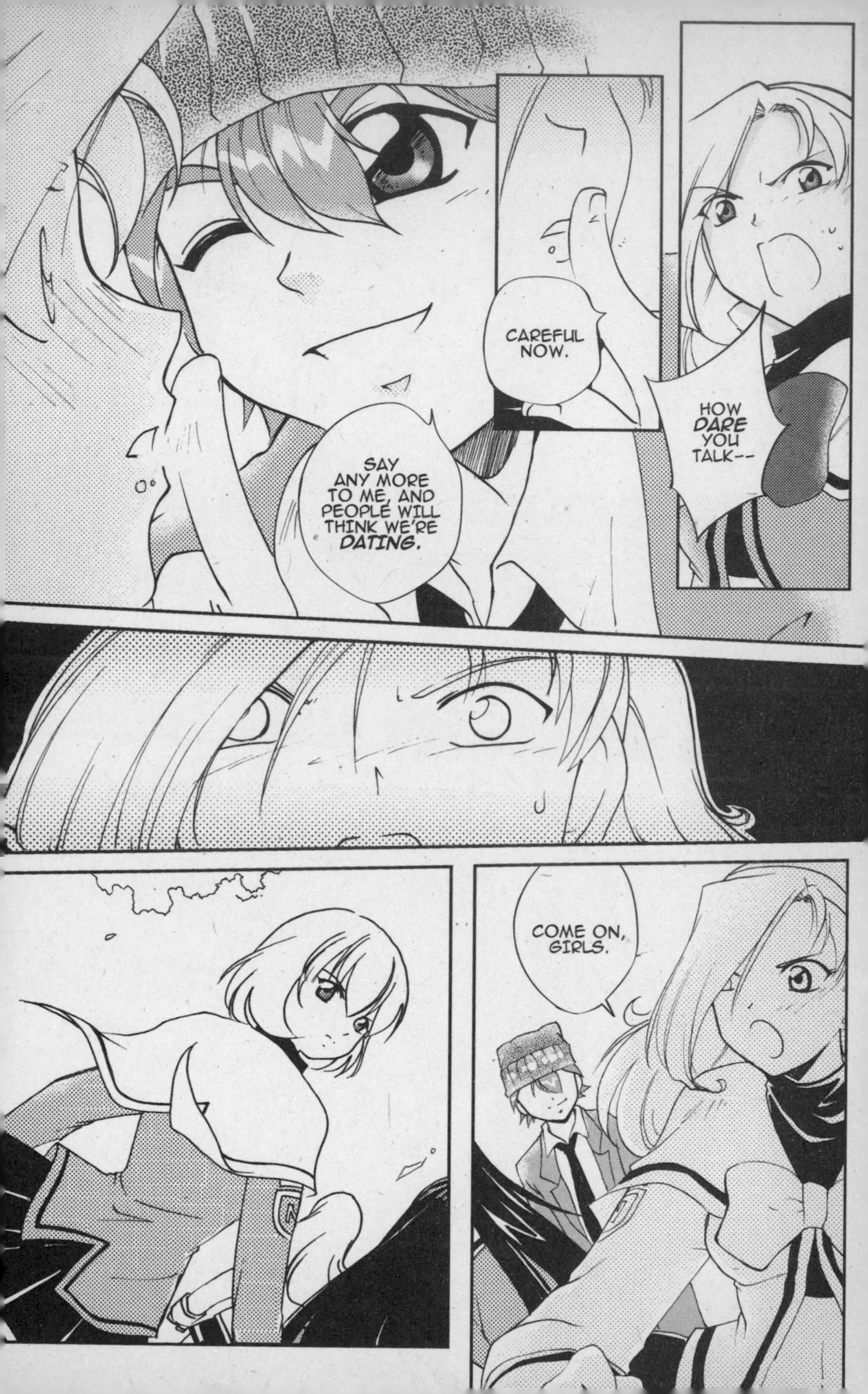
HOW DARE YOU TALK--
CAREFUL NOW.
SAY ANY MORE TO ME, AND PEOPLE WILL THINK WE'RE DATING.
COME ON, GIRLS.

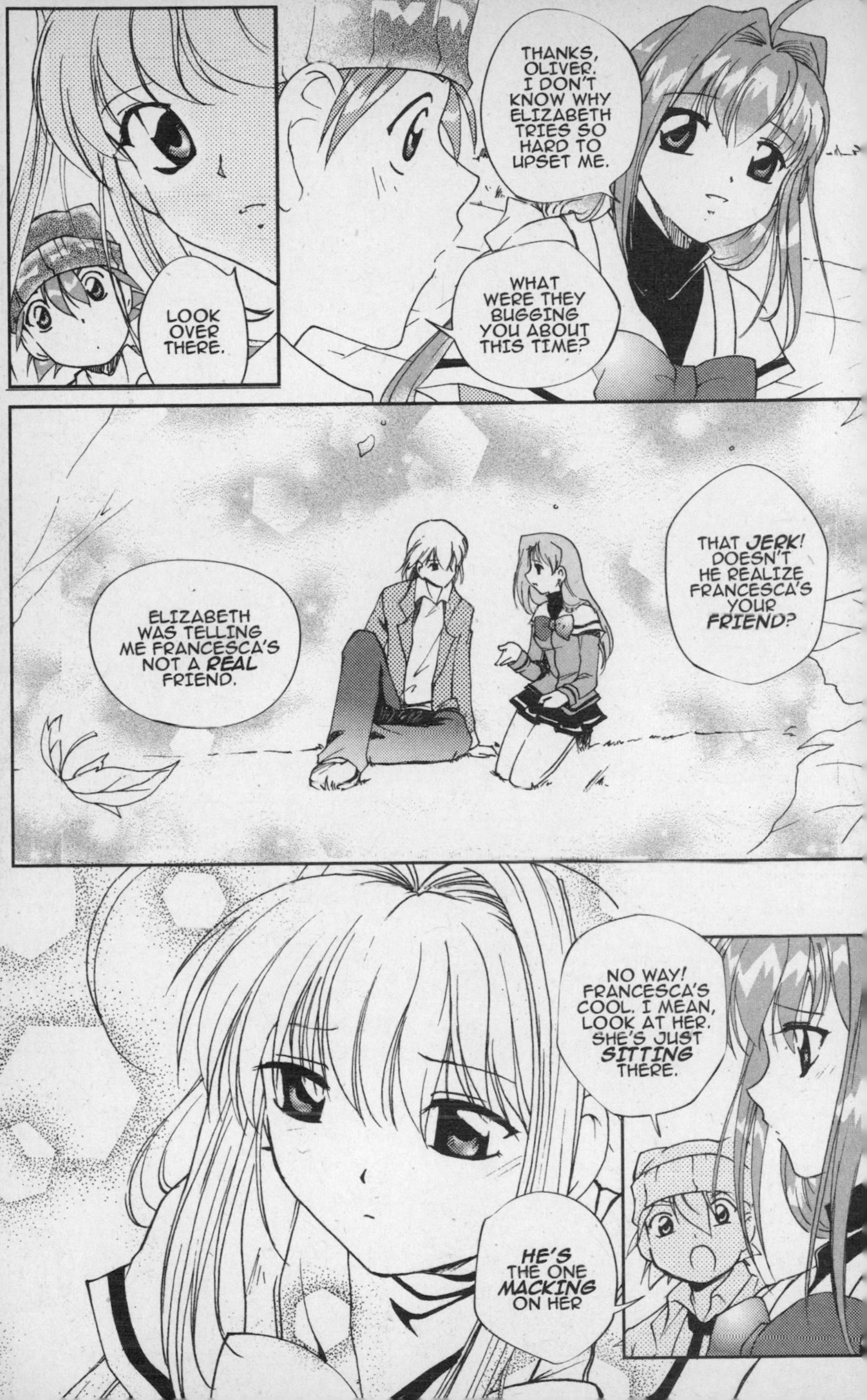
THANKS, OLIVER. I DON'T KNOW WHY ELIZABETH TRIES SO HARD TO UPSET ME.
WHAT WERE THEY BUGGING YOU ABOUT THIS TIME?
LOOK OVER THERE.
THAT JERK! DOESN'T HE REALIZE FRANCESCA'S YOUR FRIEND?
ELIZABETH WAS TELLING ME FRANCESCA'S NOT A REAL FRIEND.
NO WAY! FRANCESCA'S COOL. I MEAN, LOOK AT HER. SHE'S JUST SITTING THERE.
HE'S THE ONE MACKING ON HER

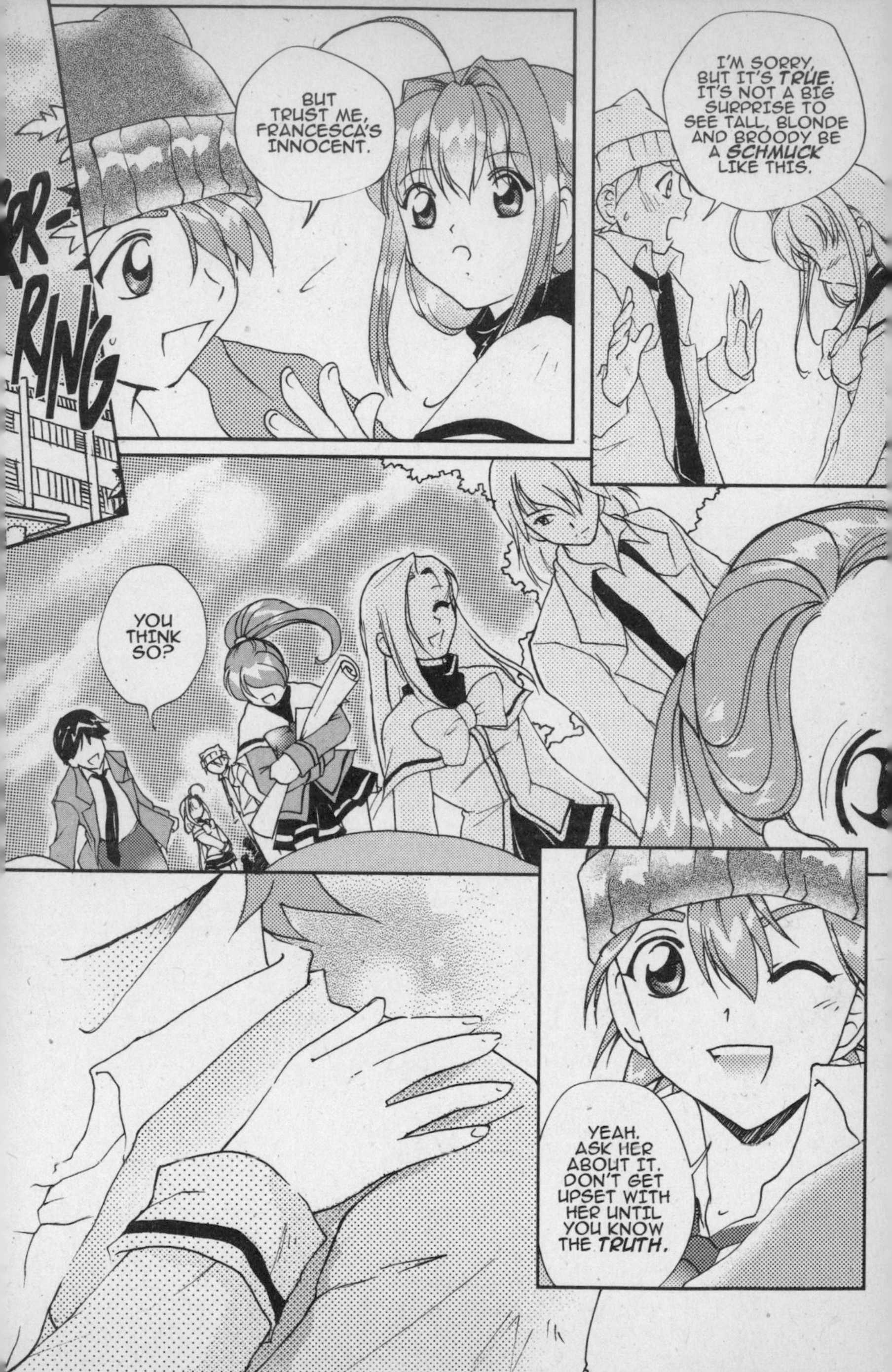
I'M SORRY, BUT IT'S TRUE. IT'S NOT A BIG SURPRISE TO SEE TALL, BLONDE AND BROODY BE A SCHMUCK LIKE THIS.
BUT TRUST ME, FRANCESCA'S INNOCENT.
RR-RING
YOU THINK SO?
YEAH. ASK HER ABOUT IT. DON'T GET UPSET WITH HER UNTIL YOU KNOW THE TRUTH.

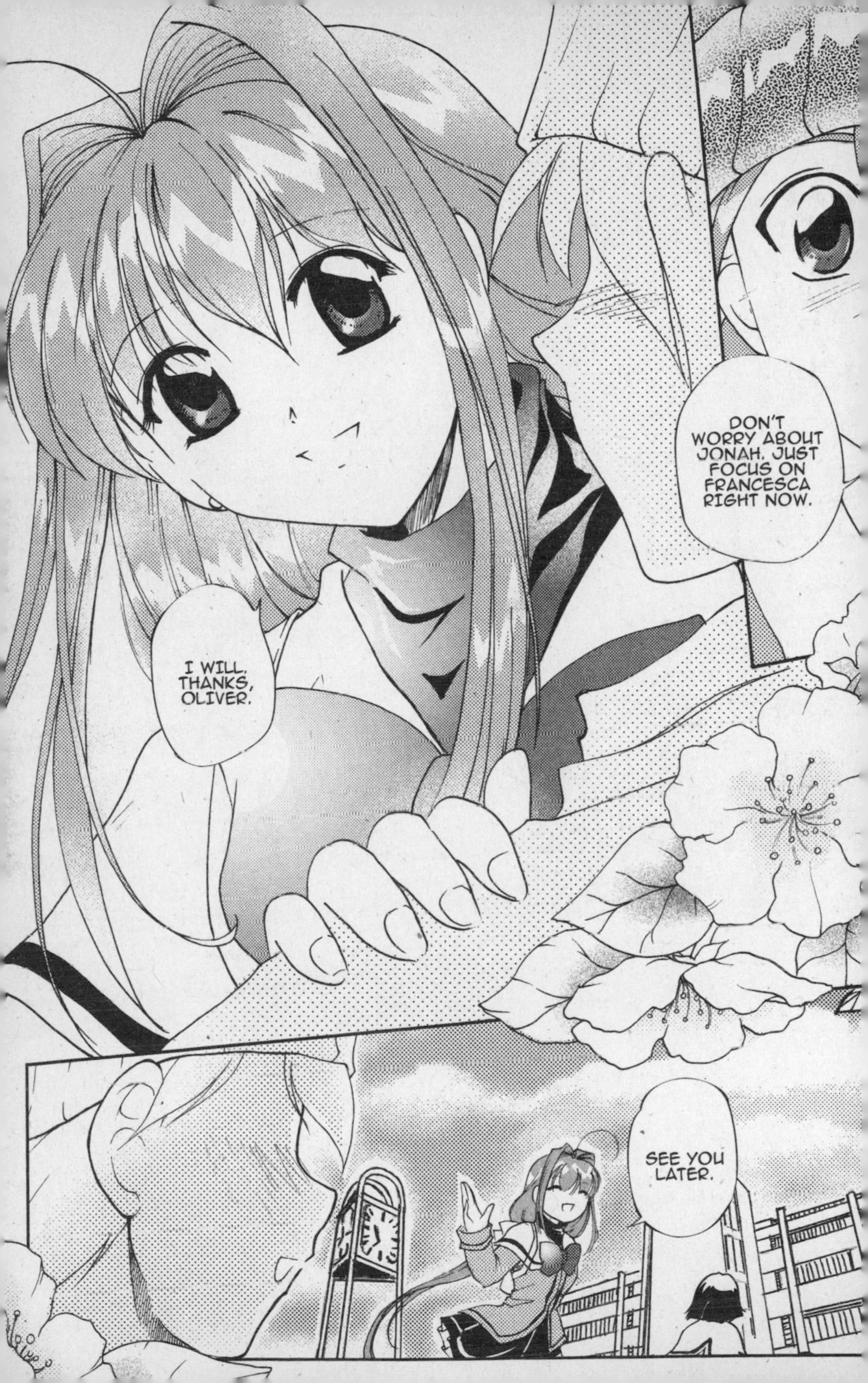
DON'T WORRY ABOUT JONAH. JUST FOCUS ON FRANCESCA RIGHT NOW.
I WILL. THANKS, OLIVER.
SEE YOU LATER.

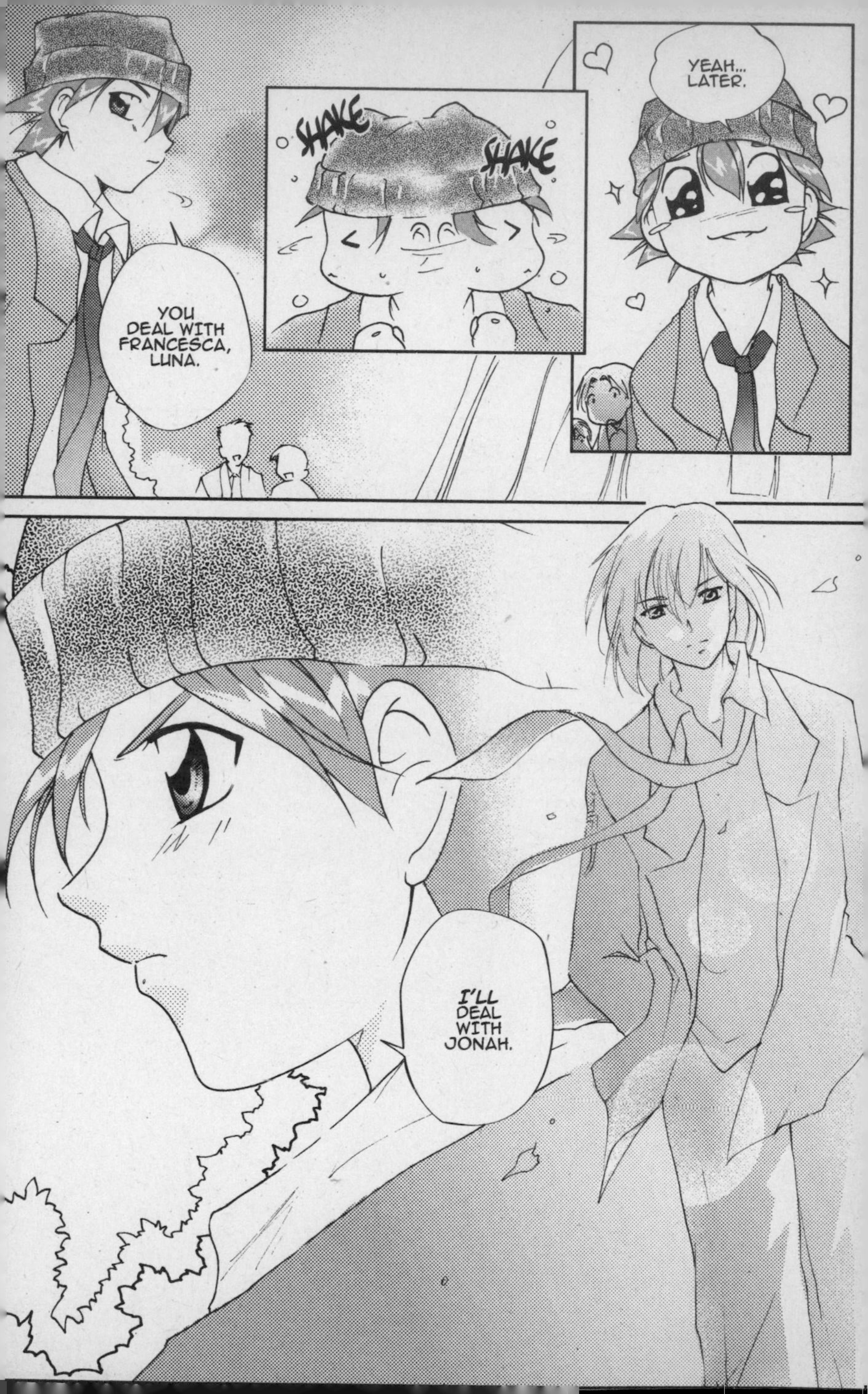
YEAH... LATER.
SHAKE
SHAKE
YOU DEAL WITH FRANCESCA, LUNA.
I'LL DEAL WITH JONAH.

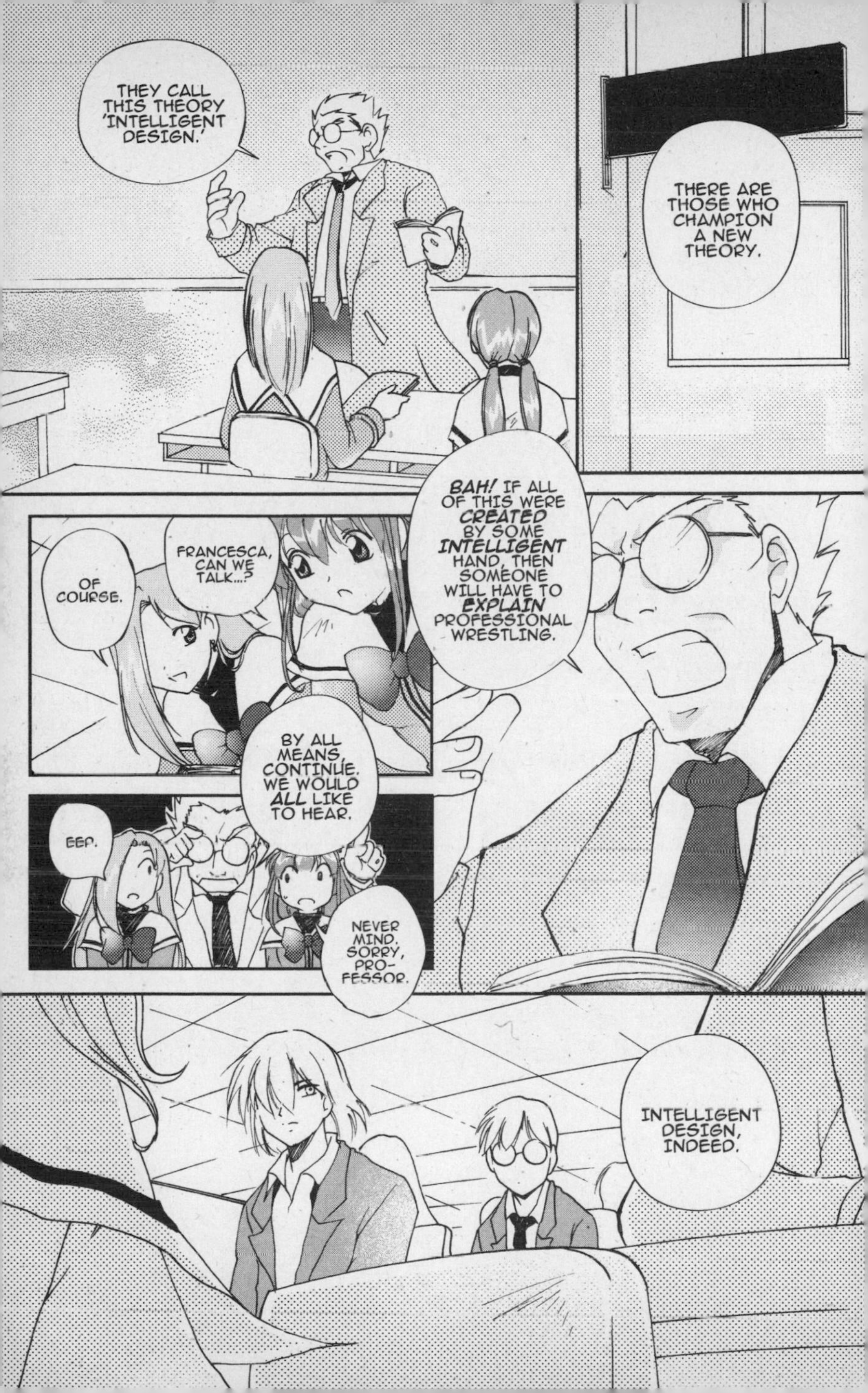
THERE ARE THOSE WHO CHAMPION A NEW THEORY.
THEY CALL THIS THEORY 'INTELLIGENT DESIGN.'
BAH! IF ALL OF THIS WERE CREATED BY SOME INTELLIGENT HAND, THEN SOMEONE WILL HAVE TO EXPLAIN PROFESSIONAL WRESTLING.
FRANCESCA, CAN WE TALK...?
OF COURSE.
BY ALL MEANS, CONTINUE. WE WOULD ALL LIKE TO HEAR.
EEP.
NEVER MIND. SORRY, PRO-FESSOR.
INTELLIGENT DESIGN, INDEED.

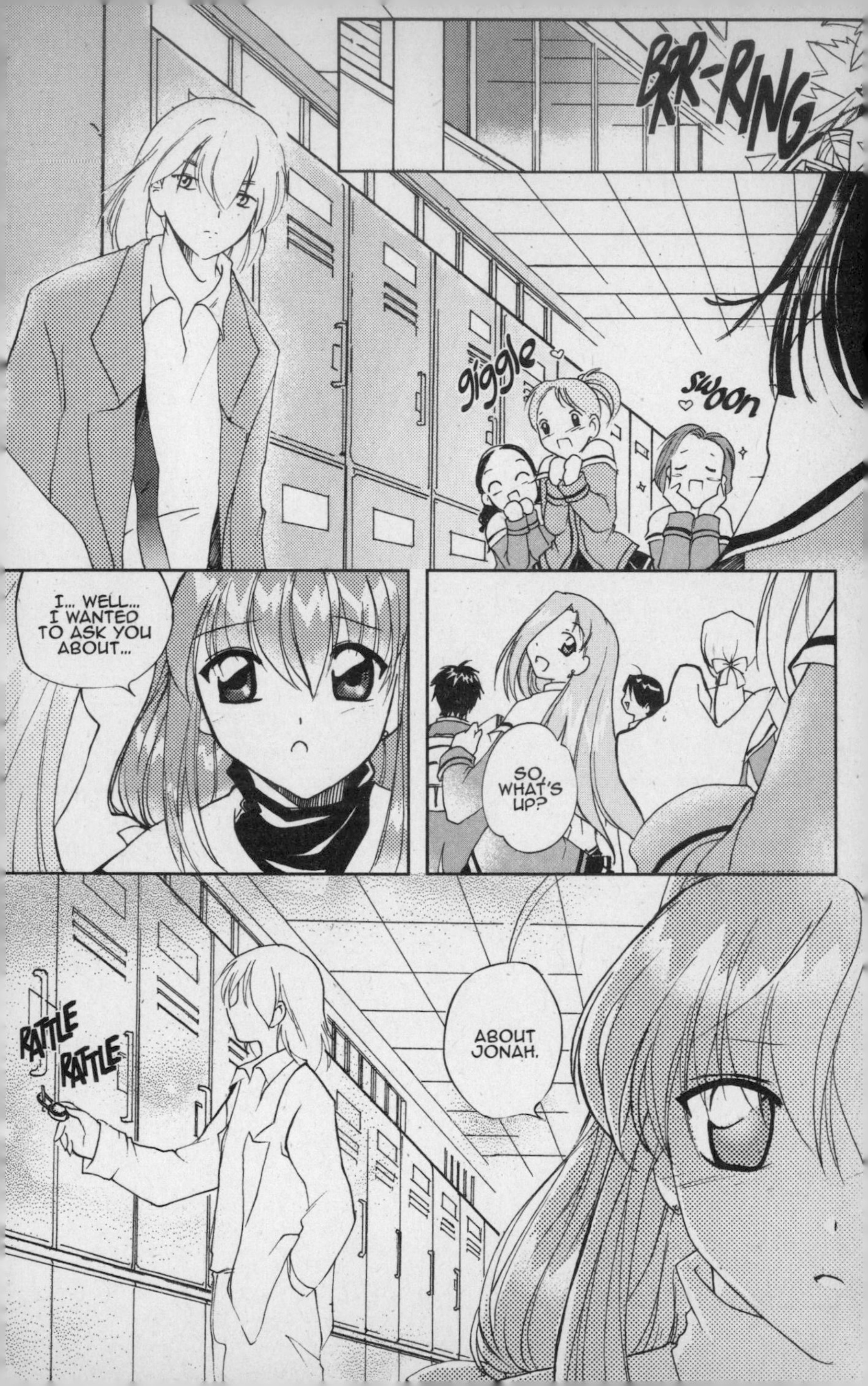
BRR-RING
swoon
giggle
SO, WHAT'S UP?
I... WELL... I WANTED TO ASK YOU ABOUT...
ABOUT JONAH.
RATTLE RATTLE

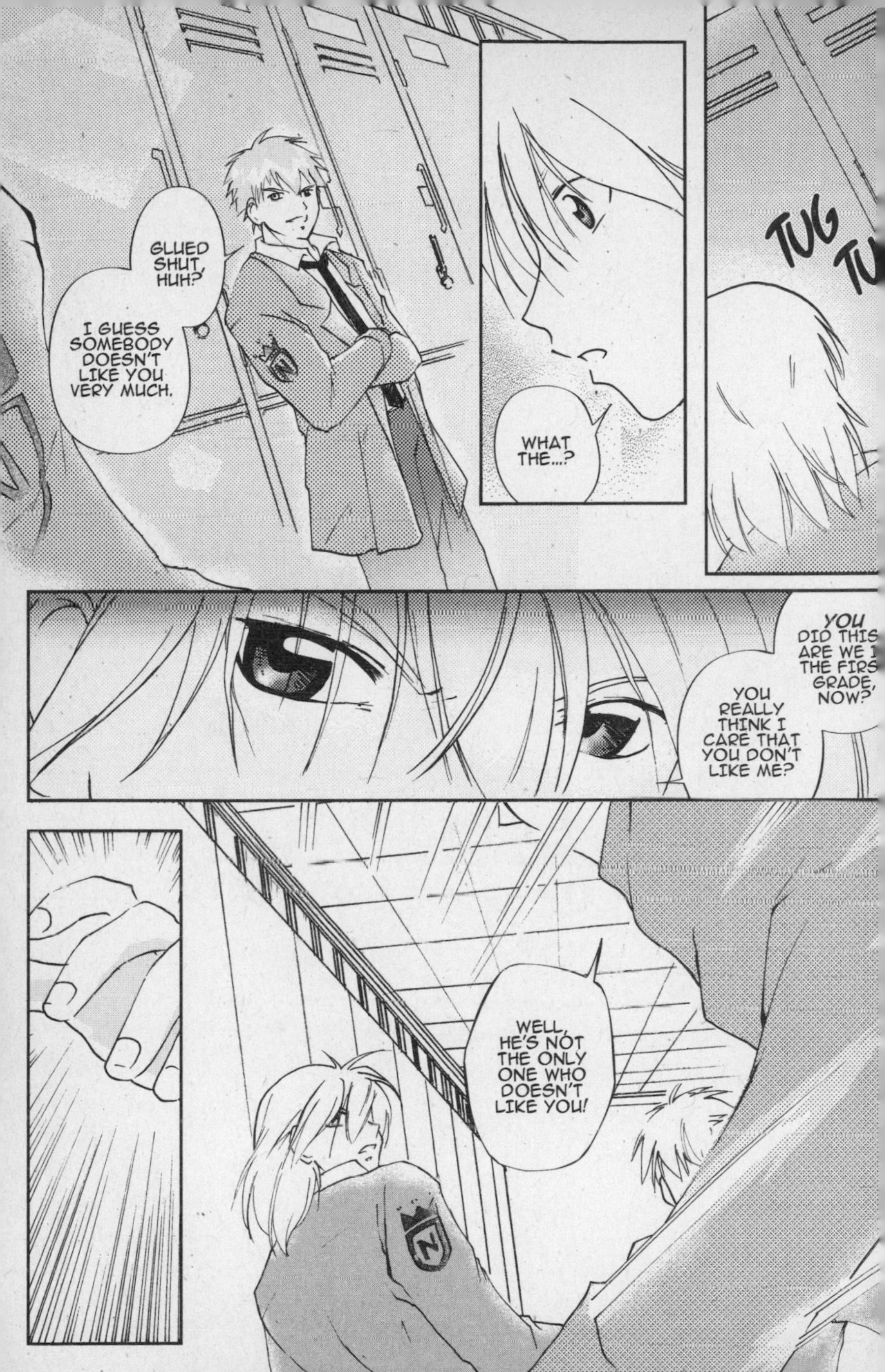
TUG TU
WHAT THE...?
GLUED SHUT, HUH?
I GUESS SOMEBODY DOESN'T LIKE YOU VERY MUCH.
YOU DID THIS ARE WE I THE FIRS GRADE, NOW?
YOU REALLY THINK I CARE THAT YOU DON'T LIKE ME?
WELL, HE'S NOT THE ONLY ONE WHO DOESN'T LIKE YOU!

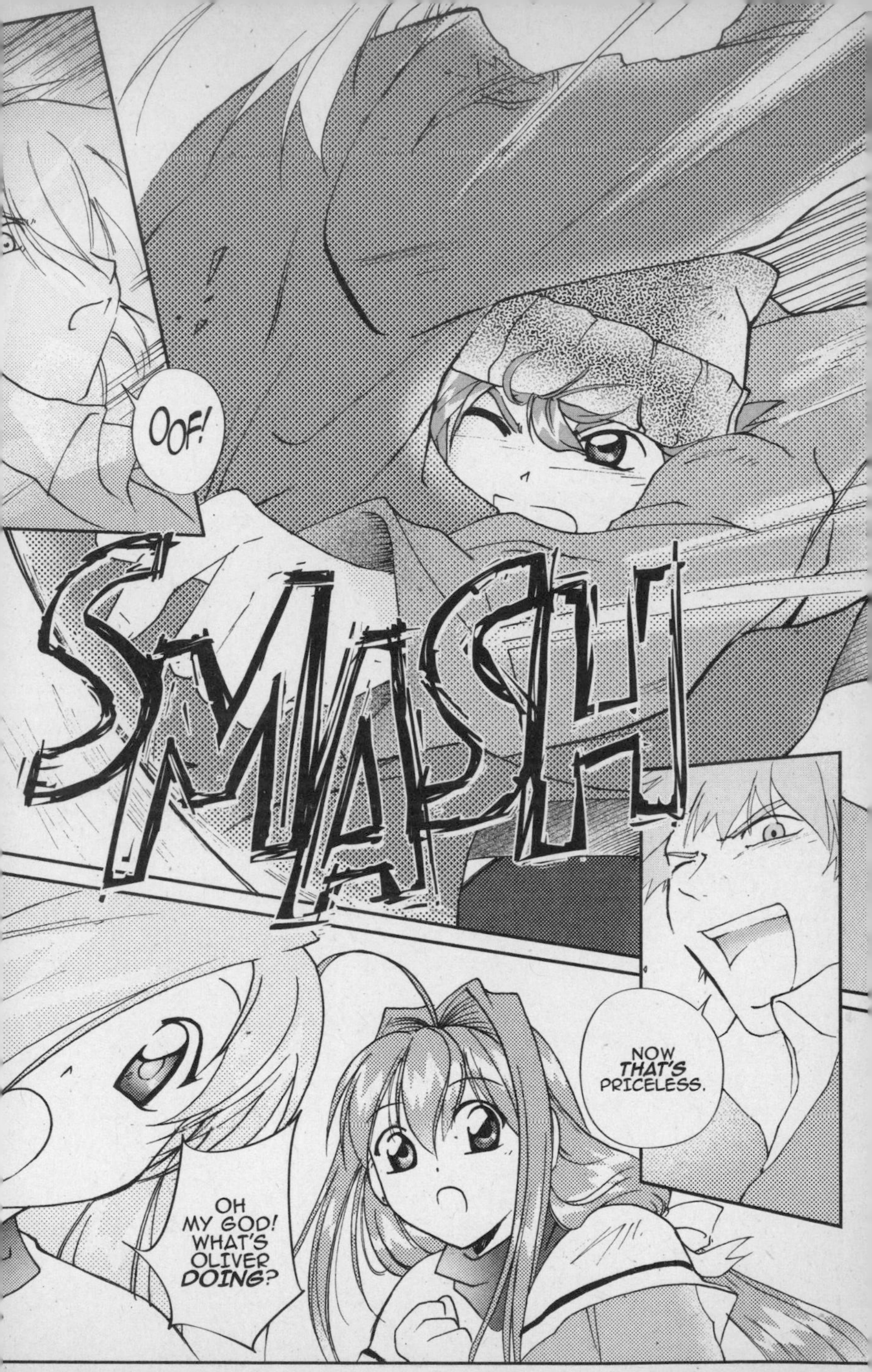
OOF!
SMASH
NOW *THAT'S* PRICELESS.
OH MY GOD! WHAT'S OLIVER *DOING?*

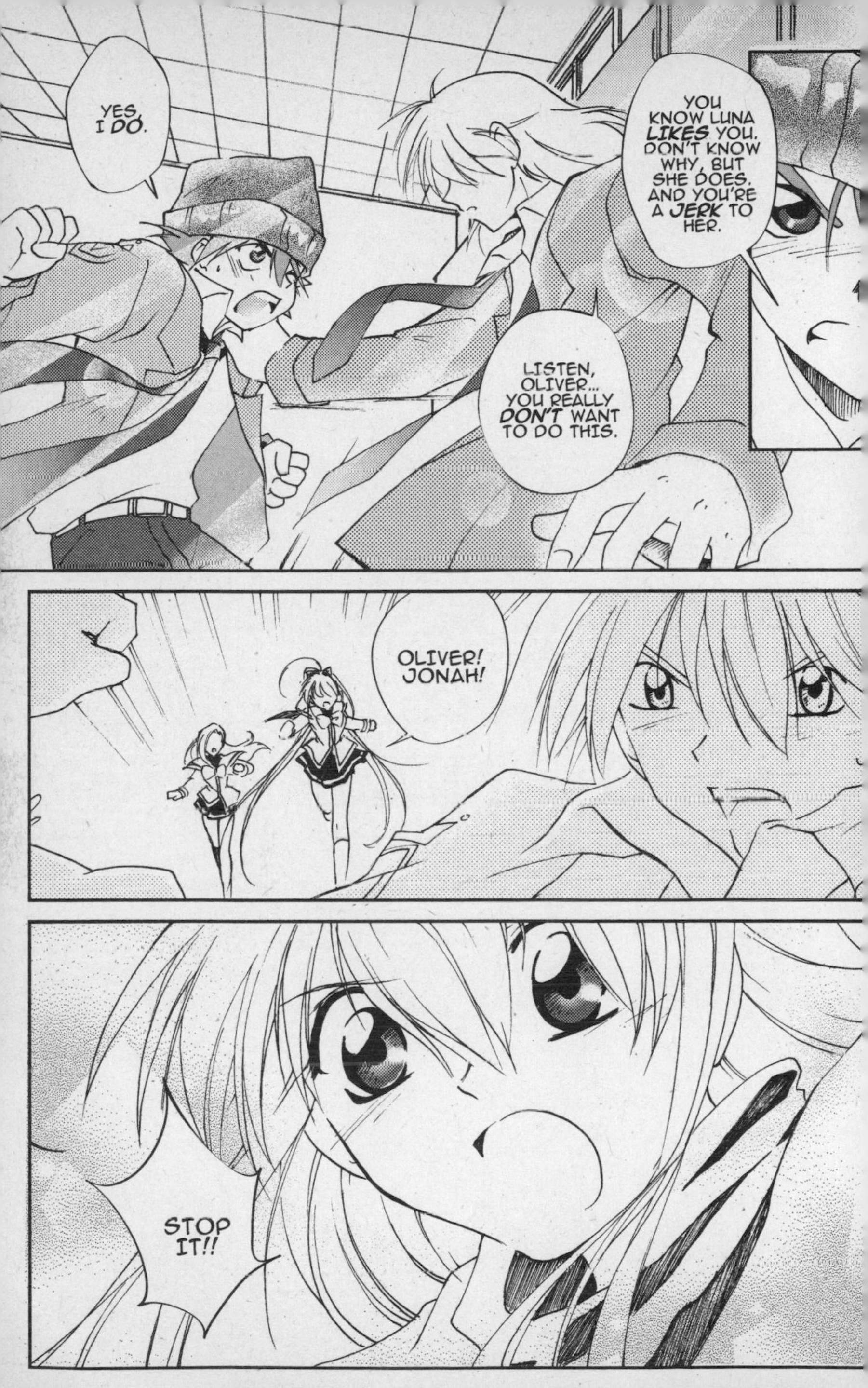
YOU KNOW LUNA LIKES YOU. DON'T KNOW WHY, BUT SHE DOES. AND YOU'RE A JERK TO HER.
LISTEN, OLIVER... YOU REALLY DON'T WANT TO DO THIS.
YES, I DO.
OLIVER! JONAH!
STOP IT!!

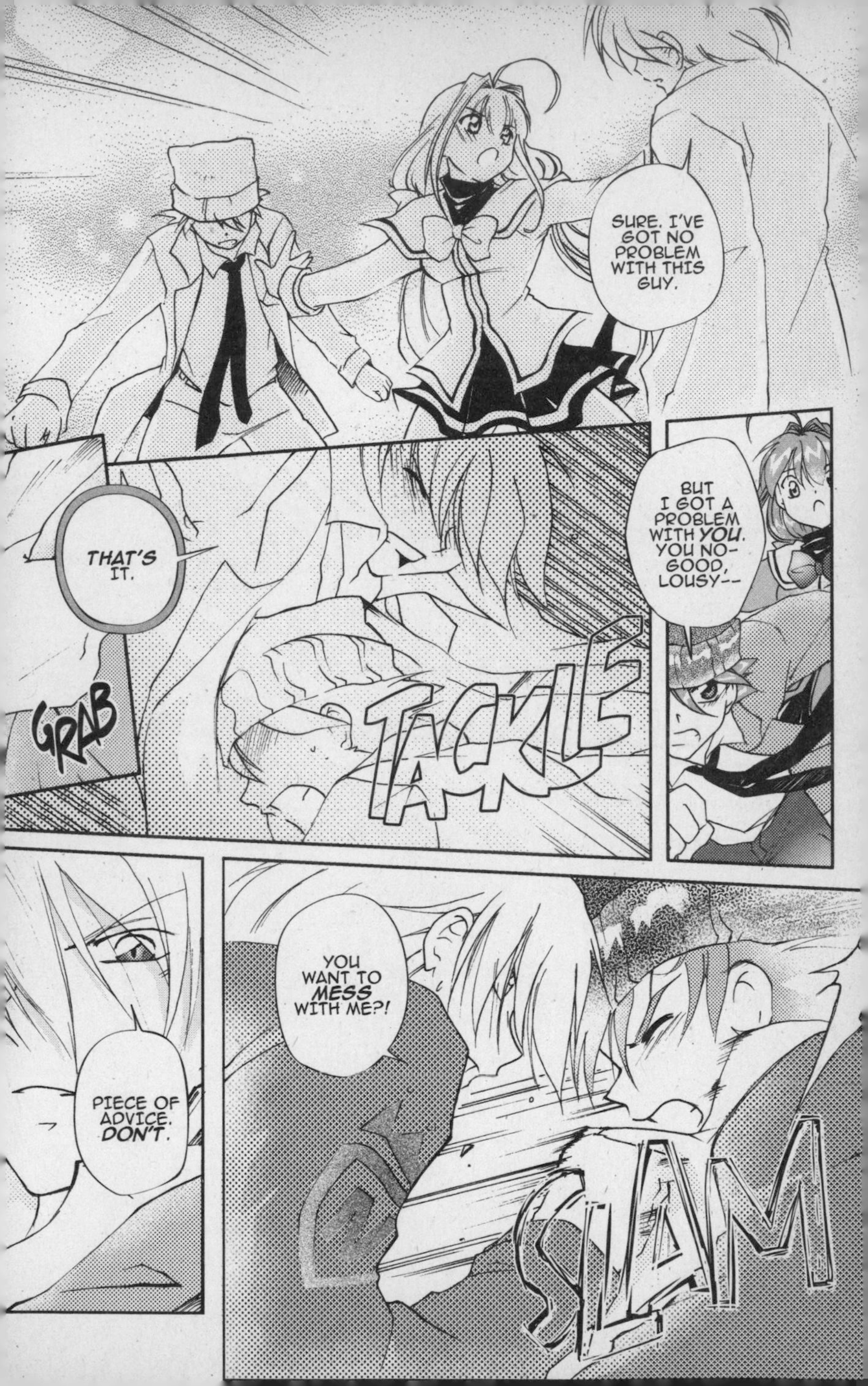
SURE, I'VE GOT NO PROBLEM WITH THIS GUY.
BUT I GOT A PROBLEM WITH *YOU*. YOU NO-GOOD, LOUSY--
THAT'S IT.
TACKLE
GRAB
YOU WANT TO *MESS* WITH ME?!
SLAM
PIECE OF ADVICE. *DON'T*.

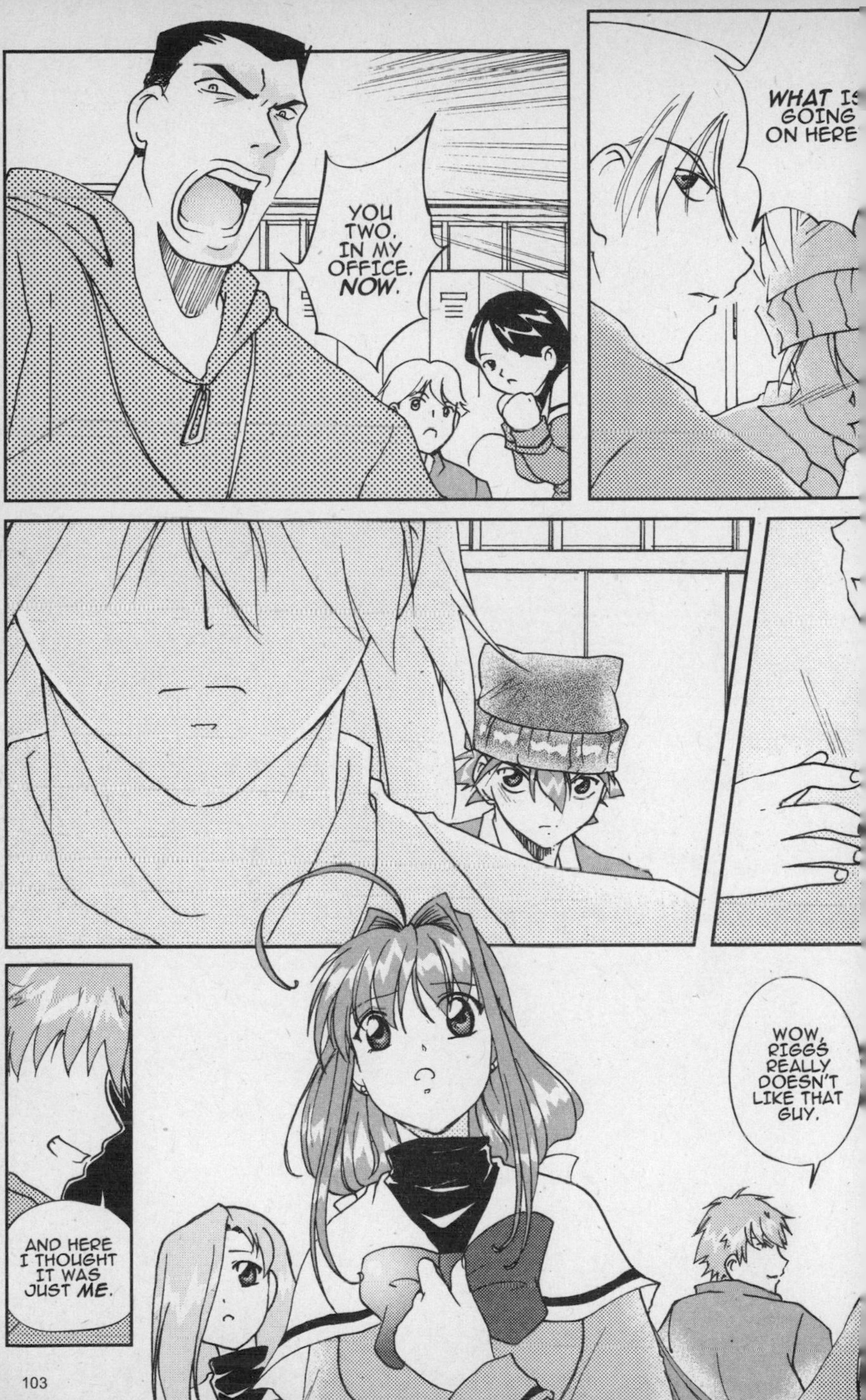
WHAT IS GOING ON HERE
YOU TWO. IN MY OFFICE. NOW.
WOW, RIGGS REALLY DOESN'T LIKE THAT GUY.
AND HERE I THOUGHT IT WAS JUST ME.

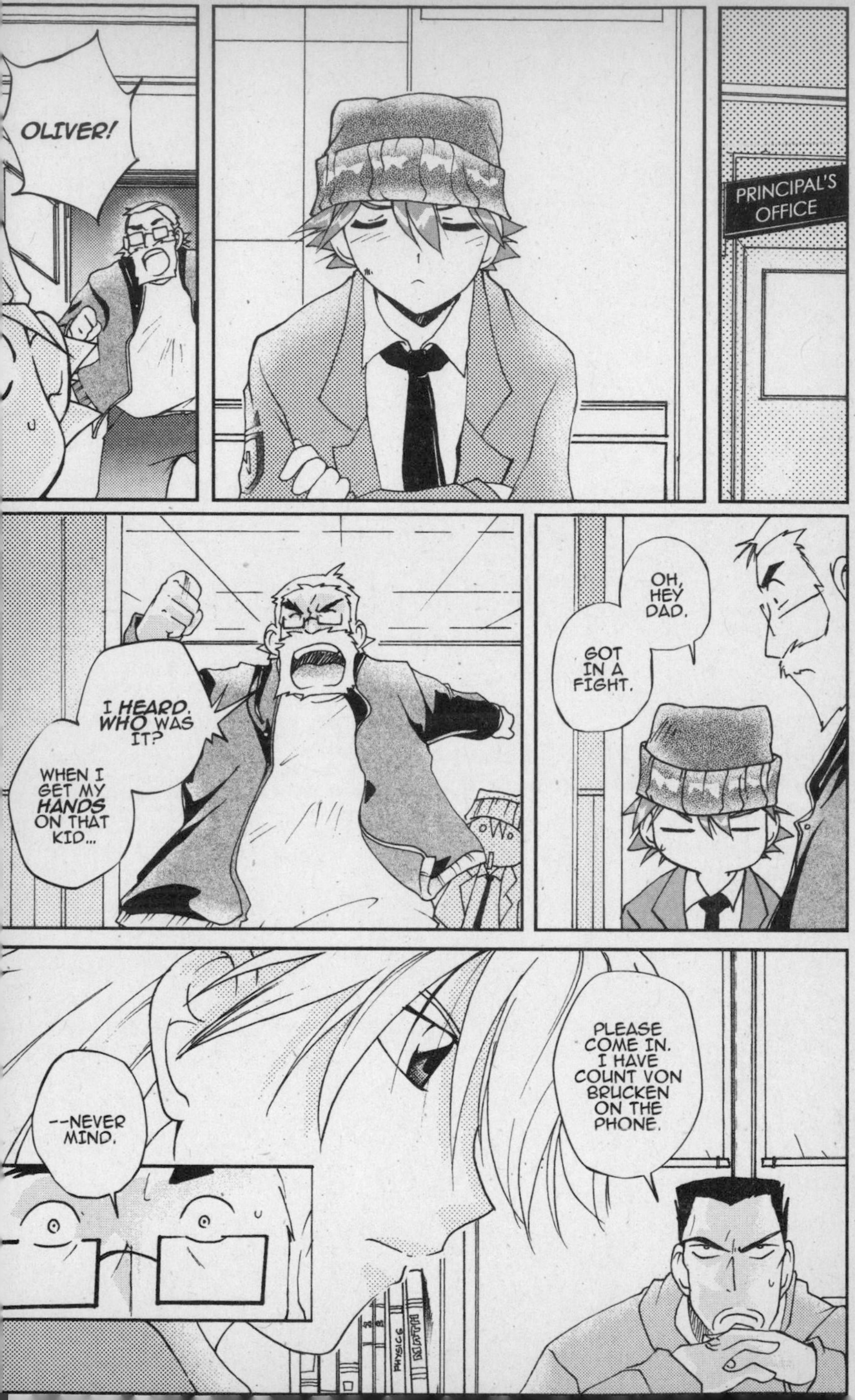
PRINCIPAL'S OFFICE
OLIVER!
OH, HEY DAD.
GOT IN A FIGHT.
I HEARD. WHO WAS IT?
WHEN I GET MY HANDS ON THAT KID...
PLEASE COME IN. I HAVE COUNT VON BRUCKEN ON THE PHONE.
--NEVER MIND.

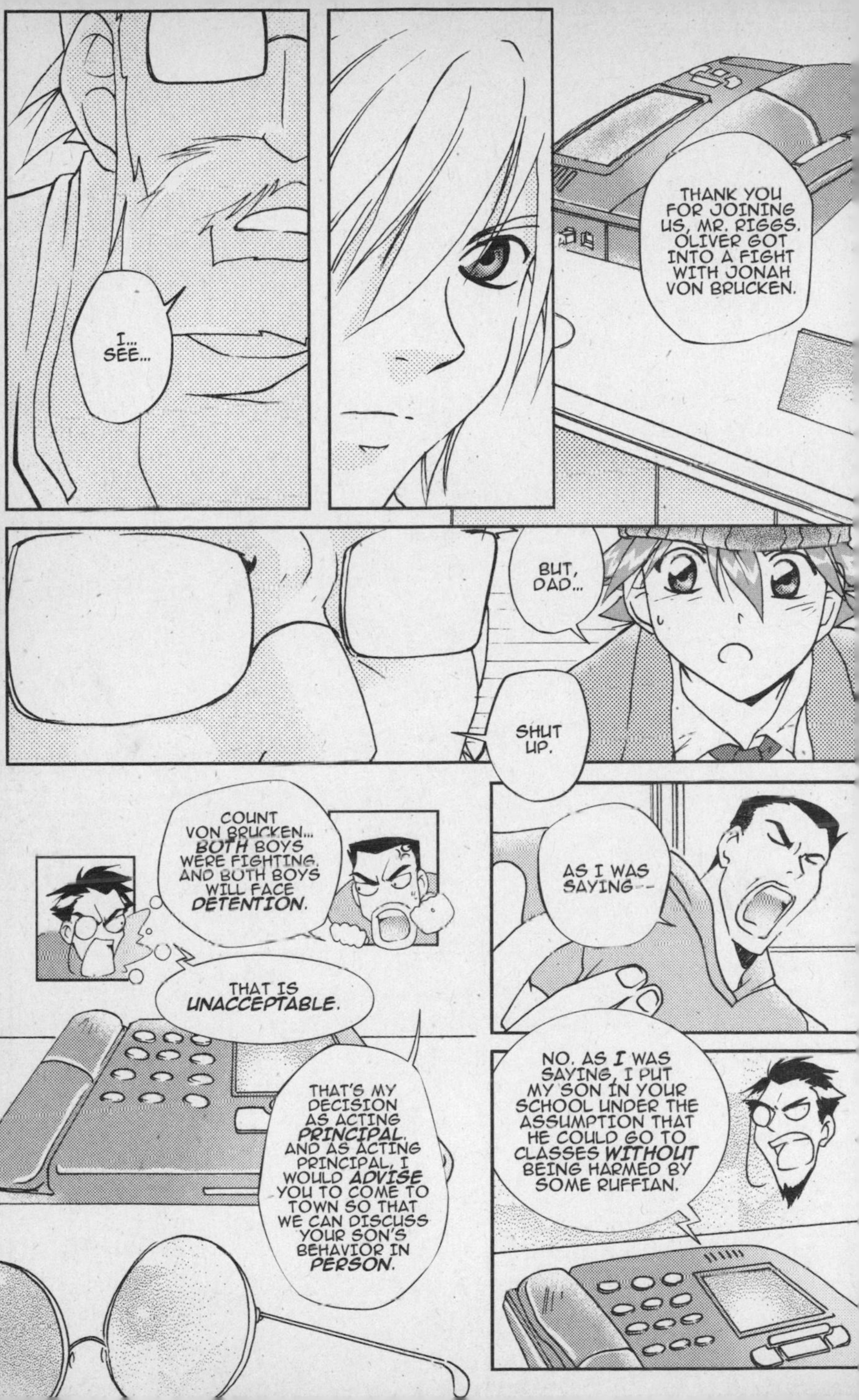
THANK YOU FOR JOINING US, MR. RIGGS. OLIVER GOT INTO A FIGHT WITH JONAH VON BRUCKEN.
I... SEE...
BUT, DAD...
SHUT UP.
AS I WAS SAYING--
COUNT VON BRUCKEN... **BOTH** BOYS WERE FIGHTING, AND BOTH BOYS WILL FACE ***DETENTION***.
THAT IS ***UNACCEPTABLE***.
NO. AS ***I*** WAS SAYING, I PUT MY SON IN YOUR SCHOOL UNDER THE ASSUMPTION THAT HE COULD GO TO CLASSES ***WITHOUT*** BEING HARMED BY SOME RUFFIAN.
THAT'S MY DECISION AS ACTING ***PRINCIPAL***. AND AS ACTING PRINCIPAL, I WOULD ***ADVISE*** YOU TO COME TO TOWN SO THAT WE CAN DISCUSS YOUR SON'S BEHAVIOR IN ***PERSON***.

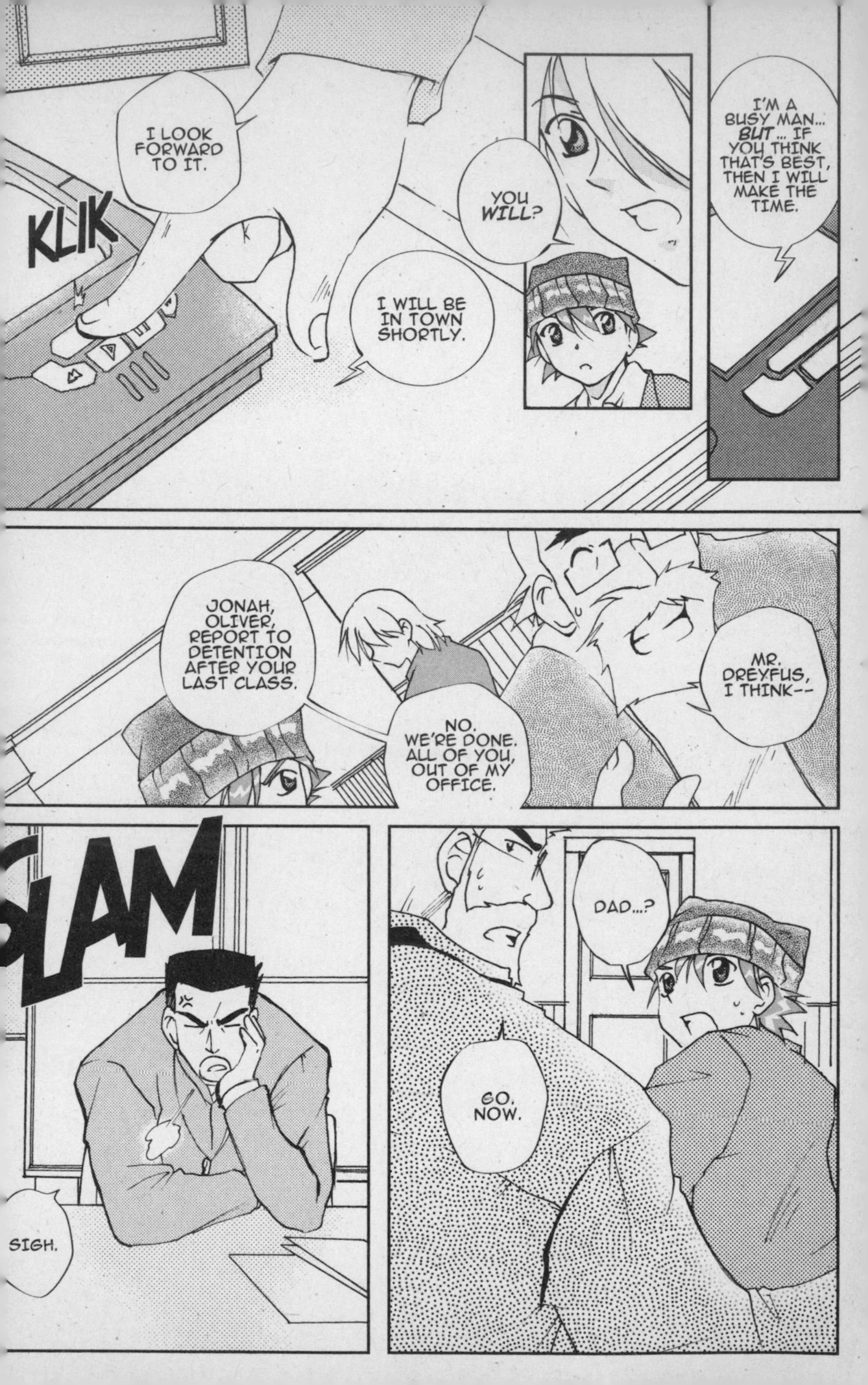
I'M A BUSY MAN... *BUT*... IF YOU THINK THAT'S BEST, THEN I WILL MAKE THE TIME.
YOU *WILL*?
I WILL BE IN TOWN SHORTLY.
I LOOK FORWARD TO IT.
KLIK
JONAH, OLIVER, REPORT TO DETENTION AFTER YOUR LAST CLASS.
MR. DREYFUS, I THINK--
NO. WE'RE DONE. ALL OF YOU, OUT OF MY OFFICE.
DAD...?
GO. NOW.
SLAM
SIGH.

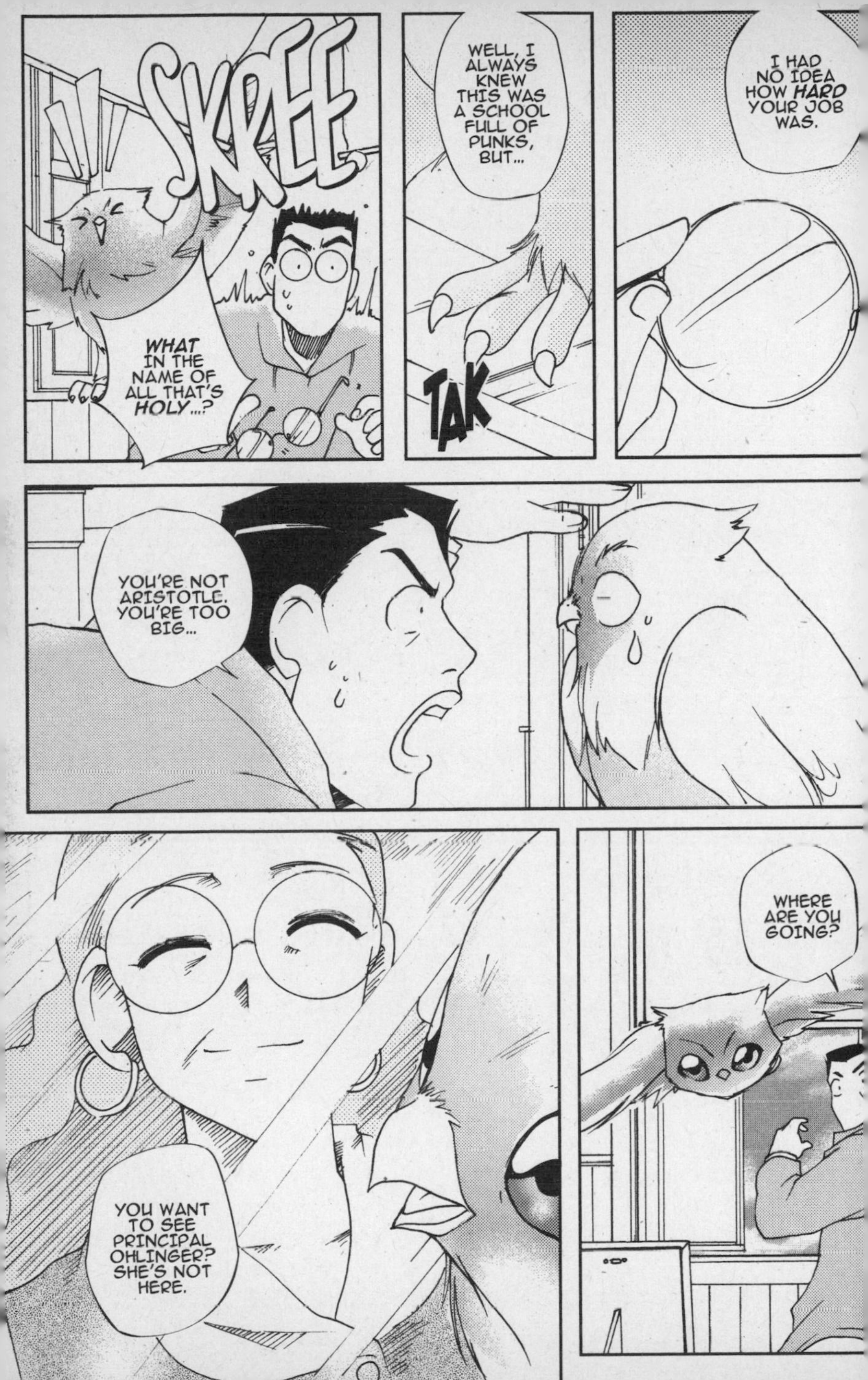
SKREE
WHAT IN THE NAME OF ALL THAT'S *HOLY*...?
WELL, I ALWAYS KNEW THIS WAS A SCHOOL FULL OF PUNKS, BUT...
TAK
I HAD NO IDEA HOW *HARD* YOUR JOB WAS.
YOU'RE NOT ARISTOTLE. YOU'RE TOO BIG...
YOU WANT TO SEE PRINCIPAL OHLINGER? SHE'S NOT HERE.
WHERE ARE YOU GOING?

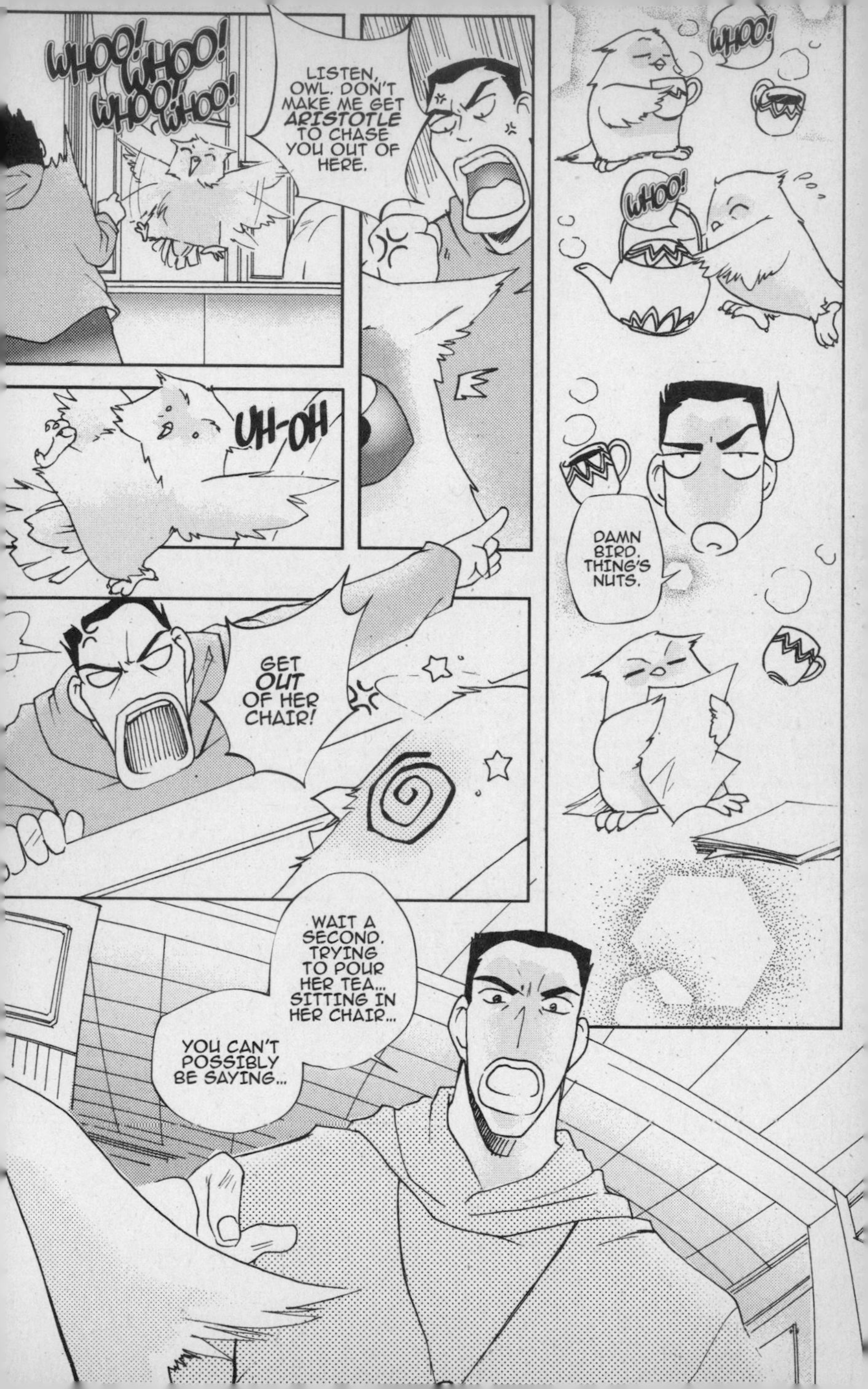
WHOO!
WHOO!
DAMN BIRD. THING'S NUTS.
LISTEN, OWL. DON'T MAKE ME GET *ARISTOTLE* TO CHASE YOU OUT OF HERE.
WHOO! WHOO! WHOO! WHOO!
UH-OH
GET *OUT* OF HER CHAIR!
WAIT A SECOND. TRYING TO POUR HER TEA... SITTING IN HER CHAIR...
YOU CAN'T POSSIBLY BE SAYING...

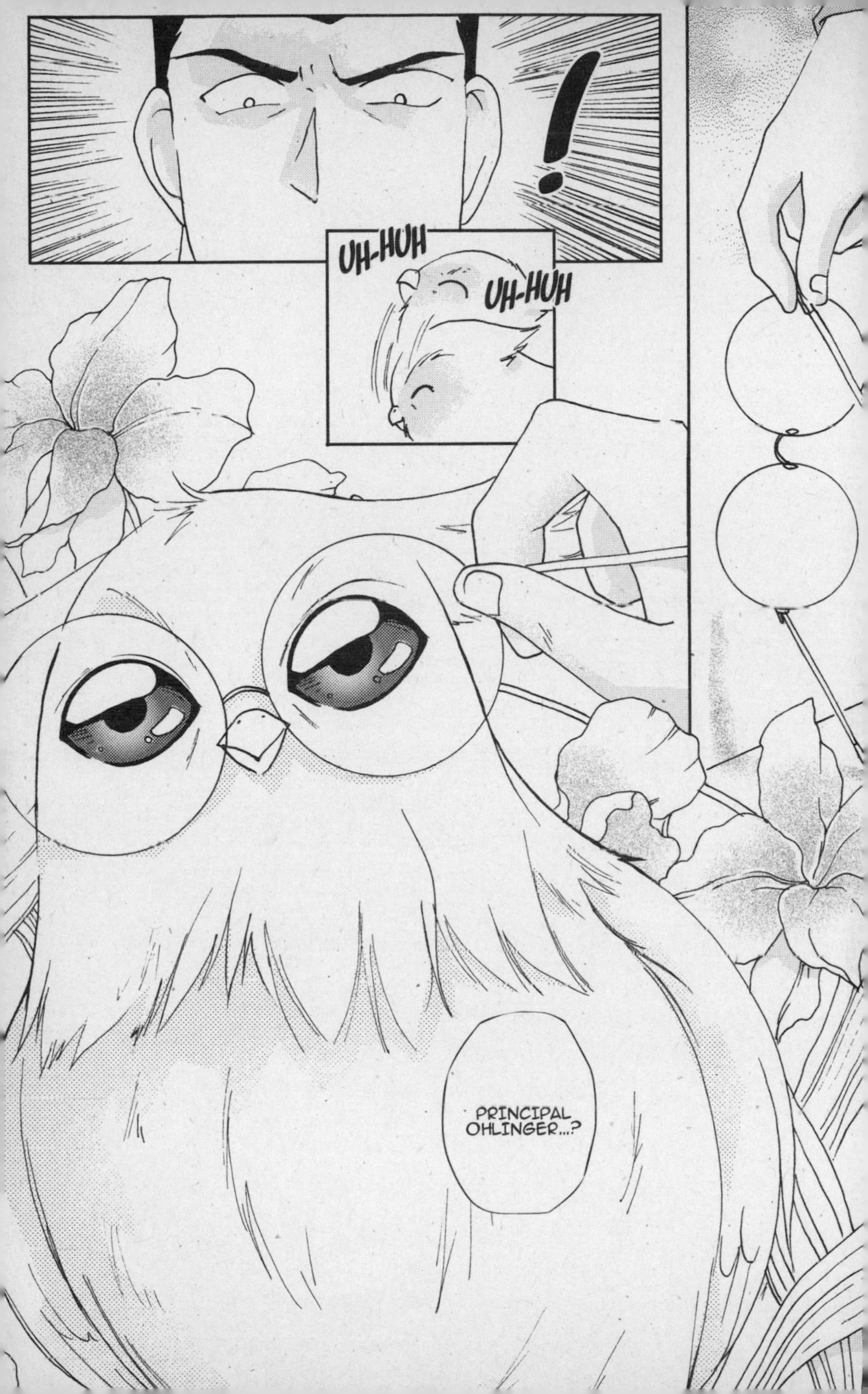
!
UH-HUH
UH-HUH
PRINCIPAL OHLINGER...?

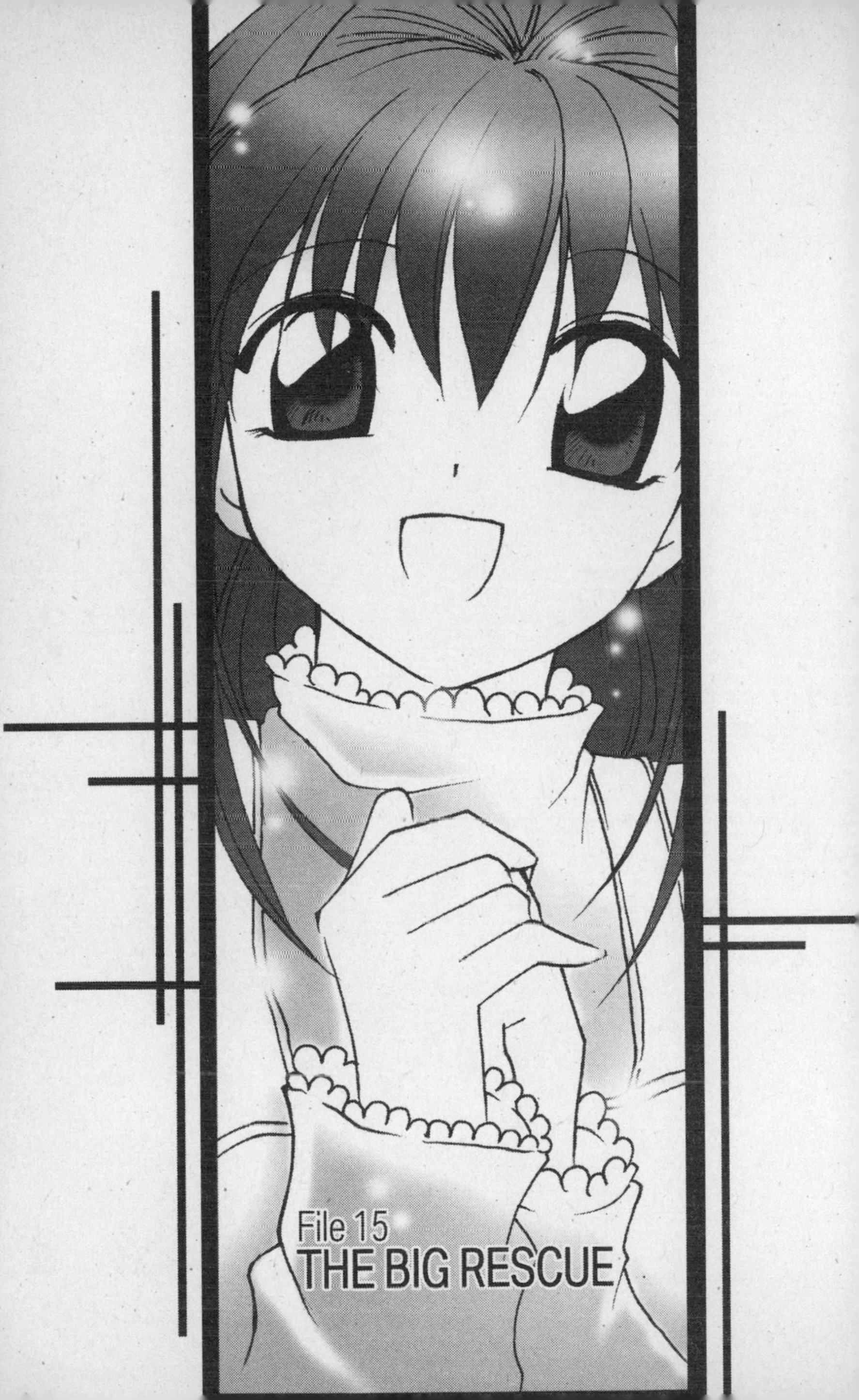
File 15
THE BIG RESCUE

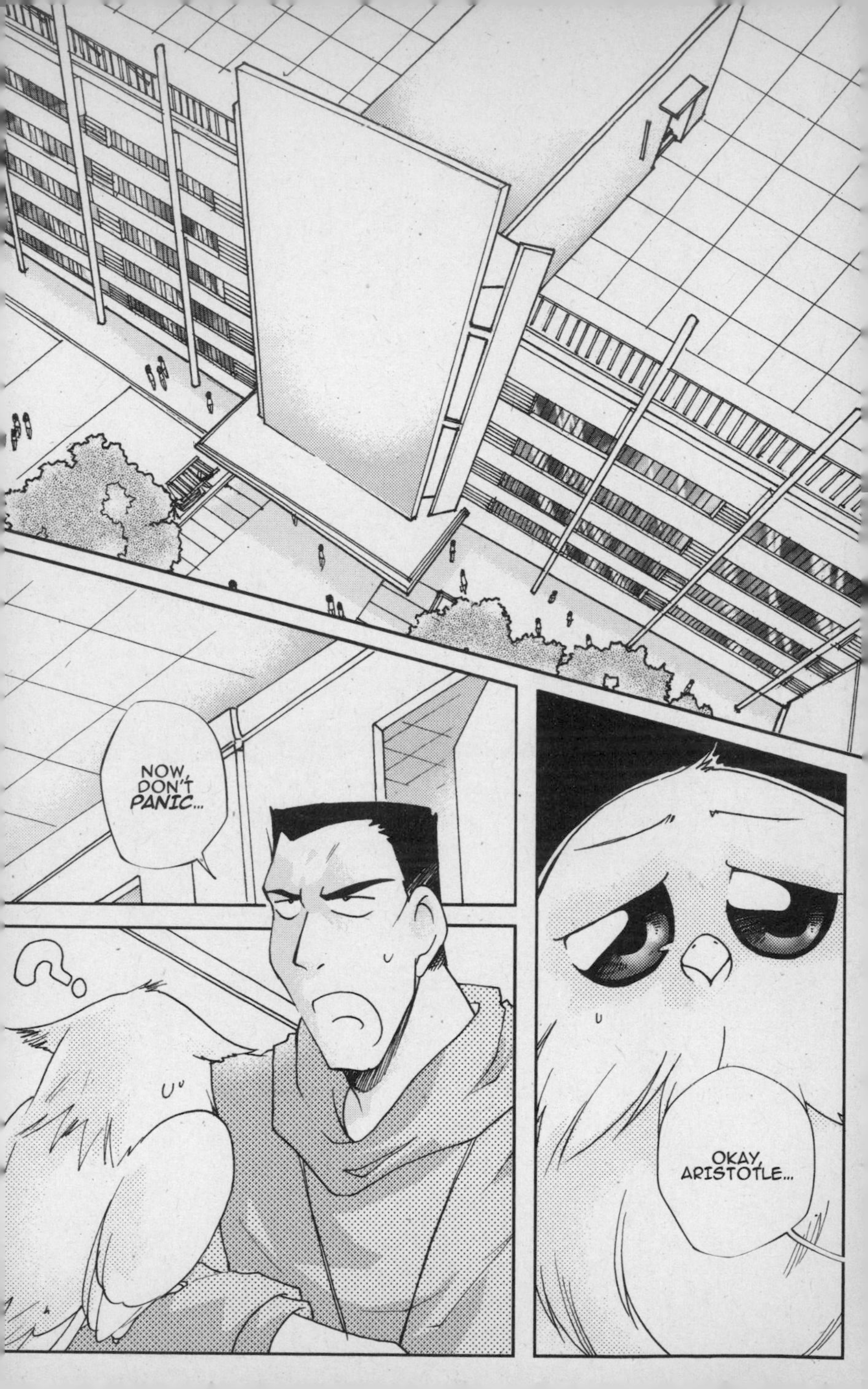
OKAY, ARISTOTLE...
NOW, DON'T PANIC...
?

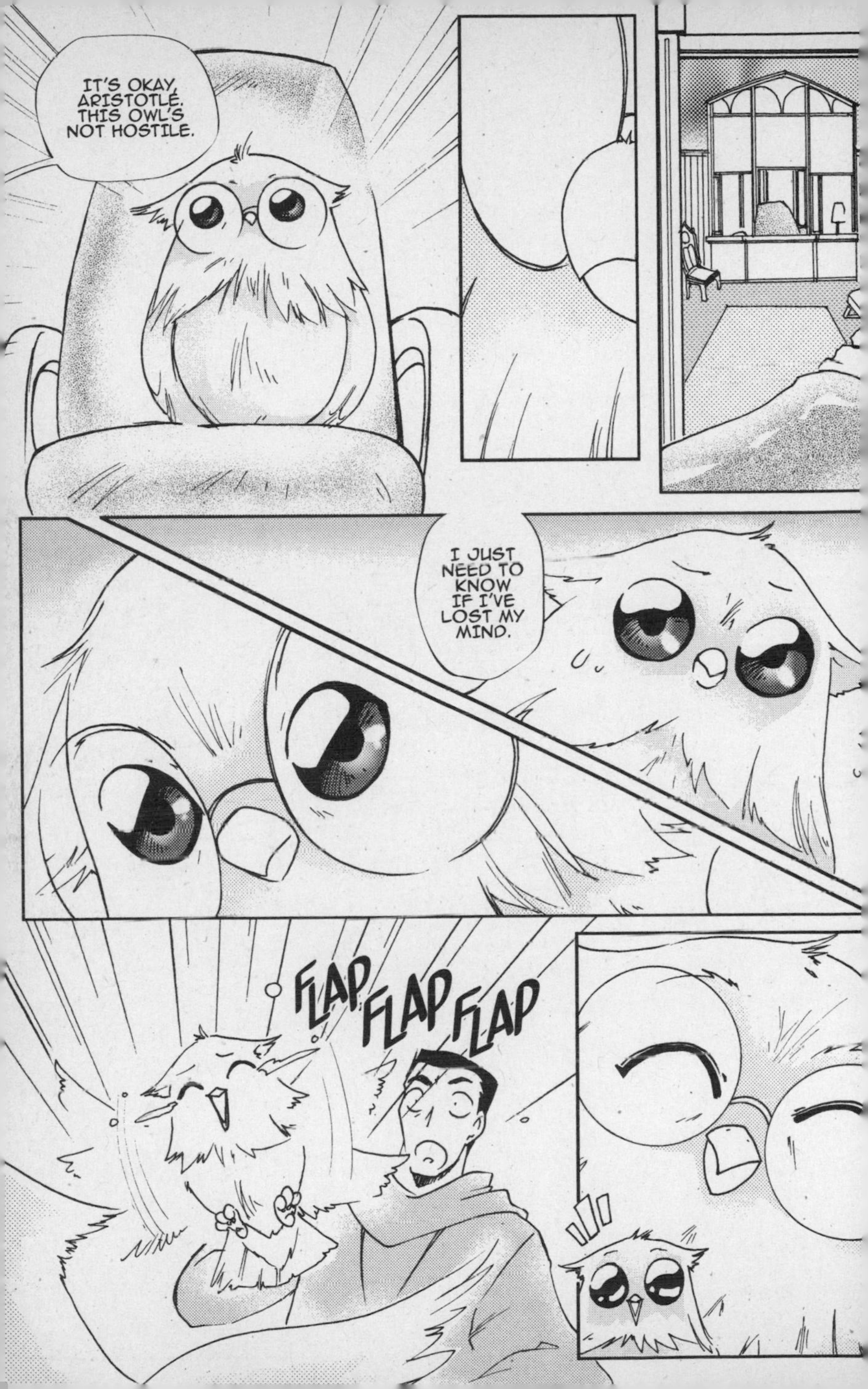
IT'S OKAY, ARISTOTLE. THIS OWL'S NOT HOSTILE.
I JUST NEED TO KNOW IF I'VE LOST MY MIND.
FLAP FLAP FLAP

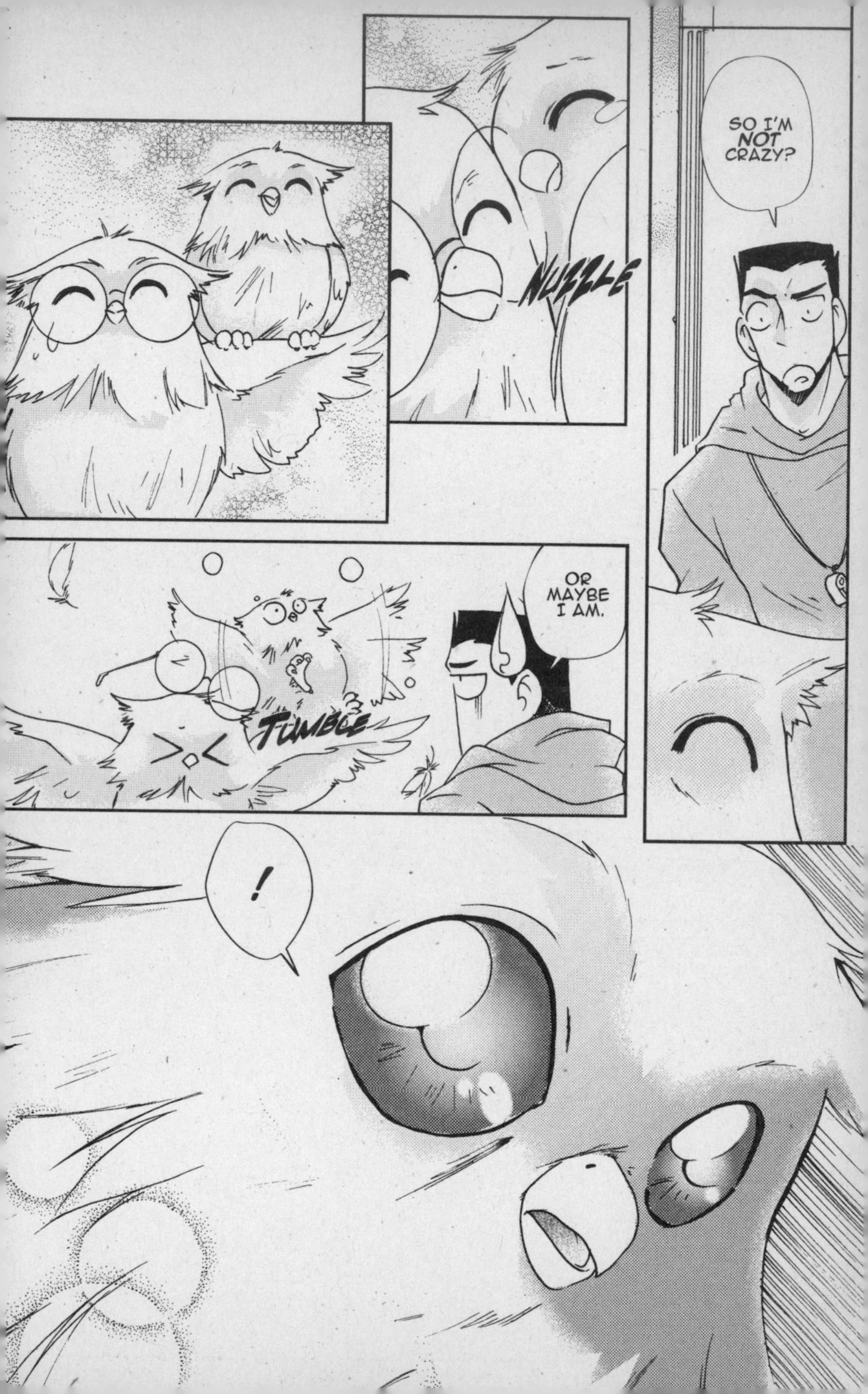

SO I'M NOT CRAZY?
NUZZLE
OR MAYBE I AM.
TUMBLE
!

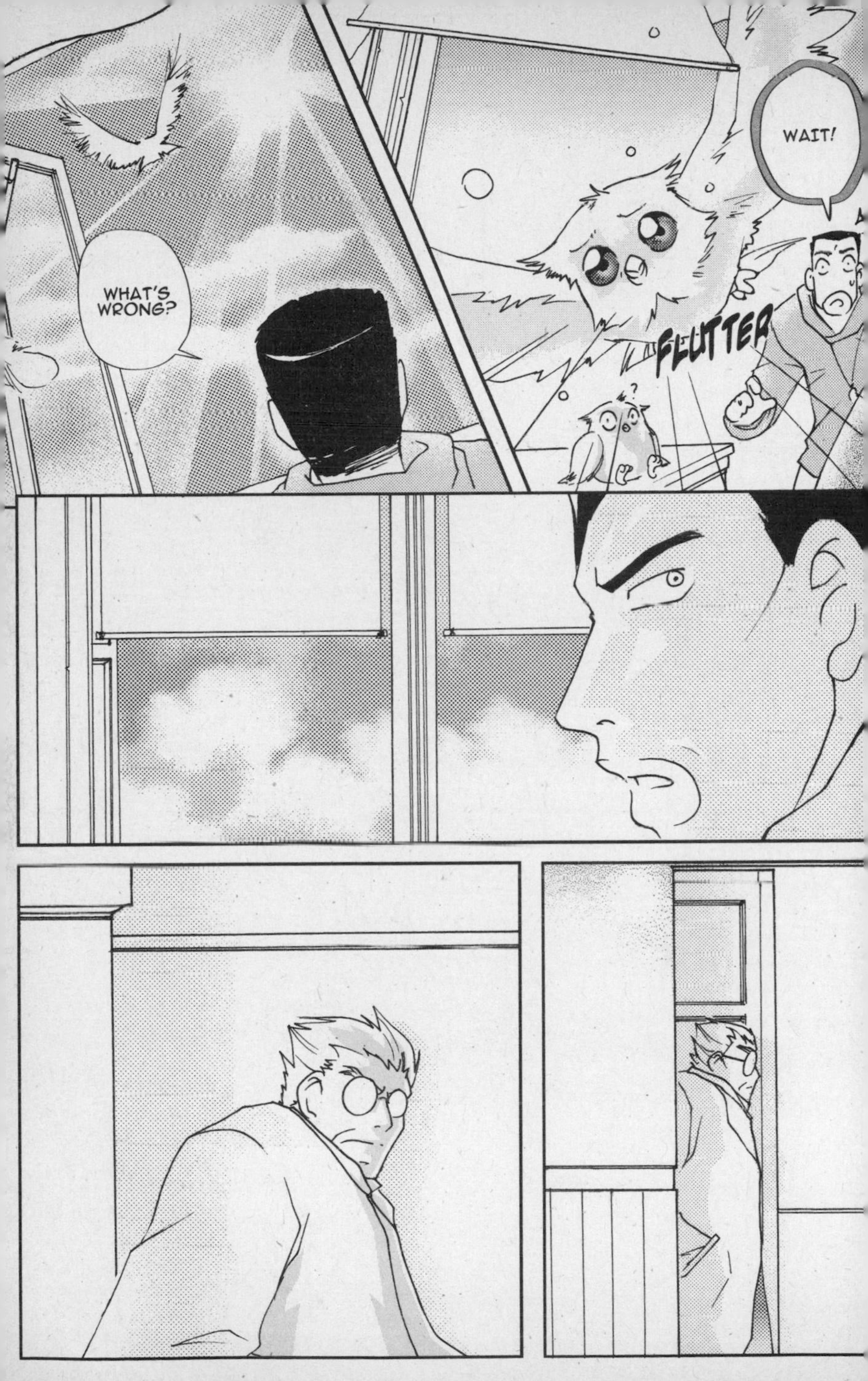
WAIT!
FLUTTER
WHAT'S WRONG?

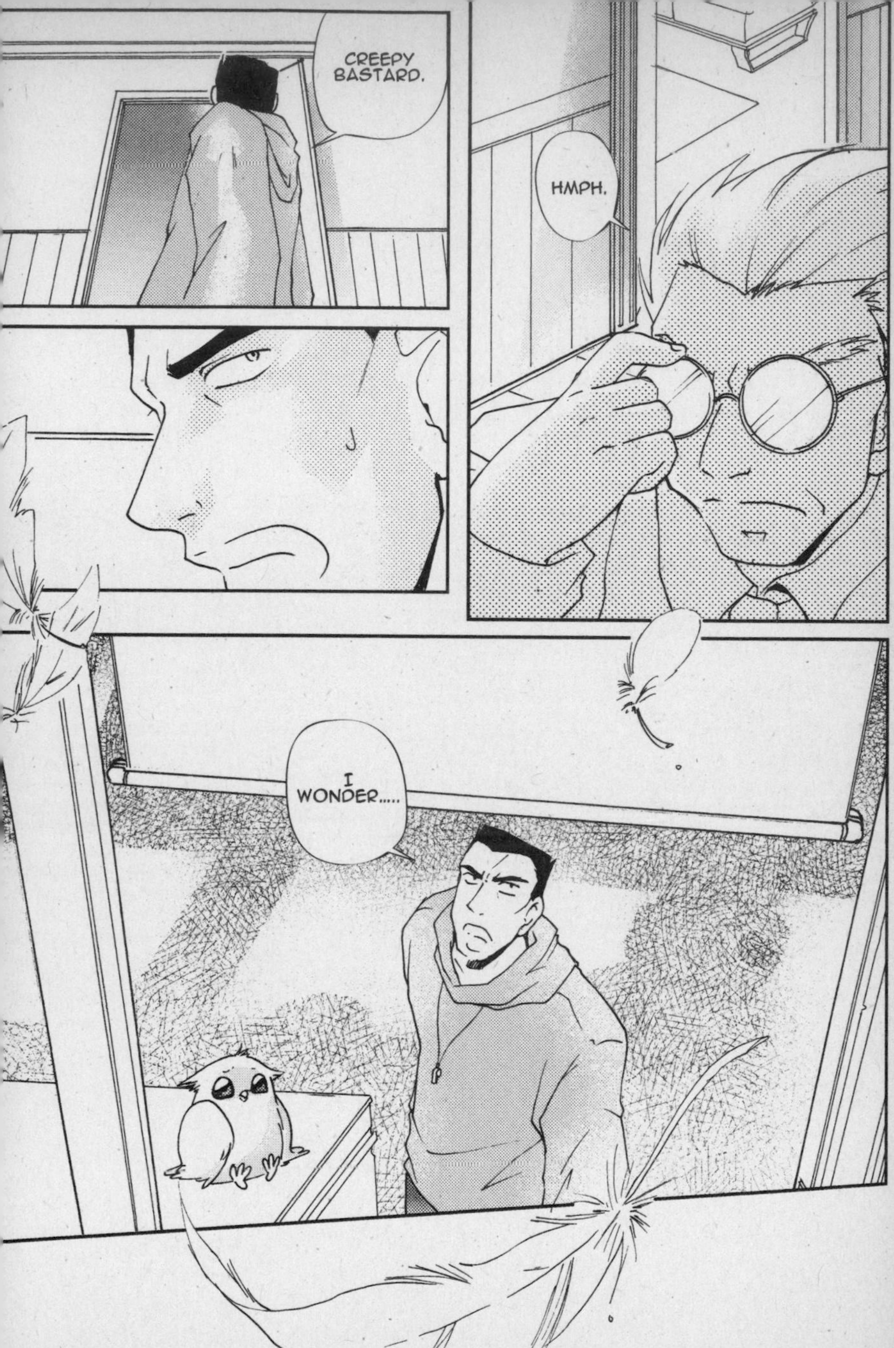
HMPH.
CREEPY BASTARD.
I WONDER.....

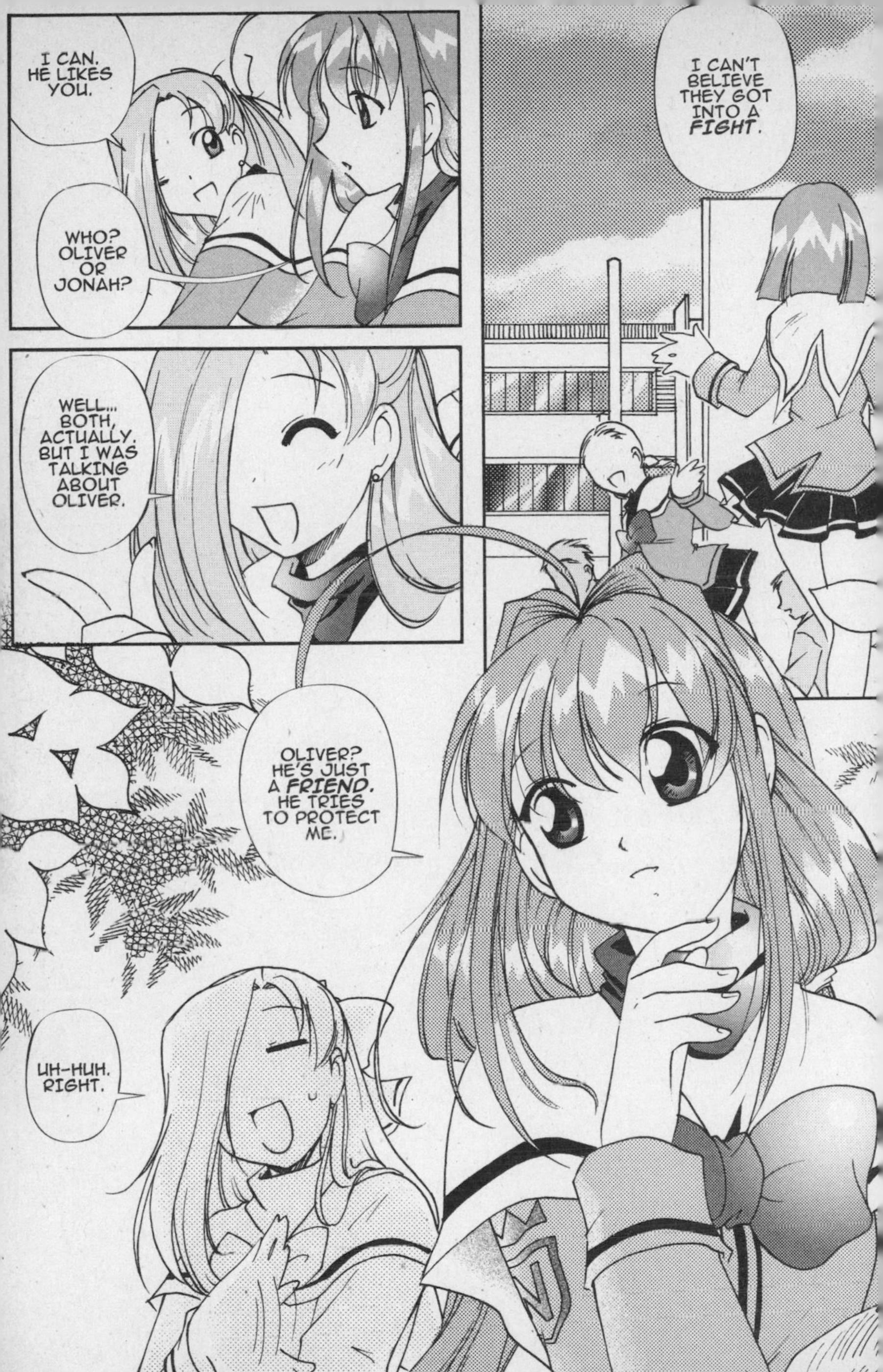
I CAN'T BELIEVE THEY GOT INTO A FIGHT.
I CAN. HE LIKES YOU.
WHO? OLIVER OR JONAH?
WELL... BOTH, ACTUALLY. BUT I WAS TALKING ABOUT OLIVER.
OLIVER? HE'S JUST A FRIEND. HE TRIES TO PROTECT ME.
UH-HUH. RIGHT.

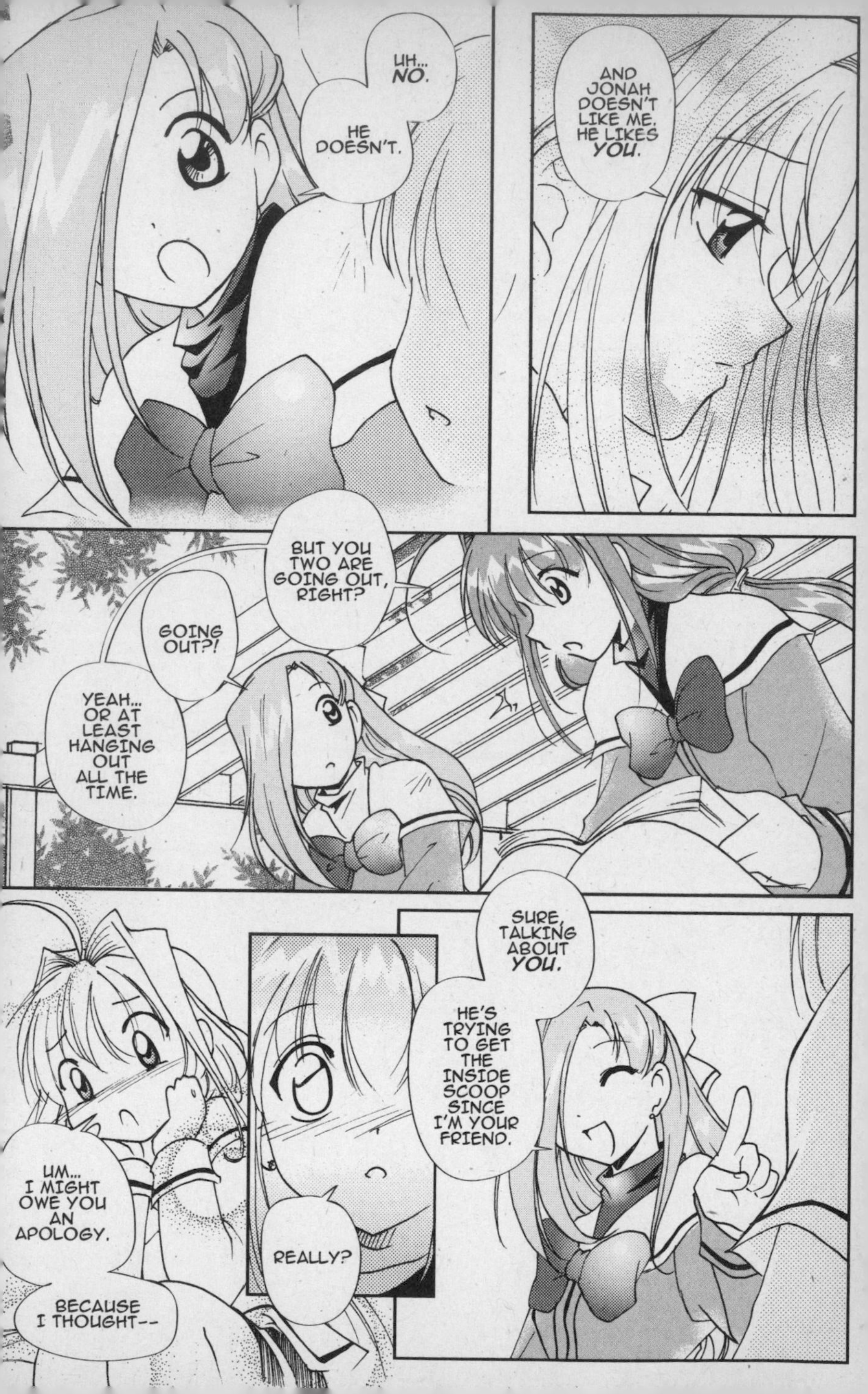
AND JONAH DOESN'T LIKE ME. HE LIKES YOU.
UH... NO.
HE DOESN'T.
BUT YOU TWO ARE GOING OUT, RIGHT?
GOING OUT?!
YEAH... OR AT LEAST HANGING OUT ALL THE TIME.
SURE, TALKING ABOUT YOU.
HE'S TRYING TO GET THE INSIDE SCOOP SINCE I'M YOUR FRIEND.
REALLY?
UM... I MIGHT OWE YOU AN APOLOGY.
BECAUSE I THOUGHT--

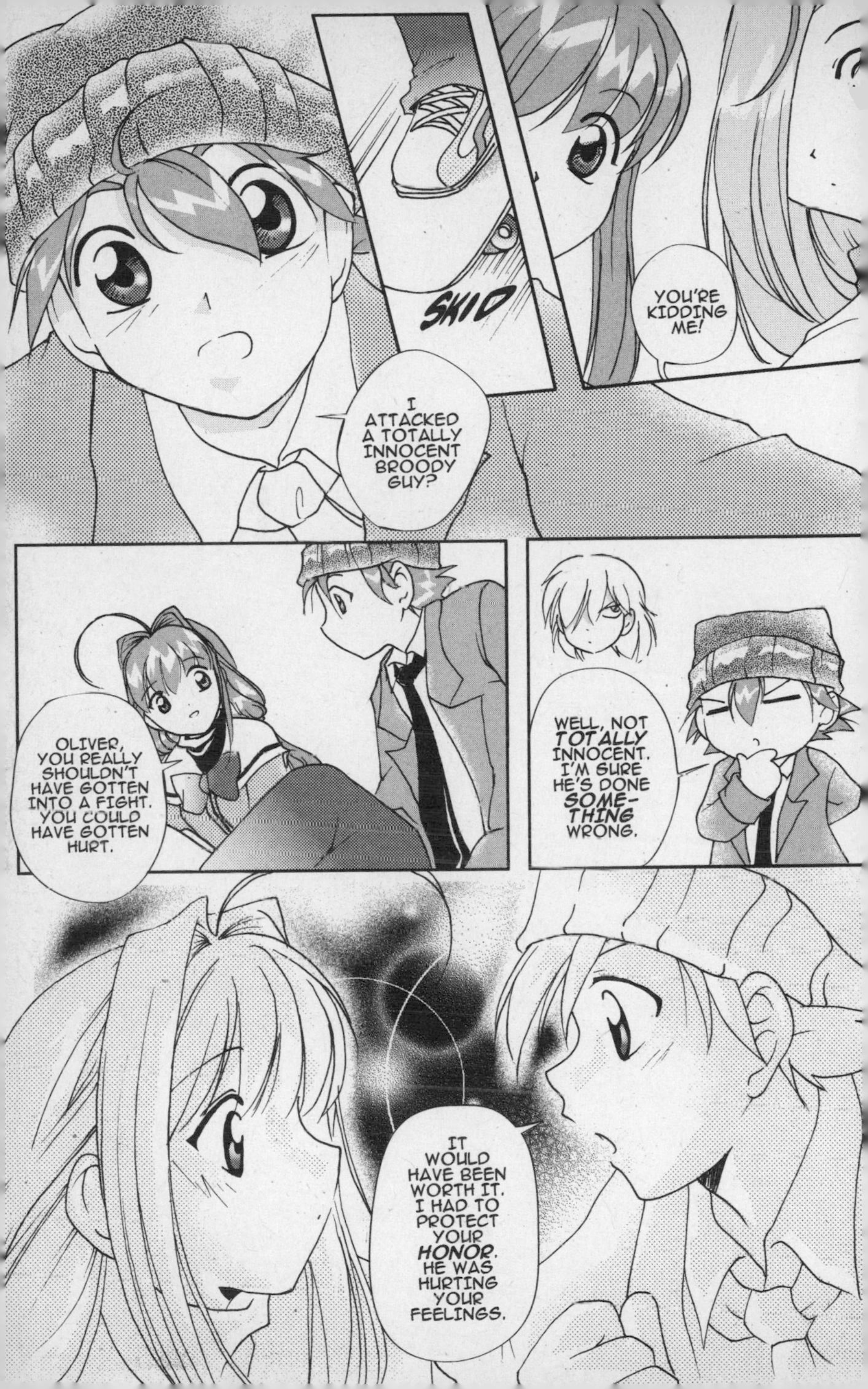
YOU'RE KIDDING ME!
SKID
I ATTACKED A TOTALLY INNOCENT BROODY GUY?
WELL, NOT *TOTALLY* INNOCENT. I'M SURE HE'S DONE ***SOME-THING*** WRONG.
OLIVER, YOU REALLY SHOULDN'T HAVE GOTTEN INTO A FIGHT. YOU COULD HAVE GOTTEN HURT.
IT WOULD HAVE BEEN WORTH IT. I HAD TO PROTECT YOUR ***HONOR***. HE WAS HURTING YOUR FEELINGS.

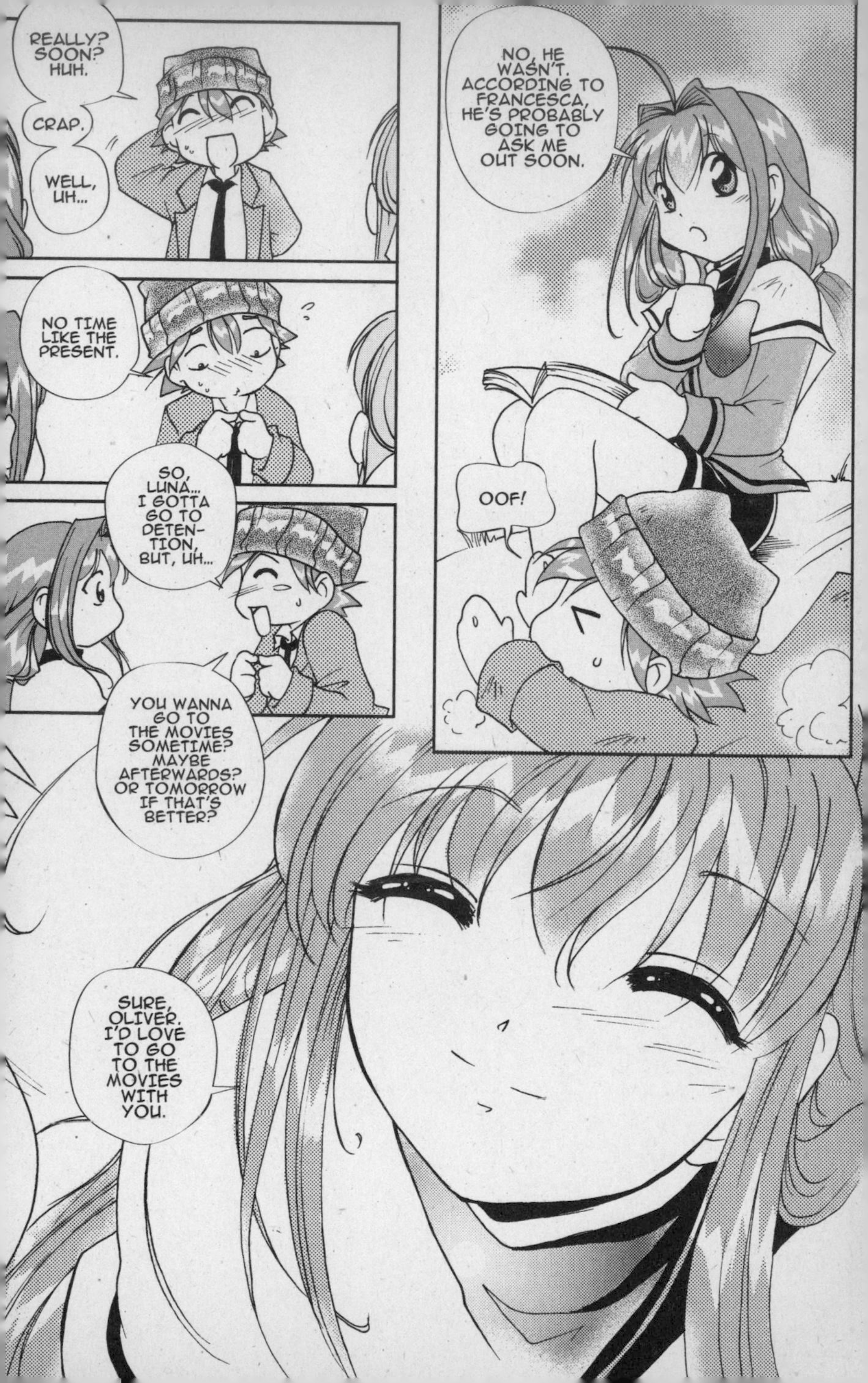
NO, HE WASN'T. ACCORDING TO FRANCESCA, HE'S PROBABLY GOING TO ASK ME OUT SOON.
OOF!
REALLY? SOON? HUH.
CRAP.
WELL, UH...
NO TIME LIKE THE PRESENT.
SO, LUNA... I GOTTA GO TO DETENTION, BUT, UH...
YOU WANNA GO TO THE MOVIES SOMETIME? MAYBE AFTERWARDS? OR TOMORROW IF THAT'S BETTER?
SURE, OLIVER. I'D LOVE TO GO TO THE MOVIES WITH YOU.

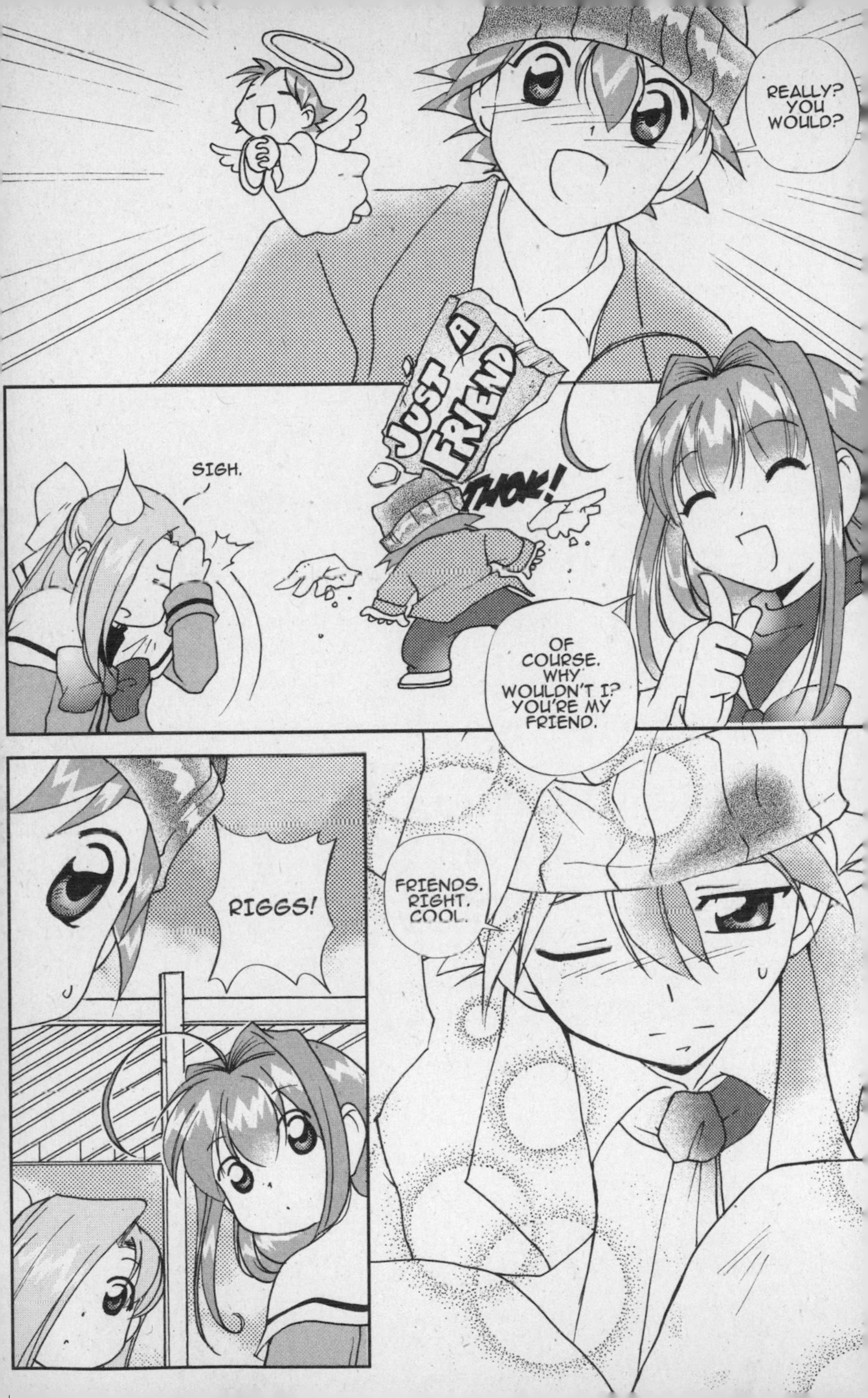
REALLY? YOU WOULD?
OF COURSE. WHY WOULDN'T I? YOU'RE MY FRIEND.
JUST A FRIEND
THOK!
SIGH.
FRIENDS. RIGHT. COOL.
RIGGS!

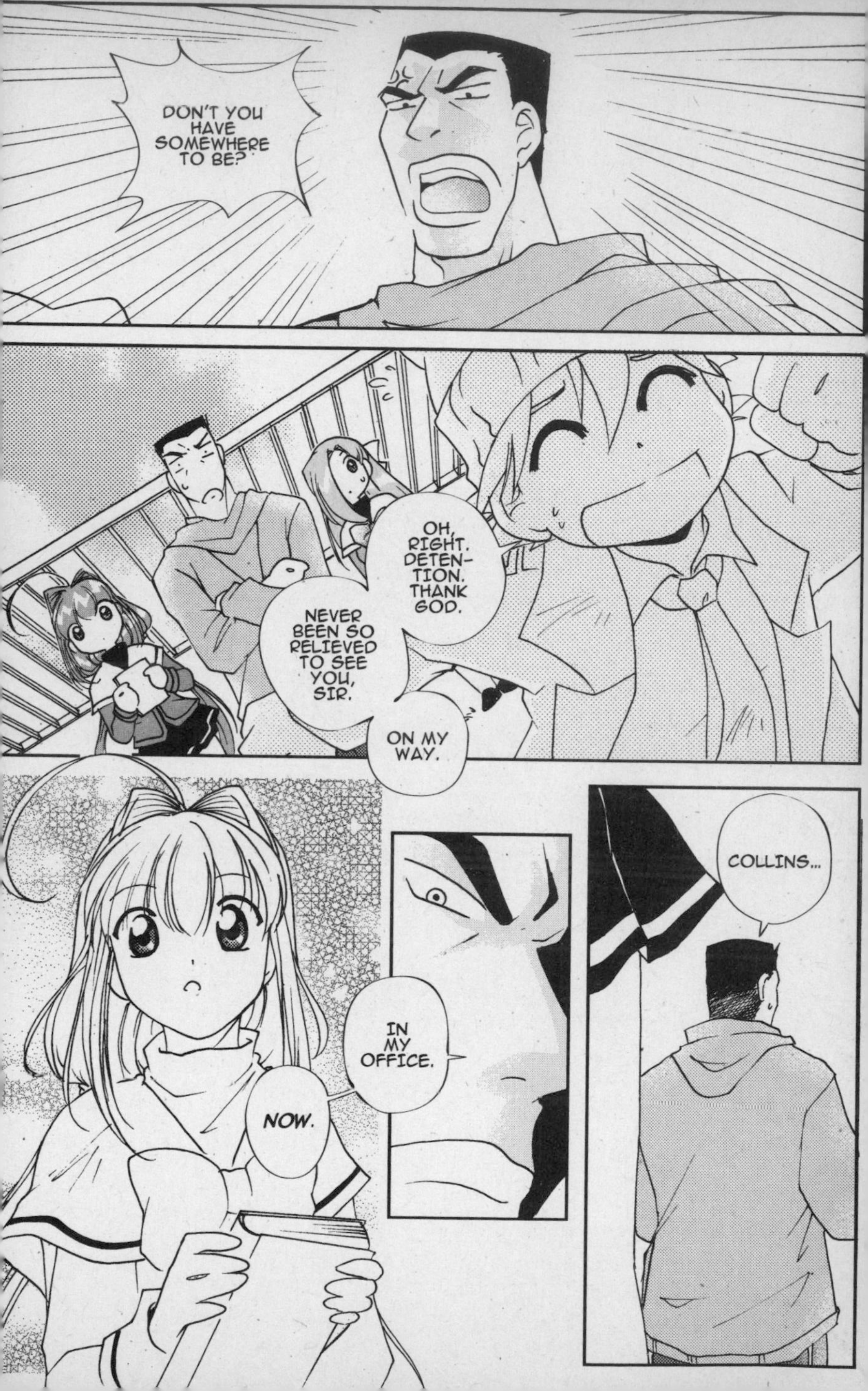
DON'T YOU HAVE SOMEWHERE TO BE?
OH, RIGHT. DETENTION. THANK GOD.
NEVER BEEN SO RELIEVED TO SEE YOU, SIR.
ON MY WAY.
COLLINS...
IN MY OFFICE.
NOW.

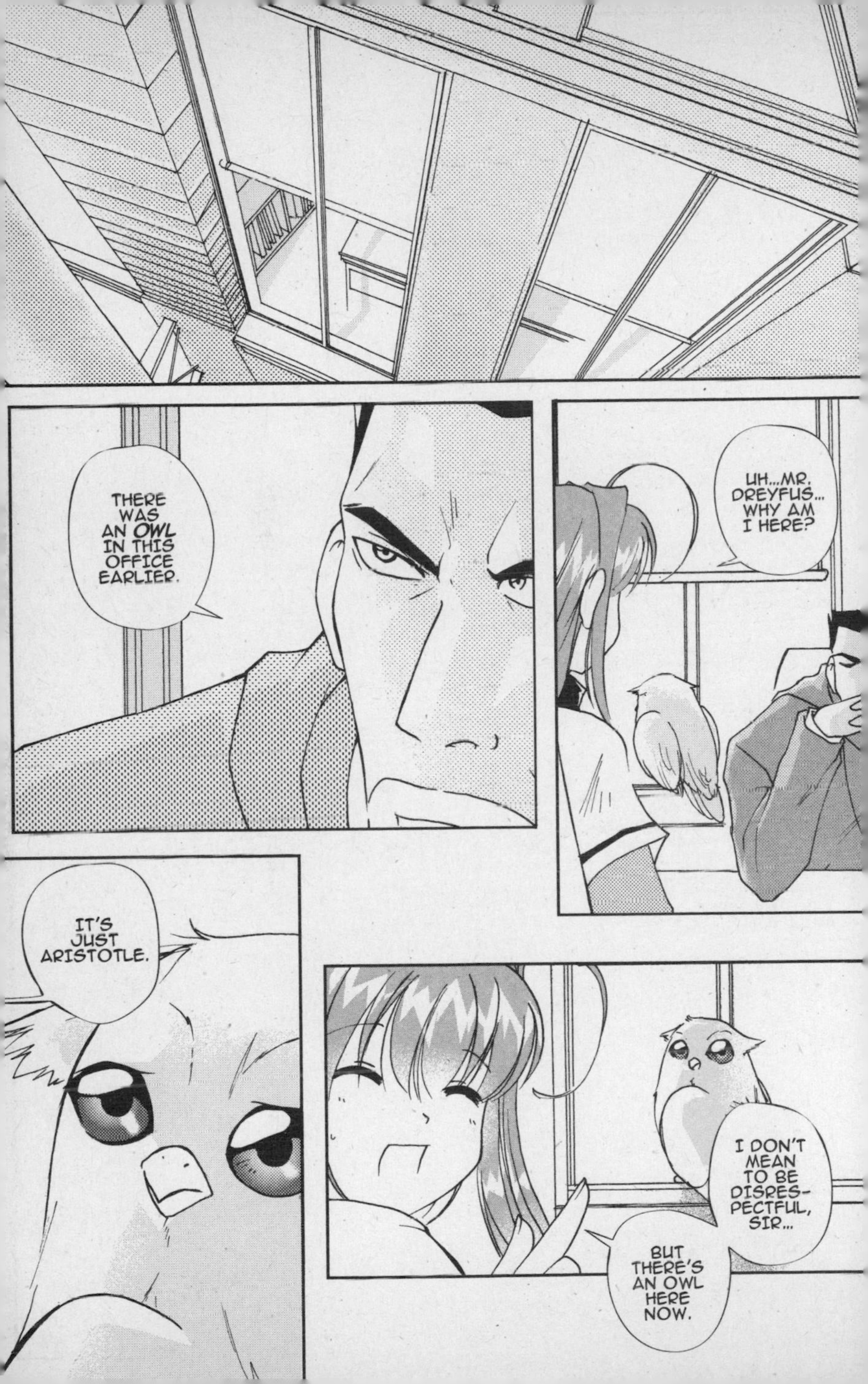
UH...MR. DREYFUS... WHY AM I HERE?
THERE WAS AN *OWL* IN THIS OFFICE EARLIER.
I DON'T MEAN TO BE DISRES-PECTFUL, SIR...
BUT THERE'S AN OWL HERE NOW.
IT'S JUST ARISTOTLE.

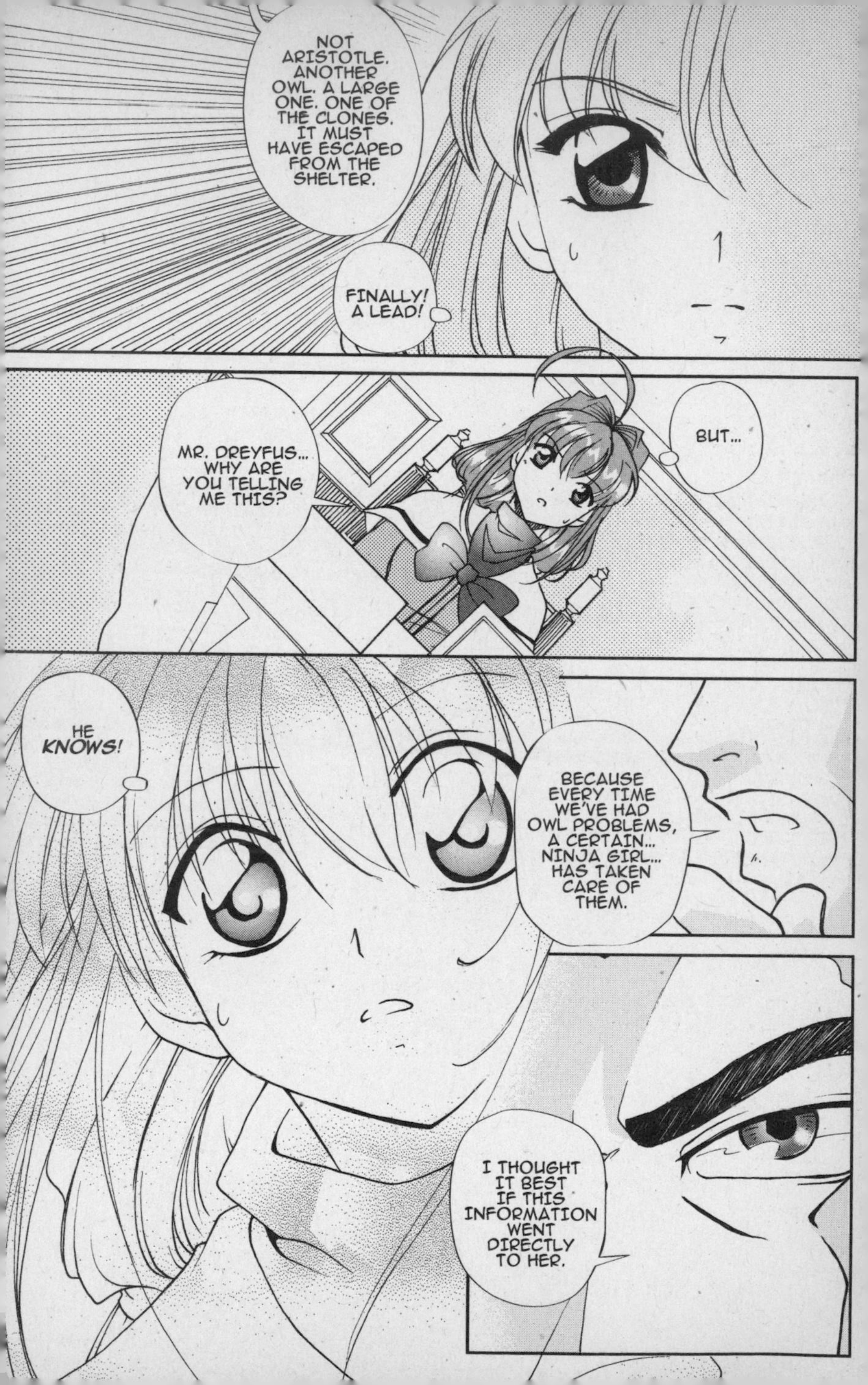
NOT ARISTOTLE. ANOTHER OWL. A LARGE ONE. ONE OF THE CLONES. IT MUST HAVE ESCAPED FROM THE SHELTER.
FINALLY! A LEAD!
BUT...
MR. DREYFUS... WHY ARE YOU TELLING ME THIS?
BECAUSE EVERY TIME WE'VE HAD OWL PROBLEMS, A CERTAIN... NINJA GIRL... HAS TAKEN CARE OF THEM.
I THOUGHT IT BEST IF THIS INFORMATION WENT DIRECTLY TO HER.
HE **KNOWS!**

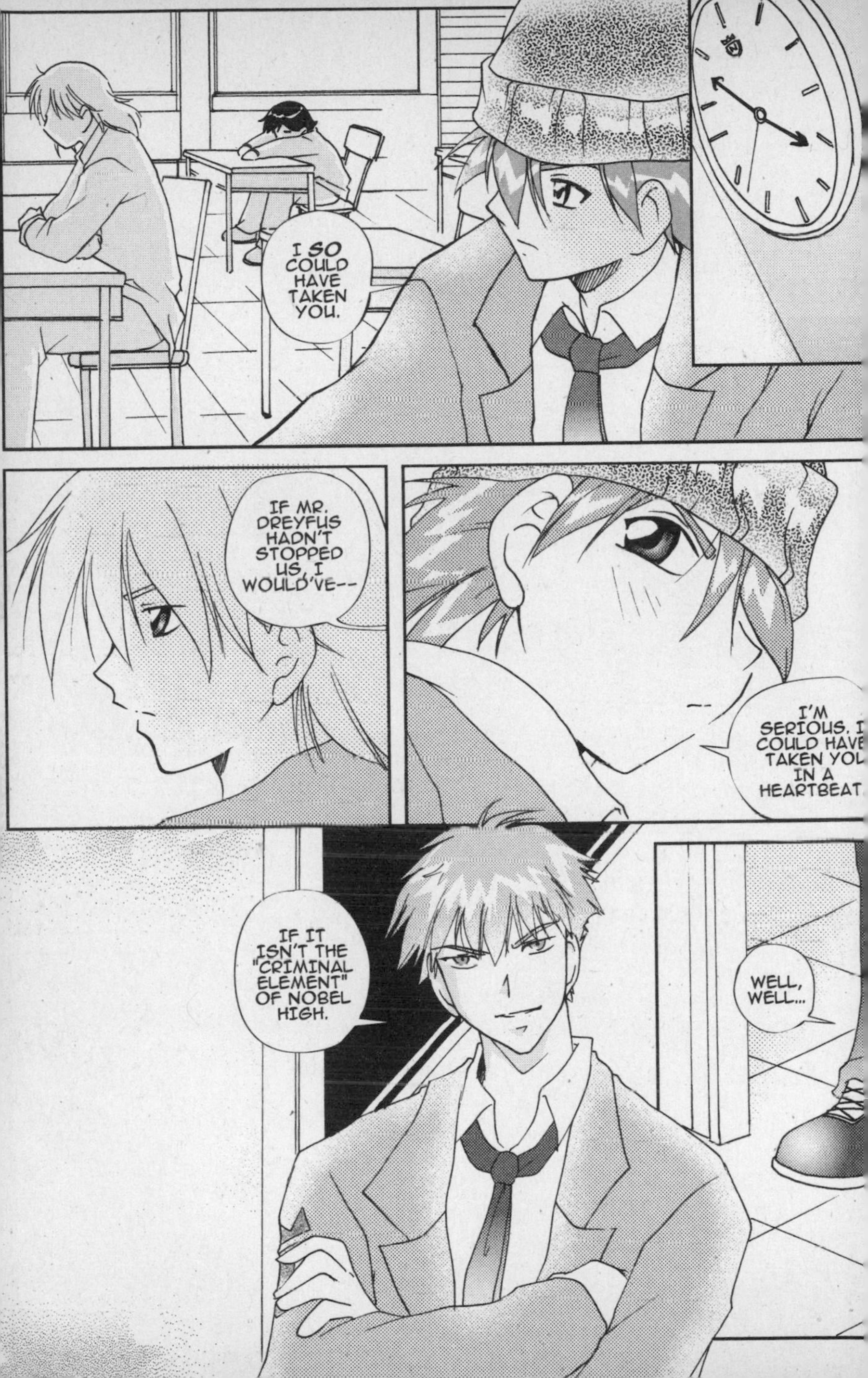
I SO COULD HAVE TAKEN YOU.
I'M SERIOUS. I COULD HAVE TAKEN YOU IN A HEARTBEAT.
IF MR. DREYFUS HADN'T STOPPED US, I WOULD'VE--
WELL, WELL...
IF IT ISN'T THE "CRIMINAL ELEMENT" OF NOBEL HIGH.

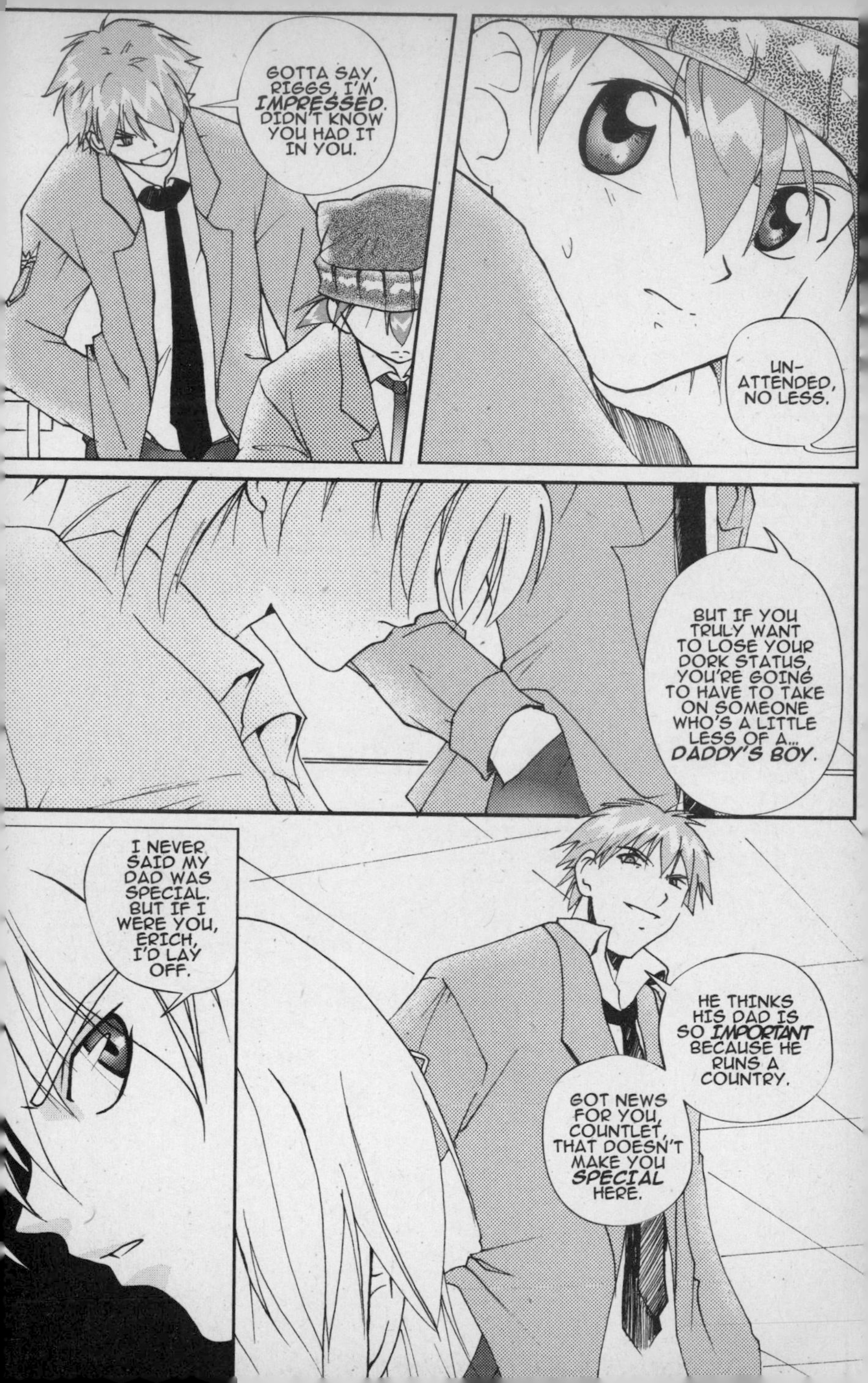
UN-ATTENDED, NO LESS.
GOTTA SAY, RIGGS, I'M *IMPRESSED*. DIDN'T KNOW YOU HAD IT IN YOU.
BUT IF YOU TRULY WANT TO LOSE YOUR DORK STATUS, YOU'RE GOING TO HAVE TO TAKE ON SOMEONE WHO'S A LITTLE LESS OF A... *DADDY'S BOY*.
HE THINKS HIS DAD IS SO *IMPORTANT* BECAUSE HE RUNS A COUNTRY.
GOT NEWS FOR YOU, COUNTLET, THAT DOESN'T MAKE YOU *SPECIAL* HERE.
I NEVER SAID MY DAD WAS SPECIAL. BUT IF I WERE YOU, ERICH, I'D LAY OFF.

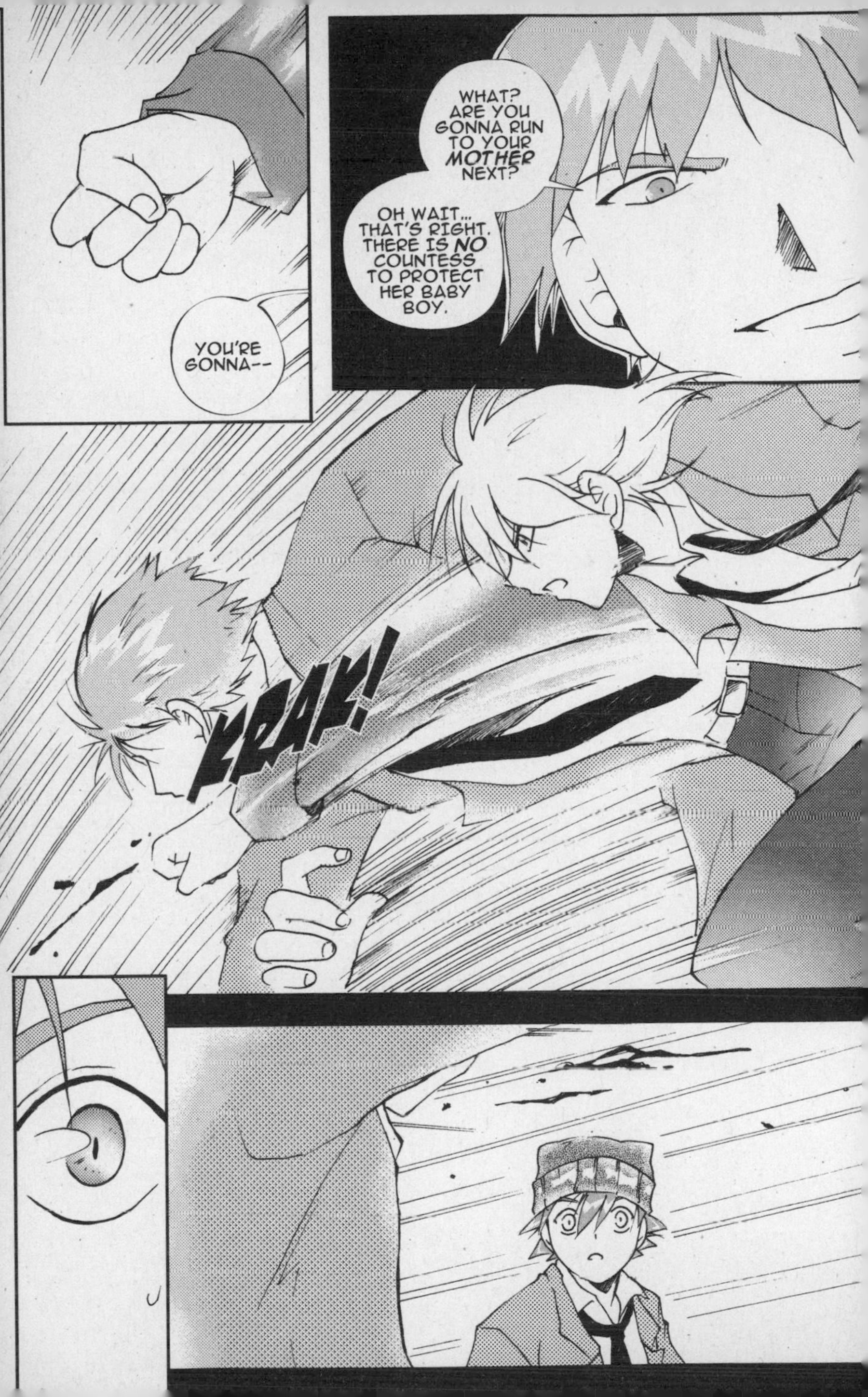
WHAT? ARE YOU GONNA RUN TO YOUR *MOTHER* NEXT?
OH WAIT... THAT'S RIGHT. THERE IS *NO* COUNTESS TO PROTECT HER BABY BOY.
YOU'RE GONNA--
KRAK!

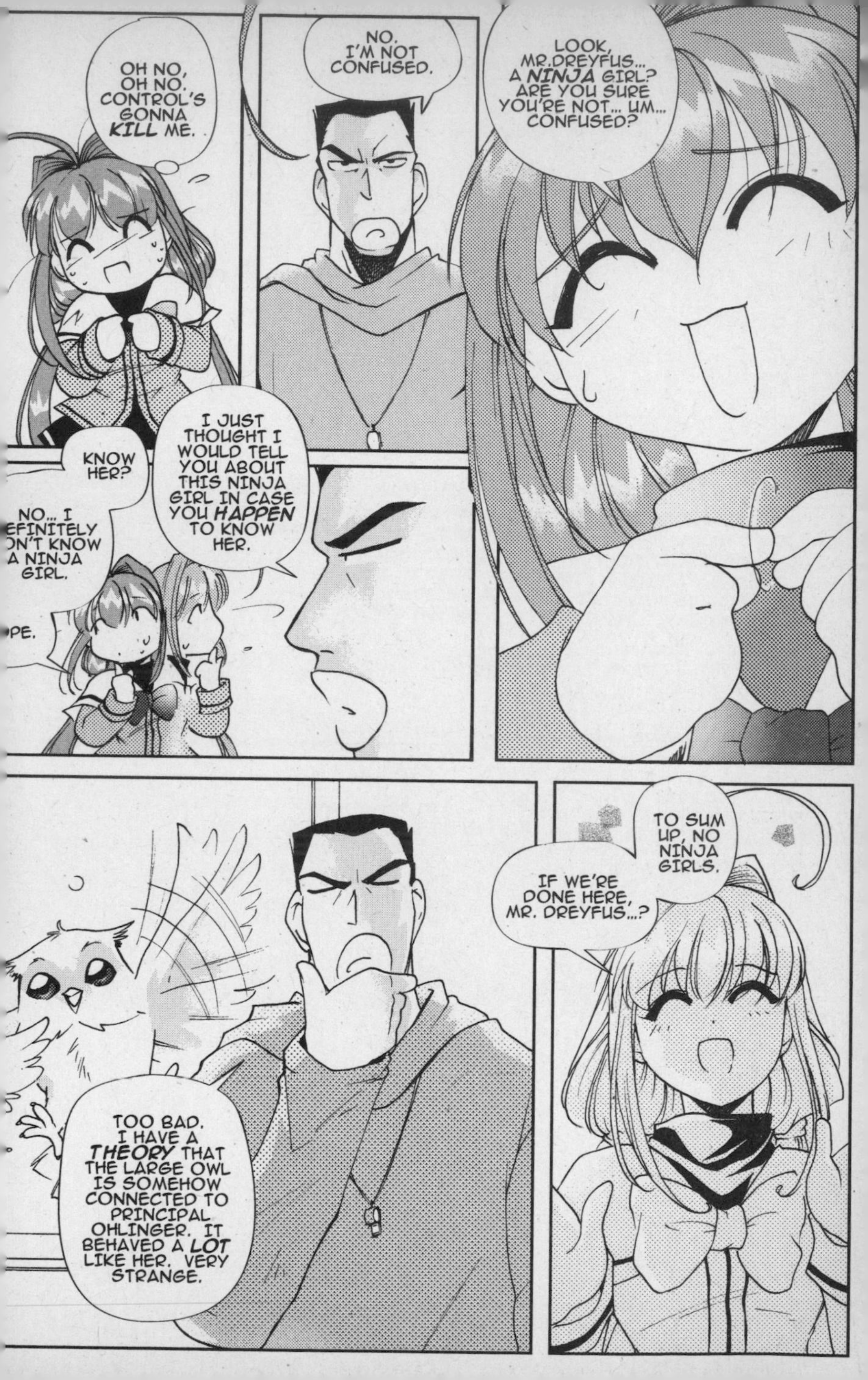
LOOK, MR.DREYFUS... A NINJA GIRL? ARE YOU SURE YOU'RE NOT... UM... CONFUSED?
NO, I'M NOT CONFUSED.
OH NO, OH NO. CONTROL'S GONNA KILL ME.
I JUST THOUGHT I WOULD TELL YOU ABOUT THIS NINJA GIRL IN CASE YOU HAPPEN TO KNOW HER.
KNOW HER?
NO... I EFINITELY ON'T KNOW A NINJA GIRL.
PE.
TO SUM UP, NO NINJA GIRLS.
IF WE'RE DONE HERE, MR. DREYFUS...?
TOO BAD. I HAVE A THEORY THAT THE LARGE OWL IS SOMEHOW CONNECTED TO PRINCIPAL OHLINGER. IT BEHAVED A LOT LIKE HER. VERY STRANGE.

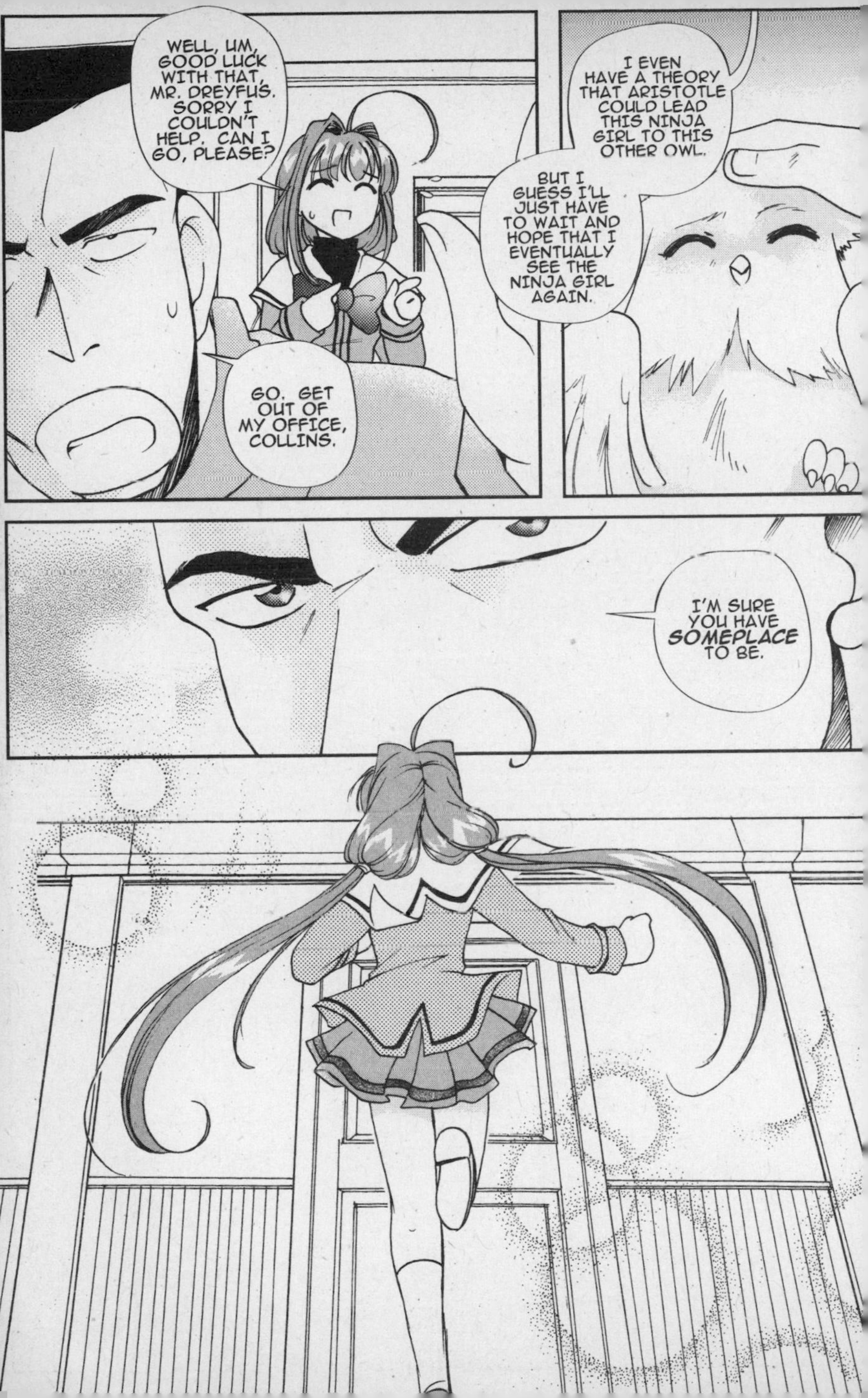
I EVEN HAVE A THEORY THAT ARISTOTLE COULD LEAD THIS NINJA GIRL TO THIS OTHER OWL.
BUT I GUESS I'LL JUST HAVE TO WAIT AND HOPE THAT I EVENTUALLY SEE THE NINJA GIRL AGAIN.
WELL, UM, GOOD LUCK WITH THAT, MR. DREYFUS. SORRY I COULDN'T HELP. CAN I GO, PLEASE?
GO. GET OUT OF MY OFFICE, COLLINS.
I'M SURE YOU HAVE **SOMEPLACE** TO BE.

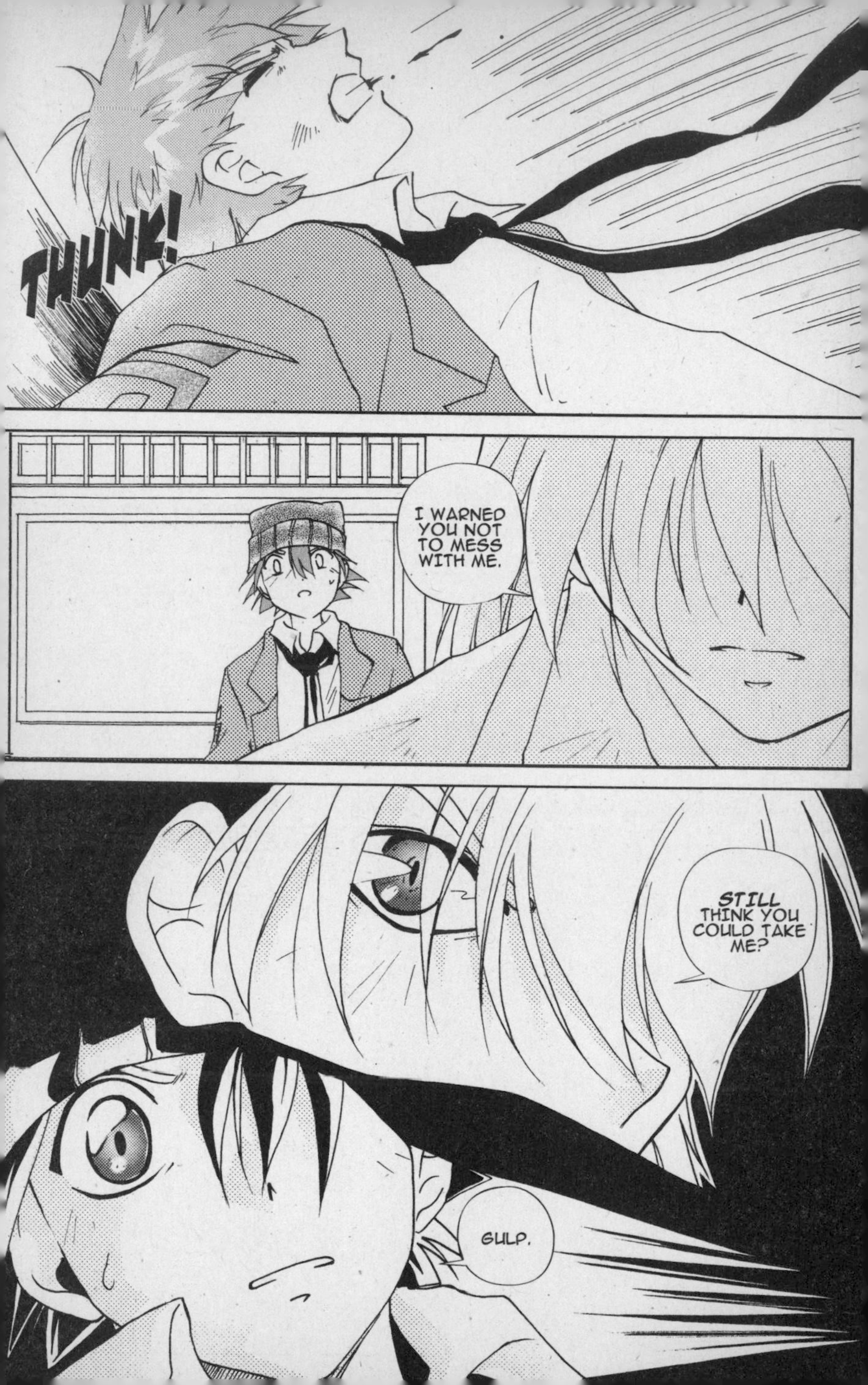
THUNK!
I WARNED YOU NOT TO MESS WITH ME.
STILL THINK YOU COULD TAKE ME?
GULP.

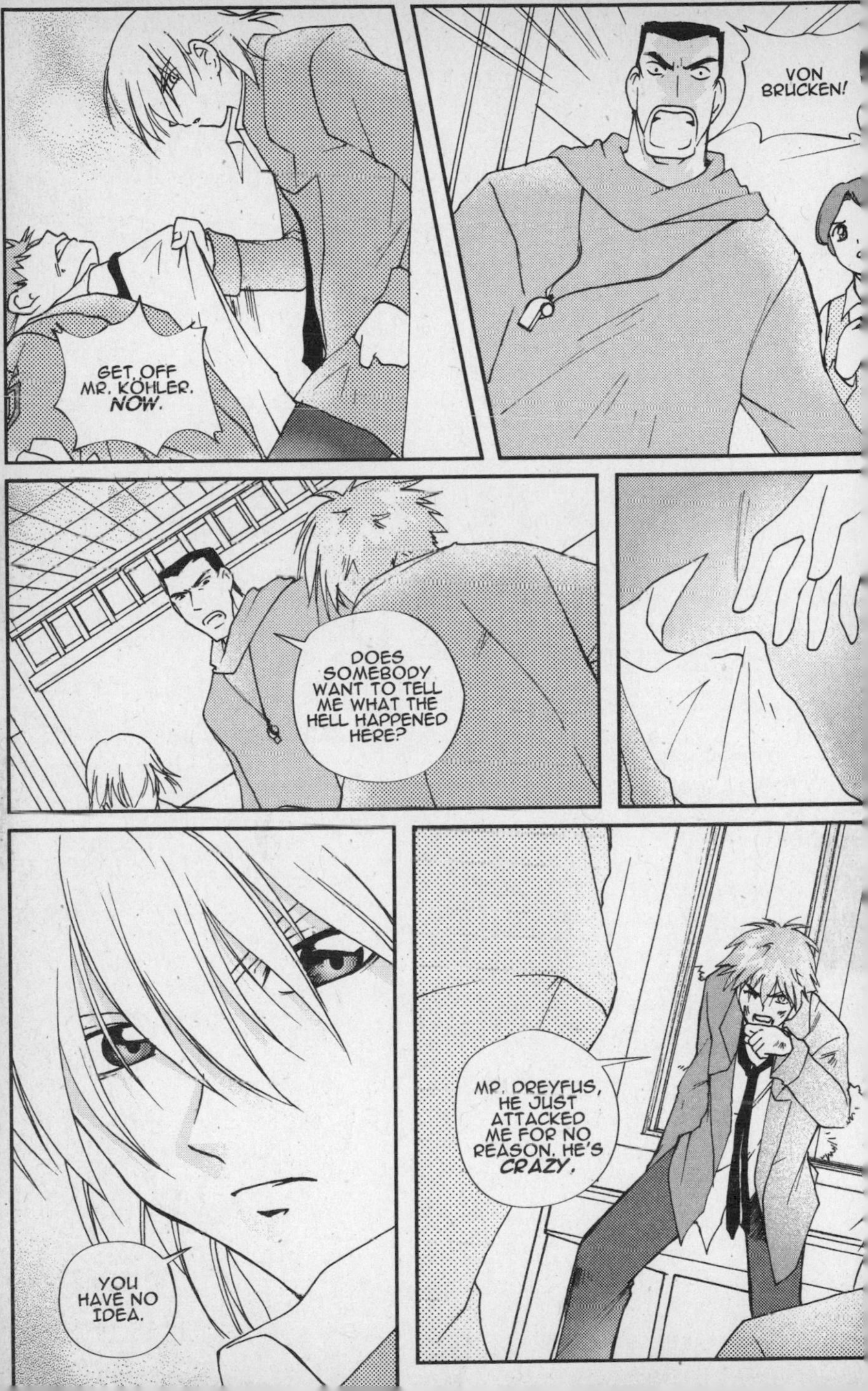
VON BRUCKEN!
GET OFF MR. KÖHLER. *NOW*.
DOES SOMEBODY WANT TO TELL ME WHAT THE HELL HAPPENED HERE?
MR. DREYFUS, HE JUST ATTACKED ME FOR NO REASON. HE'S *CRAZY*.
YOU HAVE NO IDEA.

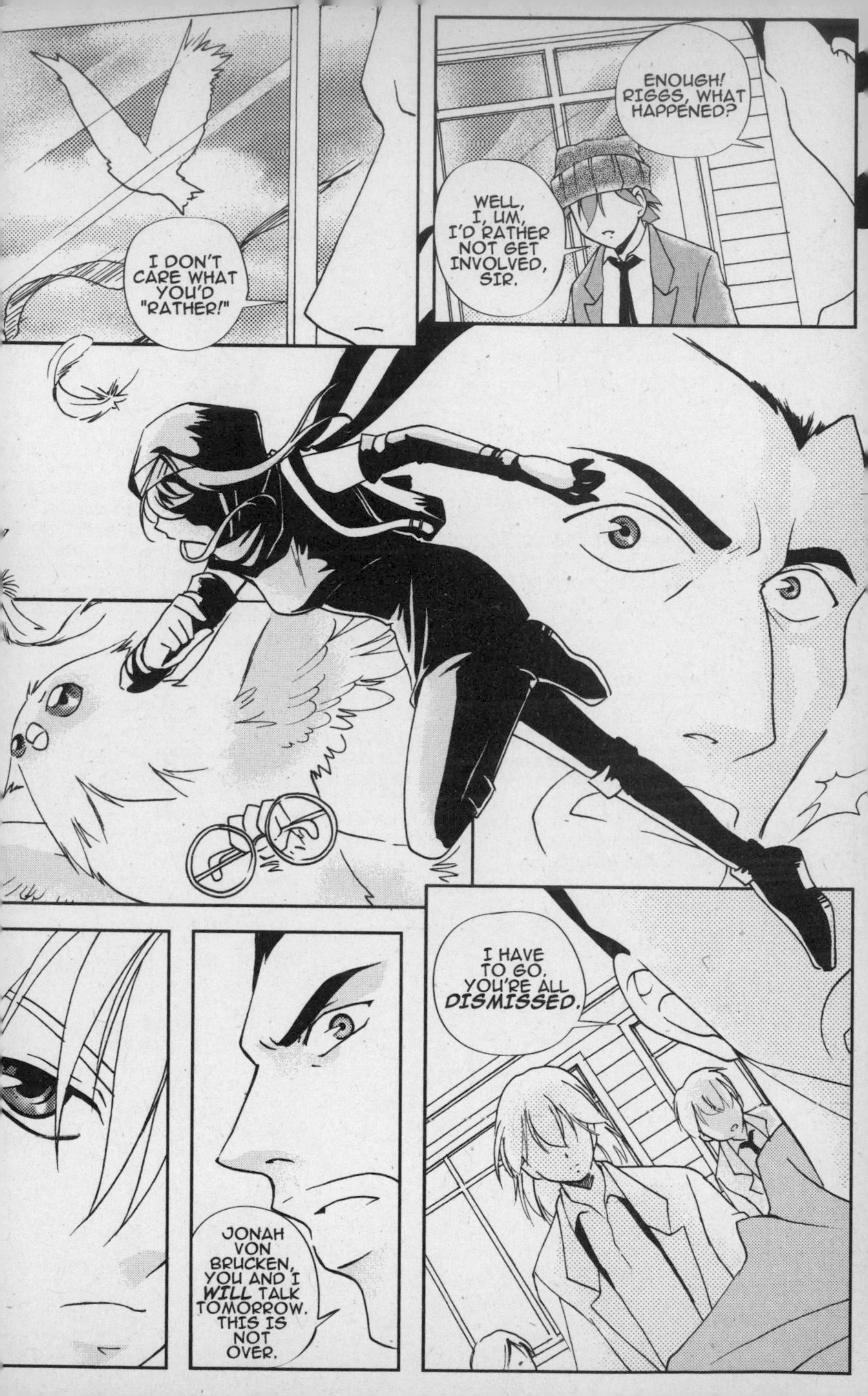
ENOUGH! RIGGS, WHAT HAPPENED?
WELL, I, UM, I'D RATHER NOT GET INVOLVED, SIR.
I DON'T CARE WHAT YOU'D "RATHER!"
I HAVE TO GO. YOU'RE ALL **DISMISSED.**
JONAH VON BRUCKEN, YOU AND I ***WILL*** TALK TOMORROW. THIS IS NOT OVER.

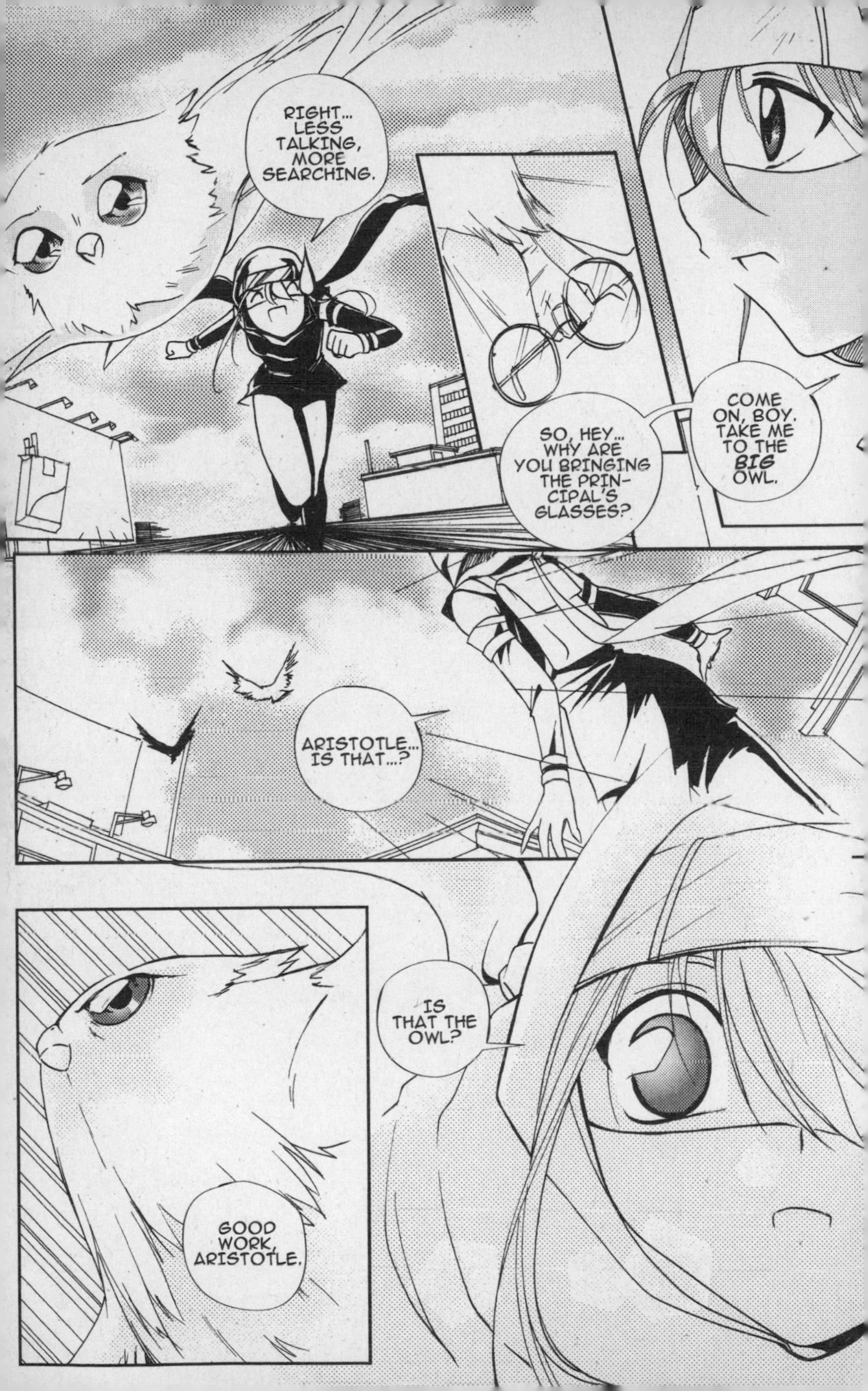
COME ON, BOY. TAKE ME TO THE *BIG* OWL.
SO, HEY... WHY ARE YOU BRINGING THE PRIN-CIPAL'S GLASSES?
RIGHT... LESS TALKING, MORE SEARCHING.
ARISTOTLE... IS THAT...?
IS THAT THE OWL?
GOOD WORK, ARISTOTLE.

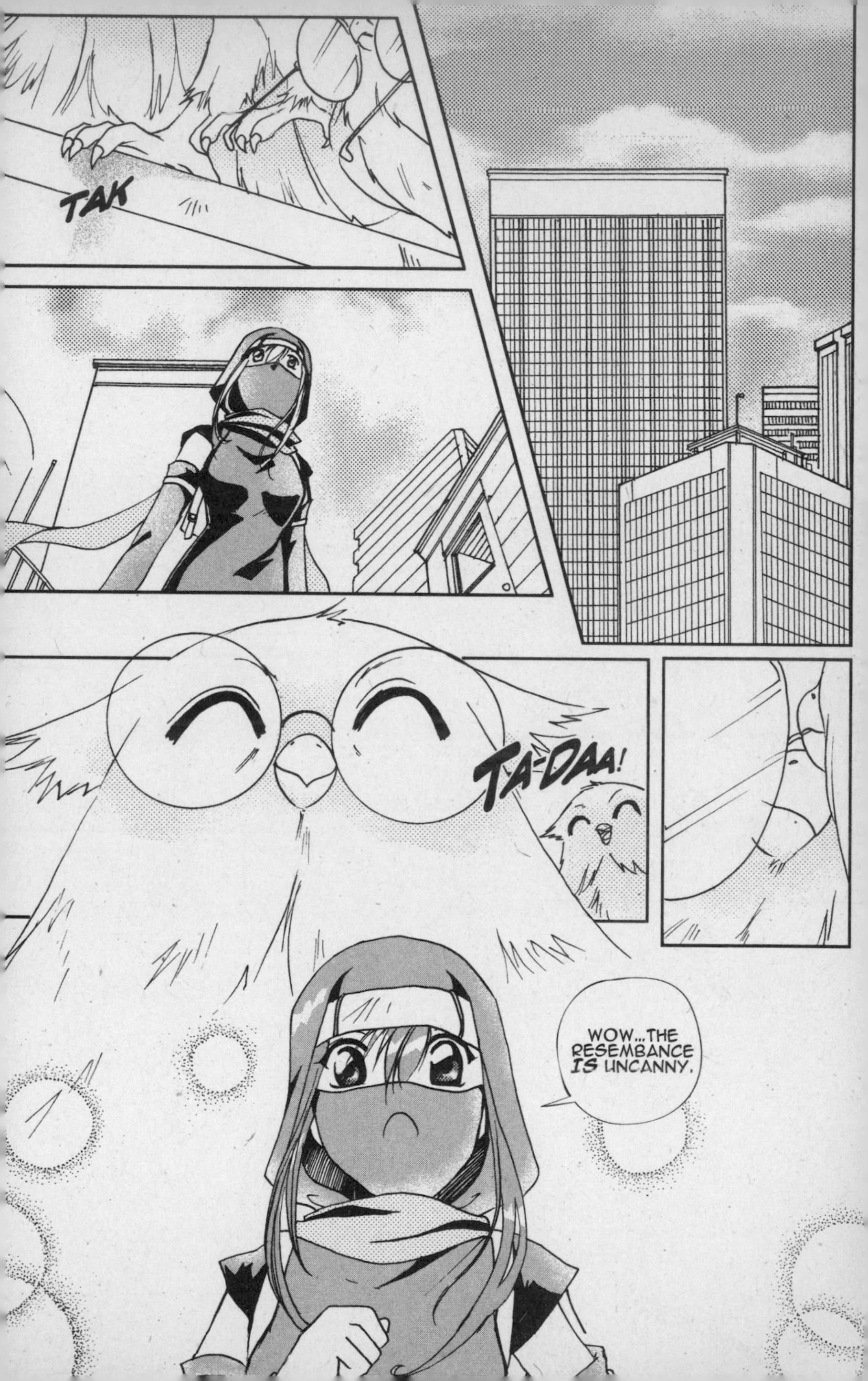
TAK
TA-DAA!
WOW...THE RESEMBANCE IS UNCANNY.

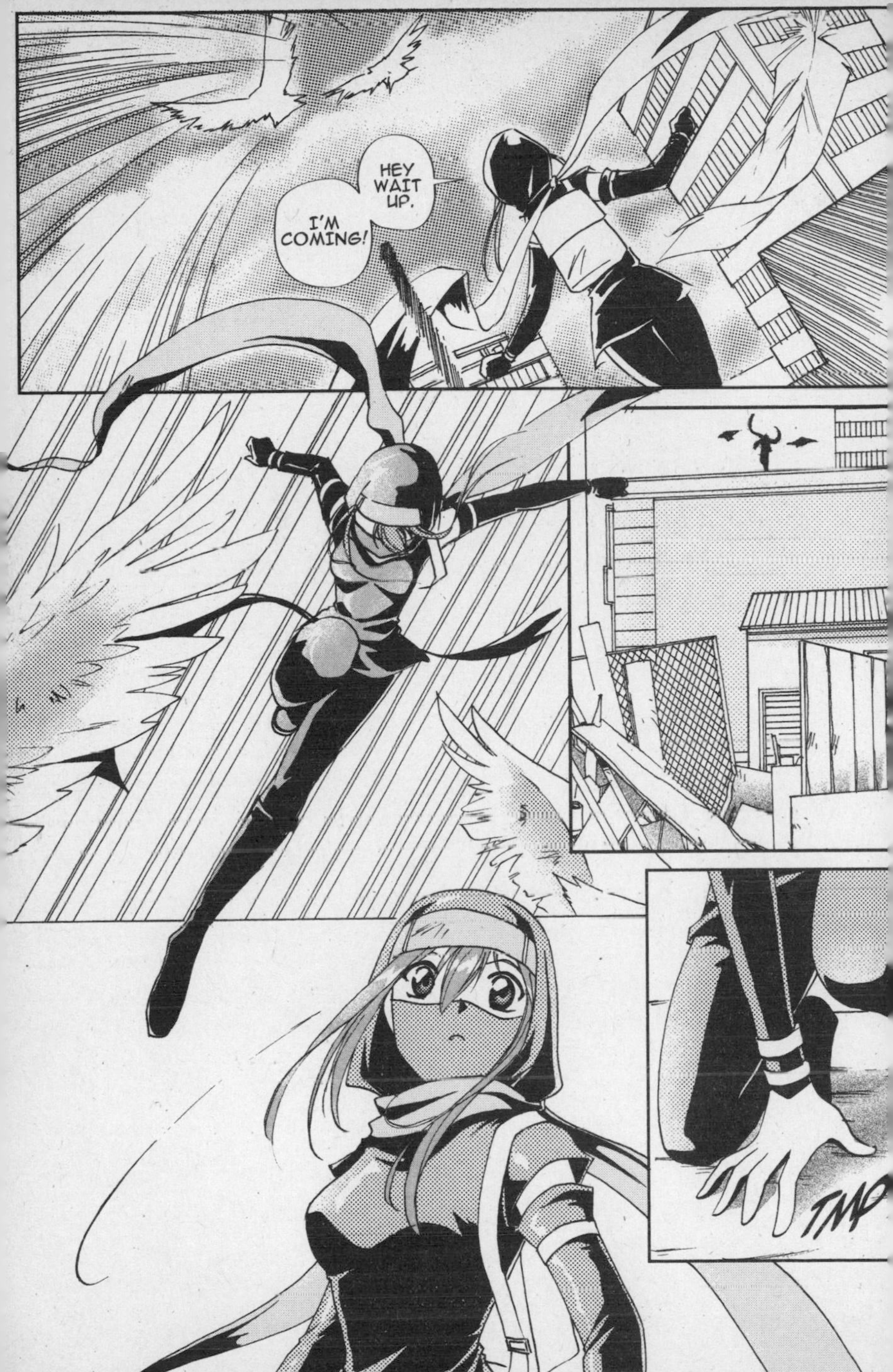
HEY WAIT UP.
I'M COMING!
TMP

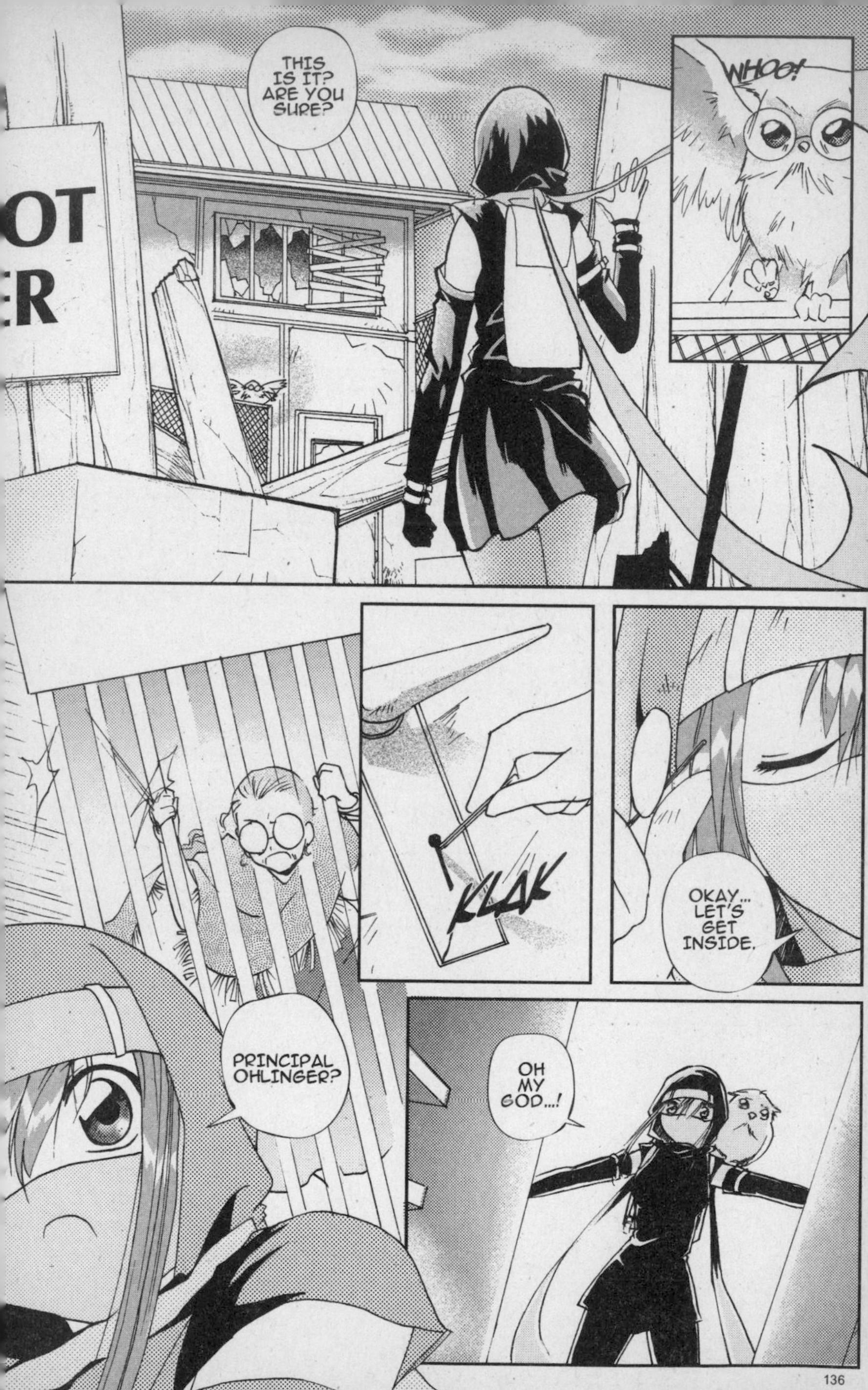
WHOO!
THIS IS IT? ARE YOU SURE?
OT
ER
OKAY... LET'S GET INSIDE.
KLAK
OH MY GOD...!
PRINCIPAL OHLINGER?

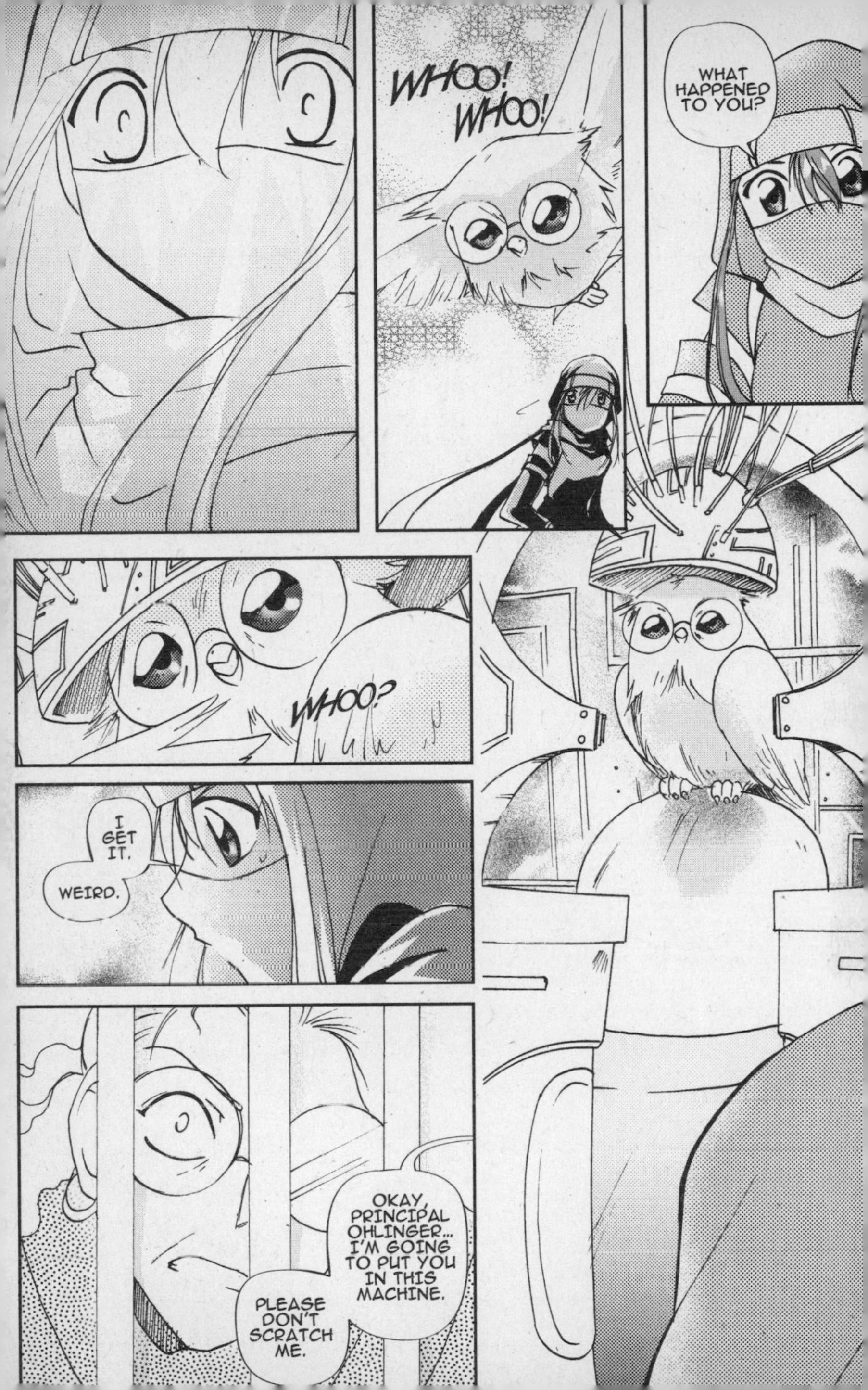
WHAT HAPPENED TO YOU?
WHOO! WHOO!
WHOO?
I GET IT.
WEIRD.
OKAY, PRINCIPAL OHLINGER... I'M GOING TO PUT YOU IN THIS MACHINE.
PLEASE DON'T SCRATCH ME.

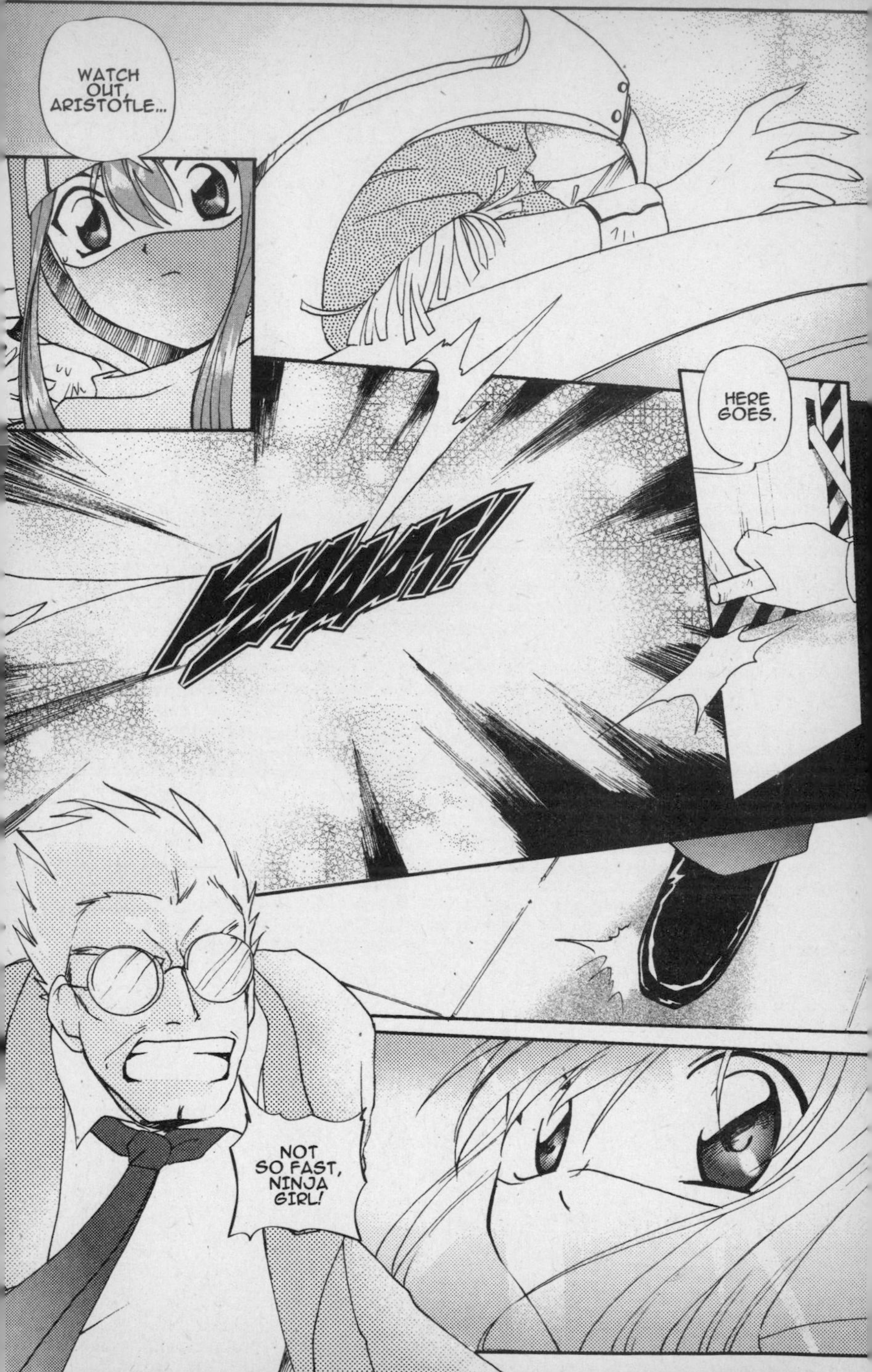
WATCH OUT, ARISTOTLE...
HERE GOES.
NOT SO FAST, NINJA GIRL!

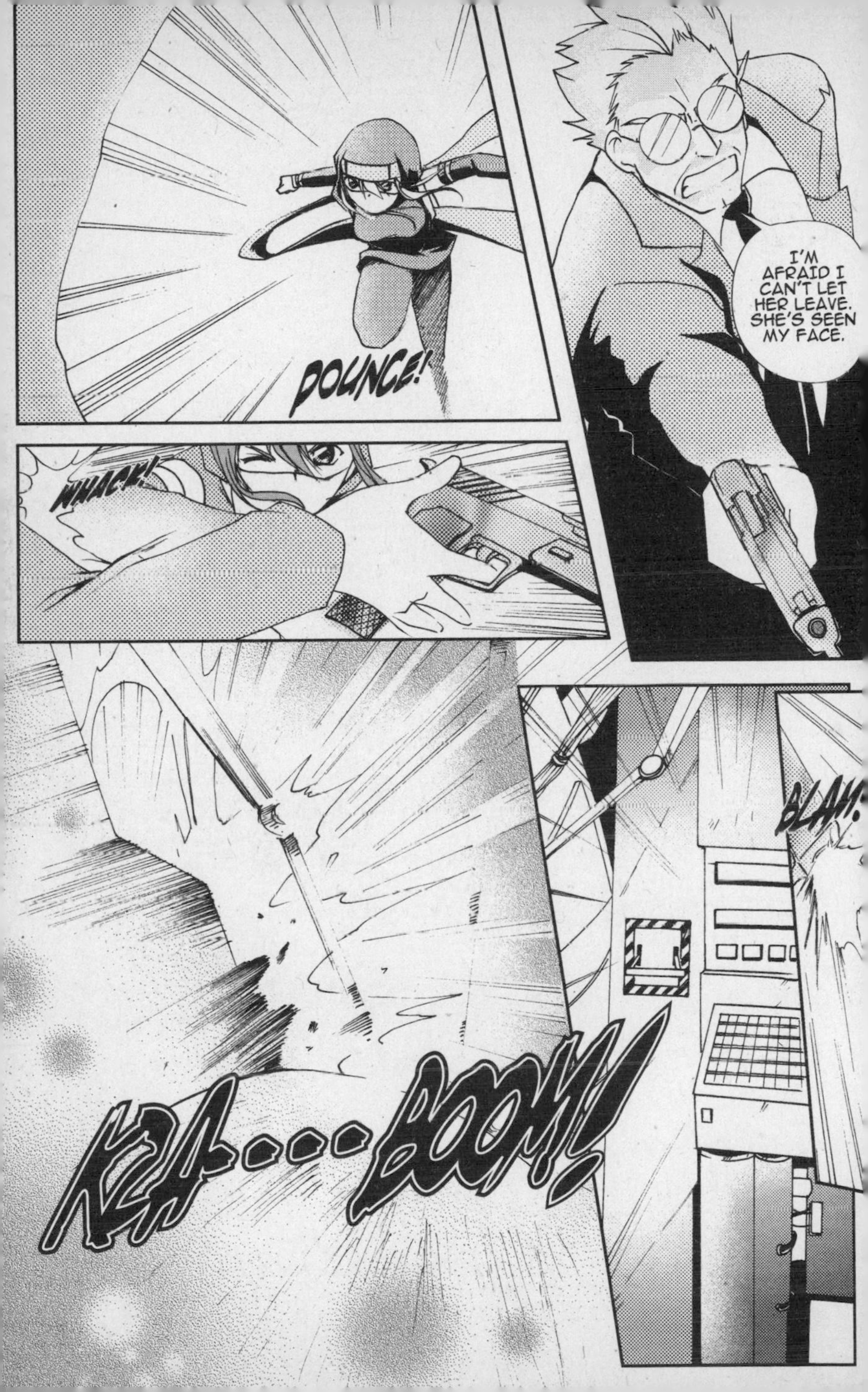
I'M AFRAID I CAN'T LET HER LEAVE. SHE'S SEEN MY FACE.
POUNCE!
WHACK!
BLAM!
KRA...BOOM!

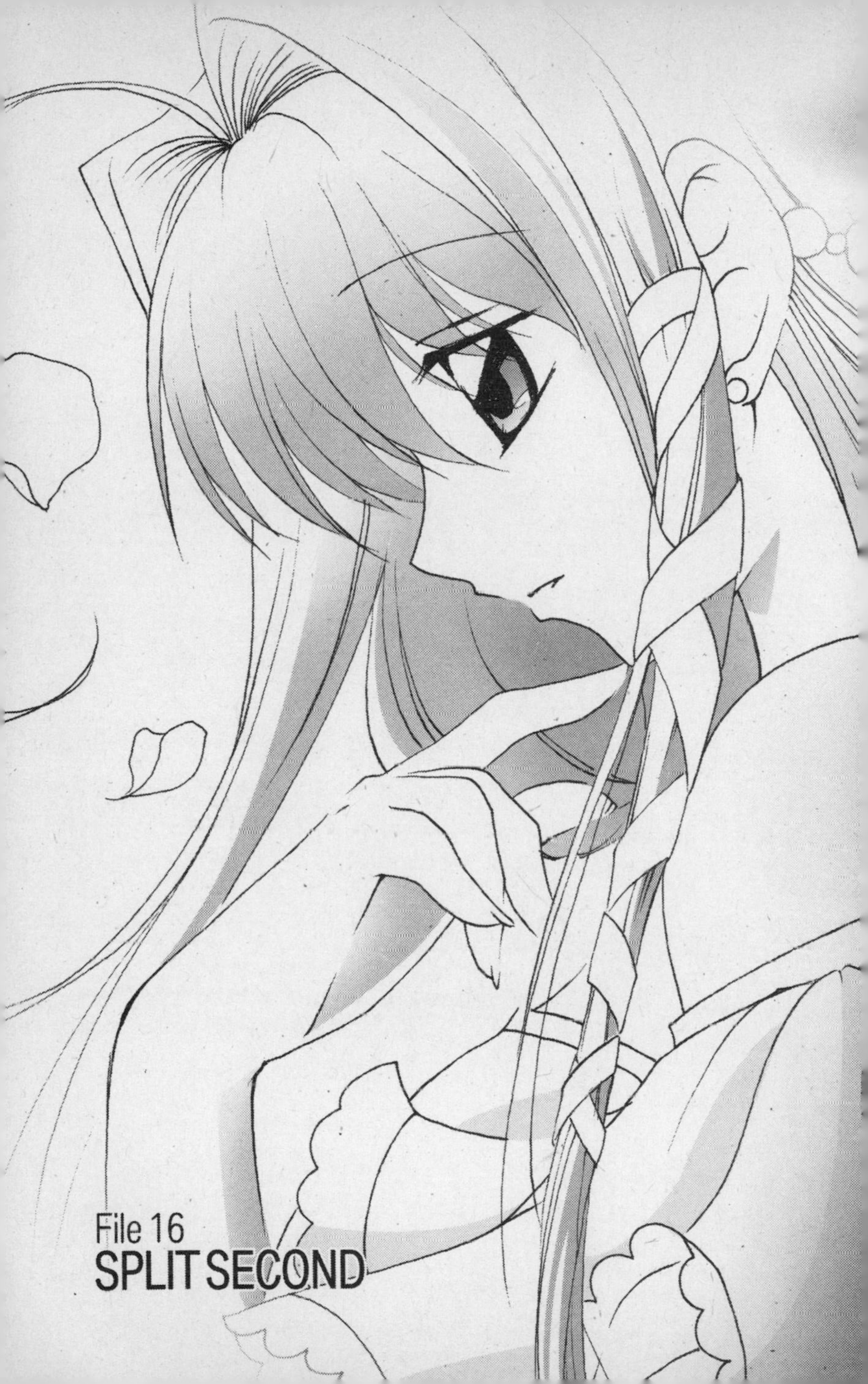

File 16

SPLIT SECOND

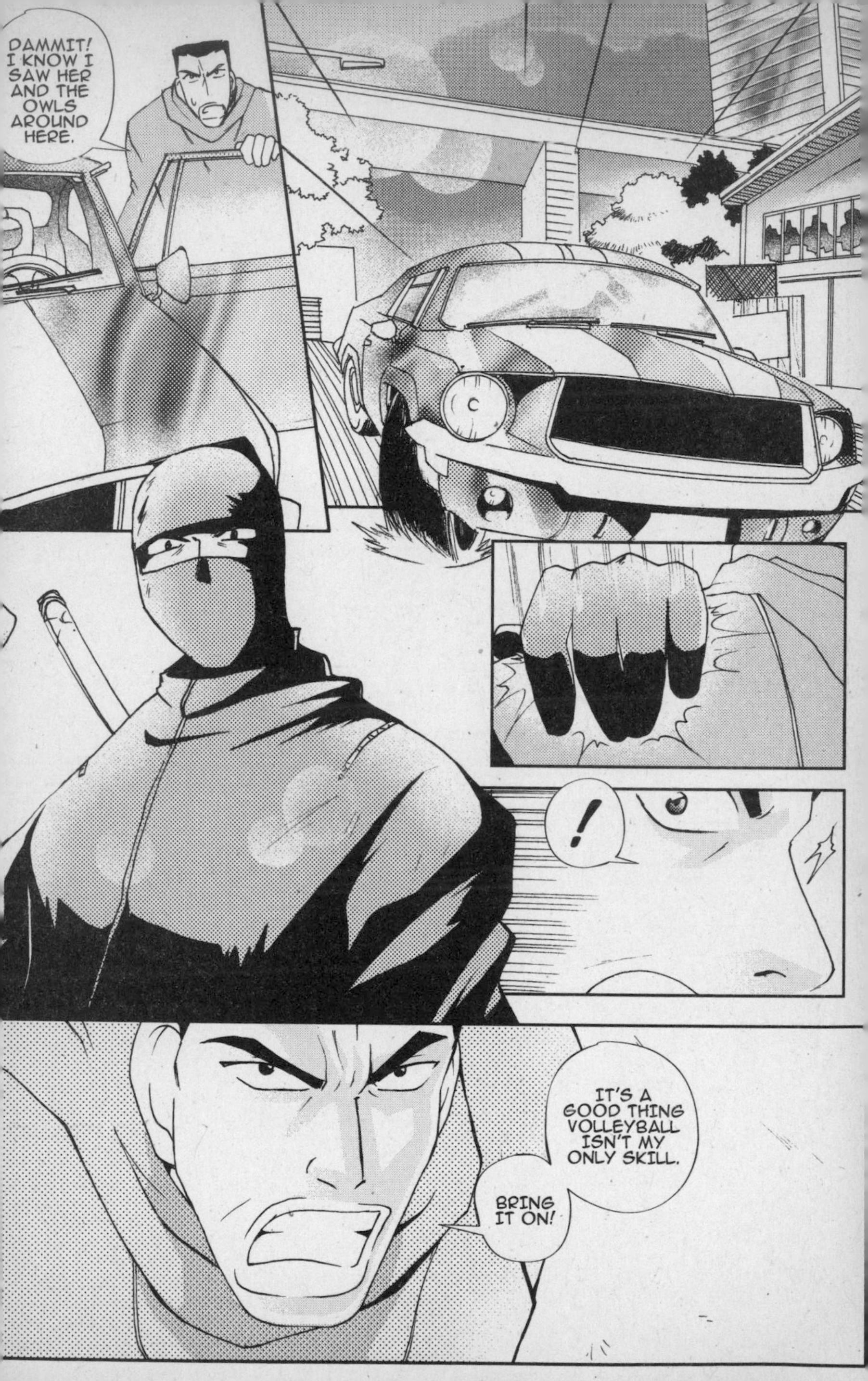
DAMMIT! I KNOW I SAW HER AND THE OWLS AROUND HERE.
!
IT'S A GOOD THING VOLLEYBALL ISN'T MY ONLY SKILL.
BRING IT ON!

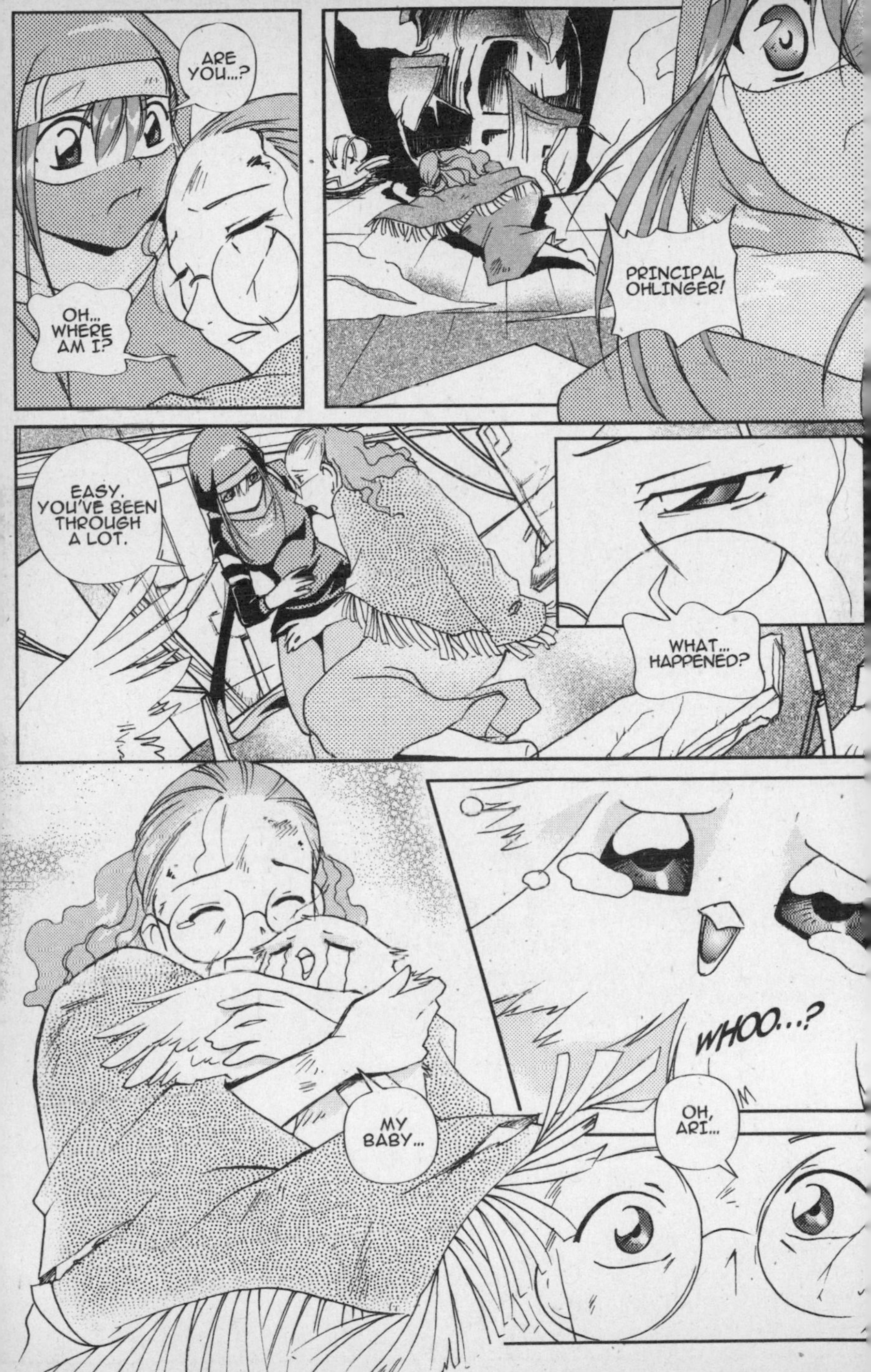
PRINCIPAL OHLINGER!
ARE YOU...?
OH... WHERE AM I?
WHAT... HAPPENED?
EASY. YOU'VE BEEN THROUGH A LOT.
WHOO...?
OH, ARI...
MY BABY...

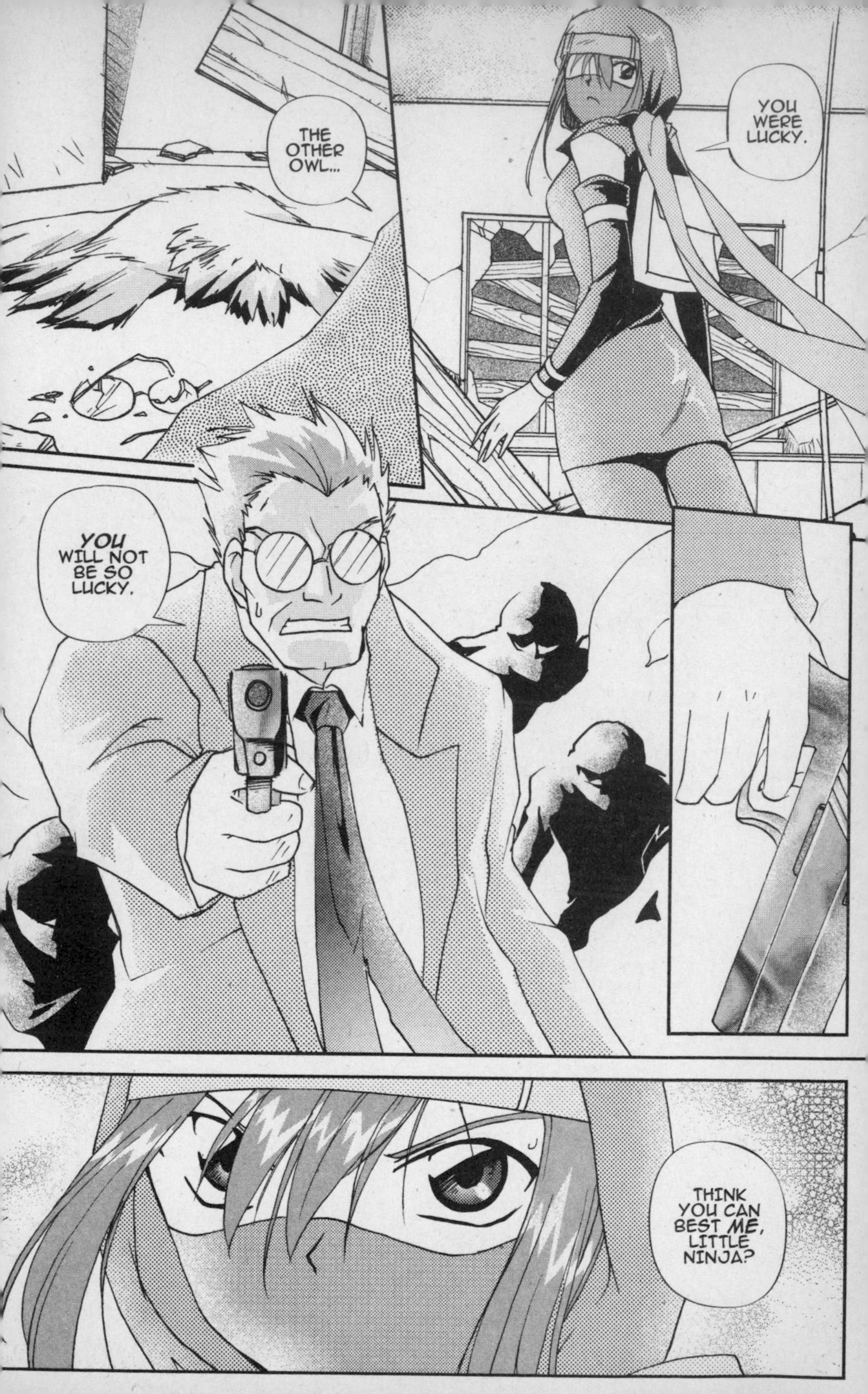
YOU WERE LUCKY.
THE OTHER OWL...
YOU WILL NOT BE SO LUCKY.
THINK YOU CAN BEST *ME*, LITTLE NINJA?

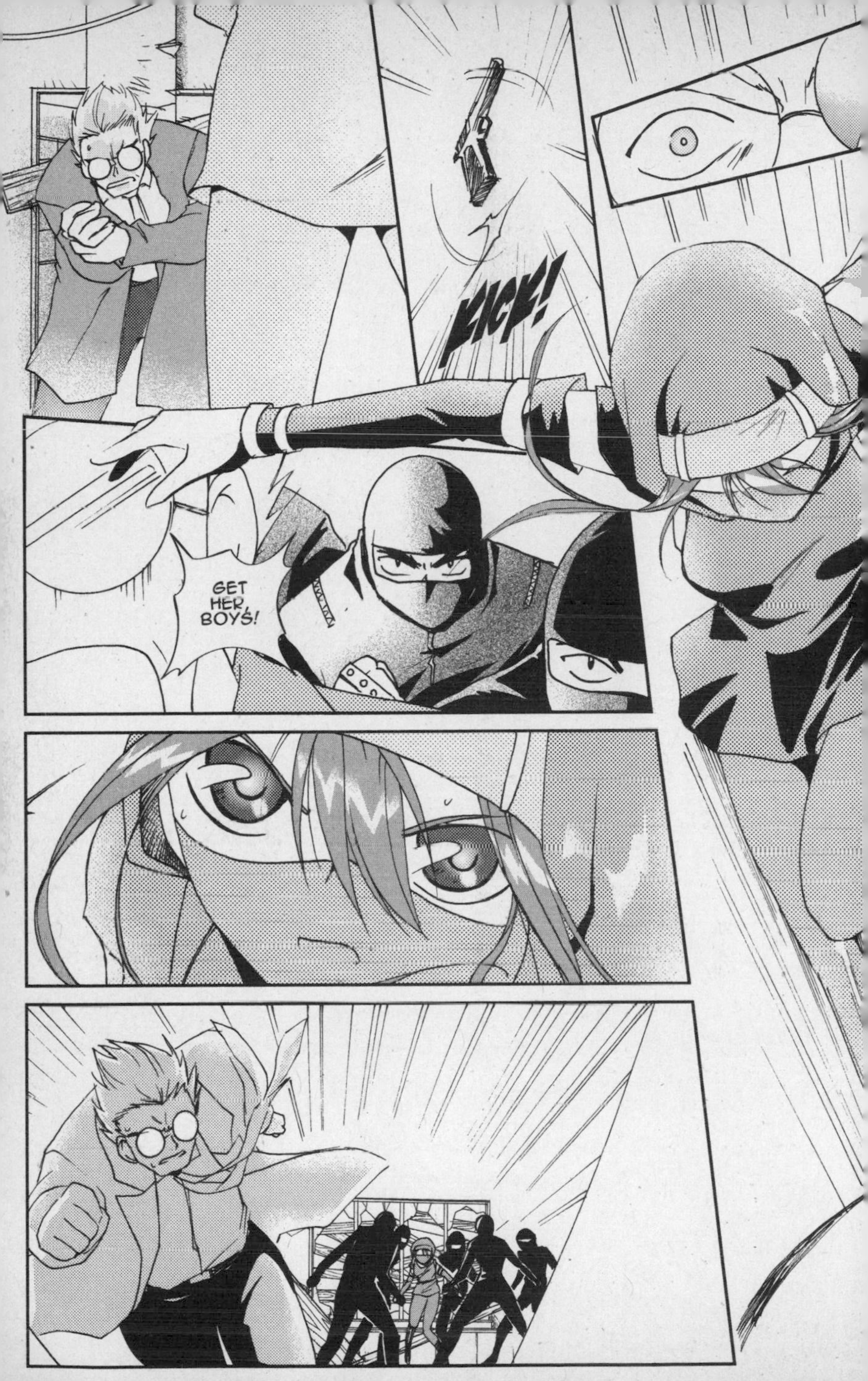
KICK!
GET HER, BOYS!

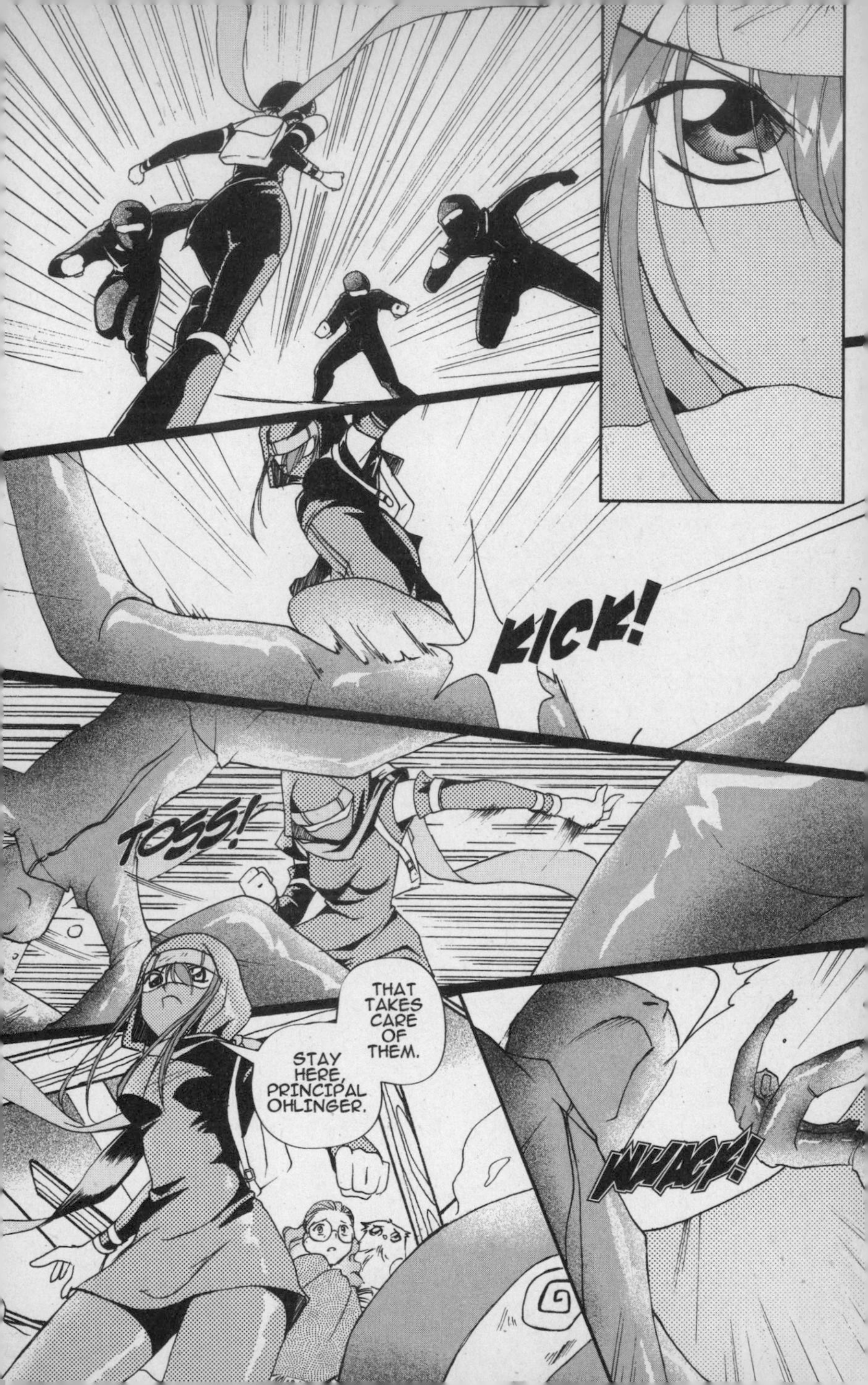
KICK!
TOSS!
WHACK!
THAT TAKES CARE OF THEM.
STAY HERE, PRINCIPAL OHLINGER.

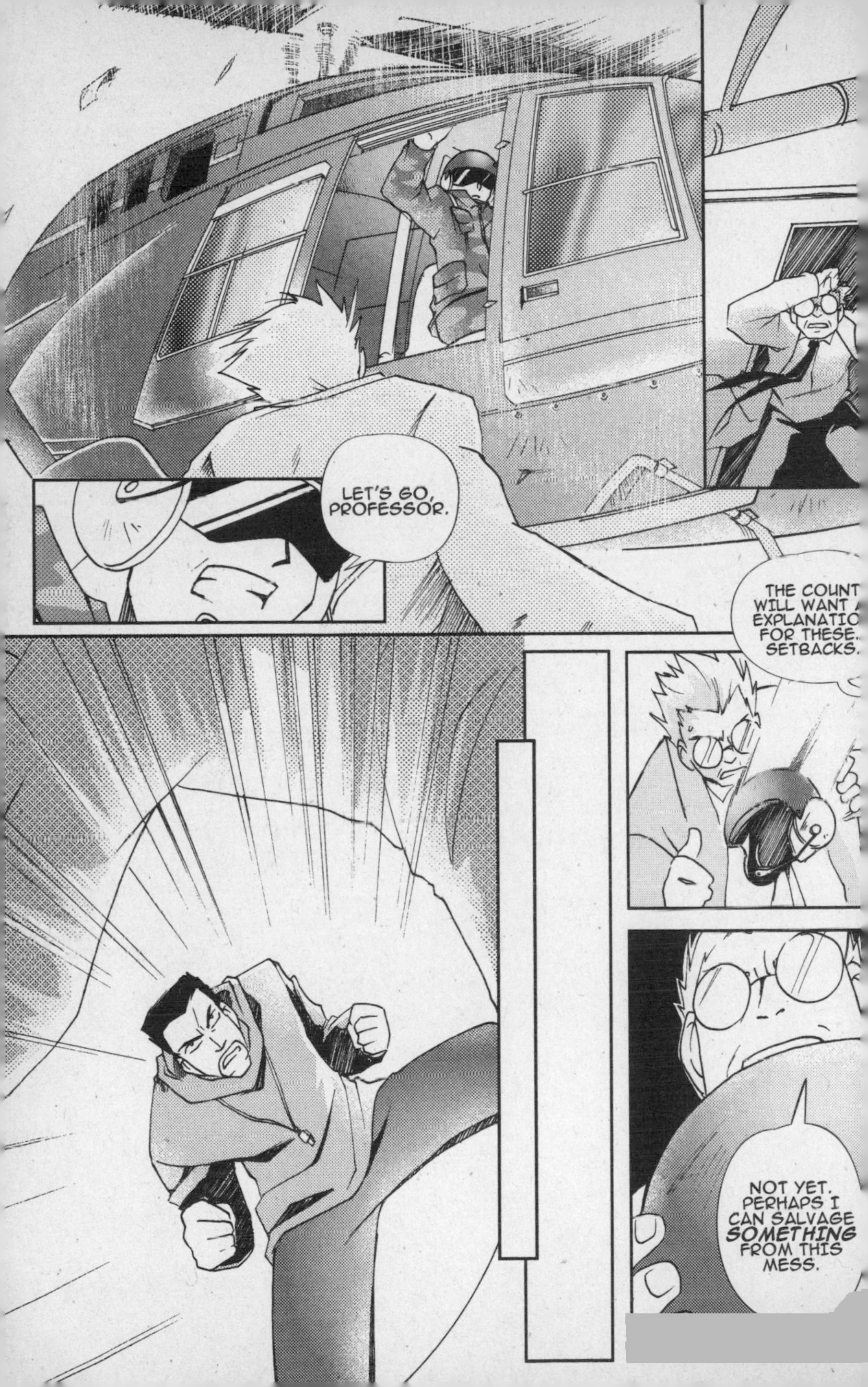
LET'S GO, PROFESSOR.
THE COUNT WILL WANT A EXPLANATIO FOR THESE... SETBACKS.
NOT YET. PERHAPS I CAN SALVAGE *SOMETHING* FROM THIS MESS.

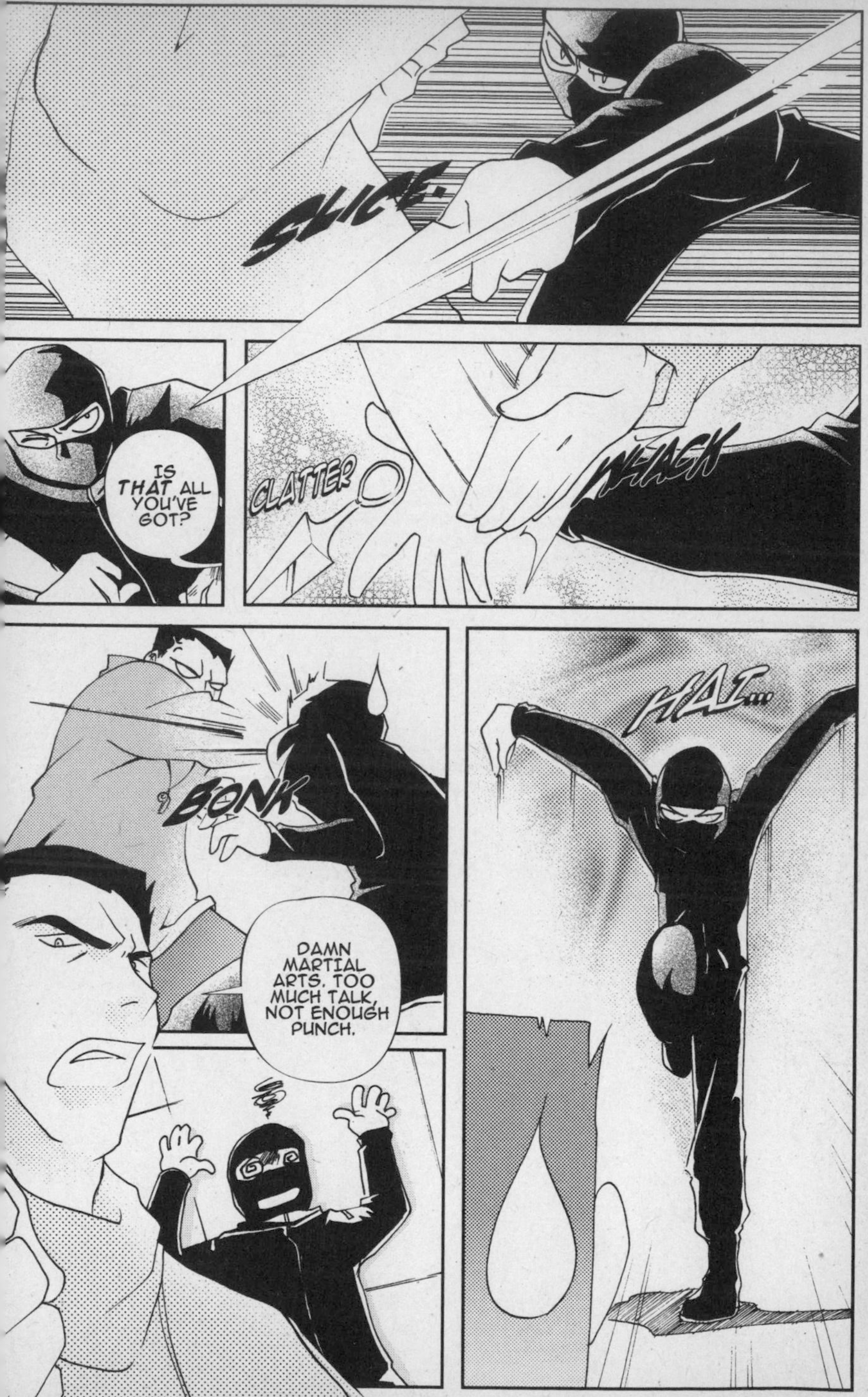
SLICE
WHACK
CLATTER
IS THAT ALL YOU'VE GOT?
HAI...
BONK
DAMN MARTIAL ARTS. TOO MUCH TALK, NOT ENOUGH PUNCH.

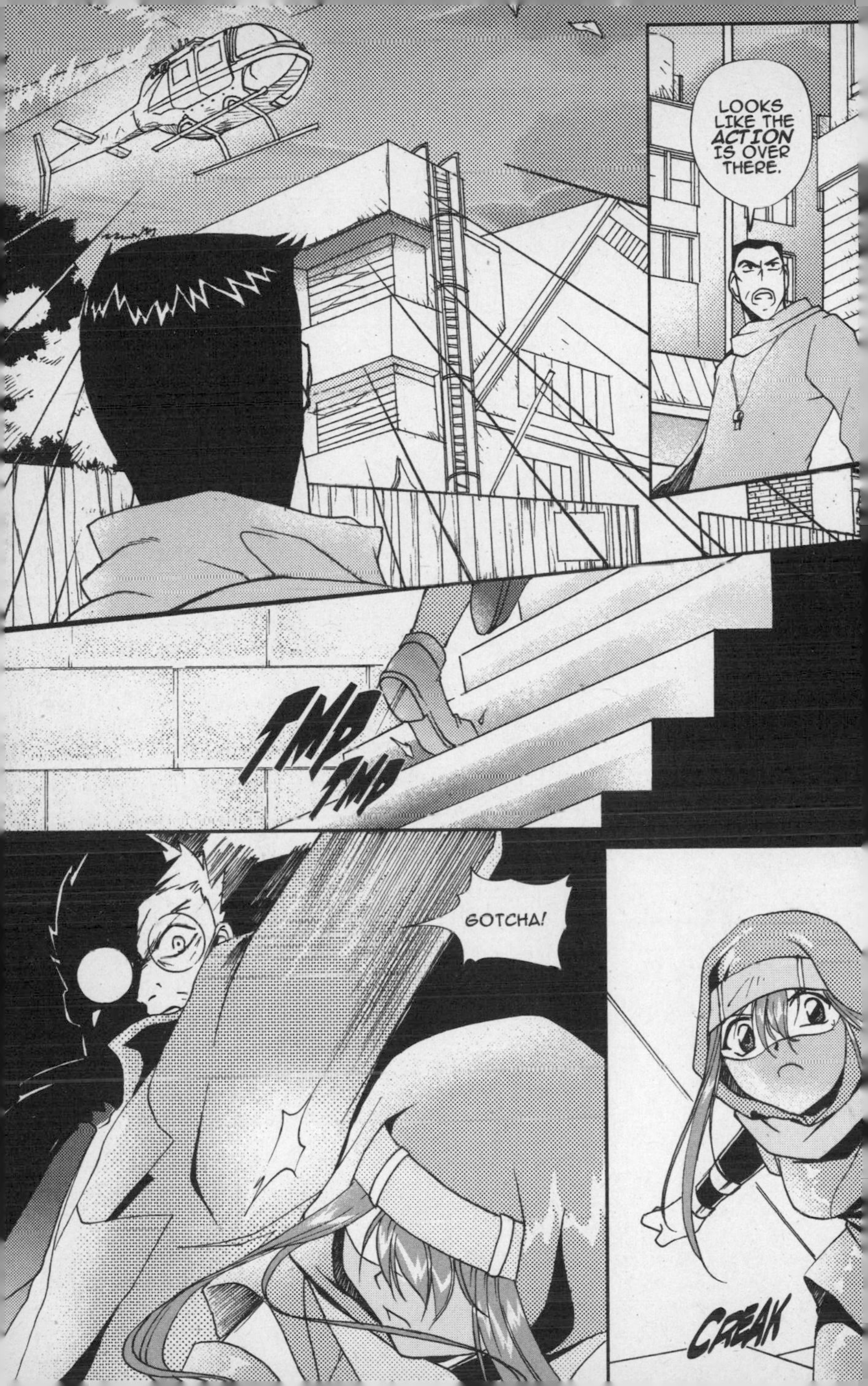
LOOKS LIKE THE ACTION IS OVER THERE.
TMP TMP
GOTCHA!
CREAK

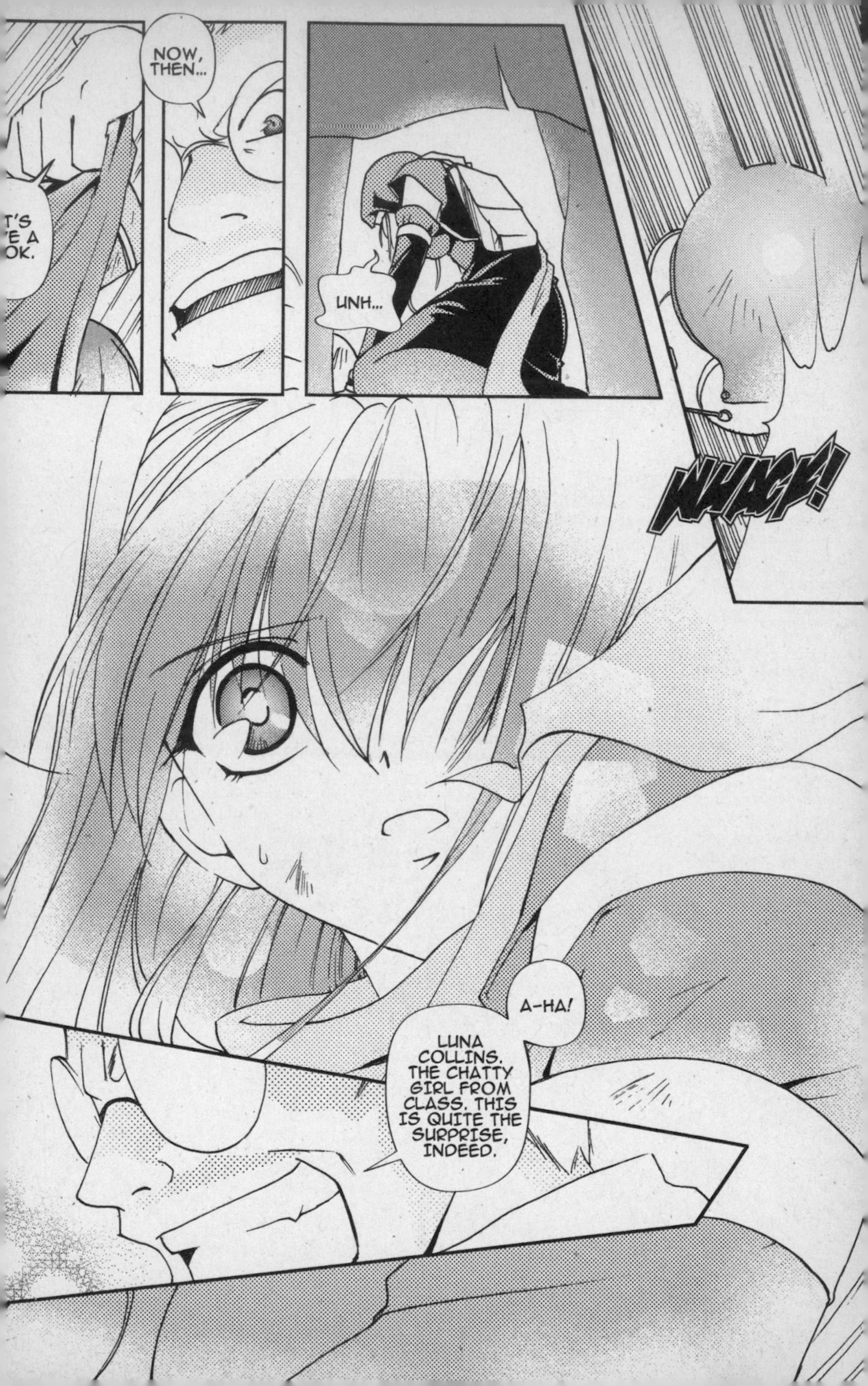
WHACK!
UNH...
NOW, THEN...
A-HA!
LUNA COLLINS. THE CHATTY GIRL FROM CLASS. THIS IS QUITE THE SURPRISE, INDEED.

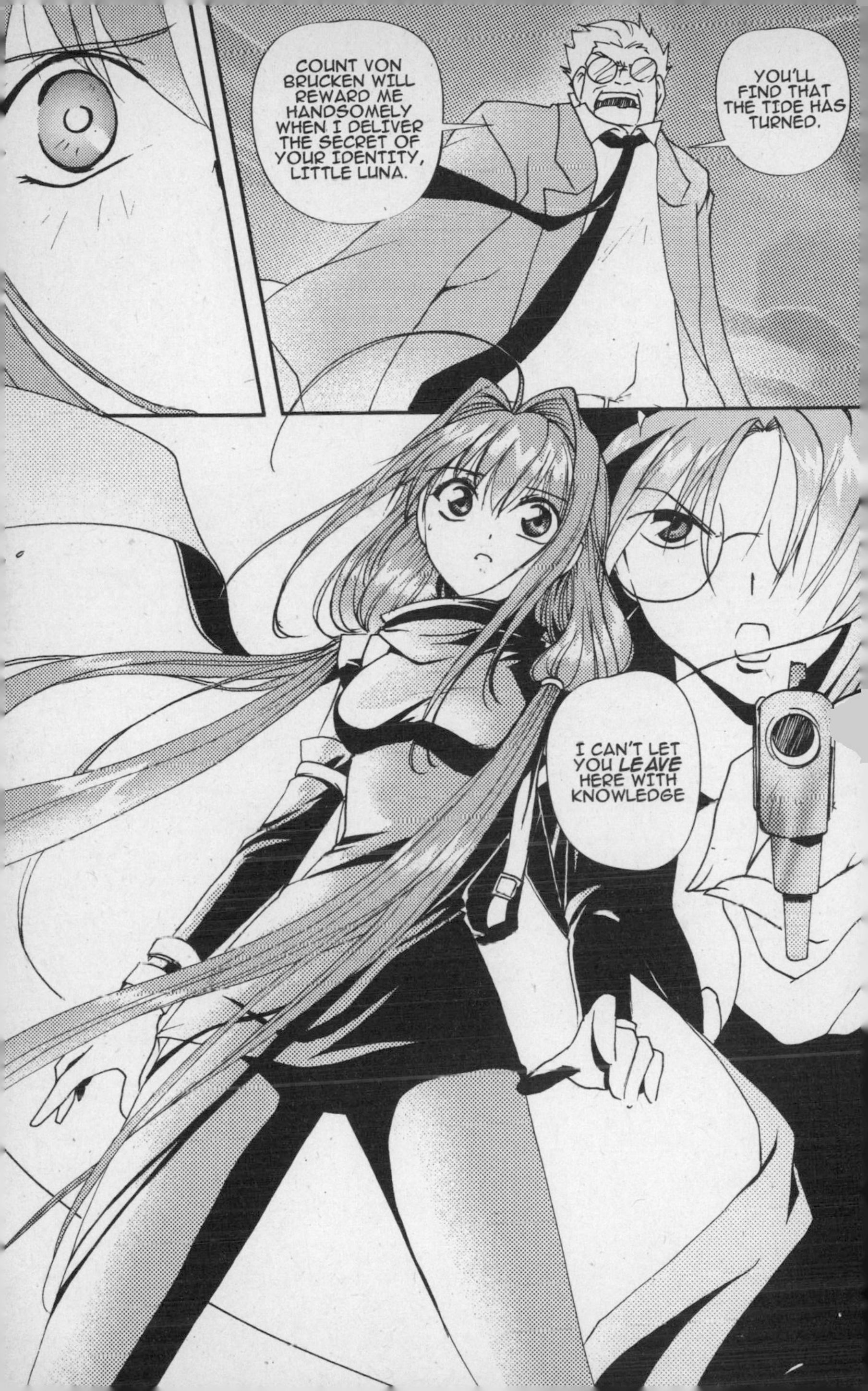
YOU'LL FIND THAT THE TIDE HAS TURNED.
COUNT VON BRUCKEN WILL REWARD ME HANDSOMELY WHEN I DELIVER THE SECRET OF YOUR IDENTITY, LITTLE LUNA.
I CAN'T LET YOU *LEAVE* HERE WITH KNOWLEDGE

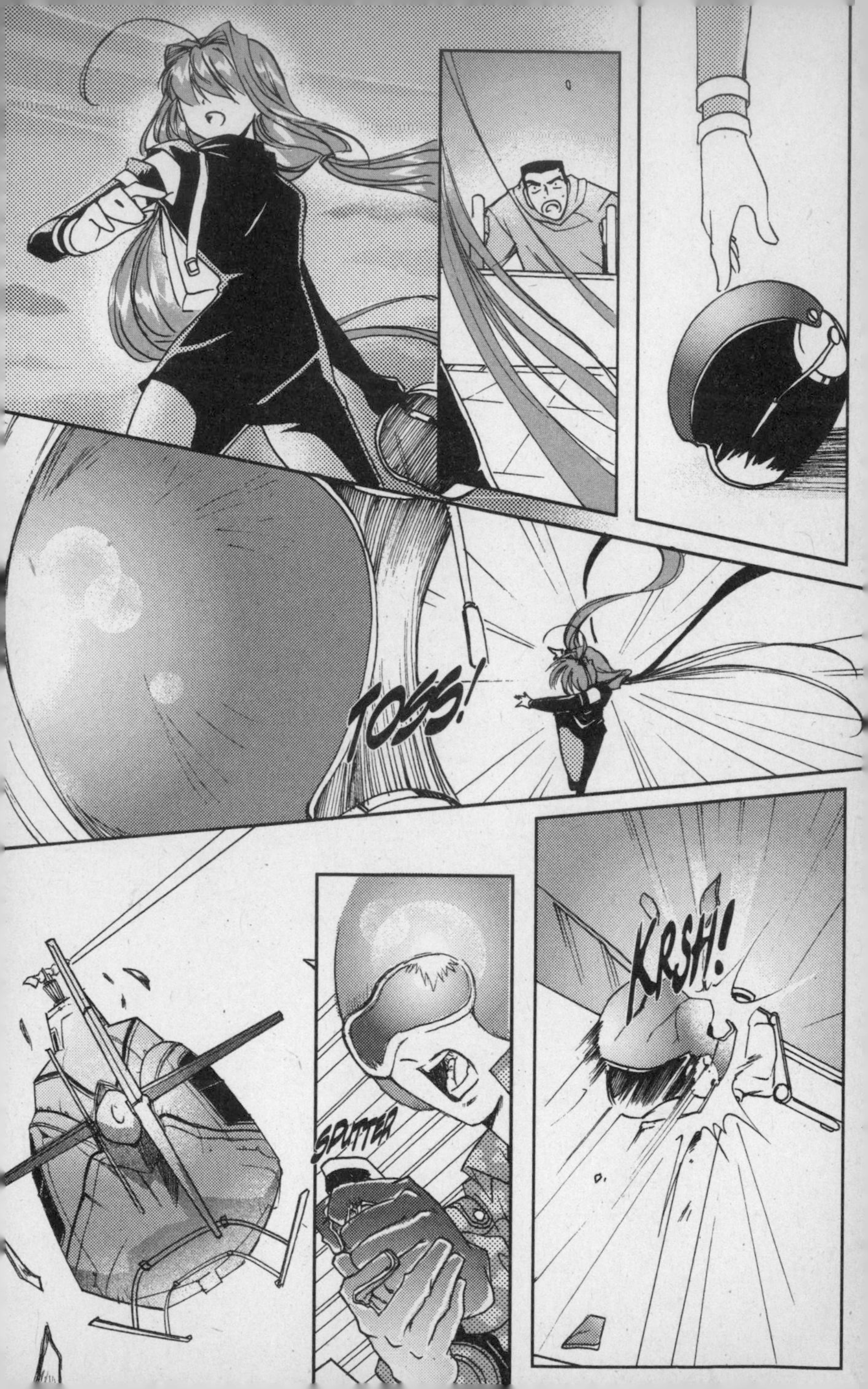
TOSS!
KRSH!
SPUTTER

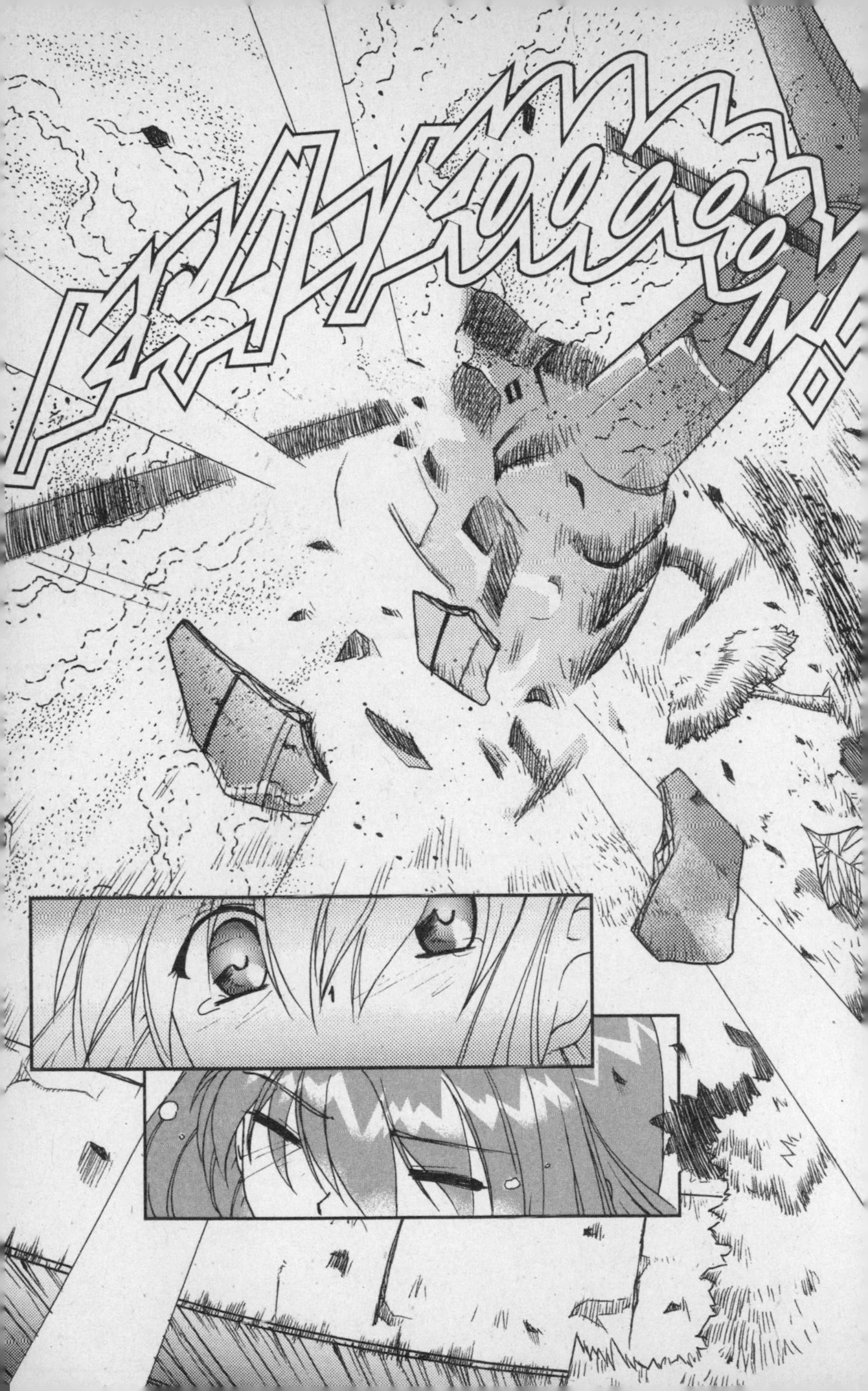

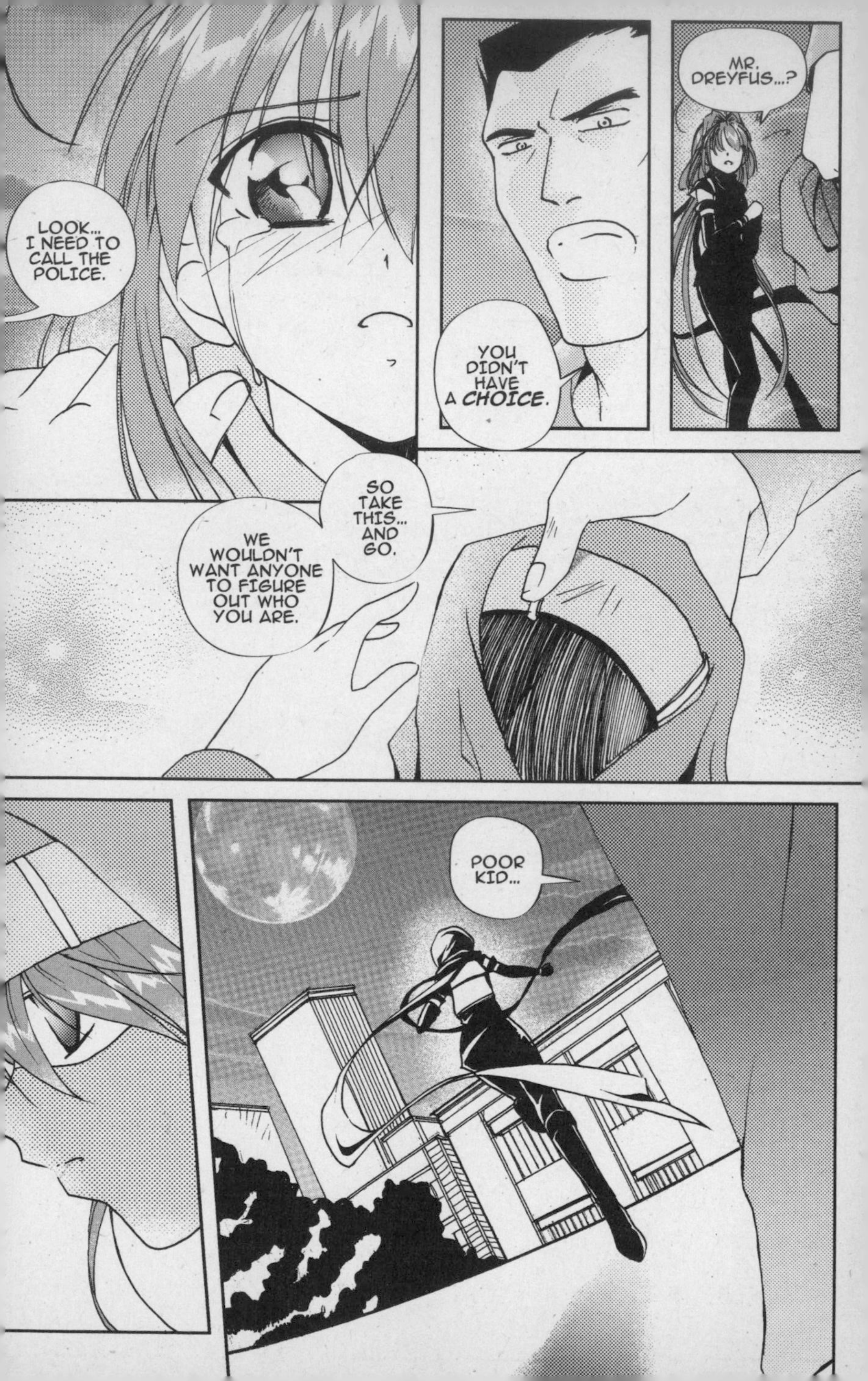
MR. DREYFUS...?
YOU DIDN'T HAVE A CHOICE.
LOOK... I NEED TO CALL THE POLICE.
SO TAKE THIS... AND GO.
WE WOULDN'T WANT ANYONE TO FIGURE OUT WHO YOU ARE.
POOR KID...

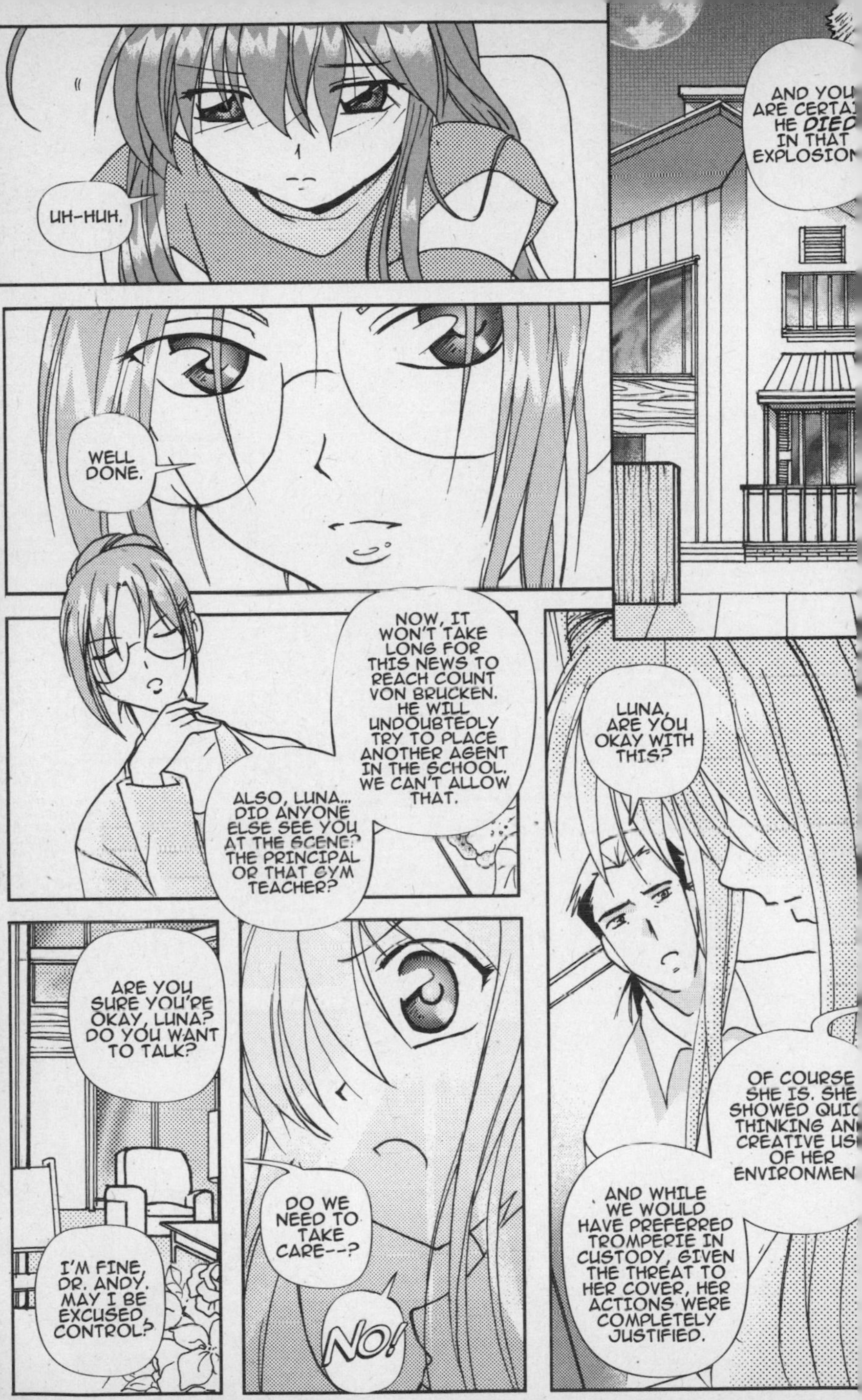
AND YOU ARE CERTAI HE *DIED* IN THAT EXPLOSION
UH-HUH.
WELL DONE.
LUNA, ARE YOU OKAY WITH THIS?
OF COURSE SHE IS. SHE SHOWED QUIC THINKING AN CREATIVE US OF HER ENVIRONMEN
AND WHILE WE WOULD HAVE PREFERRED TROMPERIE IN CUSTODY, GIVEN THE THREAT TO HER COVER, HER ACTIONS WERE COMPLETELY JUSTIFIED.
NOW, IT WON'T TAKE LONG FOR THIS NEWS TO REACH COUNT VON BRUCKEN. HE WILL UNDOUBTEDLY TRY TO PLACE ANOTHER AGENT IN THE SCHOOL. WE CAN'T ALLOW THAT.
ALSO, LUNA... DID ANYONE ELSE SEE YOU AT THE SCENE? THE PRINCIPAL OR THAT GYM TEACHER?
DO WE NEED TO TAKE CARE--?
NO!
ARE YOU SURE YOU'RE OKAY, LUNA? DO YOU WANT TO TALK?
I'M FINE, DR. ANDY. MAY I BE EXCUSED, CONTROL?

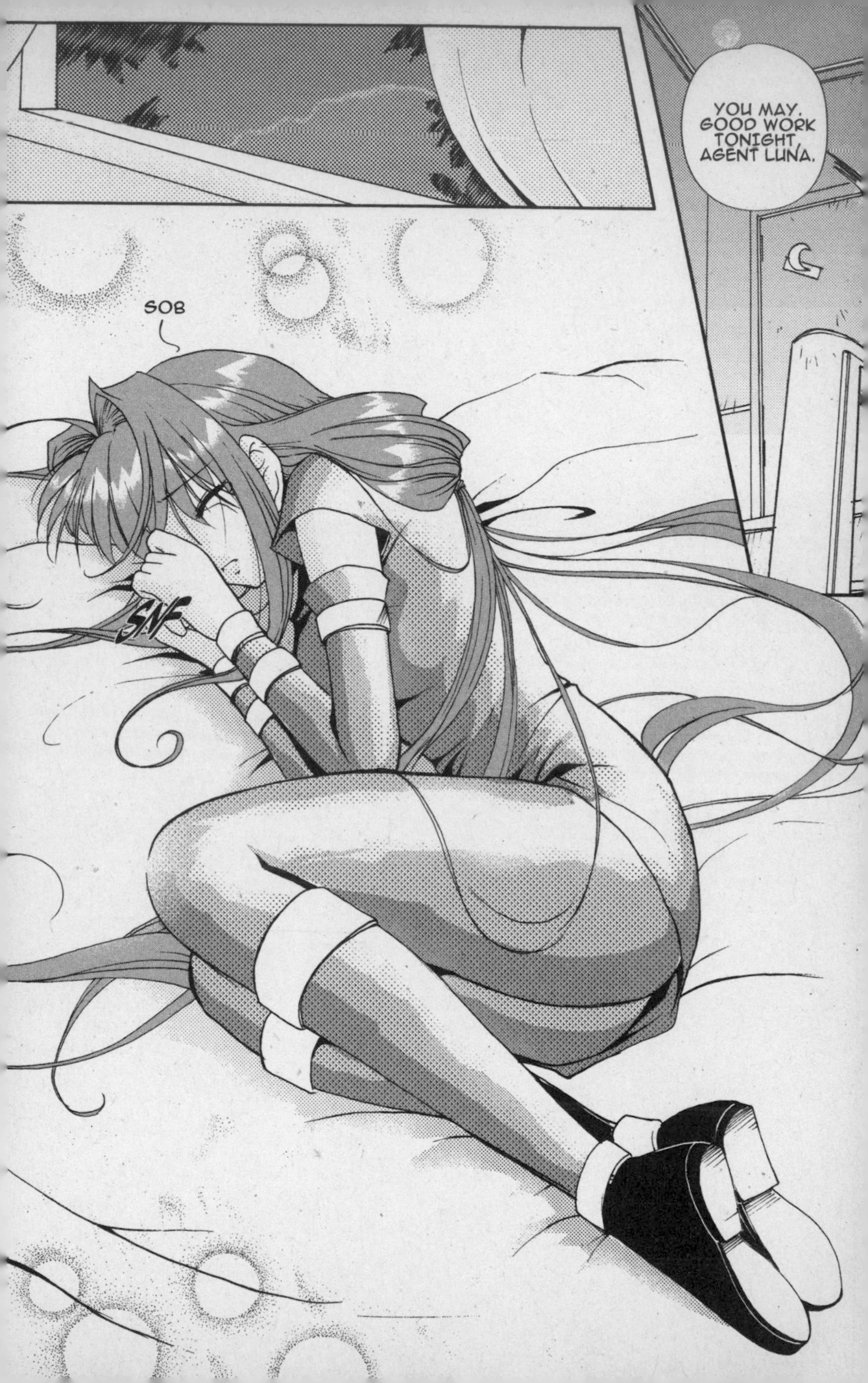
YOU MAY. GOOD WORK TONIGHT, AGENT LUNA.
SOB
SNF

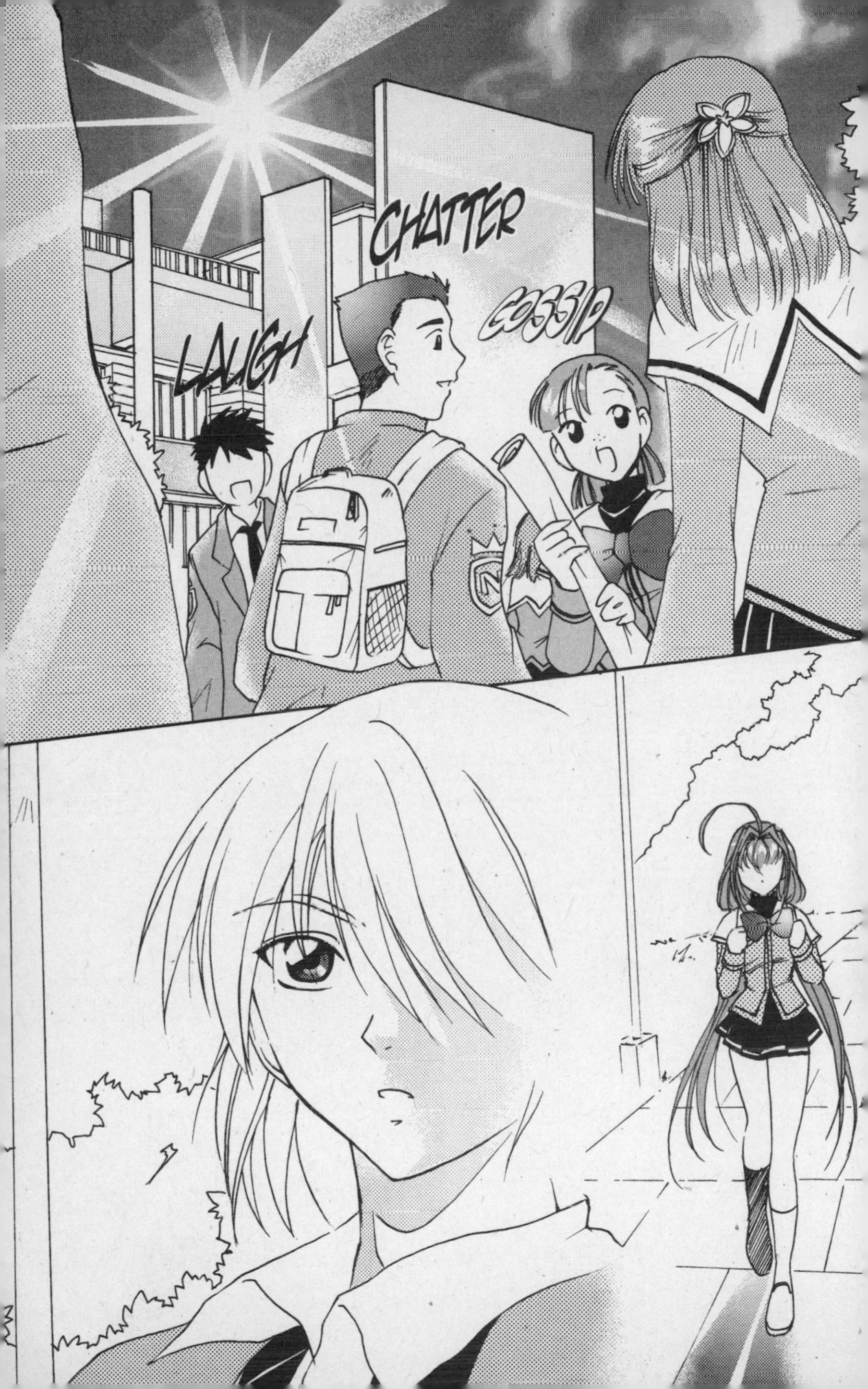
CHATTER
GOSSIP
LAUGH

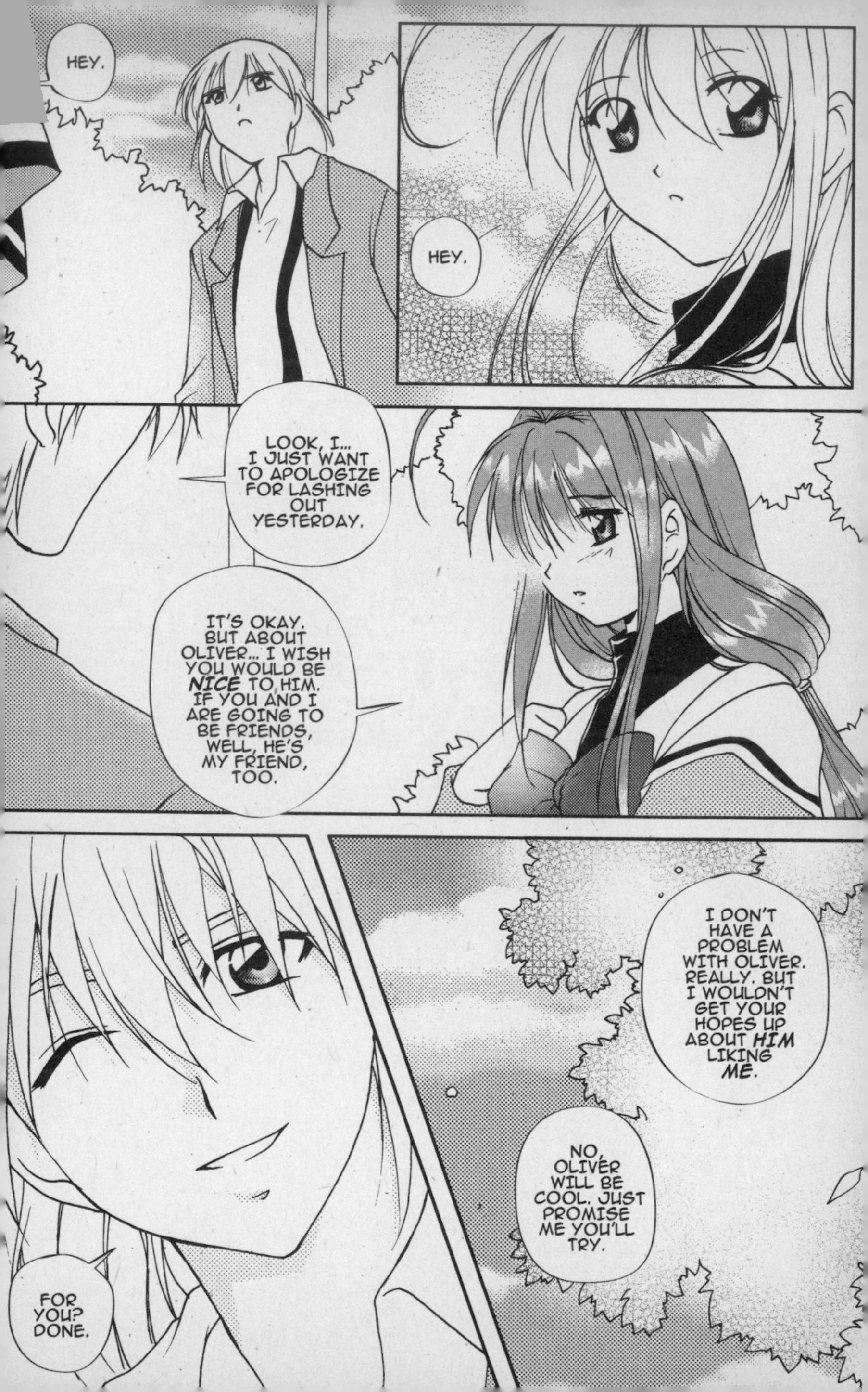
HEY.
HEY.
LOOK, I... I JUST WANT TO APOLOGIZE FOR LASHING OUT YESTERDAY.
IT'S OKAY. BUT ABOUT OLIVER... I WISH YOU WOULD BE NICE TO HIM. IF YOU AND I ARE GOING TO BE FRIENDS, WELL, HE'S MY FRIEND, TOO.
I DON'T HAVE A PROBLEM WITH OLIVER. REALLY. BUT I WOULDN'T GET YOUR HOPES UP ABOUT HIM LIKING ME.
NO, OLIVER WILL BE COOL. JUST PROMISE ME YOU'LL TRY.
FOR YOU? DONE.

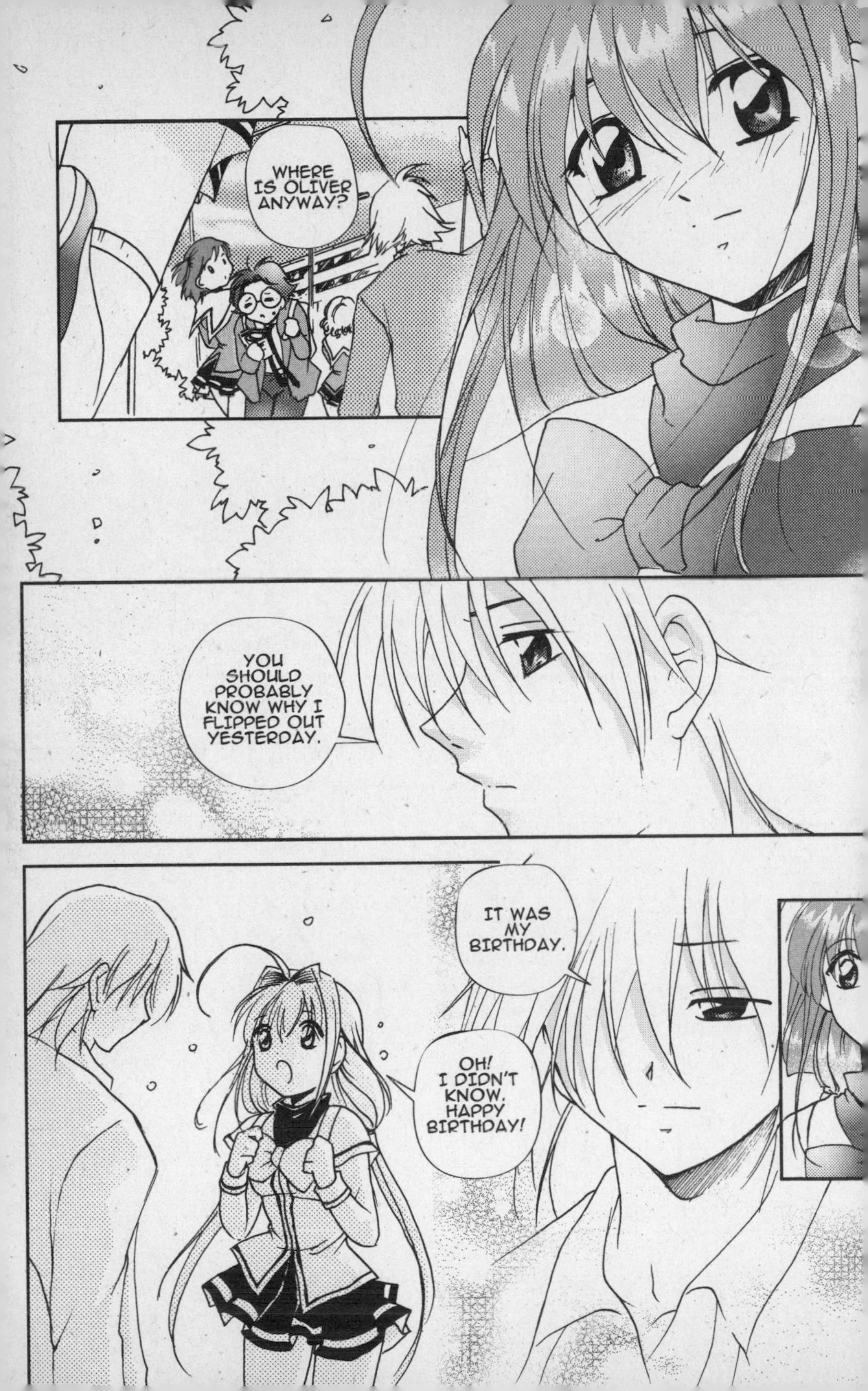
WHERE IS OLIVER ANYWAY?
YOU SHOULD PROBABLY KNOW WHY I FLIPPED OUT YESTERDAY.
IT WAS MY BIRTHDAY.
OH! I DIDN'T KNOW. HAPPY BIRTHDAY!

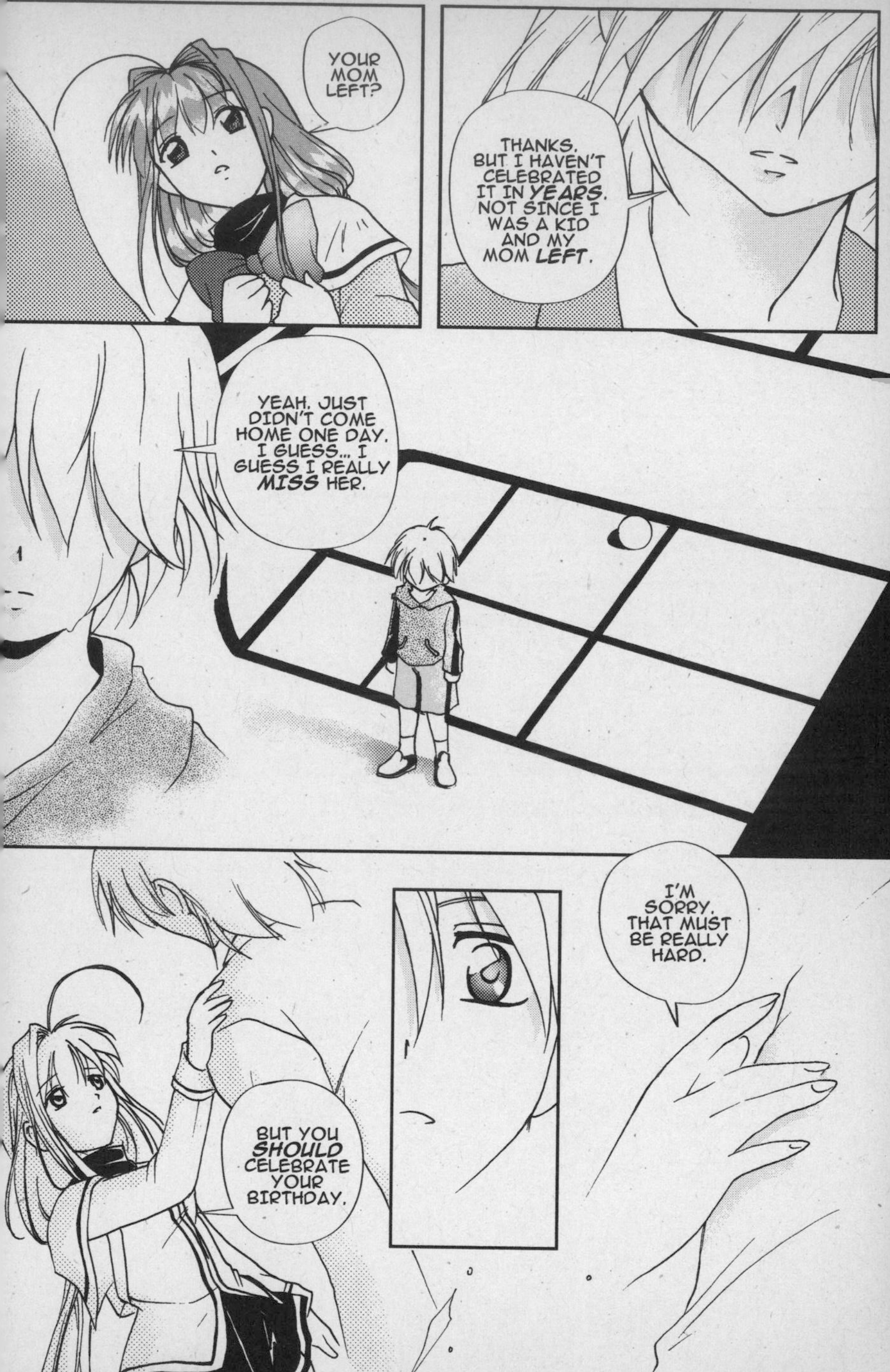
THANKS. BUT I HAVEN'T CELEBRATED IT IN YEARS. NOT SINCE I WAS A KID AND MY MOM LEFT.
YOUR MOM LEFT?
YEAH. JUST DIDN'T COME HOME ONE DAY. I GUESS... I GUESS I REALLY MISS HER.
I'M SORRY. THAT MUST BE REALLY HARD.
BUT YOU SHOULD CELEBRATE YOUR BIRTHDAY.

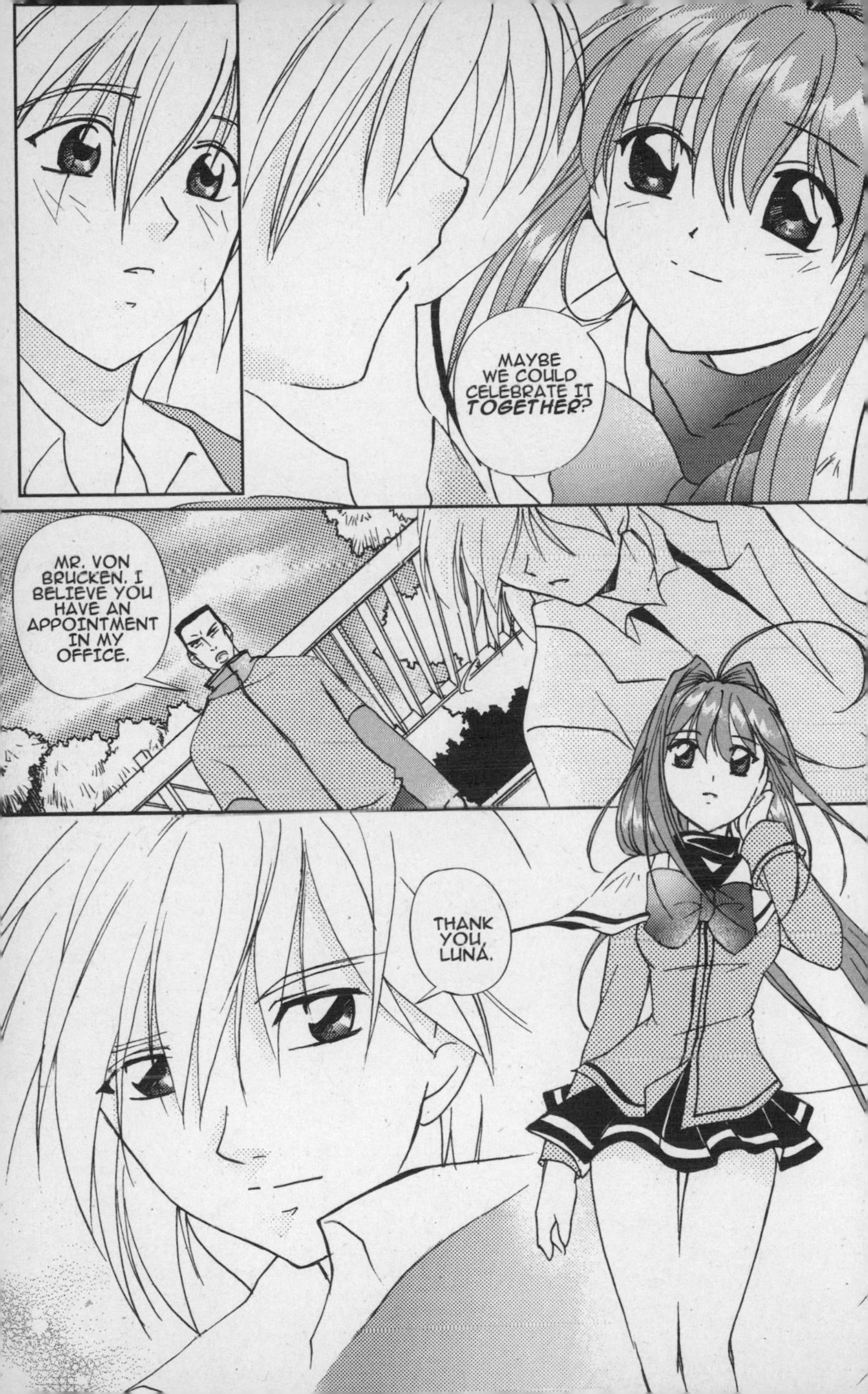
MAYBE WE COULD CELEBRATE IT TOGETHER?
MR. VON BRUCKEN. I BELIEVE YOU HAVE AN APPOINTMENT IN MY OFFICE.
THANK YOU, LUNA.

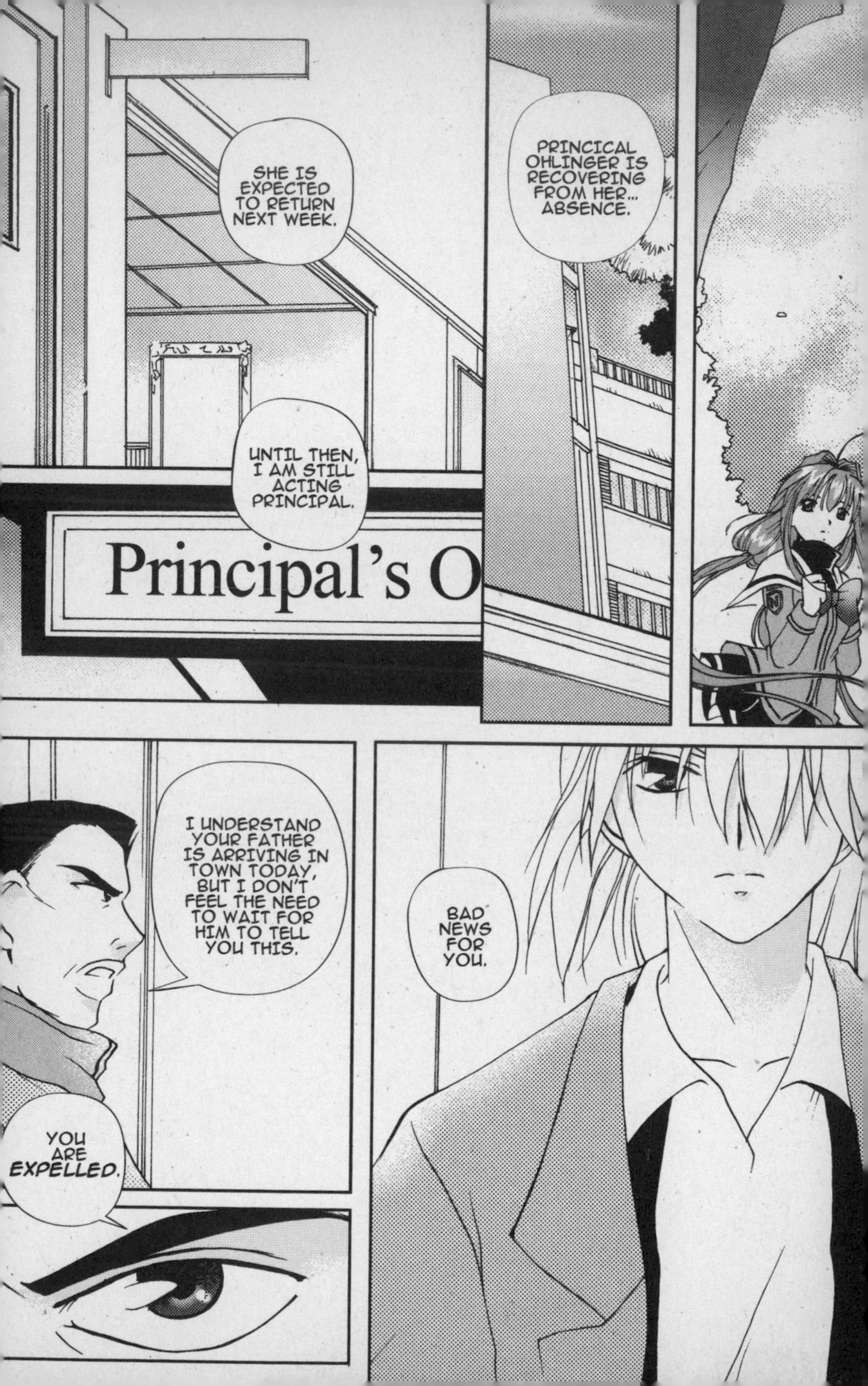
PRINCICAL OHLINGER IS RECOVERING FROM HER... ABSENCE.
SHE IS EXPECTED TO RETURN NEXT WEEK.
UNTIL THEN, I AM STILL ACTING PRINCIPAL.
Principal's O
BAD NEWS FOR YOU.
I UNDERSTAND YOUR FATHER IS ARRIVING IN TOWN TODAY, BUT I DON'T FEEL THE NEED TO WAIT FOR HIM TO TELL YOU THIS.
YOU ARE EXPELLED.

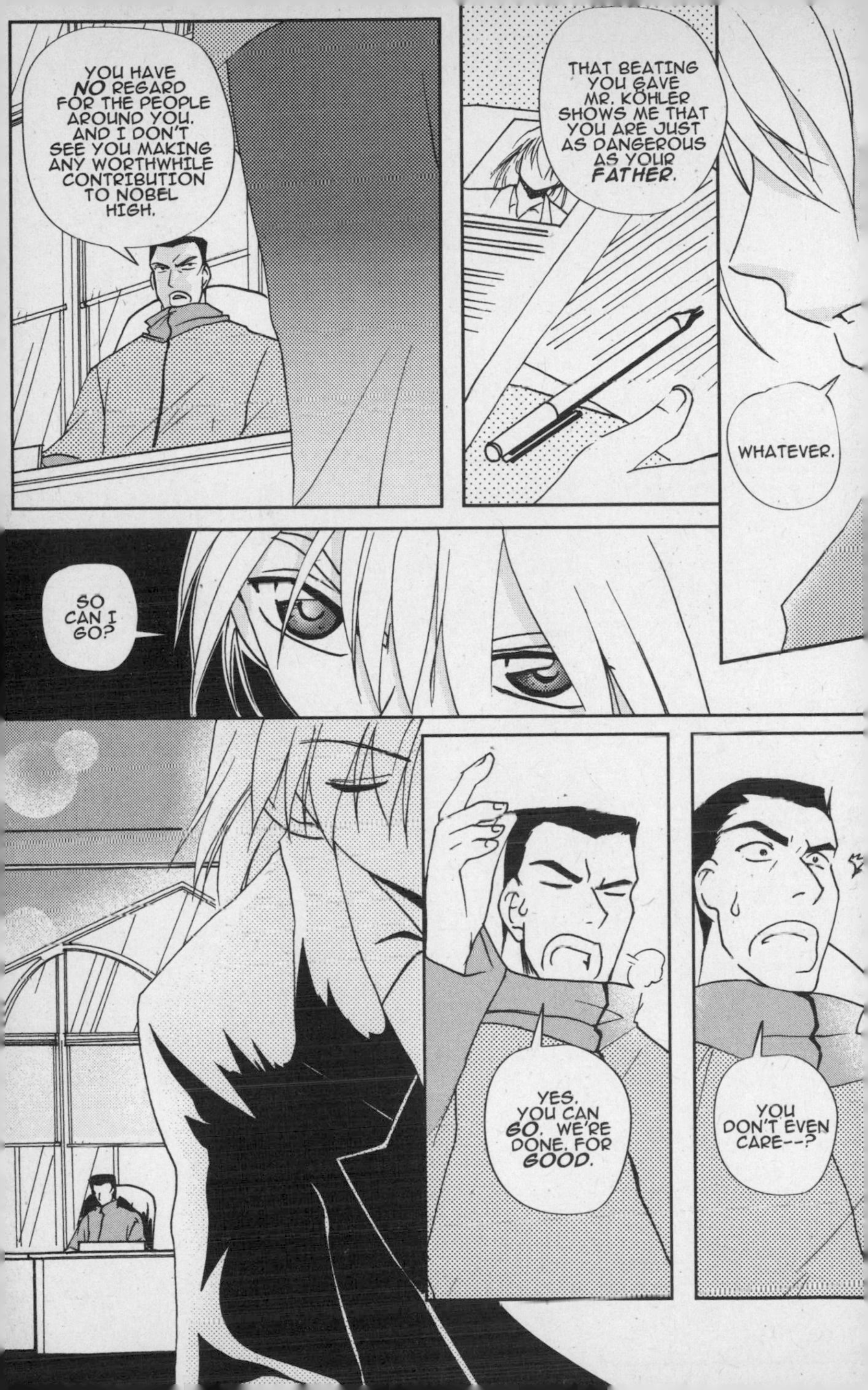
WHATEVER.
THAT BEATING YOU GAVE MR. KOHLER SHOWS ME THAT YOU ARE JUST AS DANGEROUS AS YOUR FATHER.
YOU HAVE NO REGARD FOR THE PEOPLE AROUND YOU. AND I DON'T SEE YOU MAKING ANY WORTHWHILE CONTRIBUTION TO NOBEL HIGH.
SO CAN I GO?
YOU DON'T EVEN CARE--?
YES. YOU CAN GO. WE'RE DONE. FOR GOOD.

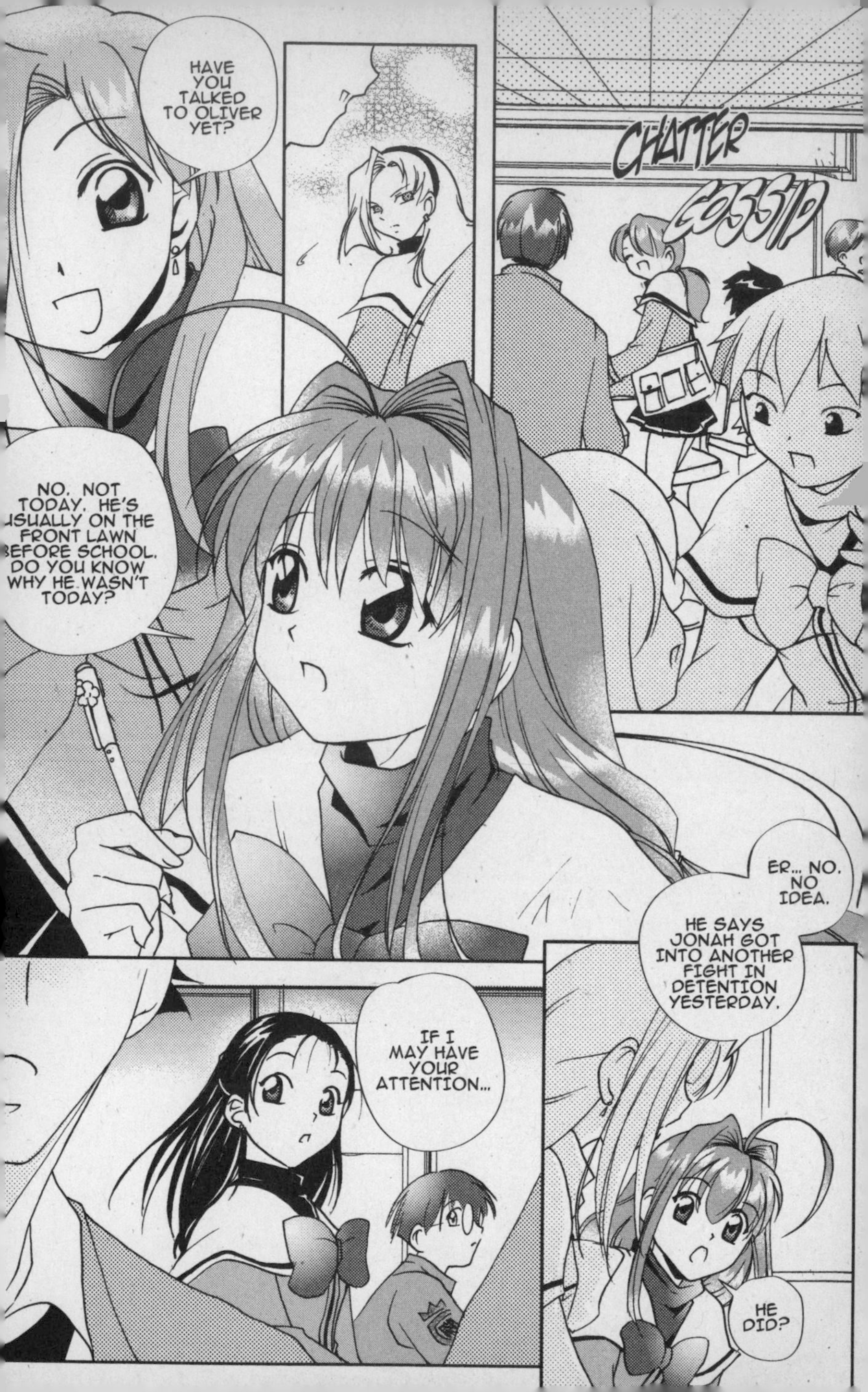
CHATTER
GOSSIP
HAVE YOU TALKED TO OLIVER YET?
NO. NOT TODAY. HE'S USUALLY ON THE FRONT LAWN BEFORE SCHOOL. DO YOU KNOW WHY HE WASN'T TODAY?
ER... NO. NO IDEA.
HE SAYS JONAH GOT INTO ANOTHER FIGHT IN DETENTION YESTERDAY.
HE DID?
IF I MAY HAVE YOUR ATTENTION...

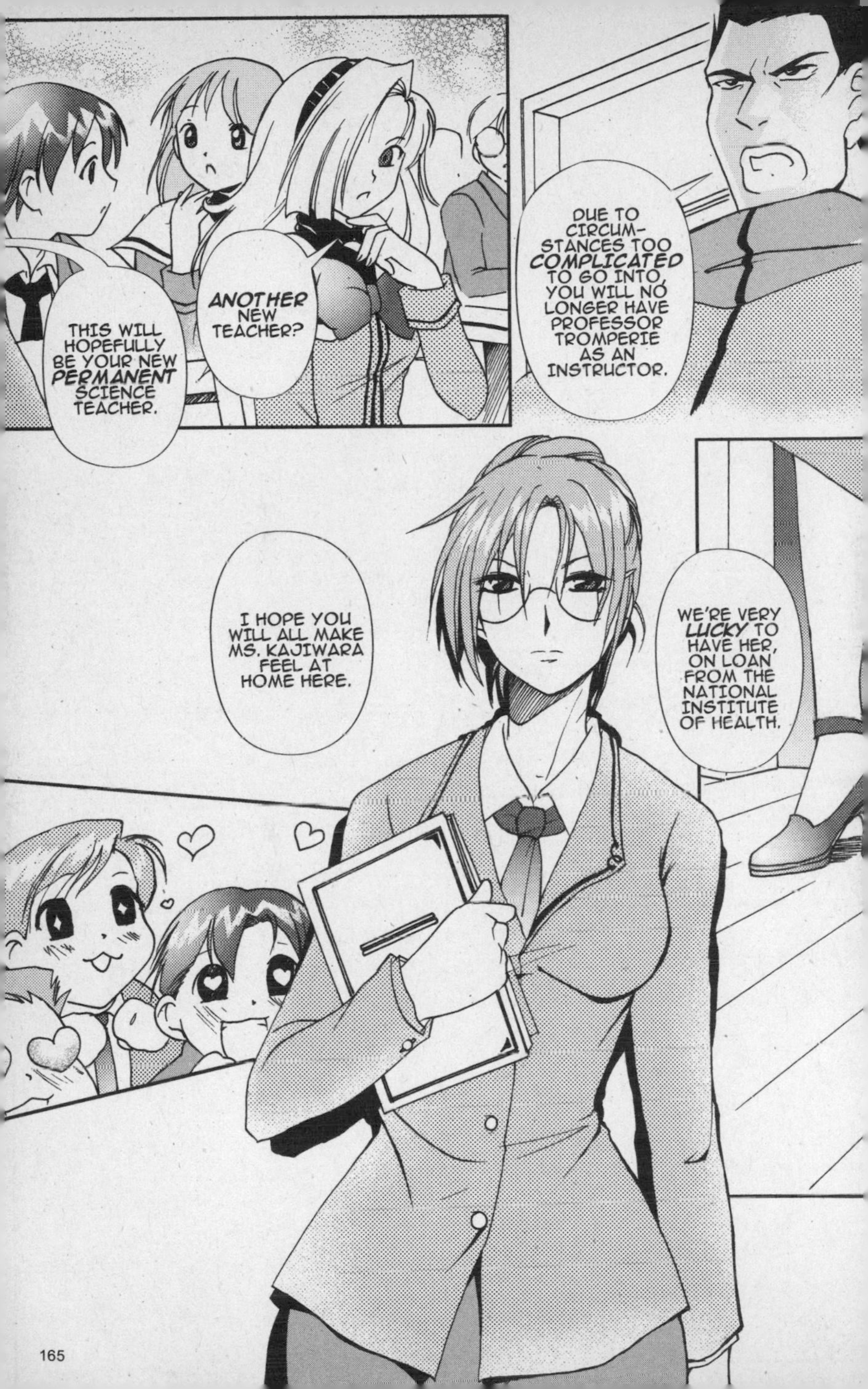
DUE TO CIRCUM-STANCES TOO COMPLICATED TO GO INTO, YOU WILL NO LONGER HAVE PROFESSOR TROMPERIE AS AN INSTRUCTOR.
ANOTHER NEW TEACHER?
THIS WILL HOPEFULLY BE YOUR NEW PERMANENT SCIENCE TEACHER.
WE'RE VERY LUCKY TO HAVE HER, ON LOAN FROM THE NATIONAL INSTITUTE OF HEALTH.
I HOPE YOU WILL ALL MAKE MS. KAJIWARA FEEL AT HOME HERE.

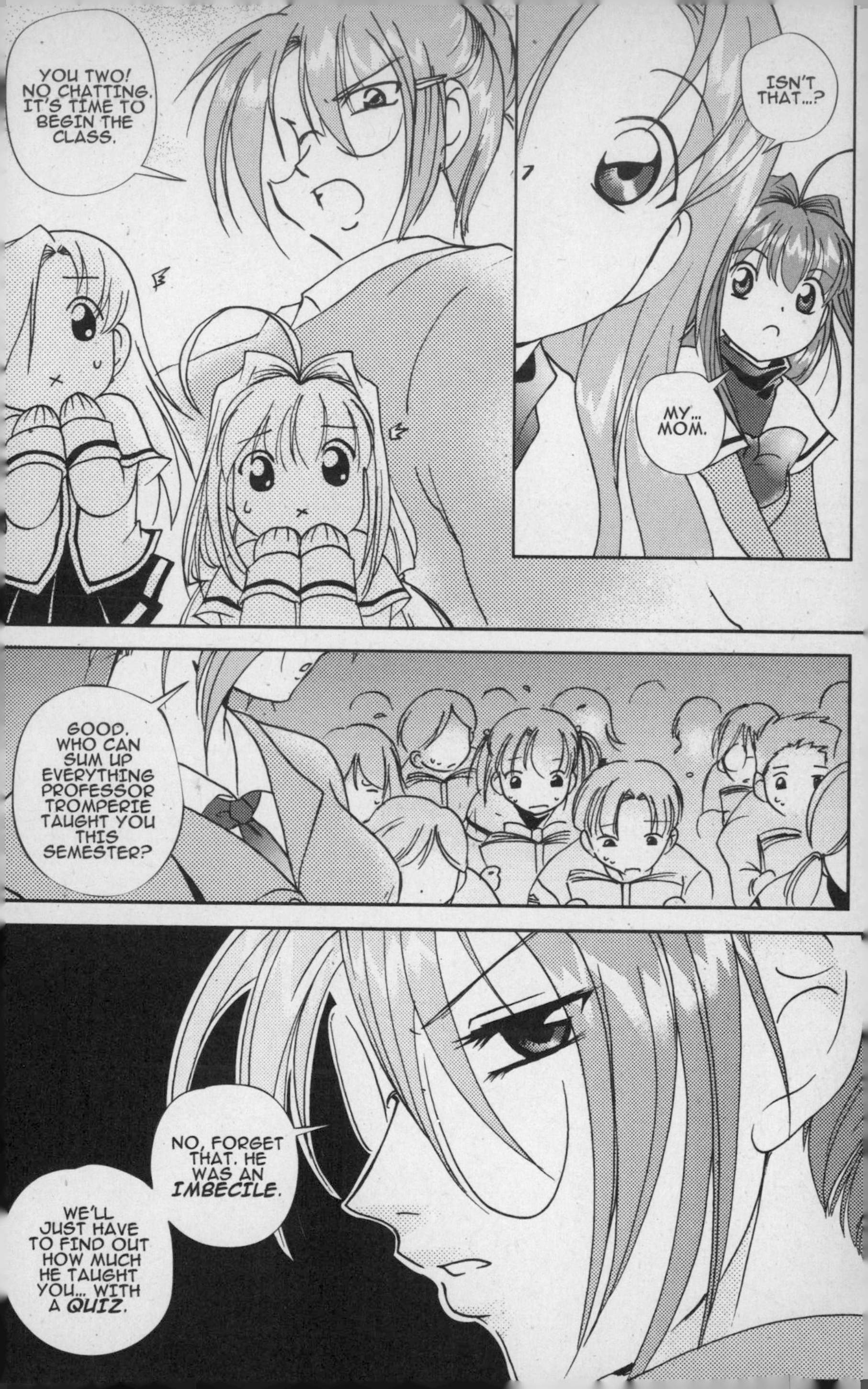
ISN'T THAT...?
MY... MOM.
YOU TWO! NO CHATTING. IT'S TIME TO BEGIN THE CLASS.
GOOD. WHO CAN SUM UP EVERYTHING PROFESSOR TROMPERIE TAUGHT YOU THIS SEMESTER?
NO, FORGET THAT. HE WAS AN *IMBECILE*.
WE'LL JUST HAVE TO FIND OUT HOW MUCH HE TAUGHT YOU... WITH A **QUIZ**.

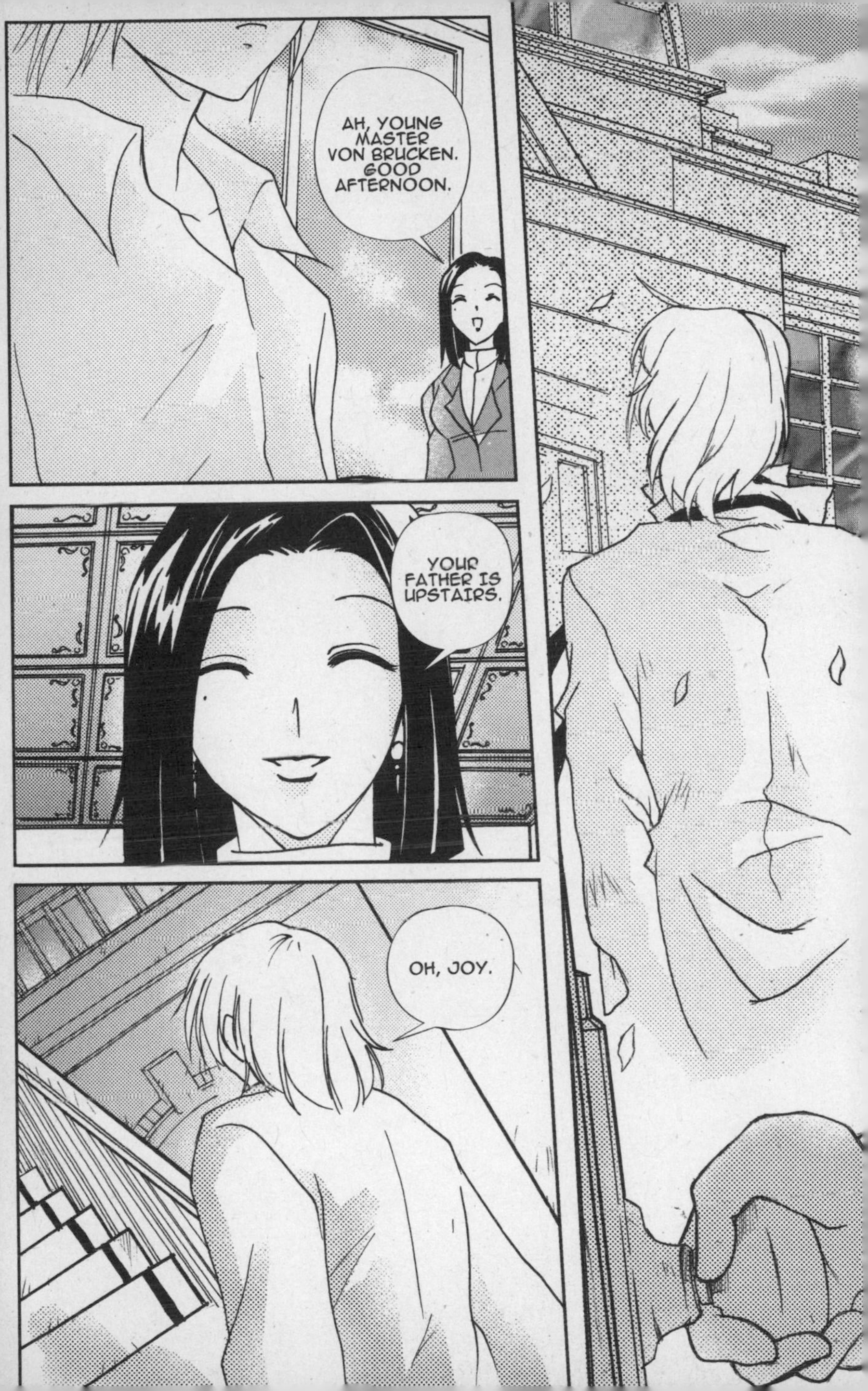
AH, YOUNG MASTER VON BRUCKEN. GOOD AFTERNOON.
YOUR FATHER IS UPSTAIRS.
OH, JOY.

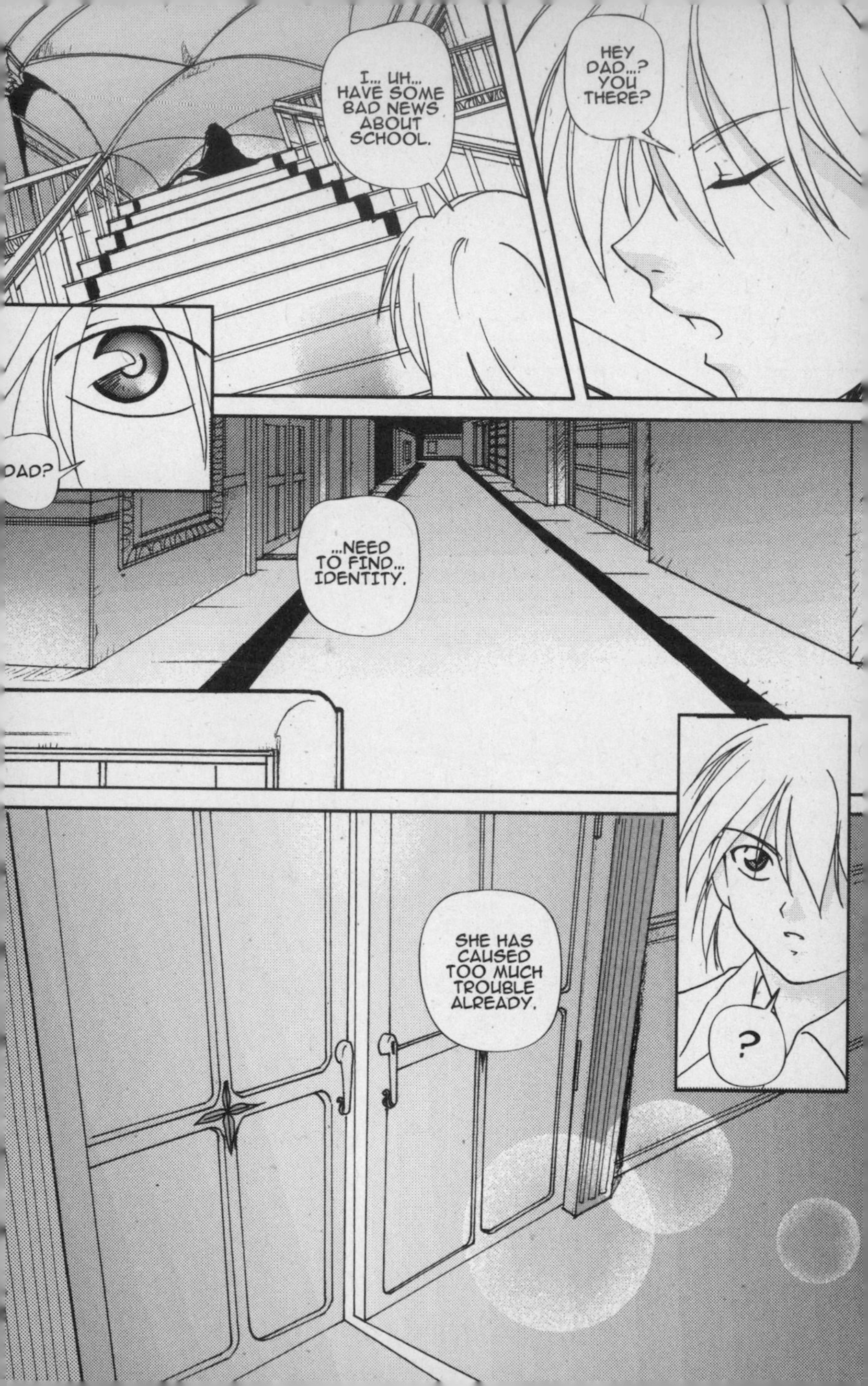
HEY DAD...? YOU THERE?
I... UH... HAVE SOME BAD NEWS ABOUT SCHOOL.
DAD?
...NEED TO FIND... IDENTITY.
SHE HAS CAUSED TOO MUCH TROUBLE ALREADY.
?

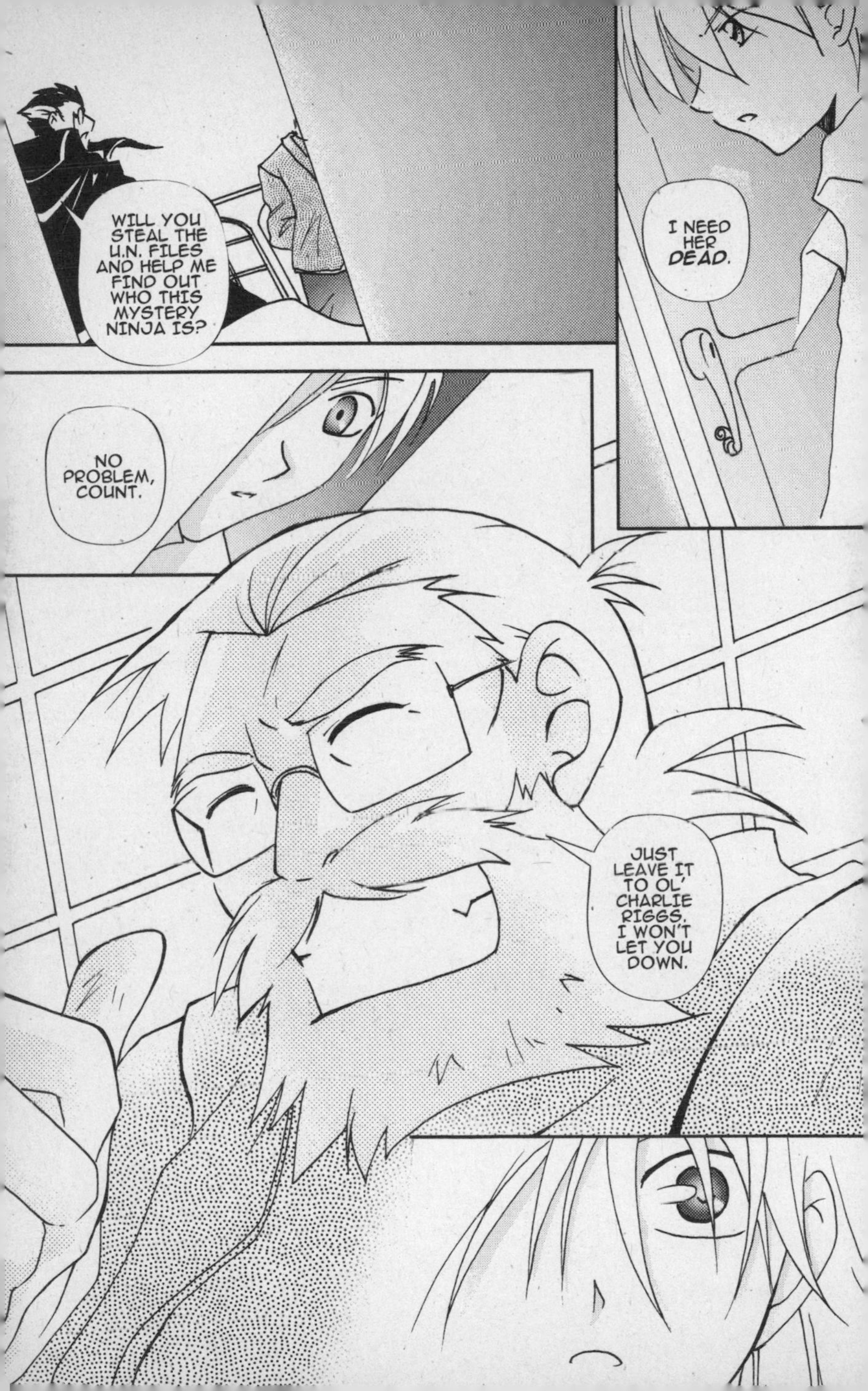
I NEED HER *DEAD*.
WILL YOU STEAL THE U.N. FILES AND HELP ME FIND OUT WHO THIS MYSTERY NINJA IS?
NO PROBLEM, COUNT.
JUST LEAVE IT TO OL' CHARLIE RIGGS. I WON'T LET YOU DOWN.

MEMORANDUM

TO: OUR READERS
FROM: NUNZIO DEFILIPPIS AND CHRISTINA WEIR
RE: AMAZING AGENT LUNA

Welcome back to Nobel High School.

Volume Three of Amazing Agent Luna is upon us, and Shiei's work keeps getting better and better, doesn't it? We didn't think it was possible, but she's done better work here than last time around.

This is the volume where the secrets and the deceptions begin to swirl. Things are going to get tricky for young Agent Luna, and her friends, and here's where a lot of that starts.

The trick with this book has always been to strike the balance between a spy story and a fish-out-of-water high school story. We've spent two volumes focusing on the second part. That's not going away, but the spy story is going to start taking center stage for a bit.

So we worried that the tone of the book would shift. After all, there's death in spy stories, and we don't want anyone being thrown when Luna's mission gets into life and death stakes. This was the volume where we had to strike the new balance. How do we put the darkness in, without hurting the fun mood that we worked so hard to establish in Volumes 1 & 2?

Fortunately, we took this as a challenge, and not a problem. But we got a big assist from Shiei. She keeps the book looking so open and fun, yet manages to capture the action scenes and the gravity of the stakes. To get what we mean, look at the first chapter of this volume. The rules have changed, but it's still Luna. Perfect.

So, we hope everyone goes along for the ride. It may have just gotten more bumpy, but hey… that's a good thing, right?

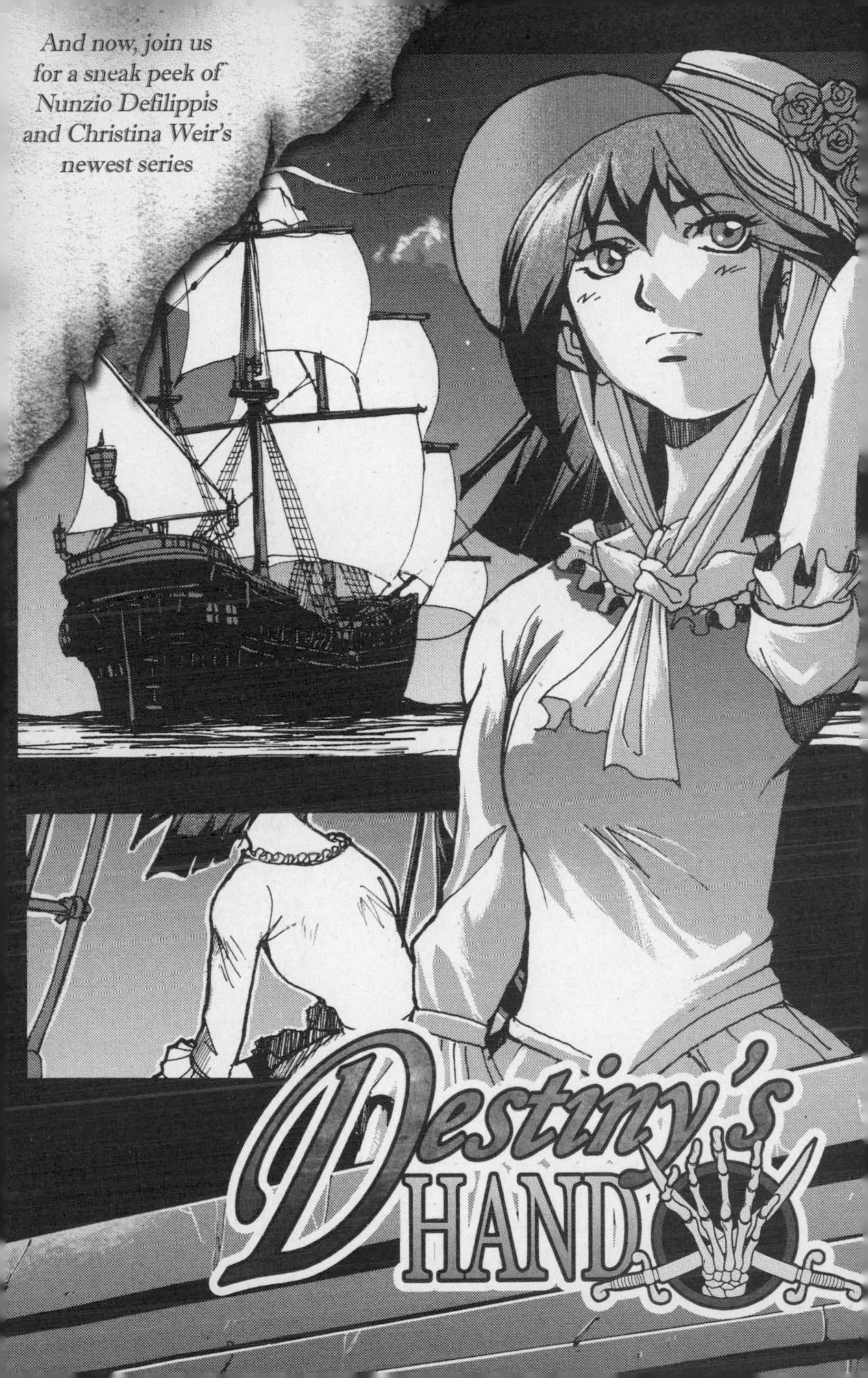
And now, join us for a sneak peek of Nunzio Defilippis and Christina Weir's newest series
Destiny's
HAND

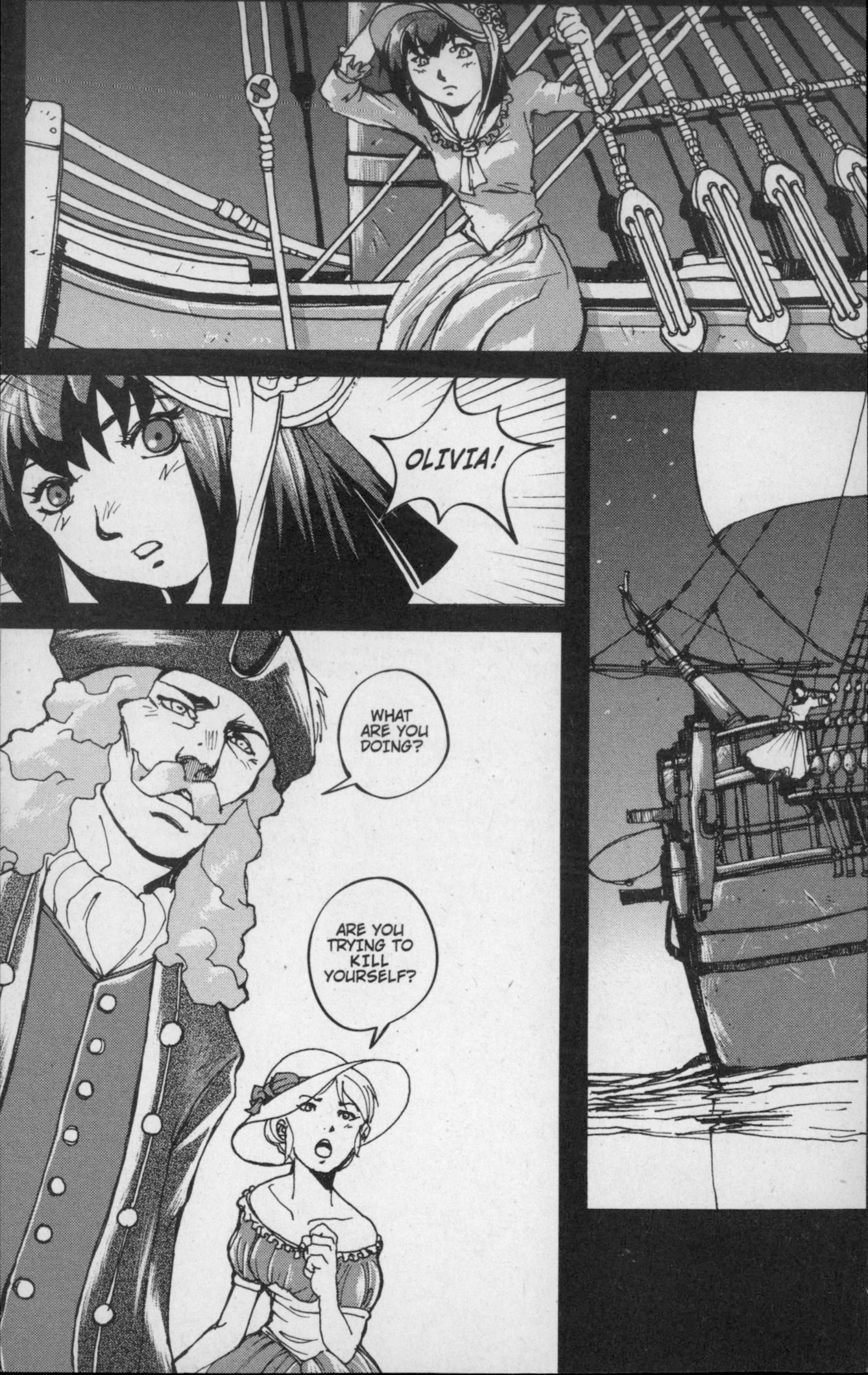
OLIVIA!
WHAT ARE YOU DOING?
ARE YOU TRYING TO KILL YOURSELF?

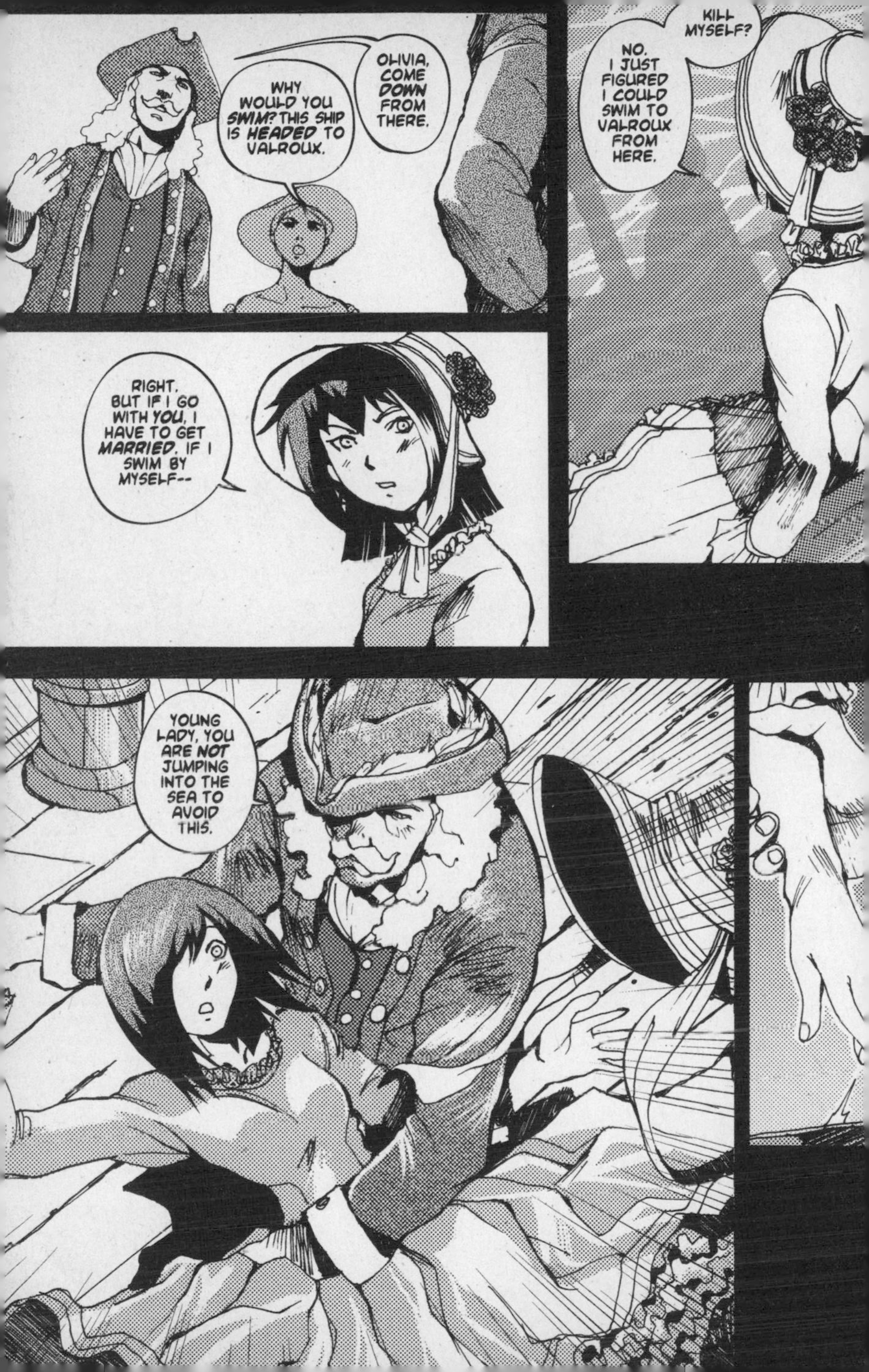
KILL MYSELF?
NO. I JUST FIGURED I COULD SWIM TO VALROUX FROM HERE.
OLIVIA, COME DOWN FROM THERE.
WHY WOULD YOU SWIM? THIS SHIP IS HEADED TO VALROUX.
RIGHT, BUT IF I GO WITH YOU, I HAVE TO GET MARRIED. IF I SWIM BY MYSELF--
YOUNG LADY, YOU ARE NOT JUMPING INTO THE SEA TO AVOID THIS.

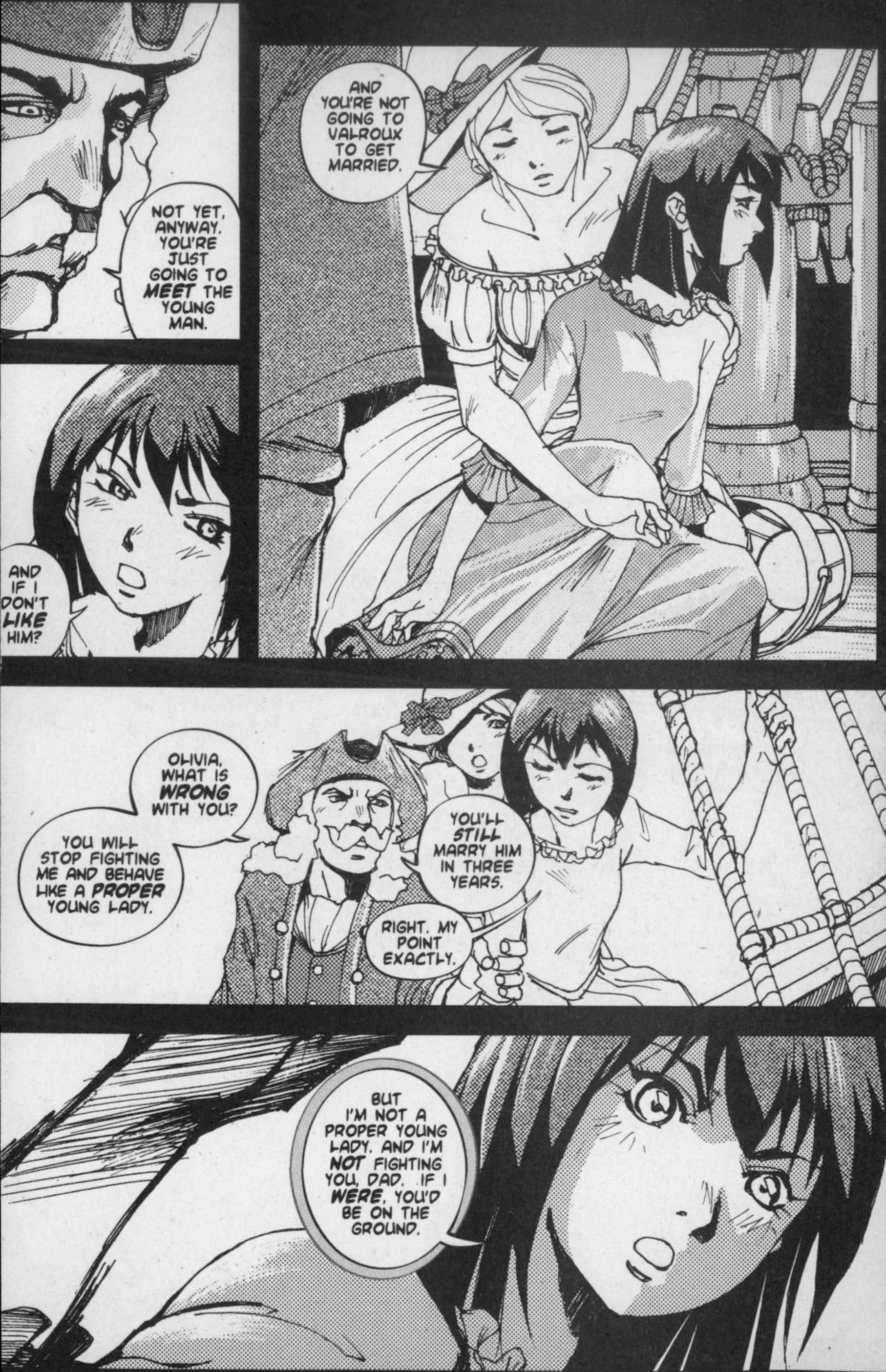
AND YOU'RE NOT GOING TO VALROUX TO GET MARRIED.
NOT YET, ANYWAY. YOU'RE JUST GOING TO MEET THE YOUNG MAN.
AND IF I DON'T LIKE HIM?
YOU'LL STILL MARRY HIM IN THREE YEARS.
RIGHT. MY POINT EXACTLY.
OLIVIA, WHAT IS WRONG WITH YOU?
YOU WILL STOP FIGHTING ME AND BEHAVE LIKE A PROPER YOUNG LADY.
BUT I'M NOT A PROPER YOUNG LADY. AND I'M NOT FIGHTING YOU, DAD. IF I WERE, YOU'D BE ON THE GROUND.

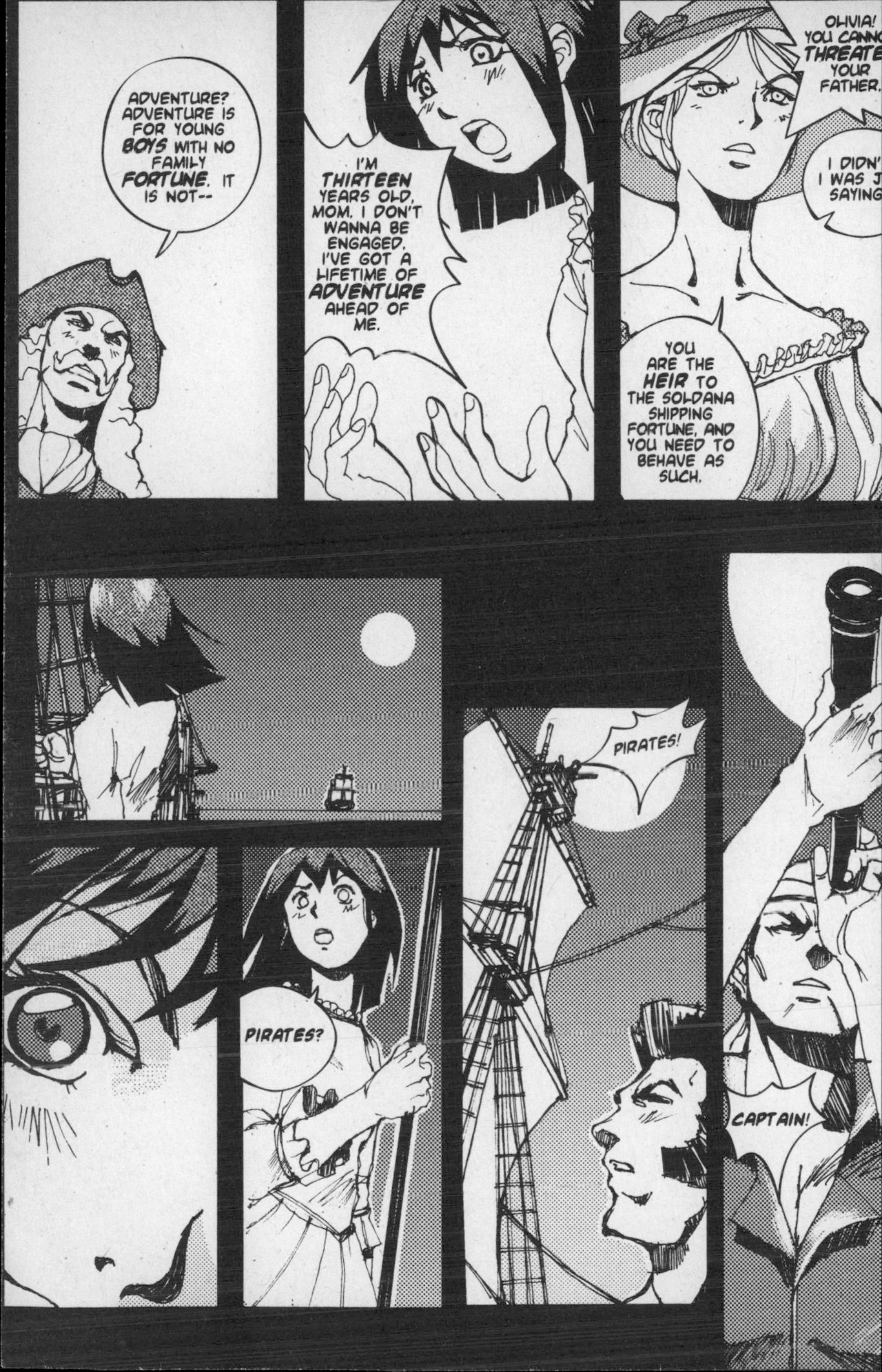
OLIVIA! YOU CANNO THREATE YOUR FATHER.
I DIDN' I WAS J SAYING
YOU ARE THE HEIR TO THE SOLDANA SHIPPING FORTUNE, AND YOU NEED TO BEHAVE AS SUCH.
I'M THIRTEEN YEARS OLD, MOM. I DON'T WANNA BE ENGAGED. I'VE GOT A LIFETIME OF ADVENTURE AHEAD OF ME.
ADVENTURE? ADVENTURE IS FOR YOUNG BOYS WITH NO FAMILY FORTUNE. IT IS NOT--
CAPTAIN!
PIRATES!
PIRATES?

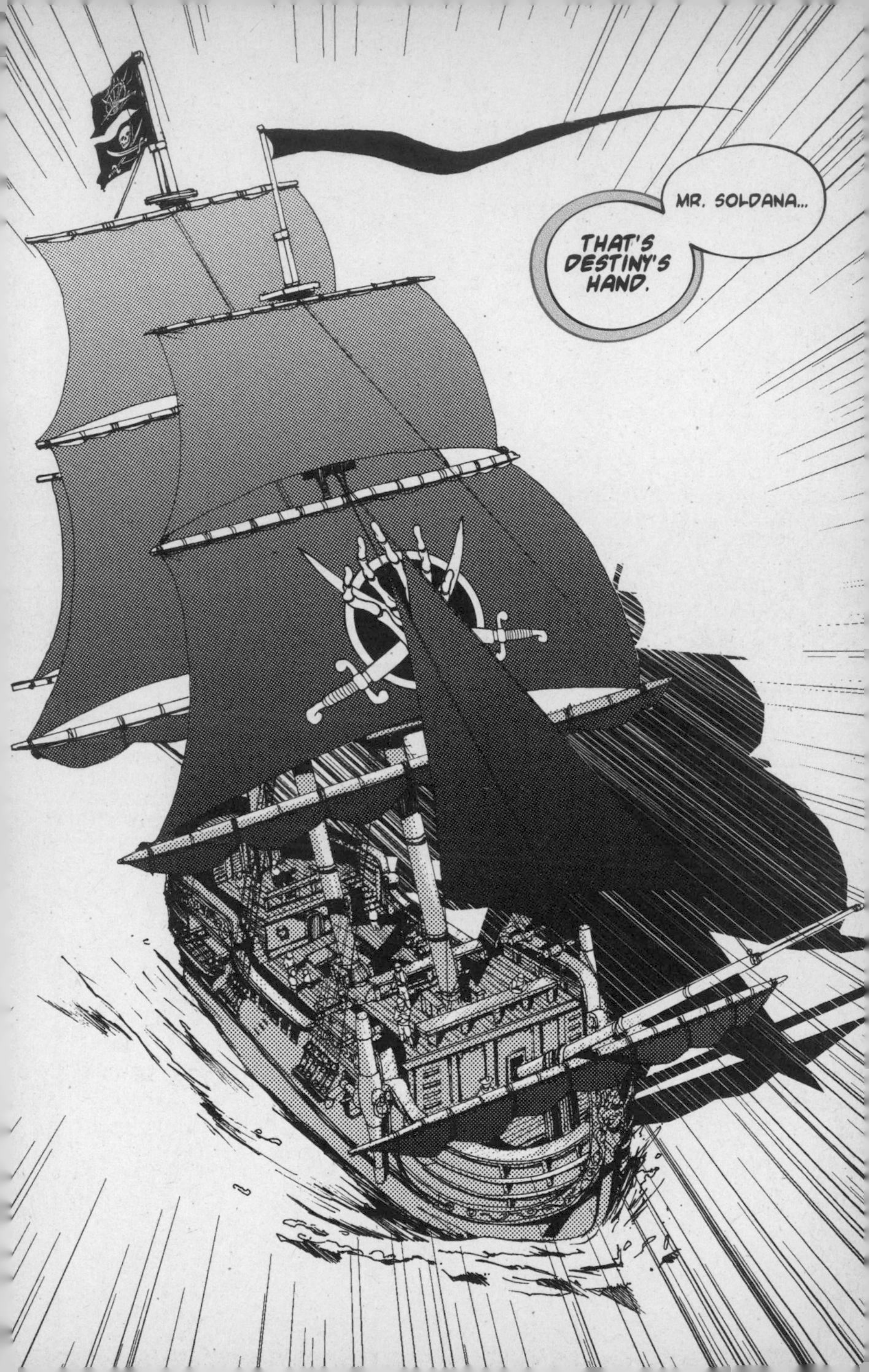
MR. SOLDANA...
THAT'S DESTINY'S HAND.

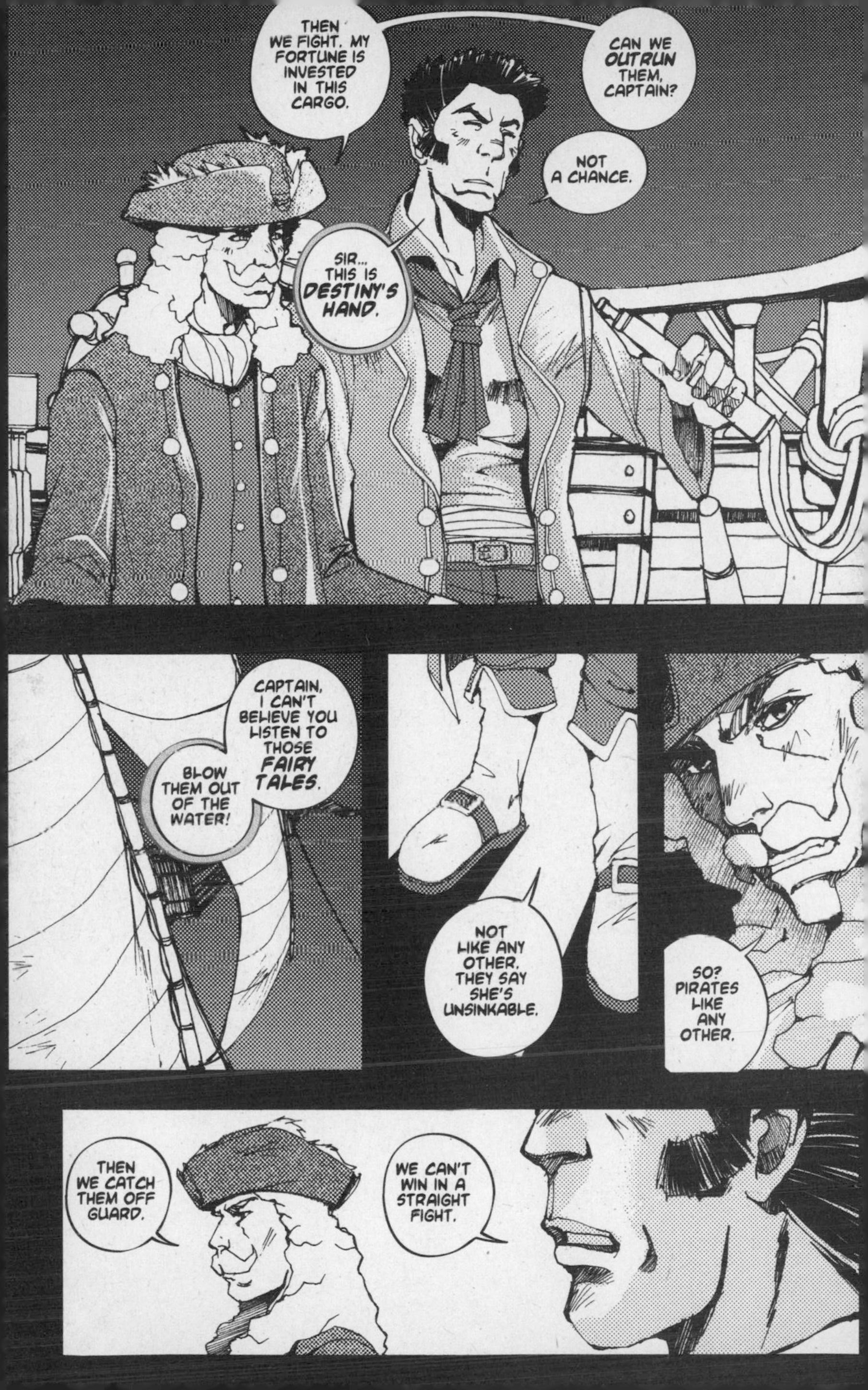
CAN WE OUTRUN THEM, CAPTAIN?
NOT A CHANCE.
THEN WE FIGHT. MY FORTUNE IS INVESTED IN THIS CARGO.
SIR... THIS IS DESTINY'S HAND.
SO? PIRATES LIKE ANY OTHER.
NOT LIKE ANY OTHER. THEY SAY SHE'S UNSINKABLE.
CAPTAIN, I CAN'T BELIEVE YOU LISTEN TO THOSE FAIRY TALES.
BLOW THEM OUT OF THE WATER!
WE CAN'T WIN IN A STRAIGHT FIGHT.
THEN WE CATCH THEM OFF GUARD.

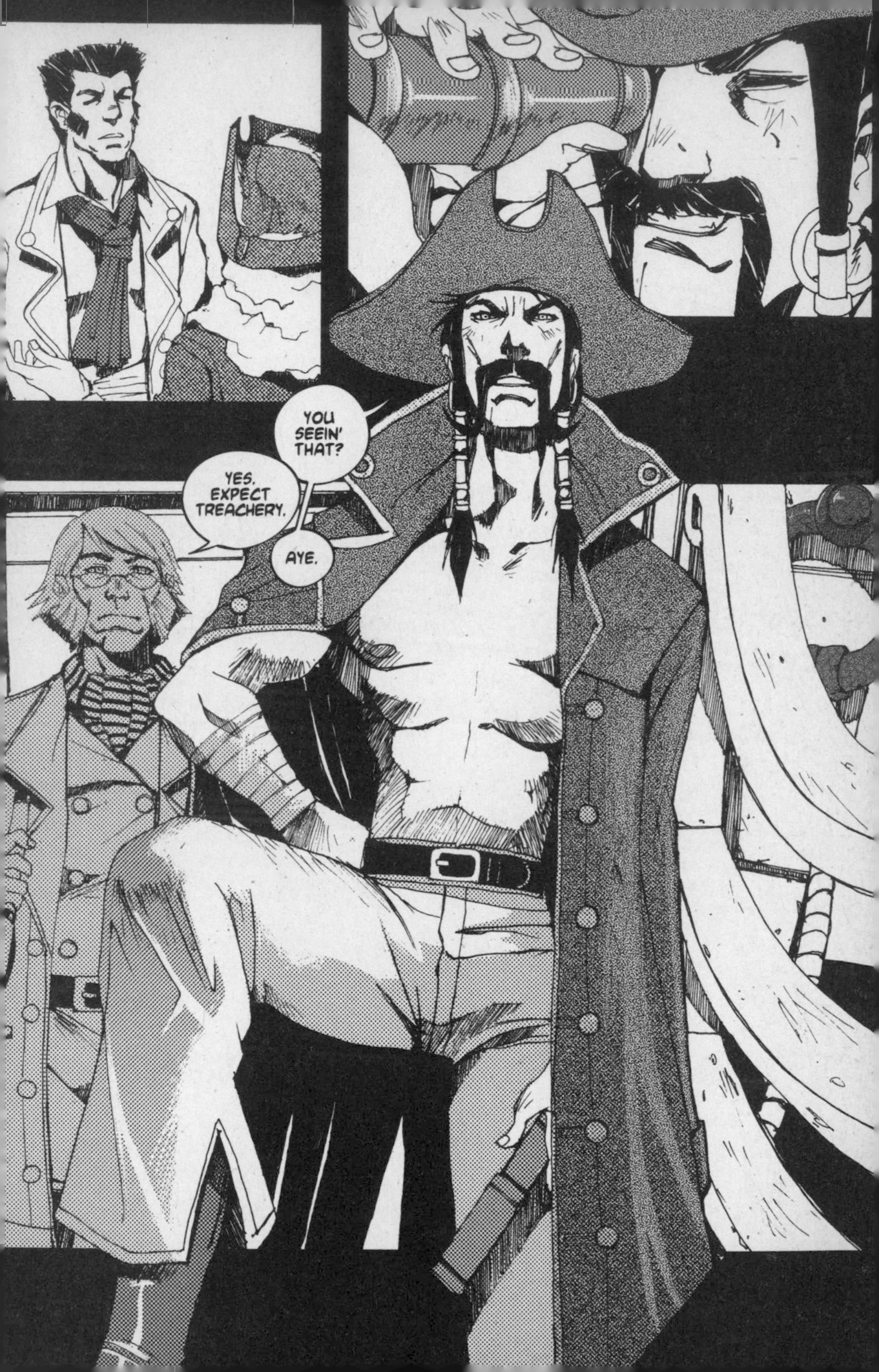
YOU SEEIN' THAT?
YES. EXPECT TREACHERY.
AYE.

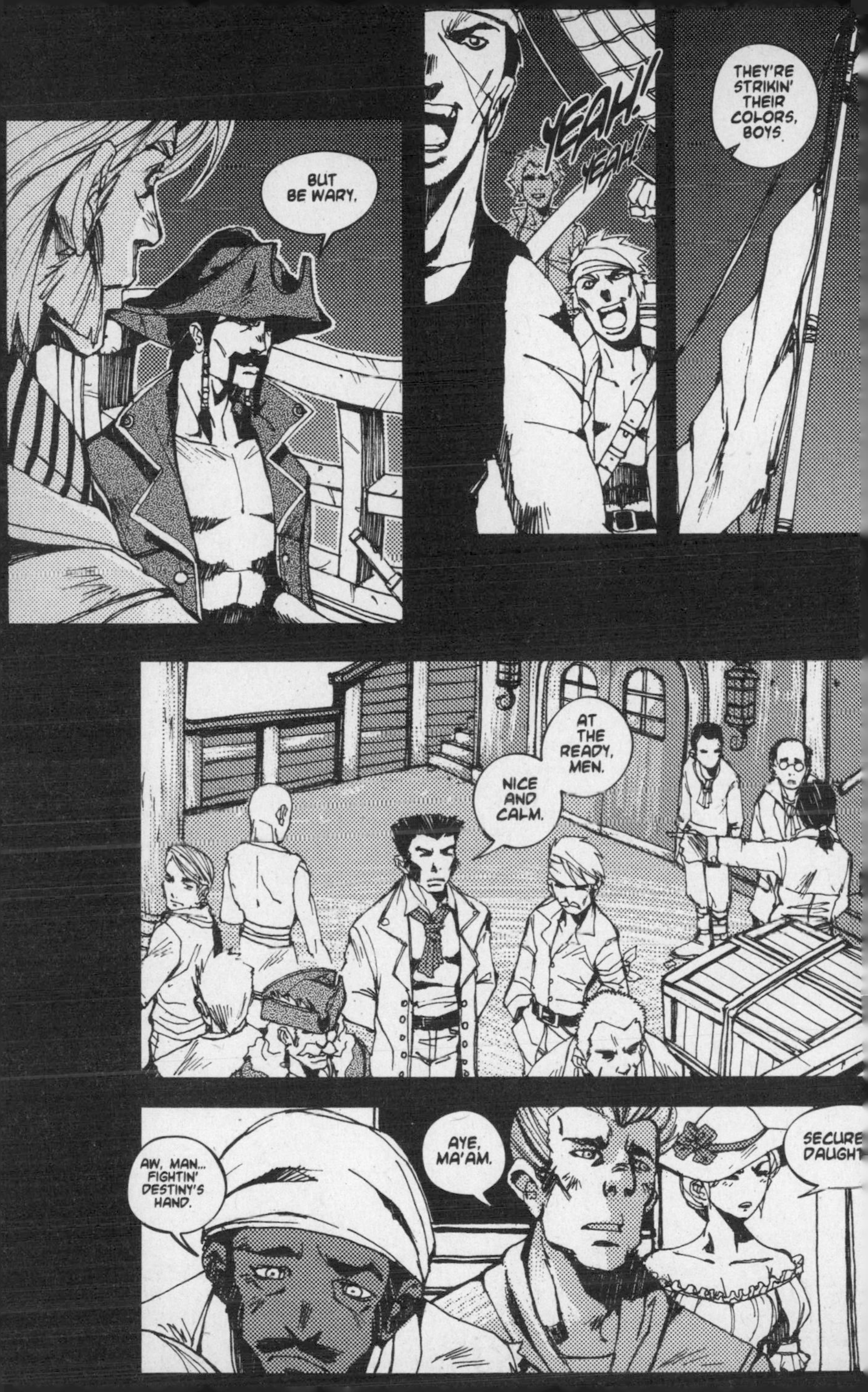
THEY'RE STRIKIN' THEIR COLORS, BOYS.
YEAH! YEAH!
BUT BE WARY.
AT THE READY, MEN.
NICE AND CALM.
SECURE DAUGHT
AYE, MA'AM.
AW, MAN... FIGHTIN' DESTINY'S HAND.

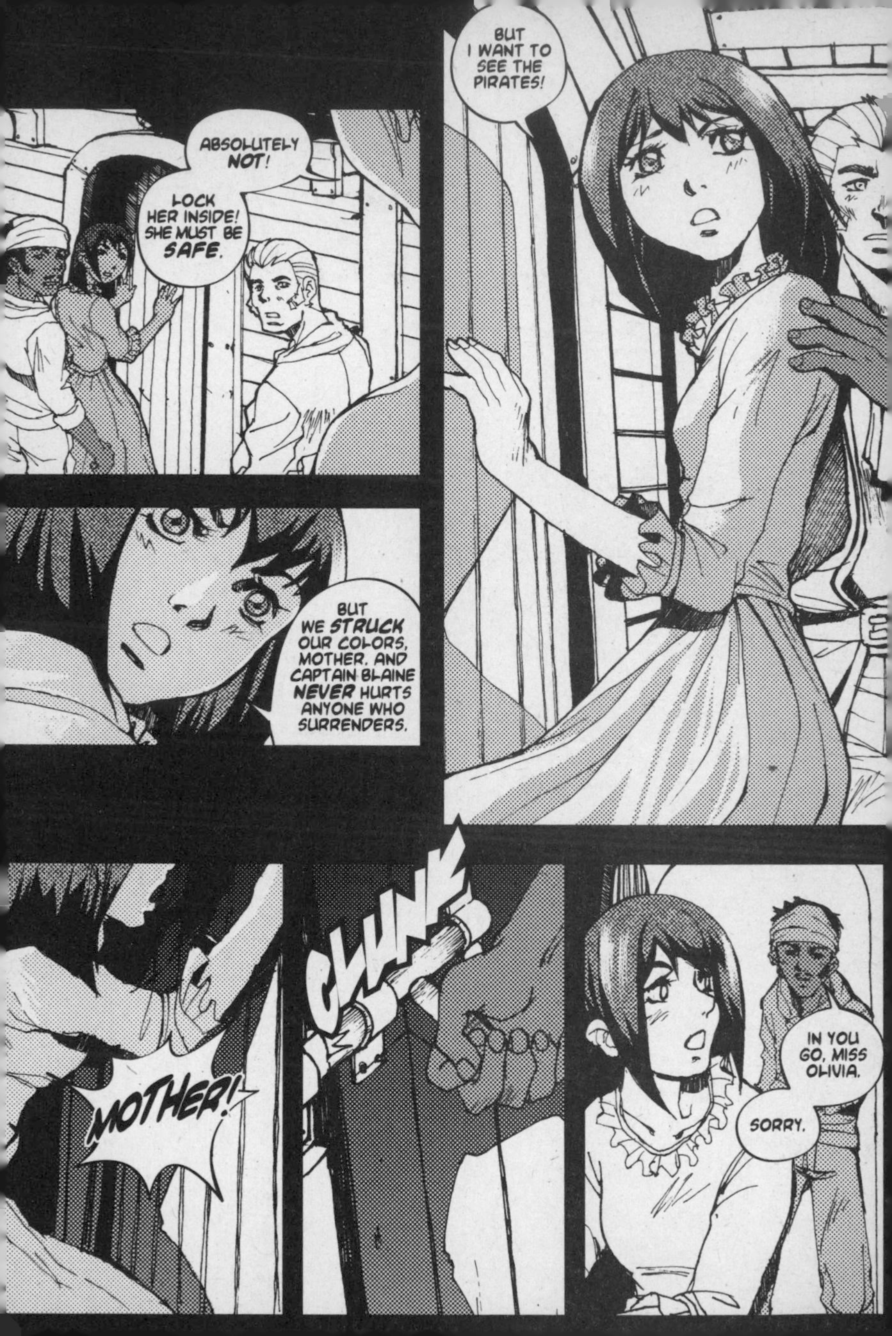
BUT I WANT TO SEE THE PIRATES!
ABSOLUTELY NOT!
LOCK HER INSIDE! SHE MUST BE SAFE.
BUT WE STRUCK OUR COLORS, MOTHER. AND CAPTAIN BLAINE NEVER HURTS ANYONE WHO SURRENDERS.
IN YOU GO, MISS OLIVIA.
SORRY.
CLUNK
MOTHER!

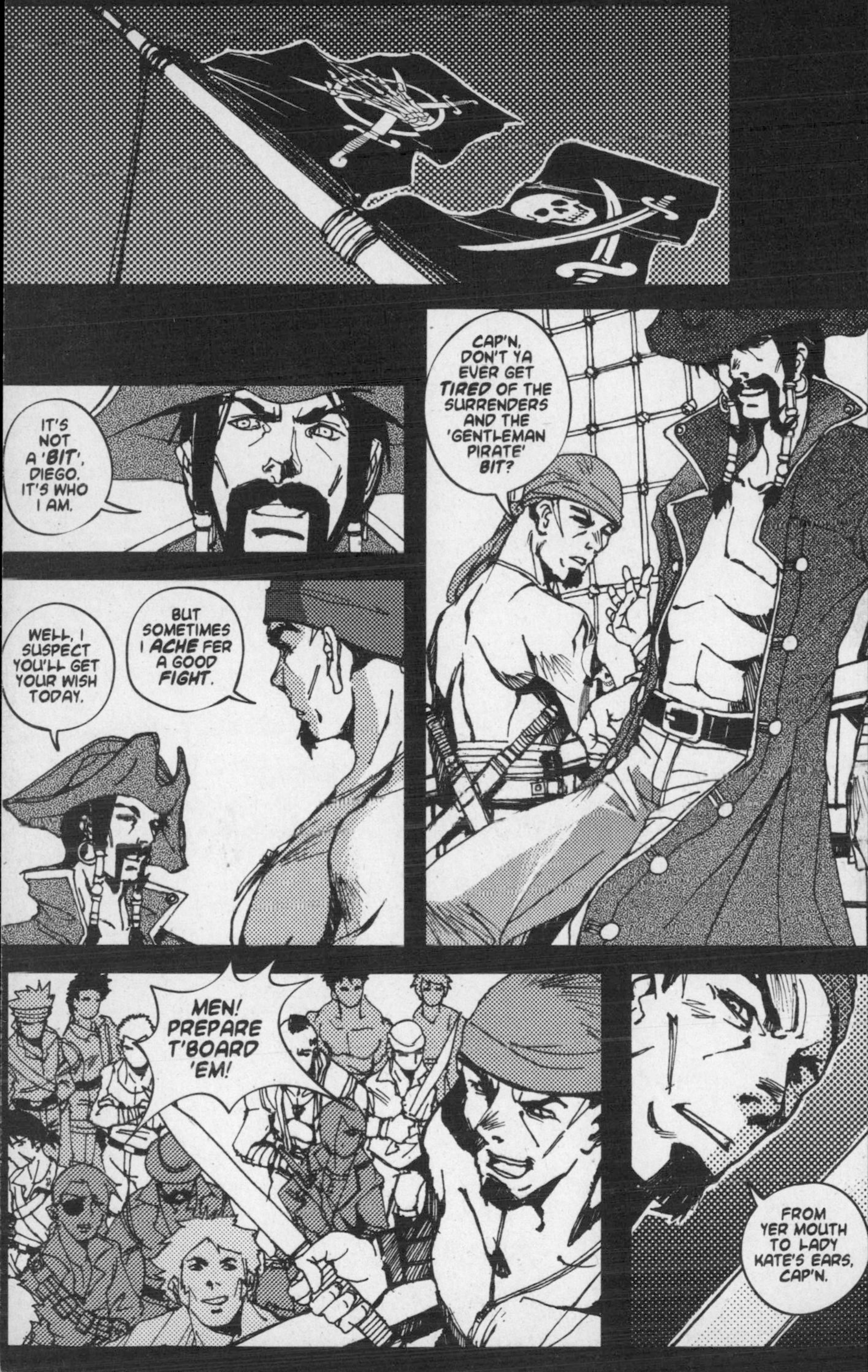
CAP'N, DON'T YA EVER GET TIRED OF THE SURRENDERS AND THE 'GENTLEMAN PIRATE' BIT?
IT'S NOT A 'BIT', DIEGO. IT'S WHO I AM.
BUT SOMETIMES I ACHE FER A GOOD FIGHT.
WELL, I SUSPECT YOU'LL GET YOUR WISH TODAY.
FROM YER MOUTH TO LADY KATE'S EARS, CAP'N.
MEN! PREPARE T'BOARD 'EM!

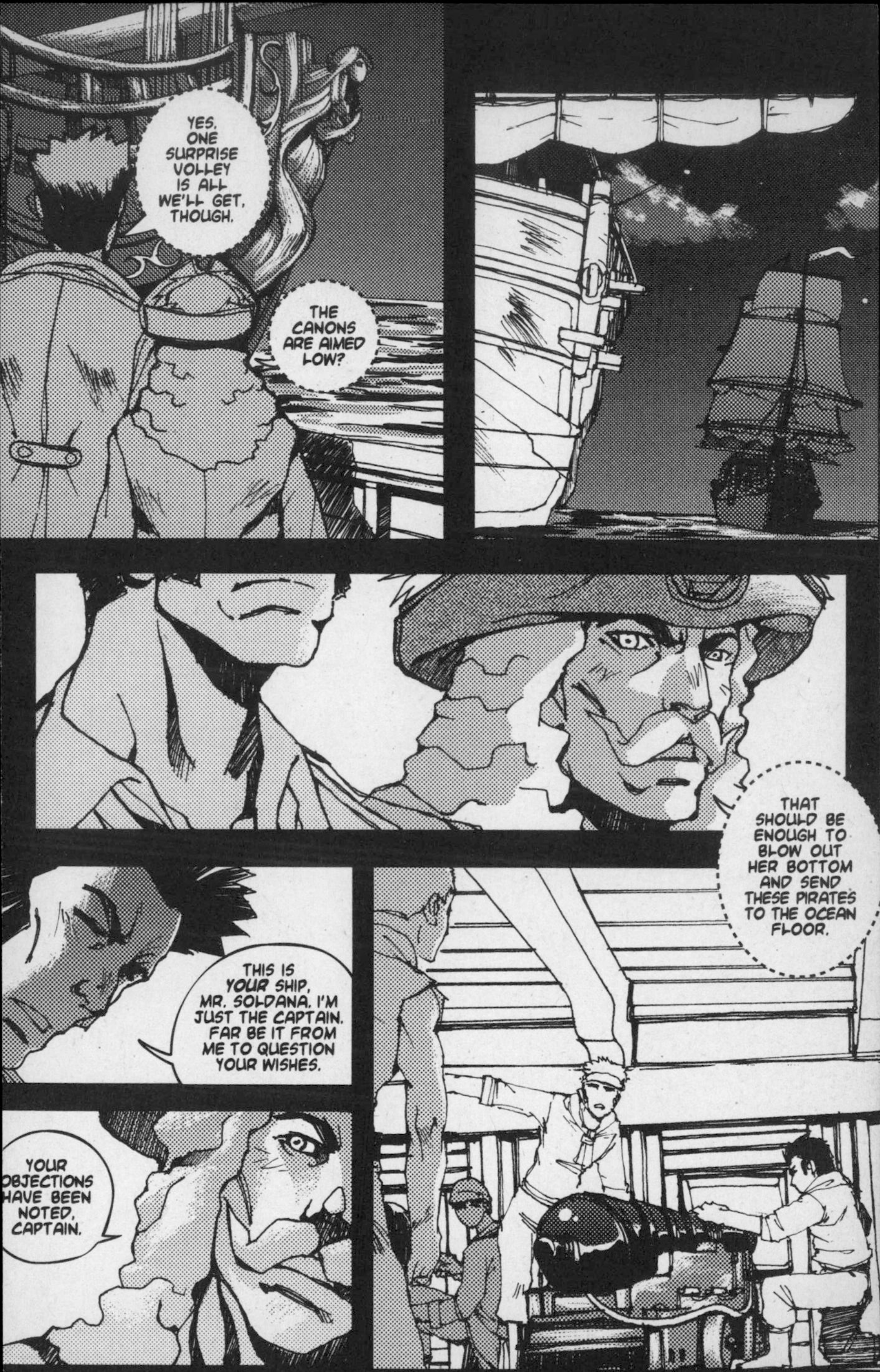
YES, ONE SURPRISE VOLLEY IS ALL WE'LL GET, THOUGH.
THE CANONS ARE AIMED LOW?
THAT SHOULD BE ENOUGH TO BLOW OUT HER BOTTOM AND SEND THESE PIRATES TO THE OCEAN FLOOR.
THIS IS YOUR SHIP, MR. SOLDANA. I'M JUST THE CAPTAIN. FAR BE IT FROM ME TO QUESTION YOUR WISHES.
YOUR OBJECTIONS HAVE BEEN NOTED, CAPTAIN.

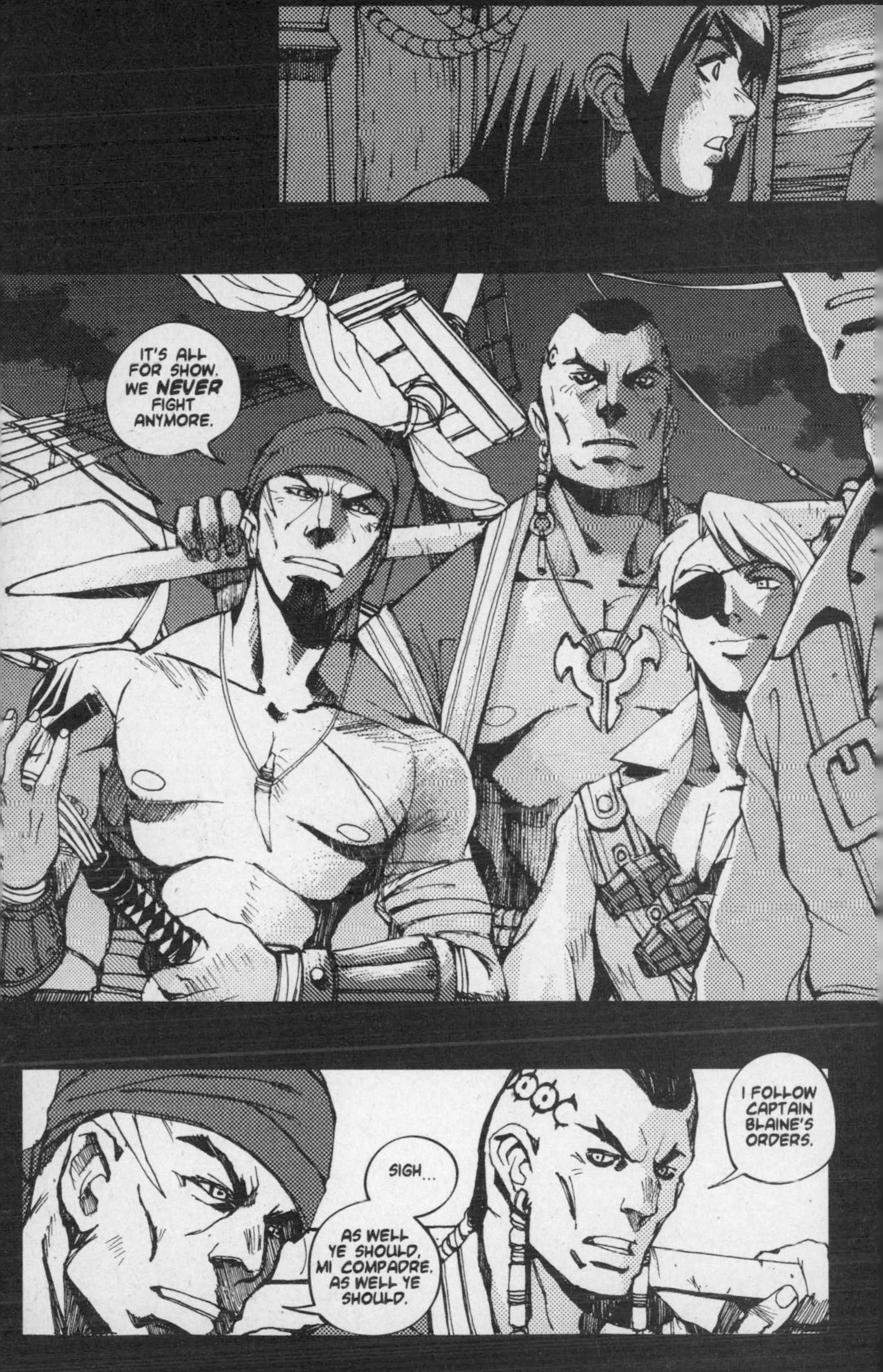
IT'S ALL FOR SHOW. WE **NEVER** FIGHT ANYMORE.
I FOLLOW CAPTAIN BLAINE'S ORDERS.
SIGH...
AS WELL YE SHOULD, MI COMPADRE. AS WELL YE SHOULD.

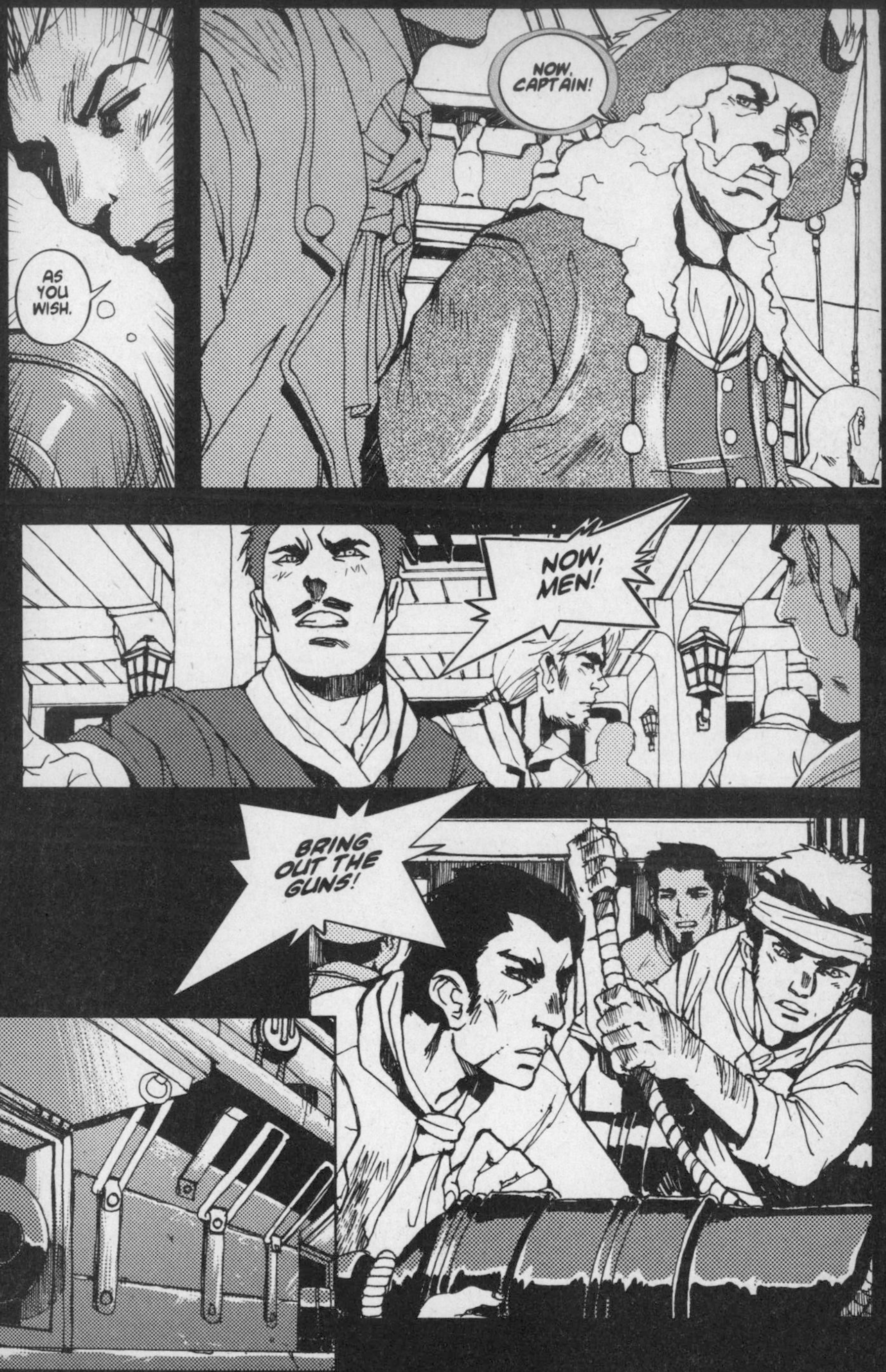
NOW, CAPTAIN!
AS YOU WISH.
NOW, MEN!
BRING OUT THE GUNS!

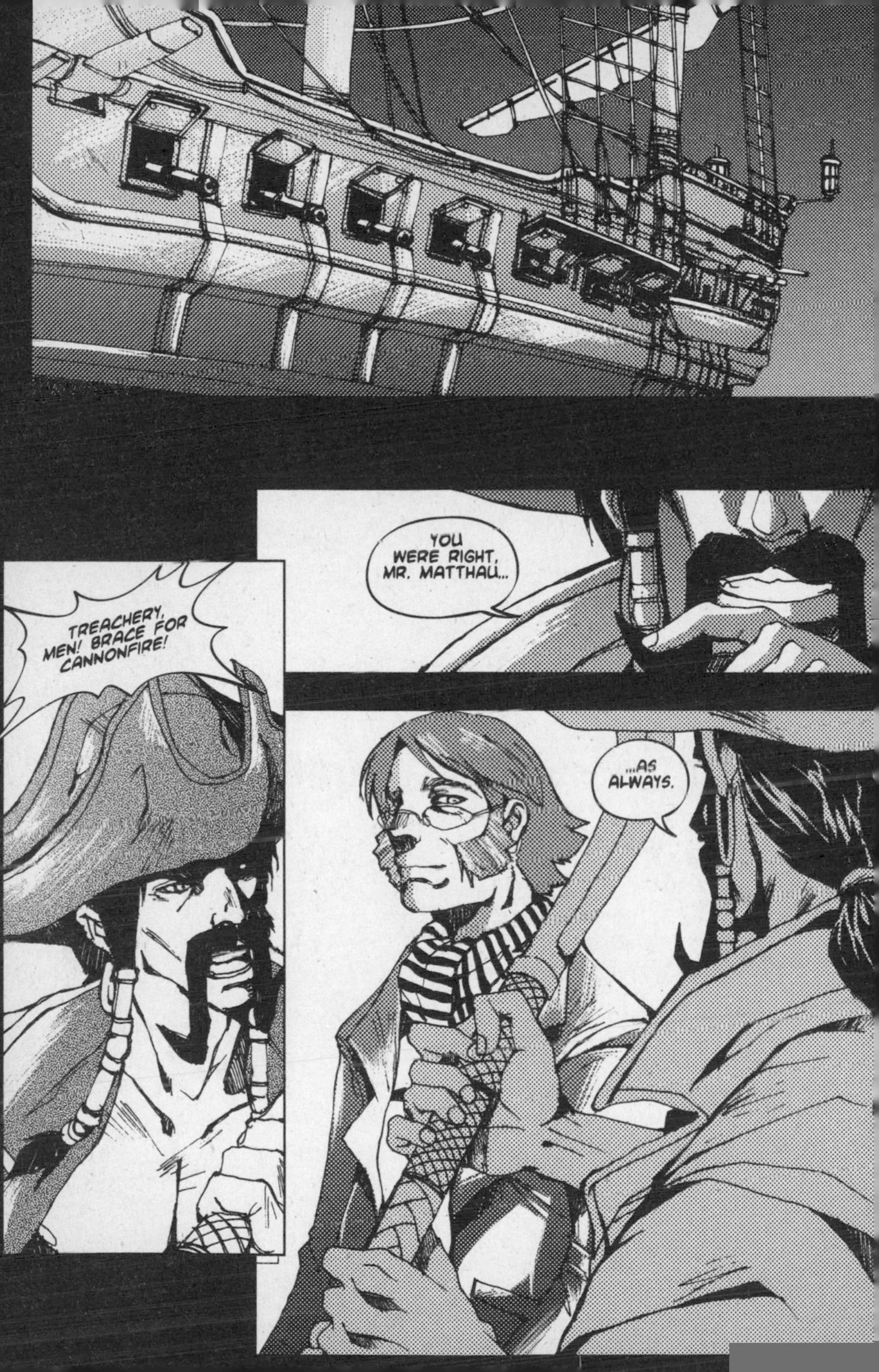
YOU WERE RIGHT, MR. MATTHAU...
...AS ALWAYS.
TREACHERY, MEN! BRACE FOR CANNONFIRE!

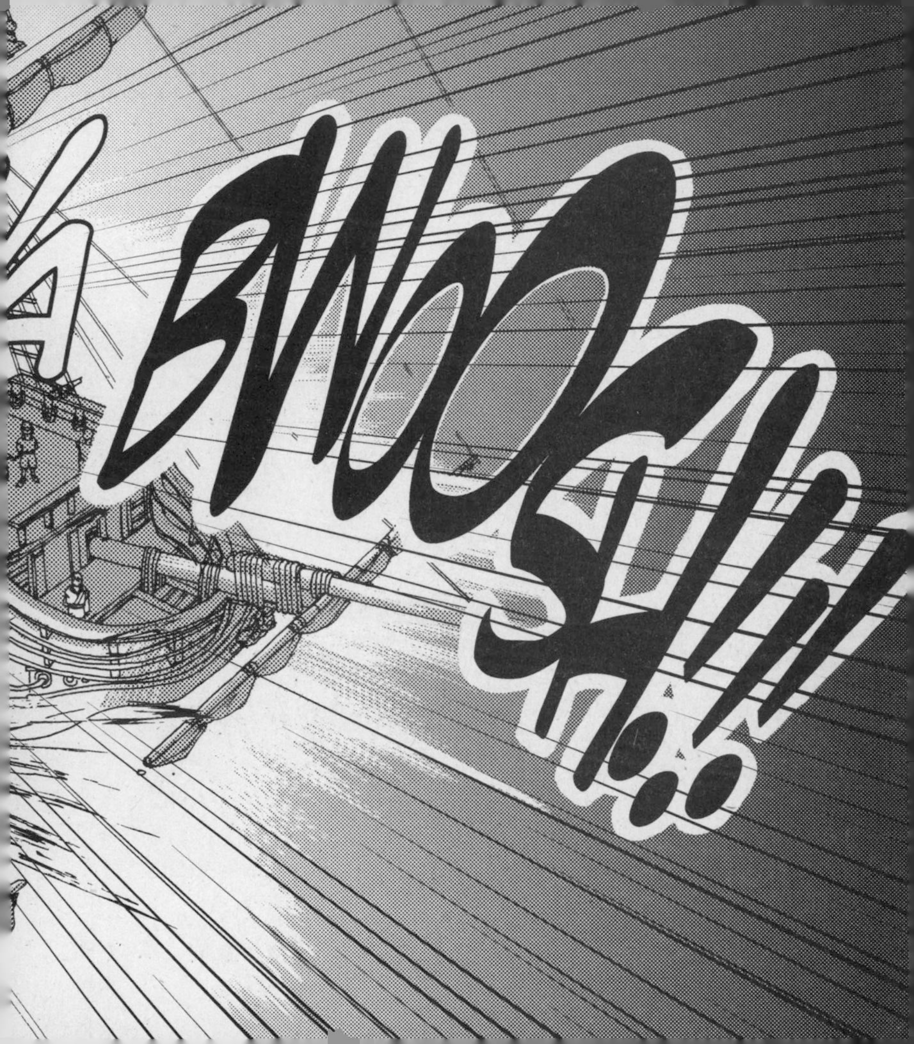
BWOOSH!!

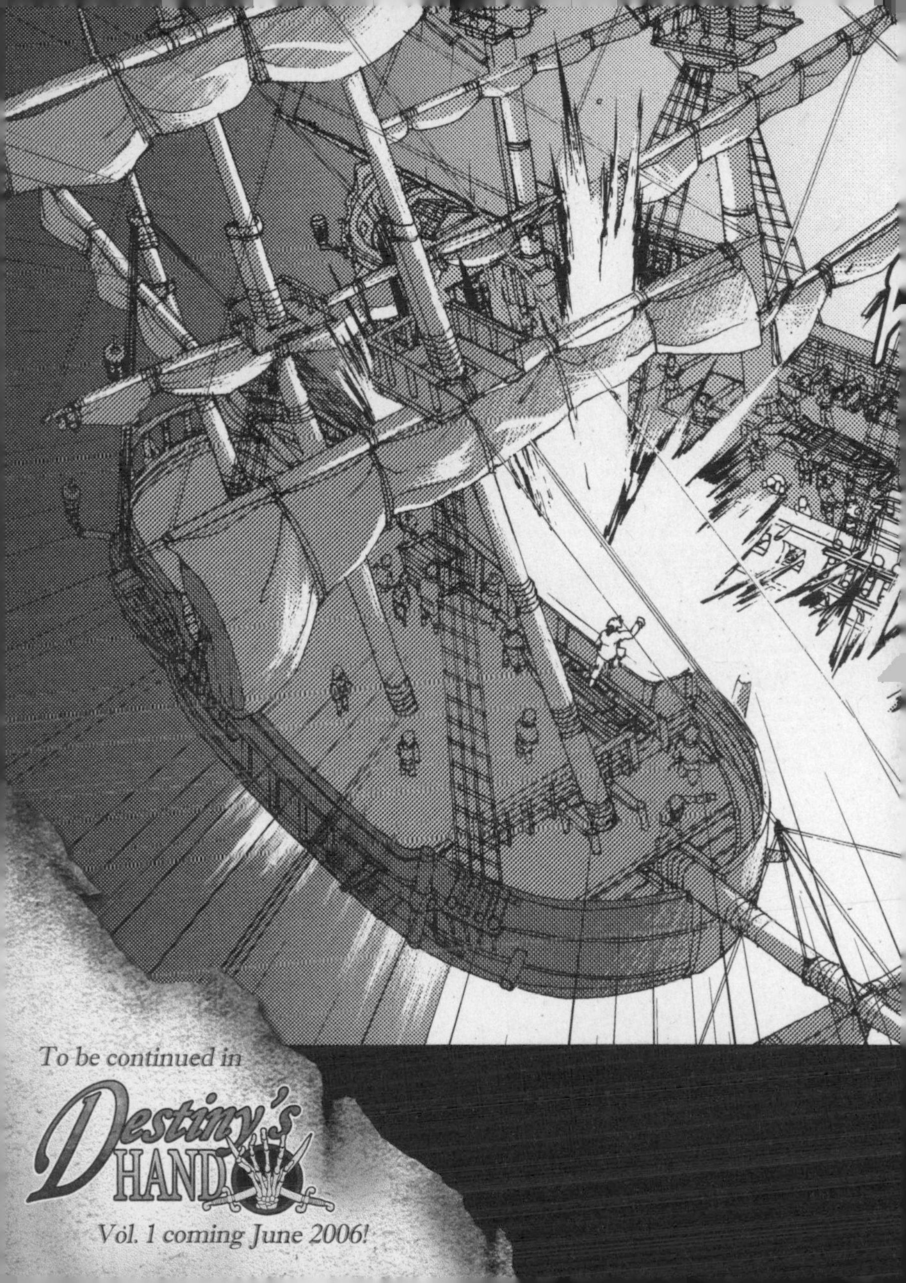
To be continued in
Destiny's
HAND
Vol. 1 coming June 2006!

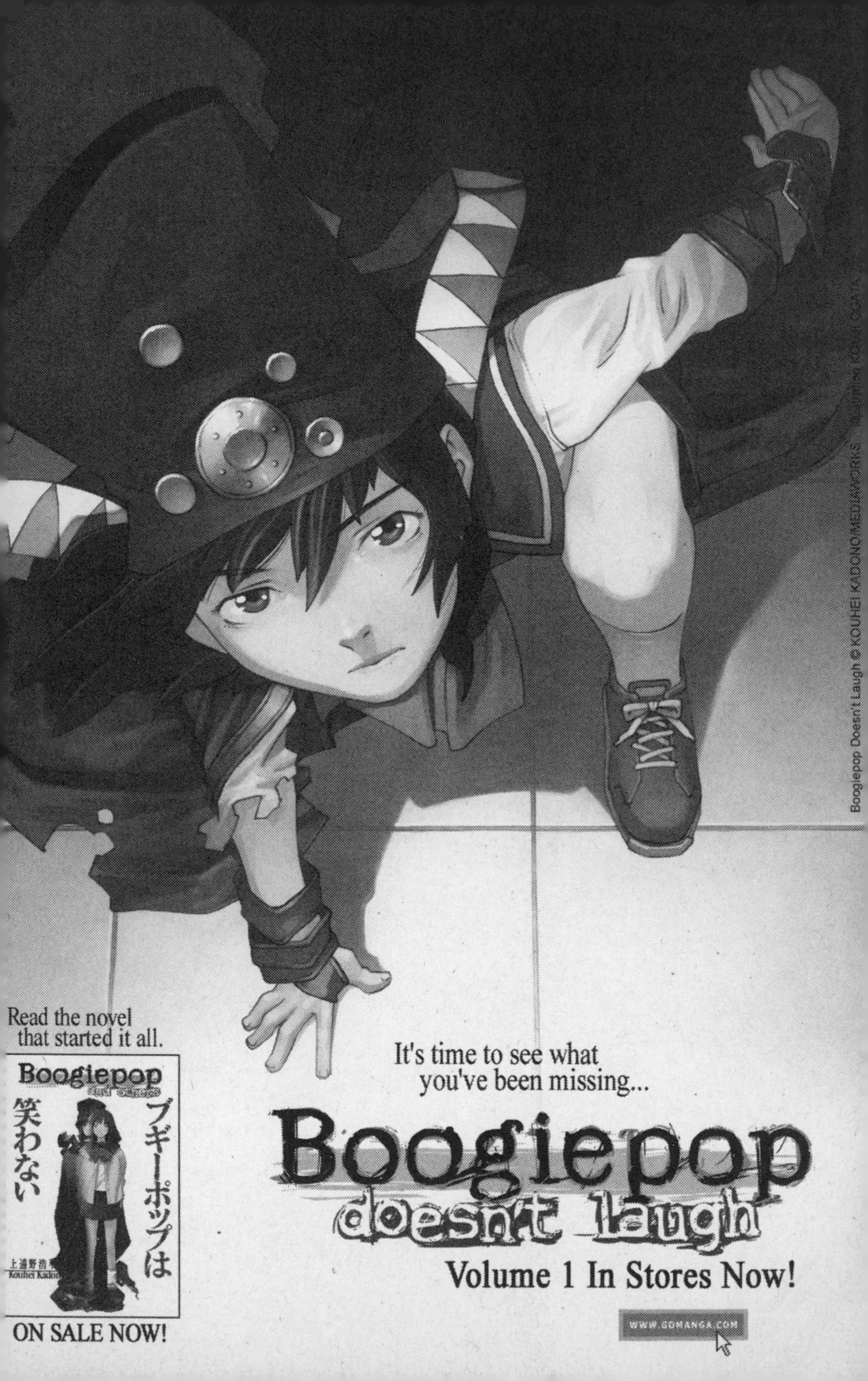
Read the novel
that started it all.
Boogiepop
ブギーポップは
笑わない
ON SALE NOW!
It's time to see what
you've been missing...
Boogiepop
doesn't laugh
Volume 1 In Stores Now!
WWW.GOMANGA.COM
Boogiepop Doesn't Laugh © KOUHEI KADONO/MEDIAWORKS

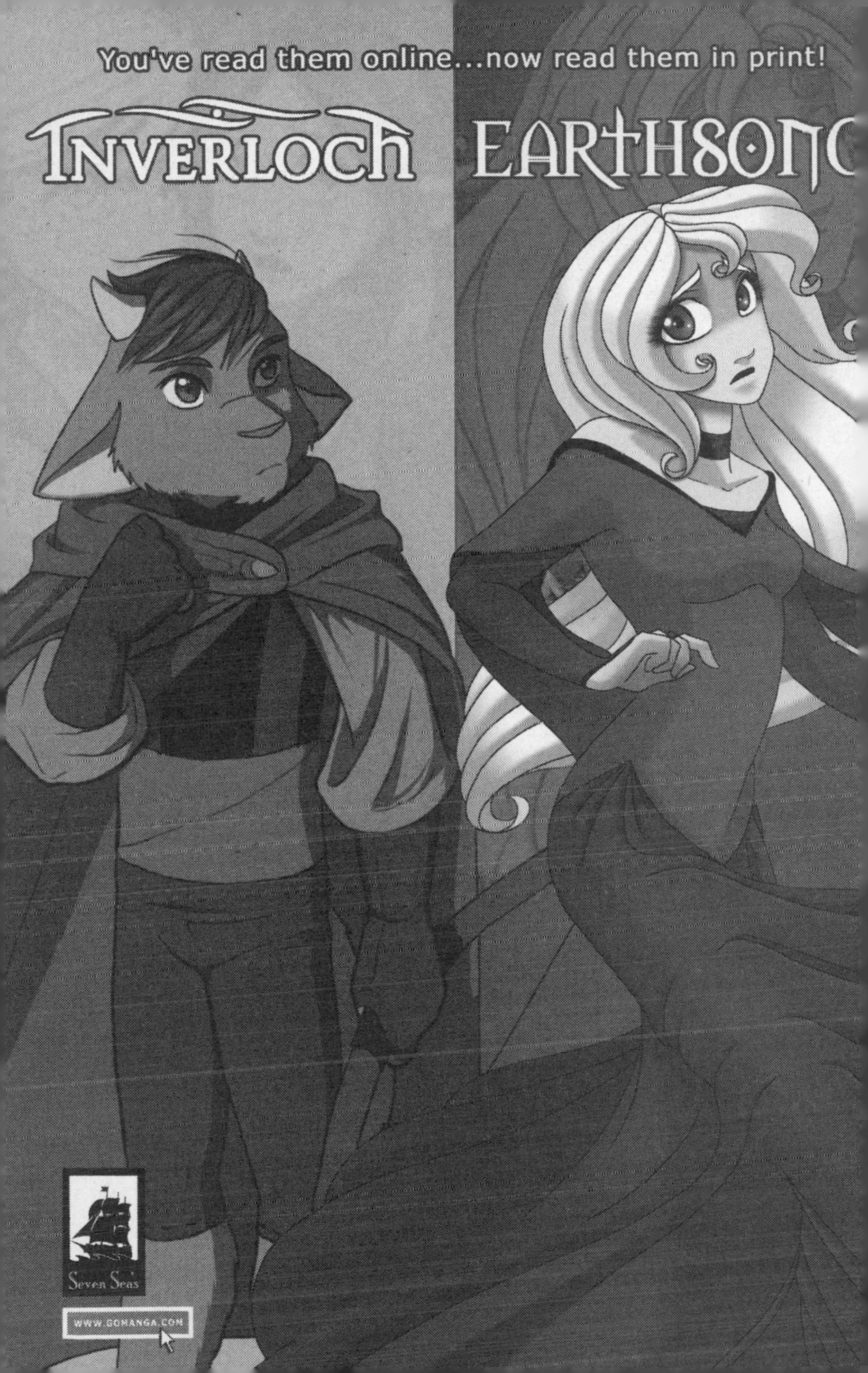
You've read them online...now read them in print!
INVERLOCH
EARTHSONG
Seven Seas
WWW.GOMANGA.COM

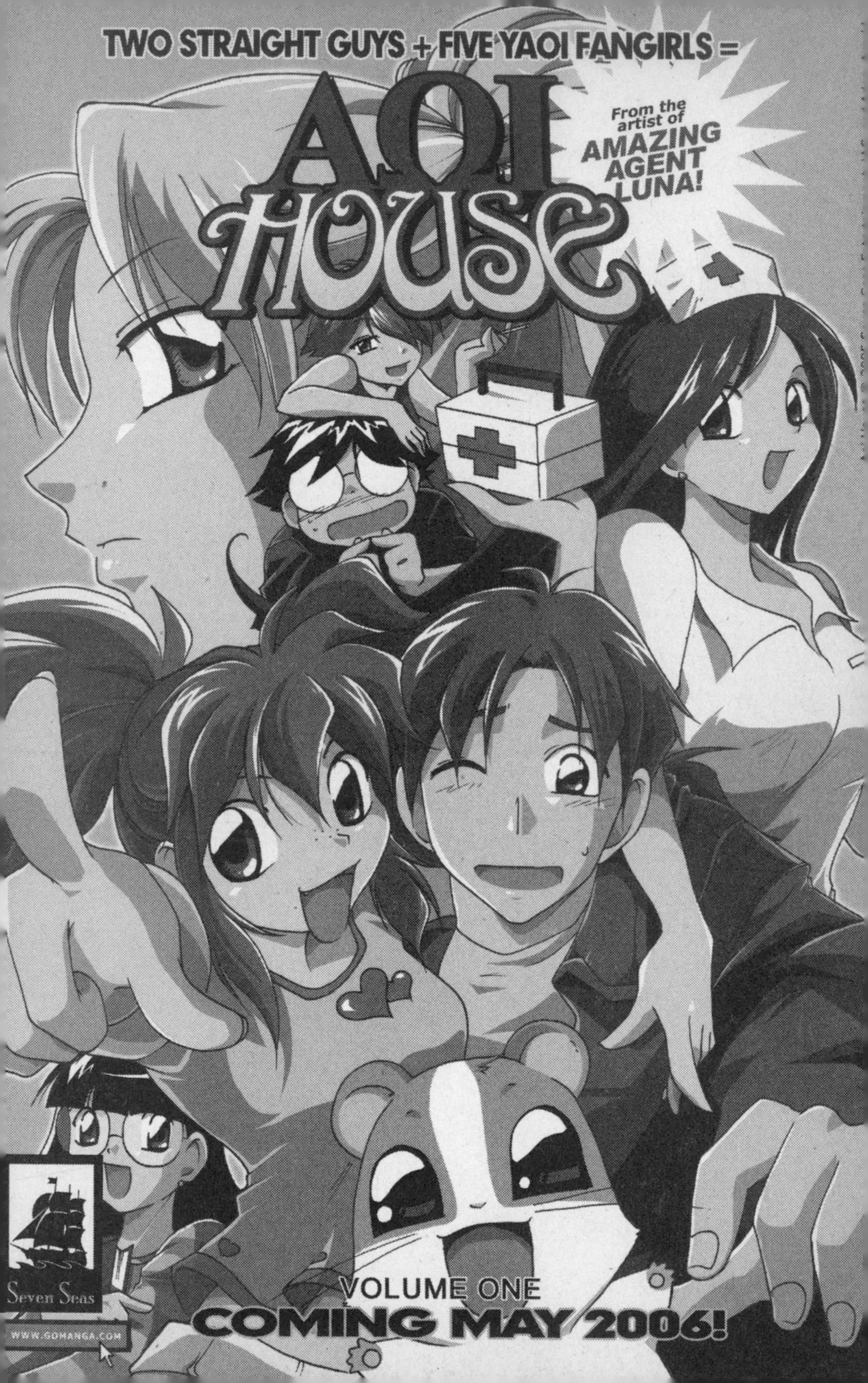

TWO STRAIGHT GUYS + FIVE YAOI FANGIRLS =
AOI HOUSE
From the artist of AMAZING AGENT LUNA!
Seven Seas
WWW.GOMANGA.COM
VOLUME ONE
COMING MAY 2006!

THE END

YOU'RE READING THE WRONG WAY

This is the last page of
Amazing Agent Luna Volume 3.

This book reads from right to left, Japanese style. To read from the beginning, flip the book over to the other side, start with the top right panel, and take it from there.

If this is your first time reading manga, just follow the diagram. It may seem backwards at first, but you'll get used to it! Have fun!